Labour Regulation in the 21st Century: In Search of Flexibility and Security

ADAPT LABOUR STUDIES BOOK-SERIES

International School of Higher Education in Labour and Industrial Relations

ADAPT (www.adapt.it) is a non-profit organisation founded in 2000 by Professor Marco Biagi with the aim of promoting studies and research in the field of labour law and industrial relations from an international and comparative perspective. Our purpose is to encourage and implement a new approach to academic research, by establishing ongoing relationships with other universities and advanced studies institutes, and promoting academic and scientific exchange programmes with enterprises, institutions, foundations and associations. In collaboration with the **Marco Biagi Centre for International and Comparative Studies** (www.csmb.unimore.it), ADAPT set up the International School of Higher Education in Labour and Industrial Relations, a centre of excellence which is accredited at an international level for research, study and the postgraduate programmes in the area of industrial and labour relations.

Labour Regulation in the 21st Century: In Search of Flexibility and Security

Edited by

Tomas Davulis and Daiva Petrylaitė

CAMBRIDGE SCHOLARS PUBLISHING

Labour Regulation in the 21st Century:
In Search of Flexibility and Security,
Edited by Tomas Davulis and Daiva Petrylaitė

This book first published 2012

Cambridge Scholars Publishing

12 Back Chapman Street, Newcastle upon Tyne, NE6 2XX, UK

British Library Cataloguing in Publication Data
A catalogue record for this book is available from the British Library

ISBN (10): 1-4438-3663-X, ISBN (13): 978-1-4438-3663-0

TABLE OF CONTENTS

Chapter Two: Particularly Problematic Labour Law Issues

Chapter Three: Social Security Law

LIST OF ILLUSTRATIONS

LIST OF TABLES

In Search of Flexibility and Flexicurity

Tomas Davulis and Daiva Petrylaitė

In modern society, labour relations are complicated and heterogeneous, as they reflect both the present state of the market economy and more general rules governing everyday life. Even the smallest social or economic changes may affect labour relations, which may inevitably give rise to antagonism, disagreement and conflict among the parties. Therefore, the increasing role of labour relations and that of the individual actors is characterised by new aspects determining contemporary social phenomena and processes, e.g. the definition of the social market economy.

Nowadays, the contemporary western world not only considers the relationships that take place within the market economy—which are based on the production and exchange of goods—but it also takes account of the adoption of certain principles—i.e. the freedom and initiative of economic activities and the right of private ownership—thus examining the social nature of such market relations.

At the end of the 21th century, new challenges for labour law have arisen. Increasing globalisation processes, the technological revolution, the establishment of new forms of employment, business relocation, and the nearly unlimited potential of the usage of information technologies in labour processes have resulted in a number of preconditions for the individualisation of labour relations.

Relevant issues resulting from the industrial revolution period and matters in terms of production have made room for technological innovation and new ways of handling relations in our consumer society. Therefore, today it is important to address not only the labour market relations and commitment of the state to ensure free economic activities, but also to deal with the social needs that require predetermined governmental measures to restrict free market relations, as a way of implementing shared objectives and values arising out of dialogue and cooperation of the social partners.

Besides free and independent, the relations within the market economy should also be socially motivated. The state has the opportunity—and the duty—to limit the relations of the market economy so as to achieve certain social goals.

Both at a European and national level, striking the balance between security and flexibility of employment should be the core challenge of the labour market when developing relevant policy strategies. In considering the goal of the European Union to become the most competitive and dynamic knowledge economy in the world—capable of sustainable economic growth with more and better jobs and greater social cohesion—the mission of the Community should reflect the effort to strengthen both flexibility and security in the labour market. The commitment of EU employers and employees to adapt to the volatile labour market conditions leads to safeguard jobs. More specifically, this means to balance both flexibility and security to combine these two fundamental goals, with current theories on industrial relations and labour law that are called into question. While acknowledging the role of labour laws in protecting the rights and interests of employees, this function should be understood in a broader sense as a task to safeguard common interests, in order to benefit employers and employees, and all those individuals who have been forced out of the labour market.

CHAPTER ONE:

LOOKING FOR FLEXIBILITY AND SECURITY OF THE LABOUR MARKET

TACKLING THE ECONOMIC CRISIS: LABOUR LAW IN LITHUANIA

TOMAS DAVULIS AND DAIVA PETRYLAITĖ

1. Introduction

The global financial crisis that erupted in 2008 had a profound impact in many industries. Once again, economic difficulties have demonstrated the close interdependence between labour law and the economic system. The scope of the commitments placed by labour law on the workforce can also be expressed in economic terms, because it directly affects the price of the services rendered and goods supplied in the global economy. During economic downturns, the set of labour market policy becomes not only an economic but also a fiscal instrument. If, for any reason currency devaluation is not possible, similar results could be achieved by labour law devaluation. Politicians following this logic undertook Europe-wide measures devised to enhance competitiveness of local employers through a reduction of workforce costs, especially those relating to the requirements set forth by labour law norms. It was also claimed that those measures were aimed at promoting employment and reducing unemployment rates.

At the current stage of economic development and when considering national realities, the response of labour law varies, though most legislations show a trend towards "loosening" the legal norms governing labour relations, by watering down mandatory legal norms or easing the standards of conduct required by these norms. On the basis of these considerations, the authors aim at providing a reply to the question of whether changes in labour law prompted by economic difficulties represent a new paradigm shift in Lithuanian labour law. This is because labour law norms arise not as a result of a targeted and politically-driven implementation of social policy—e.g. the measures liberalising labour relations, updating legal regulation and filling legal vacuum—but as a result of an adjustment of completely different interests and negotiations on the basis of mutual trade.

2. The Role of Labour Law in the Modern Social Market Economy

The search for social justice becomes apparent in the practice of the legal regulation of labour relations. While adopting labour laws and setting the limits of regulation of labour relations, the State should take into consideration societal basic expectations. That is why today, particular emphasis is placed on the possibility to resort to contractual regulation of labour relations, thus narrowing the limits of the imperative provisions. The international community also regards labour law as an undisputable regulator of the balance of power between capital and labour. For example, with the view to implementing the objectives of the Lisbon Strategy, the Communication from the Commission "Towards Common Principles of Flexicurity: More and Better Jobs through Flexibility and Security"[1] points out that the adaptation to the changed economic and social conditions requires a more flexible labour market combined with levels of security that address simultaneously the new needs of employers and employees. However, Europe is not adjusting to the shocks that are imposed on its economy as well as it could. This is also the case in Lithuania. Undoubtedly, the capability to adapt not only depends on the will of labour market entities themselves, but also on the opportunities they are provided with. The degree of optionality in regulating the labour market directly impacts on the opportunities for flexible adaptation to market changes in the manner of easing or aggravating such opportunities. Therefore in 2006, calling the society for a public debate about the future of labour law, the Commission of European Communities published the Green Paper "Modernising Labour Law to Meet the Challenges of the 21st Century",[2] which states that:

> The modernization of labour law constitutes a key element for the success of the adaptability of workers and enterprises. This objective needs to be pursued in the light of the Community's objectives of full employment, labour productivity and social cohesion.

[1] European Commission. 2007. *Towards Common Principles of Flexicurity: More and Better Jobs Through Flexibility and Security, (2007) 359 final.* Brussels: European Commission.

[2] European Commission. 2006. *Green Book on Modernising the Labour Law in order to Cope with the Challenges of the 21st Century COM* (2006) 708 final. Brussels: European Commission.

The paper points out that collective agreements should play a major role in regulating the relationship between labour and the social environment, thus not just limiting them to complementing working conditions already defined by law. They serve as an important tool in adjusting legal principles to specific economic situations and dealing with particular circumstances of specific sectors. Developments in social dialogue at national, industry and enterprise level, geared towards introducing new forms of internal flexibility, have also demonstrated how workplace rules can be adapted to changing economic realities. Therefore, today's European society and decision-makers have to pay particular attention to the implementation of an innovative model of collective labour relations, i.e. in order to create an EU system of collective labour relations coordinated on a uniform basis, which—though not being unified—should be based on similar norms and values. On the other hand, individual Member States should also seek not to diverge from this integral European system of collective labour relations. Accordingly, Europe should act as a catalyst to unite different existing systems.

3. National Approach to Labour Law

With regard to this aspect, Lithuania appears to be still following the trends of the last decade, with the idea of individualism in labour relations being obtruded by all mass media. Unfortunately, this idea is getting more and more entrenched in the society. The theory and practice of collective relations are described as "out of style", outdated and lagging behind social and economic changes of life.[3] Changing Economic, social and political might inevitably be used in regulating particular issues related to labour relations, labour and social conditions in specific areas—e.g. in industrial branches and regions. Nowadays, we cannot any longer confine ourselves to the national relations of economic and social life. In the context of recent growth of flexibility of the labour market either at a local or global level, both separate enterprises and national legal systems must—in order to survive under the new conditions of competition—take over global trends in the legal regulation of labour relations, create certain working and business conditions that would ensure the implementation of and the balance between protective and economic functions of labour law, while acknowledging the independence of the parties to labour relations and creating the widest possible opportunity for taking autonomous

[3] These neo-liberal ideas are particularly actively propagated by the Free Market Institute: www.lrinka.lt.

decisions on fundamental economic and social issues.[4] Neo-liberal ideas, which are more and more loudly manifesting in Lithuania, suggest narrowing the ambit of collective agreements and promote leaving to the parties the discretionary power in terms of working hours, wages and other important conditions of work. Obviously, such a position negates the collective nature of labour relations in full and confronts itself with the very nature of labour law, by denying the basic function of this branch of law, i.e., its protective function. Without denying the role of labour laws in safeguarding the rights and interests of the employee, today this function should be understood on a wider scale: labour law is supposed to protect not only the interests of working staff on an individual basis, but assume a wider task of safeguarding all people involved in gainful employment as well as those who are unemployed. This can be done only by increasing the levels of flexibility of the regulation of labour relations, e.g. by reducing the role of regulatory control and increasing that of collective agreements. Yet, it should not be overlooked that legal regulation at a national level, though introducing some restrictions on business, conduct and other freedoms, serves for the implementation of the State's function as that of a public arbiter, i.e., certain restrictions are imposed with the view to securing the public interest. Therefore, it is necessary to support the principal requirement of trade unions to liberalise the area of collective labour relations in Lithuania, i.e., to extend the autonomy of the parties to labour relations and to provide them with wider opportunities of collective actions. This would create conditions for refusing excessively detailed statutory regulation of labour relations and for more flexible regulation of the specifics of labour relations. Collective agreements would be able to react more expeditiously to changes in labour relations and changing interests of employees and employers, as compared to the state's legal instruments. Such a shift in the regulation of labour relations from central control to autonomy of the social partners would considerably contribute to flexibility of labour relations, at the same time ensuring adequate social security of employees.

---

[4] Petrylaitė, D. 2007. "Kolektyviniai darbo santykiai amžių sandūroje: uždaviniai ir galimybės [Collective Labour Relations in the Centuries Crossing: Tasks and Possibilities]," *Teisė*, No. 65:112.

4. Economic Crisis and Amendments to the Labour Code

After reforming national labour law by adopting the Labour Code on 22 June 2002, which became effective in 2003,[5] the Government made an attempt to improve it. Although several articles were amended frequently, as few as two amendments to the Labour Code which are of a broad scope and cover a number of articles, namely, the amendment of 12 May 2005[6] and the amendment of 13 May 2008,[7] are worthy of mention. These amendments, which had been drafted by competent scholars, representatives of social partners formed by the Seimas Committee on Social Affairs and Labour, address the issues of improvement of the Labour Code from the inside, focusing on some inconsistencies of the legislator, the legal vacuum revealed by case law, and the harmonization of national law with EU Law. Therefore, the Labour Code actually preserved the original structure and reflected the "demarcation line"[8] identified at the stage of adoption, thus balancing the interests of social groups. Hence, the regulation of labour relations remained as strict and inflexible as it was until 2002.[9]

The coalition of the right and centre party that came to power in autumn 2008 at the outbreak of the financial crisis faced a poor financial and economic situation. After almost half a decade of rapid growth of the economic and social standard, the deficit of the state budget and of the budget of the social insurance fund began to increase rapidly. The coalition viewed as the main instruments to improve the situation, the general tightening of spending (reduction of the social standard) and the creation of an economic environment favourable for employers. Therefore, the Programme of the Government of the Republic of Lithuania[10] set the goal of taking urgent action to liberalize labour relations. Under the Programme, the Government assumed the commitment to observe the principles of the *flexicurity* (secure flexibility) strategy recently promoted

---

[5] Official gazette *Valstybės žinios*, No. 64-2569, 2002.

[6] Official gazette *Valstybės žinios*, 2005, No. 67-2400.

[7] Official gazette *Valstybės žinios*, 2008, No. 63-2375.

[8] Davulis, T. 2008. "Lietuvos darbo teisės modernizavimo perspektyvos," *Jurisprudencija*, 29.

[9] See Davulis, T. 2009. "The Fifth Anniversary of the New Lithuanian Labour Code: Time to Change?" in *The Modernization of Labour Law and Industrial Relations in a Comparative Perspective*, ed. Blanpain, R. (Alphen aan den Rijn: Kluwer Law International), 360-364.

[10] Approved by Seimas of the Republic of Lithuania Resolution No. XI-52 of 9 December 2008. Official gazette *Valstybės žinios*, No. 146-5870, 2008.

by the European Commission on the example of Denmark and assist in creating a competitive workforce.

The Programme devoted considerable attention to this issue, but the main goal was given just a brief mention

> modernise labour relations regulation and increase flexibility thereof, so that they would be in line with the current economic development needs yet not impair labour conditions. Improvement of labour conditions is a key prerequisite for the reduction of the number of work accidents and vocational diseases.[11]

It remains unclear how flexibility and improvement of labour conditions, which are rather mutually incompatible, will be linked, but one could already suspect that high-sounding declarations conceal liberalisation plans.

In order to rescue the public finances of the state, the Government soon initiated the adoption of a package of ambivalently viewed amendments to laws cutting public spending and increasing a number of taxes, which were adopted almost overnight. The latter evolved into protests organised by social partners and resulted in the riot of 16 January 2009, which became an extraordinary event in a society which is not inclined towards protesting or holding strikes.[12] The control of public order, though lost only for a short while, was of crucial importance for the original plans of the Government to reform the legislation of the social sphere—the Government shifted from an ambitious one-sided rhetoric to more moderate proposals and dialogue with social partners. The standpoint of the Government in respect of liberal provisions was softened to the same extent as the willingness of political parties in power not to become involved in conflicts with social partners increased. Consequently, two laws amending the Labour Code were adopted over the period of two years and are very different both as regards the circumstances of their adoption, their term of validity, and the number of norms liberalising labour relations.

---

[11] Seimas of the Republic of Lithuania. 2008. *Resolution No. XI-52 on the Programme of the Government of the Republic of Lithuania.* Vilnius: Seimas of the Republic of Lithuania.

[12] Petrylaitė, D. 2010. "The Right to Strike in EU Member States: A Comparative Overview with Particular Reference to Lithuania," *The International Journal of Comparative Labour Law and Industrial Relations* 26, No. 4:421-434.

5. Amendments to the Labour Code in 2009: Modest Initial Attempts to Liberalise Labour Relations

This amendment was intended as a provisional measure, because it was in force only until 1 January 2011, i.e., for 18 months. Such an unusual tactic reflects an attempt by initiators of the draft to please everybody. On the one hand, the new legal norms pursue the aim of ameliorating the situation of employers under the conditions of the economic crisis; on the other hand, employees are told that these are merely temporary norms which will remain in force until the "end of the crisis". Therefore, the Government at this stage aims at maintaining social stability by provisional anti-crisis measures, rather than reforming or amending labour law provisions.

A point of departure for the proposals over regulation of labour relations offered by the Government was both the ranking of the country's economic competitiveness (e.g., *Doing business*) and the criticism of inflexible regulation of labour relations imposing limitations on businesses repeated by Lithuanian employers over years. The latter particularly deteriorated during the period of the economic hardship, when the issues of termination of employment relations, modification of employment contracts, promotion of job creation, and restructuring became topical.

Specific proposals of the Government concerning amendments to the Labour Code aimed to achieve the following goals:

1) *reduce the costs of employees' dismissal for employers*. It is not stability of labour relations, or support measures for preservation of workplaces, but facilitation of termination of such contracts that the Government viewed as likely to promote adaptation of the labour market. Lithuanian labour law traditionally stipulates a sufficiently broad protection of employees in the event of termination of employment contracts on economic grounds. Lacking willpower or political consensus on the issue of liberalisation of termination of employment contracts in individual labour relations, the Government offered to achieve this objective with the help of collective agreements. It was proposed to permit the reduction of the employee safeguards, but only if this is envisaged by the collective agreement. Thus, the collective agreement would be granted the power of regulating the terms of dismissal *in peius*, that is, reducing a strict imperative statutory regulation to the detriment of employees. This proposal was not a particularly drastic one, because it indirectly encouraged collective bargaining. Therefore, for trade unions it ought to have been even acceptable, but it was received with resistance and in the end it was implemented only partially—a collective agreement allows for reduction

by half only as regards the time limit of notification of dismissal, but not the amount of the severance pay;[13]

2) *to provide employers with the possibility of unilaterally modifying employment contracts.* The measures capable of directly reducing work costs could also be found in the area of part-time work. In the case of part-time working time, the accomplished work is remunerated for according to the principle of *pro rata temporis*, hence under the conditions of the economic crisis this saving policy seems to be highly attractive even in respect of the employees of the public sector. Although working time in part-time arrangements is considered to be a contractual provision, the Government of the Republic of Lithuania proposed that the Seimas envisaged the possibility of unilaterally amend the contractual provision on full-time daily working time. Again, it is not possible to speak about complete liberalisation, because the possibilities of amending the terms of employment must be provided for under a collective agreement rather than stipulated unilaterally. Moreover, it is proposed to empower the employer to terminate an employment contract with the employee who does not agree to part-time daily working time if this is necessary to ensure continuation of operation of an enterprise. Many serious doubts were raised over this proposal, especially in respect of its compliance with the provisions of EU Directive 97/81/EC concerning part-time work,[14] which stipulates the principle of part-time work on a voluntary basis. Nonetheless, these proposals were not adopted, although it is these proposals that revealed the lack of dynamism in employment contracts—the mechanism of amendment of the terms of employment (terms of remuneration, work time, work time regime, and so on) is not prepared for structural changes;

3) *to permit conclusion of fixed-term employment contracts with permanent workers.* Liberalisation of conclusion of fixed-term employment contracts is often referred to as an incentive of creation of jobs. It should be noted that Art. No. 109 of the Labour Code strictly regulated this issue by prohibiting conclusions of fixed-term employment contracts with permanent workers at the request of the parties to the contracts. The only exceptions were non-permanent work and special provisions in laws as well as—the element of flexibility—in collective agreements. The Parliament viewed the proposal to abolish all restrictions regarding conclusion of fixed-term employment contracts as an excessively drastic

[13] Employers were additionally granted the possibility of unilaterally deciding on periodical payment of the employees' severance pay where the severance pay exceeds five monthly wages (Art. No. 142 of the Labour Code).

[14] Official Journal L 14, 20/01/1998, 9.

one. It was rejected also for the reason that the initiators of the proposal had not provided for a mechanism of prevention of abuse of fixed-term employment contracts, which is required by EU Directive 1999/70/EC on fixed-term work.[15]

4) *to permit overtime work*. The fate of the proposal to liberalise overtime work was similar, although the goals it pursued were linked more with the overall tendencies of liberalisation of labour relations rather than with the economic crisis. Prohibition of overtime work should help maintain employment or encourage employers to create jobs. In fact, overtime work is unreasonably prohibited in Lithuania (Art. No. 150 and 151 of the Labour Code), which creates preconditions for employers and employees to conceal it. The Government attempted to take account of the intention of employees, taking shape during the period of economic growth, to permit employees to work more hours if they request so. The permission to agree on overtime work under collective agreements existed previously, but the proposal to permit individual agreements was rejected by the Parliament in 2009. Instead, the permitted duration of overtime work was increased from four hours in two days up to four hours per day (par. 1 of Art. No. 152 of the Labour Code).

The 2009 amendments to the Labour Code implemented only a part of the proposals of the Government concerning liberalisation of labour relations. Instead of radical permanent decisions, only minor amendments were made to certain provisions and were expected to remain in force for a very short period. Their effectiveness was also diminished by the fact that responsibility for putting them into practice fell on the parties to a collective agreements. The practice showed that it was naïve to expect that a large number of such collective agreements would be concluded and they would change the way labour law is conceived of.

6. Amendments to the Labour Code in 2010: Outcome of Social Dialogue

The 2009 amendments to the Labour Code were of a provisional nature, hence the issue of liberalisation of labour law did not disappear from the reform agenda. At the end of 2009, a national agreement was signed with social partners, under which the Government, while seeking to secure support for its economic reforms, assumed the commitment not to submit any unilateral proposals to the Parliament until 2011, unless they were approved by the Tripartite Council. In 2010, the Government

[15] Official Journal L 175, 10/07/1999, 43.

presented its proposals to social partners suggesting to negotiate an increase of flexibility in the field of working time and overtime work, promotion of youth employment, conclusion of fixed-term employment contracts, and guarantees to employees in the event of redundancy (notification time limits, severance pay, guarantees to specific categories of employees). The negotiations of 2010 attempted to rectify the failures of 2009. In exchange for the proposed liberalisation measures, the Government proposed to negotiate on a package of "compensation" provisions, that is, consolidation of the position of employees' representatives in enterprises (including participation in management bodies of enterprises and holding of strikes), improvement of the mechanism of labour disputes, compliance with and control of labour legislation. Employers did not produce any significantly new proposals, because their standpoint was well represented by the Government itself. Trade unions agreed to negotiate and presented their own proposals. In light of the mentioned provision of the national agreement, it should be noted that it is only thanks to active use of the negotiations method that a compromise was reached, namely, to secure approval of a new reform law—the Law Amending and Supplementing the Labour Code of 22 June 2010. Due to the fact that the law is the outcome of the social compromise, some of its provisions are clearly more favourable for employers, and others—for employees as they compensate for the losses of the latter.

6.1 Measures of Liberalisation of Labour Relations

Working time. The most decisive victory of the employer's interests can be noted in the regulation of working time. It should be pointed out that national labour laws used to regulate working time strictly. The tradition of five working days per week and eight-hour working day was inherited from Soviet labour law. It was very strict in regulating any deviations (work on rest days, overtime work, and so on). Additional restrictions were placed on employers also by the requirements of a minimum uninterrupted rest period stipulated by EU directives.[16] The increased "density" of legal norms made labour organisation complicated as employers had to ensure both an uninterrupted rest period, and the duration of a working day not exceeding 8 hours as well as the duration of a working week not exceeding 40 hours, whereas tailoring of working time

[16] See EU Directive 93/104/EC (Official Journal L 307, 13/12/1993, 18) and Directive 2003/88/EC (Official Journal L 299, 18/11/2003, 9) concerning certain aspects of working time.

to individual needs was limited. The 2010 amendments to the Labour Code introduce flexibility in respect of working time in a rather simple manner—by abolishing restrictions for the introduction of summary recording of working time in enterprises. Having regard to the opinion of representatives of employees, the employer is granted the right to unilaterally introduce summary recordings of working time in the enterprise. Certainly, such a possibility restricts the freedom of employees to plan their time (especially in respect of the employees working in several enterprises, the employees having obligations to their families), but it enables the employer to make rational use of the workforce, plan employment, and adapt to structural or seasonal fluctuations in the market.

Overtime work. Regulation of working time is also associated with another flexibility measure, namely, liberalisation of overtime work. While in 2009 employers failed to obtain permission to individually negotiate on overtime work with employees, the 2010 amendments to the law provided for such a possibility. Nevertheless, this novelty is not as liberal as it is in well-developed Western countries, as the employer is not granted the absolute right to unilaterally assign overtime work. Unless such overtime work is a *force majeure* case, it might be "subject to the request or consent of an employee". Leaving the issue of the difference between the request of the employee and the consent of the employee open to discussion, it will be necessary to decide in practice whether an *ad hoc* or a long-term consent of the employee is meant here, whether such a consent may be withdrawn, whether it is possible to give consent on one occasion and refuse to work overtime on the subsequent occasion, and so on.

Fixed-term employment contracts. The repeated attempt to liberalise the conclusion of fixed-term employment contracts in the 2010 amendments to the Labour Code was successful only partially. Trade unions offered a stout resistance to the general permission to conclude fixed-term employment contracts, but agreed on the proposal to permit conclusion of such contracts temporarily (until mid 2012) in respect of newly created workplaces.

6.2 "Compensatory Package" for Employees

It should be pointed out that along with easing the burden of employers, the 2010 amendments to the Labour Code also attained certain achievements on part of employees. Among such achievements, mention could be made of some new provisions of the Labour Code obtained "in exchange" for the liberalising provisions. The most important provision is related to strikes. In Lithuania, regulation of strikes is very stringent.[17] Trade unions were successful in adapting this procedure to suit their own needs by forcing the adoption of the provisions permitting greater freedom in declaring strikes at the sector level. It should be pointed out that sectoral bargaining and collective agreements have been subject to regulation in the Republic of Lithuania since 1994, but until 2010 there were no special norms regulating the organisation of strikes at sector level. Therefore, the decision achieved by trade unions is indeed beneficial for them—the right to take a decision on calling a strike at the sector level is granted to the trade unions of the sector and, as opposed to declaration of strikes in enterprises, voting of neither employees, nor members of a trade union is mandatory under the law. The sole restriction is the requirement that such issues must be discussed by the Tripartite Council of the Republic of Lithuania before the strike. This regulation is a large step forward in ensuring development of social dialogue in Lithuania, because it is due to the complexity of the strike mechanism that collective bargaining continuously fails to shift from the dominant level of enterprises to the sector level.[18]

An interesting novelty is provided for also in the regulation of individual employment contracts. For the first time, Lithuanian labour law envisages the suspension of an employment contract in the cases when the employer fails to comply with its obligations in respect of the employees. Where the employer fails to regularly pay wages, violates laws, collective agreements or employment contracts, Lithuanian labour law previously provided just for the right of the employee to initiate termination proceedings. The 2010 supplement to the Labour Code provides for a new possibility, namely the right to unilaterally suspend an employment contract for a period of up to three months, subject to giving a written notice to the employer three days in advance. Interestingly enough, these norms are quite strict with regards to employers. Thus, the employer is required to pay the employee compensation in the amount of the minimum wage for each day. The true essence of this amendment may be completely different, e.g. to enable employees to use this instrument of individual self-defence in place of a collective sanction (namely, a strike). The procedure for calling a strike is rather long and complicated, hence a temptation

[17] Petrylaitė, D. 2010. "The Right to Strike in EU Member States: A Comparative Overview with Particular Reference to Lithuania," *The International Journal of Comparative Labour Law and Industrial Relations* 26, No. 4:421-434.

[18] Davulis, T. 1999. "Kolektyviniai susitarimai: kolektyvinių darbo santykių reguliavimo problemos [Collective agreements: the Problems of the Regulation Collective Labour Disputes]," *Teisė* 33, No. 1:12-13.

arises to use co-ordinated suspension of an employment contract where the demands raised are of a legal nature.[19]

7. Conclusions

The new traditions of social policy decision-making and social dialogue taking shape over several decades since the re-establishment of independence determine, to a great extent, the dynamic possibilities of labour law. The Labour Code, which crowned the labour law reform carried out for over a decade and which entered into force in 2003, is viewed as a point of reference for every new legislative initiative. Therefore, any initiatives concerning amendments of the Labour Code are seen from the perspective of interests of one or another social group (employees or employers) as compared against the provisions of the Labour Code already in force. The measures focusing on liberalisation of labour relations or making them more flexible in respect of Lithuanian employers may be viewed positively taking into account a sufficiently high level of protection of employees in Lithuania inherited from the Soviet labour law, the changing factors of the economic environment, the tendencies of regulation of labour relations in other countries, and the social policy instruments of the European Union. So far, the will potential of political government determines whether the liberalisation measures implemented at the national level may be radical or moderate. The principles of advanced social dialogue are best reflected by application of the method of bargaining and exchanges with a view to ensuring changes in labour relations. The analysis of the situation in Lithuania has shown that it is evaluation of mutual proposals and a search for a compromise through negotiations alone that allow for reaching agreements on changing the current situation, which significantly facilitates passing of laws at the Parliament. The most important task in the future will be the search for measures offered in exchange, and the protection of employees' interests, rather than the identification of the labour law norms presenting an obstacle to employers and therefore requiring liberalisation. The labour law norms which are ineffective and which *de facto* worsen the legal situation of employees, as well as the provisions necessary to meet the present-day challenges of the working environment, namely, the

---

[19] Lithuania's labour law permits strikes not only requiring conclusion of a collective agreement, but also with regards to violations of labour laws, collective agreements or employment contracts, provided that these violations are of a collective nature (Art. No. 68 of the Labour Code).

sustainability of qualifications and opportunities on the labour market, the possibility to participate in management of an enterprise, the adaptation to technological progress, the protection of private life, and so on, may be viewed as such measures.

References

Davulis, T. 2009. "The Fifth Anniversary of the New Lithuanian Labour Code: Time to Change?" in *The Modernization of Labour Law and Industrial Relations in a Comparative Perspective*, ed. Blanpain, R. (Alphen aan den Rijn: Kluwer Law International), 360-364.

—. 1999. "Kolektyviniai susitarimai: kolektyvinių darbo santykių reguliavimo problemos [Collective agreements: the Problems of the Regulation Collective Labour Disputes]," *Teisė* 33, No. 1:12-13.

—. 2008. "Lietuvos darbo teisės modernizavimo perspektyvos," *Jurisprudencija*.

European Commission. 2006. *Green Book on Modernising the Labour Law in order to Cope with the Challenges of the 21st Century COM (2006) 708 final.* Brussels: European Commission.

—. 2007. *Towards Common Principles of Flexicurity: More and Better Jobs Through Flexibility and Security, (2007) 359 final.* Brussels: European Commission.

Petrylaitė, D. 2007. "Kolektyviniai darbo santykiai amžių sandūroje: uždaviniai ir galimybės [Collective Labour Relations in the Centuries Crossing: Tasks and Possibilities]," *Teisė*, No. 65:112.

—. 2010. "The Right to Strike in EU Member States: A Comparative Overview with Particular Reference to Lithuania," *The International Journal of Comparative Labour Law and Industrial Relations* 26, No. 4:421-434.

In Need of Flexicurity and Security in a Global Economy

Roger Blanpain

1. Introduction

Flexicurity is one of those fascinating concepts that everyone can agree upon. Undoubtedly, we all want to be flexible and secure. However, in order to understand what needs to be done, to ensure flexicurity works fairly, we have to look at the driving forces which govern our labour relations and the economy in which employment and workers evolve.

2. Super-capitalism

First of all, our economy is increasingly global, especially since China and India joined the free market system. More importantly, we live in an era of *super-capitalism,*[1] in that shareholder value, rather than stakeholder value, is given priority. Our economy is driven by capital investments that are expected to produce economic returns and by consumers who want the best products at the lowest price. Companies need to cut costs and to win over consumers and investors, and this leads to ongoing restructuring, relocations, dismissals, higher levels of poverty, and dual societies.

Moreover, capitalists control politicians. Ninety-thousand lobbyists in Washington can provide unlimited funding to politicians who need financial support for their campaigns. Hilary Clinton, running for President as a Democratic candidate, was sponsored by the tobacco industry, Philip Morris. That says enough.

The super-rich get richer. One percent of Americans get 25% of national wealth: lower taxes, no control of the banks and more bonuses.

[1] Friedman, T. 2009. *Hot, Flat and Crowded.* London: Penguin Books, 516; Reich, R. 2007. *Supercapitalism. The Transformation of Business, Democracy, and Everyday Life.* New York: Knopf, 272; Reich, R. 2010. *Aftershock. The Next Economy and America's Future.* New York: Knopf, 174.

Even now, in the post-crisis period, CEOs earn millions. Workers lose worldwide. Capital is global, labour is not.

3. The Financial Crisis

The recent global crisis had a lot in common with the uncontrolled activity of bankers, which caused the housing bubble in the USA, the result of a steady increase in house prices. More and more families were borrowing higher amounts of money from the banks, that secured that money by issuing mortgage-backed securities (MBSs) and collateralised debt obligations (CDOs). These are a type of structured asset-backed securities (ABS) whose value and payments are derived from a portfolio of fixed-income underlying assets. CDOs are assigned different risk classes, or tranches, whereby "senior" tranches are considered the safest securities. Interest and principal payments are made on the basis of seniority, so that junior tranches offer higher coupon payments (and interest rates) or lower prices to compensate for additional default risk. While the property prices were going up, the system functioned well. However, once prices fell, the system collapsed.[2]

Bankers took extreme risks, some behaved like gangsters. Only profits, enormous wages and extraordinary bonuses counted. No doubt, greed was the dominating force. The reason for this state of affairs is simple: the financial markets in the USA were deregulated. The motto was "The market should have the last word". We have witnessed the result of this. Clearly, there is a lack of efficient control of financial transactions at the national, European and international level as well.

4. Governments Save Banks

Since financial institutions operate globally, and many banks were in difficulty, the international financial system remained obstructed. Banks did not trust one another, and the financial flows necessary to finance both existing and new investments by enterprises ceased as well. The result of this state of affairs was the worldwide economic recession. Consumers lost confidence, and banks had to be supported by national governments. In

---

[2] See Aleksandrov, Z. "The Challenges of Globalisation and the Economic Downturn. The European Globalisation Adjustment Fund," Paper presented at Tilburg University, the Netherlands, April 2009. Driessen, B. "The Financial Crisis and Unemployment," Paper presented at Tilburg University, the Netherlands, April 2009. Wikipedia: Collateralized debt obligation.

certain countries, banks simply came under state ownership, in others enormous amounts of money were pumped into the banking system to keep it going. Meanwhile, unemployment rates increased.

5. Multinationals

Multinationals are equally global and running the show. Around 100,000 multinational companies are characterised by *centralised decision-making*. Decisions about what and where to invest are taken in faraway headquarters, bypassing local politicians and trade unions. In 2010, when GM decided to close down its Antwerp plant employing 2,900 workers, the decision was made in Detroit. The Flemish government and the "strong" Belgian trade unions were pedalling in thin air.

What is even more important is that multinational enterprises (MNEs) oversee *research and development*. Approximately 70% of research funds are provided by multinationals. In 1989, while visiting Toyota in my capacity as President of the IIRA, the enterprise had no less than 10,000 people involved in research activities. MNEs conclude research contracts with universities. Seventy percent of the technological transfer involving new technologies and production is done by multinational enterprises, and research is mostly carried out at company headquarters, which adds to the globalising effect.

Everywhere, there appears to be a deference to attract multinational investment to give momentum to jobs and new technologies. Multinationals view countries as clients, in terms of benefits that they can offer. Accordingly, the power is with the multinational groups.

A good example is the latest developments in the automobile company Fiat (January 2011).

Fiat: New contract, longer hours, shorter breaks

On 13 and 14 January 2011, over 5,000 Fiat workers at Turin's main factory voted on a new collective agreement which drastically increases hours, reduces breaks and restricts industrial action

Workers were supposedly under pressure by management with the threat of relocation if they voted against the agreement.[3]

The new agreement is essentially the same as that imposed on Fiat workers at a plant near Naples six months ago. The contract involves flexible working hours in three shifts, fewer breaks, and a ban on spontaneous strike action.

According to the details of the new agreement, instead of the former system of 10 shifts a week, workers will now be called upon to work 18 shifts. This will consist of three shifts per day beginning Monday morning at 6 a.m. and finishing on Sunday morning at 6 a.m. The rest of Sunday remains free.

Working time is officially 40 hours per week, but under the new agreement, workers can be called upon to work up to 120 hours overtime per year. Since Saturday is a normal working day, there is a provision for two days' leave every fortnight. Every working minute has been planned out in detail. In the course of every eight-hour shift, workers are entitled to just two (instead of three) breaks of 10 minutes, with meals to be taken at the end of the shift. Sick leave is to be strictly limited and sickness benefit reduced due to what the management regards as excessive absenteeism.

The new Fiat agreement seems to be contrary to the existing national collective agreement in several ways, e.g., with its stipulation of a high number of overtime hours, the strike ban and the eventual exclusion of elected representatives in the factories.

In order to circumvent the existing national agreement, Fiat has withdrawn from the employers' association, Confindustria.

---

[3] Such a threat is contrary to the OECD Guidelines for Multinational Enterprises, namely paragraph 7 of the Employment and Industrial Relations Chapter: "Enterprises should, within the framework of applicable law, regulations and prevailing labour relations and employment practices, in the context of *bona fide* negotiations with representatives of employees on conditions of employment, or while employees are exercising a right to organize, not threaten to transfer the whole or part of an operating unit from the country concerned nor transfer employees from the enterprises' component entities in other countries in order to influence unfairly those negotiations or to hinder the exercise of a right to organize".

In Turin, Fiat is planning to build a new Jeep and an Alfa Romeo in a joint venture with Chrysler. The aim is to double the production of autos. Fiat raised its stake in Chrysler from 20 to 25 percent in what has been described as a further step towards gaining full control of its US partner. The company has said it will invest €1 billion in the Fiat-Chrysler project in the parent company at Turin-Mirafiori—so long as workers vote in favour of their increased exploitation.

On 13-14 January 2011, staff at Fiat's Mirafiori plant in Turin approved a tough deal on working conditions that is to save their factory and prove key to the future of the new Fiat-Chrysler auto giant. According to a final tally of the vote, those supporting the deal obtained 54.05 percent. Turnout was 94.2 percent, with 5,119 of the plant's 5,431 employees taking part.[4]

However, the composition of the multinational group is shifting: from West to East.

6. The Colonisation of the West

There is no doubt that the EU has lost the initiative. With 500 million inhabitants, the EU has less than 7% of the world population. The East is in a position of advantage, particularly China, as it investments have an impact worldwide. Last year, the Chinese invested more than 50 billion US dollars overseas, with 33 billion in the EU. One of the most significant results of such a massive investment was the acquisition of Volvo, which still employs 22,000 employees, and it is characterised by innovative technology and expertise. These days companies in the EU are cheap, and this has led to their willingness to formalise bargains.

These takeovers are the start of a new era: the colonisation of the West by the East. The Western economy, and above all Western values are at stake. Countries in the West are accustomed to foreign investments, but until recently investors were mostly American and Japanese. Westerners conformed to the decisions of their headquarters, but these multinationals belong to democratic countries, which have respect for human rights, including trade union freedom.

Now, this state of affairs will change dramatically. The East has gained economic power, the result of Arab petrodollars and Chinese worldwide commerce.

[4] Belga "Minder rechtenomfabriekte redden" (Fewer rights to save enterprise), www.zondag.be, (accessed January 16, 2011).

Thc EU's diminished influence and power in terms of international decision-making was clearly illustrated at the Climate Summit in Copenhagen in 2010, in reference to the takeover of Volvo by the Chinese carmaker Geely. After discussing the issue for two weeks, US President Barack Obama came to an agreement with China, while European representatives watched impotently.

The Chinese are proud of their culture, and with a realisation of their power have become more determined to achieve their goals.

However, China is not a democratic country, but a communist dictatorship, where human rights are not recognised. A popular example of this is in their unwillingness to accept the Dalai Lama. There is neither trade union freedom, nor free collective bargaining. The right to privacy is unknown as well as the right to equal treatment. According to Confucius, everyone has his/her place in the hierarchy, and those at the top make decisions. There is no democratic legitimisation of decision-making and freedom of expression is dangerous for the State, as Google experienced lately. The internet is screened and the death penalty is still in force. Copyright means the right to copy, and trade secrets are not kept. China is a country with a fashion industry employing more than 10 million workers.

There are some 300 million illegal Chinese workers who out of poverty have left the countryside and work in the black market in and around big cities. They contribute to China's wealth, yet without any social rights, minimum wage or social security.

7. The New Lisbon Strategy: Europe 2020

7.1 Crisis

Europe finds itself in the post-crisis period, both economically and socially. In 2009, GDP fell by 4%, and public deficit and debt levels now correspond to 7% and over 80% of GDP, respectively. Belgium has a debt-level of almost 100%, thus the bank crisis has ruined a significant number of people.

Twenty-three million people—10% of the active population—are now unemployed. Employment rates in Europe—69% on average for those aged 20-64—are still significantly lower than in other parts of the world. Only 63% of women are working, compared to 76% of men, and the percentage of older workers (55-64) who are employed is only 46%, well below the 62% in the US and Japan. Moreover, on average Europeans work 10% fewer hours than their US or Japanese counterparts.

Demographic ageing is accelerating. As the baby-boom generation retires, the active population in the EU will start to shrink from 2013/2014. The number of people aged over 60 is now increasing twice as fast as it did before 2007—by about two million every year compared to the previous one million. A reduced working population and a higher proportion of retired people will place additional strains on our welfare systems, particularly at the time of dealing with an increase in costs for health care and retirement pensions. Undoubtedly, there is a need for Europe to come up with some ideas for reform. In March 2010, the European Commission proposed its plan for 2020,[5] that was to be approved by the European Council by June 2010.

In this connection, Europe 2020 sets out three priorities:

1) Smart growth: developing an economy based on knowledge and innovation.
2) Sustainable growth: promoting a more resource-efficient, greener and more competitive economy.
3) Inclusive growth: fostering a high-employment economy and delivering social and territorial cohesion.

To this end, the European Commission proposes the following EU targets:

1) 75% of the population aged 20-64 should be employed.
2) 20 million less people should be at risk of poverty.
3) 3% of the EU GDP should be invested in R&D.
4) The proportion of early school leavers should be no more than 10%, and at least 40% of the younger generation should obtain a tertiary degree.

7.2 A Critical Assessment

Whether this plan will succeed will mainly depend on the willingness of the 27 Member States. Indeed, the EU has no economic or social policy of its own; the main responsibility for determining these rests on the Member States.

---

[5] European Commission. 2010. *Europe 2020: A Strategy for Smart, Sustainable and Inclusive Growth.* Brussels: European Commission. http://ec.europa.eu/eu2020/index_en.htm (accessed January 16, 2011).

7.3 Lack of Social Competence

The question indeed arises as to whether the EU has sufficient competence to develop a fully-fledged European social policy. In answering this question, one needs to recall that the competence to deal with issues are those that have been transferred by the Member States to the EU and need to be exercised as indicated by the Treaty

On this point, the so-called European Social Model is extremely weak. Indeed, a number of social "core" issues are excluded from the EU competence, namely:

1) pay, the right of association, the right to strike and the right to impose lock-outs.

As for other important matters, unanimity in the European Council is required, namely:

2) social security and social protection of workers;
3) job security;
4) representation and collective defence of interests, including co-determination.

However, unanimity between 27 Member States is almost impossible.

Needless to say that the European Social Model, as far as the sphere of competence is concerned, is almost non-existent. The most negative aspect is that this will be a permanent feature as the European Treaty (TFEU) can only be amended by unanimous consent, that is difficult to reach particularly when it comes to matters of social policy.

Obviously, there are other ways to foster convergence in the social field, like the so-called "enhanced co-ordination strategy", as shown in the case of the employment guidelines, which gave rise to the devising of national action plans, pressuring Member States into conforming to these guidelines. This all-important strategy could be adopted elsewhere, for instance to implement the "Lisbon 2020" Strategy.

However, there are a number of matters that fall outside the sphere of EU competence for which unanimity is required: the enactment of binding measures on core issues such as a European minimum wage or the recognition of a collective agreement at the EU level as binding on core issues such as social security, job security, and collective bargaining.

As a matter of course, the EU does not have the essential powers to organise and establish a fully-fledged European Social Model. What is worse, the political will to further integrate in social terms is likewise lacking, and the more countries join the EU, the more difficult it becomes to muster such a political commitment.

7.4 Lack of Financial Means

Moreover, the EU Member States lack the financial means to launch a dynamic economic policy or to invest in research and development in a consistent manner. Three percent of GDP has been a goal for a long time but it has not been achieved. Due to the financial crisis, national governments have to cut expenses and save—drastic saving plans have been introduced in Greece and Spain, among others; the German government believes it needs to save €80 billion (£65.8 billion) before 2014, and the Belgian Government should save €22 billion by 2015. These measures are not welcomed by the public at large, and the same goes for measures to keep people at work longer, e.g. by raising the *retirement age*. The French proposal to increase the retirement age to 62 years encountered enormous resistance on the part of French Trade Unions.

7.5 Being Competitive

In order to maintain higher levels of competition in this global economy, it is important to diminish labour costs, provide flexible working time, and employment contracts. Minimum wages should be abolished, while the extension of collective agreements is questioned.

In 2010, the German Job Miracle was taken as a reference model,[6] particularly considering the main aspects of the German labour market:

1) the lowest unemployment rate for 18-year-olds (7%);
2) the lowest number of long-term unemployed since reunification: 900,000;
3) the highest degree of employment: 41 million workers (out of a population of 80 million);
4) higher levels of participation of workers aged 55-64 (+16%) increasing the rate for this age group to 53%;

---

[6] Prof. Dr. Spermann, A. 2010. "Job Miracle in Germany? How the Former Sick Man of Europe Got Healthy," Lecture given in Brussels, Belgium, 14 December 2010.
http://www.randstad.be/nl/informatie/informatieenservice/seminaries/conferenties/ (accessed November 7, 2011).

5) higher levels of female participation, with an increase of 6% raising the relative percentage to a 64 % participation rate
6) economic growth forecast: 3% in 2010 and 2% for 2011.

The reason for this has to be found in the so-called Hartz reforms 2002-2005: "Push and Pull Approach", the main pillars of which are:

1) merger of unemployment benefit and public assistance (since 2005);
2) a new simplified system:
   a) 12-month unemployment benefits, means test, basic income;
   b) effects: reduction of reservation wage;
3) other changes of labour market institutions:
   a) improved job placement system;
   b) deregulation of agency work;
   c) expansion of marginal employment (400 € jobs);
   d) incentives for self-employment;
   e) lowering of barriers to enter the labour market.[7]

No amendments have been made in terms of employment protection legislation. A number of critical questions arise when evaluating the successful German experience. Here, there is neither a general minimum wage nor any extension of collective agreements with *erga omnes* clauses. Further, there is no automatic indexation of wages based on the rising costs of living.

What strikes one most is the considerable number of workers with low incomes—that is those who earn less than €9.71 gross per hour (this is less than two-thirds of the average wage)—which make up less than 22% of the workforce. Especially for Central and Eastern European workers and other immigrants, wages of €3 to €5 per hour have been reported and some five million workers earn around €1,500 gross a month. A worker who makes €200 a month is entitled to up to €600 of public assistance money. The question arises as to whether Germany is evolving into a dual system similar to the American one. Is this the objective of flexicurity?

---

[7] Prof. Dr. Spermann, A. 2010. "Job Miracle in Germany? How the Former Sick Man of Europe Got Healthy," Lecture given in Brussels, Belgium, 14 December 2010, 3 and 10. http://www.randstad.be/nl/informatie/informatieenservice/seminaries/conferenties/ (accessed November 7, 2011).

8. In Summary

We live in times of super-capitalism, dominated by multinational enterprises. The main economic decisions are taken at a global and international level, bypassing local players. There is a sort of casino-banking, with labour law and employment relations that remain national. Even in the EU, labour costs are a completely national affair, resulting in cost competition between Member States and social dumping. At the same time, trade unions are getting weaker and are no match for the multinational enterprises and even national companies, which are free to relocate. Labour relations are power relations and power, alongside capital, is driving workers towards more flexibility.

What workers need is security. In this sense, another lesson learned from the crisis is that some degree of rigidity might represent a virtue in times of crisis. Where employers can dismiss at will, as in the USA, and there are no social backups, the crisis not only hits harder, but it feeds itself, because purchasing power diminishes and there are no prospects. Security for employees is, in times of economic difficulty, a must. Flexibility is a must too, but the aim should be, as it is in Denmark, to provide new job opportunities. The crisis also tells us that it is time to cut the excessive bonuses of top managers.

For the long term "more control" is needed, especially of the financial system at a national, European and international level. There is no room for bankers behaving irresponsibly. There should be enough *rigidity* to ensure income and *security* for workers. And there remains the fundamental duty to provide more *training*, as those without sufficient skills pay the hardest price for globalisation.

Nevertheless, the EU has no choice; we have to support the Lisbon Strategy, in an awareness that it will be extremely difficult to obtain "smart, sustainable and inclusive growth". The road is narrow and steep, but we must try. It is not forbidden to dream and sometimes dreams come true.

References

Aleksandrov, Z. "The Challenges of Globalisation and the Economic Downturn. The European Globalisation Adjustment Fund," Paper presented at Tilburg University, the Netherlands, April 2009.

Driessen, B. "The Financial Crisis and Unemployment," Paper presented at Tilburg University, the Netherlands, April 2009.

European Commission. 2010. *Europe 2020: A Strategy for Smart, Sustainable and Inclusive Growth.* Brussels: European Commission.

Friedman, T. 2009. *Hot, Flat and Crowded.* London: Penguin Books.

Reich, R. 2007. *Supercapitalism. The Transformation of Business, Democracy, and Everyday Life.* New York: Knopf.

—. 2010. *Aftershock. The Next Economy and America's Future.* New York: Knopf.

Spermann, A. 2010. "Job Miracle in Germany? How the Former Sick Man of Europe Got Healthy," Lecture given in Brussels, Belgium, 14 December 2010.

CORPORATE SOCIAL RESPONSIBILITY: A CONCEPT FOR THE 21ST CENTURY

MANFRED WEISS

1. Introduction

The recent financial and economic crisis affected the economy as a whole and on a global scale, with a major impact on practically all branches of activity. Markets were eroding. Positive growth rates worldwide were substituted by alarming figures for negative growth, and the effects of the crisis disappeared only slowly.

In many countries the crisis led to negative effects on the labour markets. Plant closure or at least downsizing of companies' personnel became common practice. The rate of unemployment climbed dramatically. This not only had an impact on the workers who were affected by these measures in economic terms, but there was—and to a certain extent there still is—the danger that those who stay in the companies have to constantly live with the fear of losing their job. Evidently, such level of uncertainty is not an incentive for workers' motivation and thereby for the companies' productivity. And of course, it does not affect positively the climate in the workforce. Counterproductive rivalry instead of necessary team spirit might be the undesirable outcome.

However, there were not only negative effects. The crisis also showed that countries with a pattern of cooperation involving management and workers' representatives succeeded best to minimise the negative consequences on the labour market. The crisis taught us that, in order to successfully manage a sustainable employment situation, it is necessary to develop strategies which not only please management or shareholders, but strike a fair balance between the diverging interests of all stakeholders with a view to promote sustainability. This, however, implies that attitudes and conceptual models in many countries are to be changed. And it also implies that the processes of mass lay-offs and similar procedures of downsizing and restructuring are not viewed as isolated phenomena but related to an overall business concept.

Since the effects of the crisis were more or less the same all over the world, the debate on feasible company strategies has become an international one, disconnected from domestic peculiarities. Such a company strategy is an important element of what is presently called the necessity for a "Global New Deal". This presents a great opportunity for companies to learn from one another so as to prevent repeating mistakes from the past, and to be better prepared to overcome crises.

Corporate Social Responsibility (CSR)—as a point of orientation—might be the concept companies should strive for in order to be equipped to cope with the challenges of the 21st century. Whether and to what extent this is the case is a difficult question to which here no ready-made and detailed answers are given. My intention is much more modest, namely to simply indicate the direction and avenues that companies may take. The events which led to the crisis have taught us about the lack of comprehensive concepts in which available instruments and measures are to be embedded. Therefore, CSR first will be discussed in a rather abstract way before later on drawing more concrete conclusions arising from the concept.

2. The Concept of Corporate Social Responsibility

Before dealing with the impact of CSR on rethinking and re-evaluating companies' strategies, it seems necessary to firstly identify this often quoted concept which has made a very impressive career worldwide in the last few years, at least on a rhetorical level. The many documents issued by the International Labour Organization (ILO)[1] and by the European Union (EU)[2] on this topic are a helpful tool in this respect.

According to the available material there seems to be consensus that CSR is a concept whereby companies integrate social and environmental concerns in their business operations and in their interaction with their stakeholders on a voluntary basis. It is about enterprises deciding to go beyond minimum legal requirements and obligations stemming from collective agreements in order to address societal needs. Through CSR enterprises of all sizes, in cooperation with their stakeholders, can

---

[1] See for example Murray, J. 2004. "Corporate Social Responsibility: An Overview of Principles and Practice," ILO Working Paper No. 34, Geneva: ILO; and Hopkins, M. 2004. "Corporate Social Responsibility: An Issues Paper," ILO Working Paper No. 27, Geneva: ILO.

[2] See in particular Commission of the European Communities. 2001. *Green Paper—Promoting a European Framework for Corporate Social Responsibility, COM (2001) 366 final.* Brussels: European Commission.

reconcile economic, social and environmental ambitions. This concept is based on the assumption that sustainable business success cannot be achieved solely through maximising short-term profits, but instead through market-oriented—yet responsible—behaviour. Companies have to be aware that they can contribute to sustainable development by managing their operations in such a way as to enhance economic growth and increase competitiveness, whilst ensuring environmental protection and promoting social responsibility.

Or to be even more specific: the concept of CSR offers an alternative to the view of the protagonists of deregulation—among them for a long time also influential international financial institutions such as the World Bank, the International Monetary Fund (IMF) and regional development banks—who stress negative economic effects of measures of social policy.[3] This latter view is not only one-dimensional because it exclusively focuses on economic efficiency but it proved to be wrong as extended empirical research demonstrates.

Even if many long-term benefits are indirect and difficult to measure, empirical evidence shows that fair labour conditions result in improved health and human capital which increases the productivity potential of workers. In particular, it shows that fair working conditions result in improved motivation and willingness of workers for high performance.

Long-term and stable relationships between the worker and the company provide incentives to companies to invest in workers' training because the company is able to recover returns from it. Job security provides incentives to workers to share their knowledge and skills with colleagues, especially with young people and apprentices. In addition, it allows workers to cooperate and increase productivity without fearing the loss of their job. Also at the macro-economic level, empirical evidence is available for a positive effect of decent working conditions on trade competitiveness and growth.[4]

In short and to make the point, the underlying idea of CSR makes us aware that the protagonists of deregulation suffer of a reality gap. Social policy is an essential input to a functioning market economy as well as

---

[3] For a summary of this Approach see Sengenberger, W. 2006. "International Labour Standards in the Globalized Economy: Obstacles and Opportunities for Achieving Progress," in *Globalization and the Future of Labour Law,* eds. Craig, D. R., and S. M. Lynck, (Cambridge: Cambridge University Press), 331 et seq.

[4] For a comprehensive synthesis of the available research on the beneficial effects of International Labour Standards see Sengenberger, W. 2002. *Globalization and Social Progress: The Role and Impact of International Labour Standards.* Bonn: Friedrich Ebert Stiftung.

comprehensive and sustainable economic development. Therefore, CSR should be considered as a form of investment in institutions which not only have a positive effect for themselves on the long run, but they positively impact the stability and the development of society as a whole.

However, the economic dimension is only one among others. If we are talking about CSR, we are predominantly talking about aspects of human dignity as it is expressed by the actual program of the International Labour Organization (ILO) on decent work for all. The fundamental rights perspective is playing an ever more important role. The famous statement from the ILO's Philadelphia Declaration that "labour is not a commodity" is still valid and indicates that market rules are not sufficient to meet the needs of decent work corresponding to human dignity.

If now an attempt is made to deconstruct the very complex definition of CSR, the following five basic elements can be identified:

1) CSR tries to link in particular two pillars: the social dimension and economic efficiency. In my sketchy remarks, in order to reduce complexity I have excluded the third pillar of this concept—that is the environmental one—even if this aspect is of utmost importance for the society as a whole. The basic idea of CSR is that economic and social considerations are not separate entities but depend on each other in a somehow symbiotic way. Integrating these two elements means that a synergy effect can be reached that improves the effects for both sides. Thereby, protective standards and decent working conditions are no longer perceived merely as a cost but as an investment in sustainable economic efficiency.

2) The focus on shareholder-value as the decisive criterion for business operations is to be replaced by the concept of stakeholder value, which refers to a conglomerate of actors in which employee interests—as well as consumer and public interests, as for example environmental concerns—are included. Optimising all of them is an ambitious goal. This, in my view, is the most decisive change of paradigm.

3) The short-term perspective is to be replaced by long-term strategies focussing on stability and sustainability of companies. Thereby short-time effects in stock markets are becoming less relevant than in the past.

4) At least in principle, CSR is not supposed to substitute but merely to supplement legal rules. The existence of law (legislation, collective agreements) and an efficient enforcement machinery to implement it allows CSR to develop strategies above this level. However, if a legal structure providing the necessary minimum of labour standards is lacking—which is not only the case in developing countries—it is also implied by the concept of CSR that such a minimum is to be respected. In

other words: the range of the companies' tasks according to the concept of CSR depends on the already existing legal platform in a given country.

5) Finally CSR is—at least in principle and to a certain extent—a voluntary exercise, not to be imposed on companies. It is supposed to be the result of their free choice. Of course, free choice in this area is sometimes the result of events which put pressure on companies. When, for example, Multinational Enterprises (MNE) of the textile and sportswear industries finally agreed to establish codes of conduct to be respected, also in developing countries in which they operate, this in some cases was the result of consumer boycotts in their home countries, efficiently organised by quite militant Non Governmental Organisations (NGO). Or often such codes were established simply to improve the company's image. Nevertheless, all these companies in the very end act by their choice.

3. Corporate Social Responsibility and Minimum Standards

Even if above CSR is described as a voluntary strategy to be implemented by the companies also in the absence of law, it does not mean that legal patterns would not be helpful. The more hard law pushes the companies already in the direction of CSR, the more workers can rely on the implementation of the concept. Therefore, the question arises whether and in how far there is already an international floor of rights on which CSR can be built up.

The development of international labour standards is the main task of the ILO since its foundation more than 90 years ago. Its achievements in this area undoubtedly are a success story which barely can be overestimated. Almost 200 conventions and even more recommendations, covering all kinds of aspects of Labour Law and Social Security Law, are an impressive output.[5]

An example which is of particular interest in the context of CSR may be the Convention No. 158 of 1982, supplemented by Recommendation No. 166 of the same year, on "Termination of Employment at the Initiative of the Employer". This convention refers to situations of restructuring the company and downsizing personnel. Even if it does not distinguish between individual and collective dismissals, it is important to stress that

---

[5] See for a comprehensive overview on the ILO's standard setting activities Rubin, N., ed. 2005. *Code of International Labour Law.* 2 volumes, Cambridge: Cambridge University Press.

in its second part it contains provisions concerning termination of employment for economic, technological, structural or similar reasons. A closer look shows that here the focus is on mass lay-offs. According to the general part of the convention, unilateral termination is allowed only if there is a valid reason for such termination connected with the capacity or conduct of the worker or based on the operational requirements of the undertaking, establishment or service (Art. No. 4). This undoubtedly is a ban of the concept of employment at will. The convention also entitles workers who consider that his or her employment has been unjustifiably terminated to appeal against that termination to an impartial body, be it a court, a labour tribunal, an arbitration committee or an arbitrator (Art. No. 8). In addition, the convention contains procedural requirements on distribution of the burden of proof and on minimum terms of notice on severance pay. The specific provisions for mass lay-offs contain two additional requirements: First, the employer has to inform the competent authority in the respective country (Art. No. 14). Secondly, and more importantly, the employer has to provide workers' representatives

> in good time with relevant information including the reasons for the termination contemplated, the number and categories of workers likely to be affected and the period over which the terminations are intended to be carried out [and give them] as early as possible an opportunity for consultation on measures to be taken to avert or to minimise the terminations and measures to mitigate the adverse effects of any terminations on the workers concerned such as finding alternative employment (Art. No. 13).

It should be added that there is Convention No. 135 of 1971, supplemented by Recommendation No. 143 of the same year, concerning the protection and facilities to be afforded to workers' representatives in the undertaking, allowing them to do their job efficiently and without fear, an aspect which will be treated in more detail later on. In short: all these conventions and recommendations try to promote cooperation between management and labour in case of restructuring enterprises.

Instead of giving further examples it might rather be stressed that the set of conventions should not be taken as a mirror of reality. In legal terms, conventions are considered to be international treaties which are to be ratified in order to be binding for the member countries. There, however, a significant problem arises. The Member States' inclination to ratify is unfortunately rather low, and this is particularly true for developing countries. The reason seems to be that they are afraid of competitive disadvantages in case of ratification. On the whole, 60 percent of the Member States of the ILO ratified less than a quarter of the conventions and more than 20 percent of the Member States even less than one tenth.[6]

In 1998, the ILO made an attempt by the well-known Declaration on Fundamental Labour Rights to make sure that at least the Member States abide to four core fundamental rights contained up to then in 7 conventions. These core fundamental rights are freedom of association including the right to collective bargaining, prohibition of forced labour, prohibition of child labour and prohibition of discrimination for all kind of reasons. These rights are to be applied in all Member States and no ratification is needed. A follow-up procedure in the declaration paves new ways for implementation. However, there is an ongoing debate pleading for extension of this list of core fundamental rights, for example, by a right to a living wage or by a right to health and safety.

The ratification record, however, is not the only problem. The major problem lies in the discrepancy between ratification and implementation in actual practice. It has to be kept in mind that, particularly in developing countries, there is a lack of administrative and infrastructural preconditions for such a factual implementation. Monitoring mechanisms are available only to a limited extent. In many cases trade unions are much too weak to function as a monitoring actor. Governments are quite often not very much interested in implementation in actual practice because they are afraid of losing competitive advantages which they see in low labour costs and a low level of workers' rights, the result of a narrow-minded perspective.

The monitoring machinery of the ILO is likewise inefficient. There are rather sophisticated procedures,[7] but their effect is rather modest. This has mainly to do with the fact that the material for monitoring is provided by reports which are written by the Member States themselves. Trade unions and employers' associations are entitled to cooperate in the elaboration of these reports. This, however, does not change the fact that these reports remain problematic since also these organisations are often not eager to list up domestic deficiencies in these reports. But even where the reports are correct and where deficiencies of implementation are discovered by the monitoring bodies of the ILO, the monitoring procedure is merely built on the principle of mobilisation of shame. The idea is that for mere image reasons a member state accused in such a way will further on be rule abiding. Whether this expectation is met remains more than doubtful.

---

[6] Hepple, B. 2005. *Labour Laws and Global Trade.* Oxford/Portland: Cambridge University Press, 35.

[7] For details see Servais, J. M. 2005. *International Labour Law*, The Hague: Kluwer Law International, 24 et seq.

It is because of such deficiencies—whose list could be easily extended—that private actors such as Multinational Enterprises (MNE) and other companies are supposed to develop strategies on their own to meet the requirements of CSR. The instruments to achieve this goal are codes of conduct. Long ago a framework for such codes of conduct was devised by international institutions. The forerunner in this context was the Organization for Economic Cooperation and Development (OECD) which passed already in 1976 "The OECD Guidelines for Multinational Enterprises", last amended in 2006. The ILO followed one year later in 1977 by its "Tripartite Declaration of Principles on Multinational Enterprises and Social Policy", last revised in 2007 and presently in the stage of further revision. And the latest of these codes is the United Nations' (UN) "Global Compact", issued in 1999 by Kofi Annan, at the time the UN Secretary-General. Even if the already mentioned economic and political power of the MNE was the reason for the development of the OECD and ILO guidelines, their title is somehow misleading. They are explicitly only addressed to MNE. However, they are intended to cover companies in general, not only MNE. They do not want to create gaps between MNE and domestic companies, even if it has turned out that this is a futile hope. In reality, there is segmentation between these two categories of enterprises.

These "external" guidelines were mainly meant to enrich the fantasy of management in the MNE in elaborating so called private codes of conduct. Such codes have become numerous and are mainly the product of the last two decades. They are in practice confined to MNE, thereby creating gaps between their working conditions and those of domestic companies.

Even if these codes are by no means homogeneous, they all refer to the core fundamental rights as contained in the already mentioned ILO Declaration of 1998. As for the rest, there are big differences between them. Even more significant are the differences between different branches of activity.[8] To give just an example: in the textile industry the main emphasis is on child labour, whereas in the chemical industry or in the transport sector it is on health and safety. Many codes simply refer to the

---

[8] For an example of such branch specific codes see van Liemt, G. 2000. "Codes of Conduct and International Subcontracting: A 'Private' Road towards Ensuring Minimum Labour Standards in Export Industries," in *Multinational Enterprises and the Social Challenges of the 21st Century*, ed. Blanpain, R. (The Hague / London / Boston: Kluwer Law International), 167 et seq.

whole set of ILO standards as well as to the law of the respective host country whose wording often has nothing to do with actual practice there.[9]

It should be mentioned that not only the contents of the codes are very different from each other but also the genesis of these codes. Originally most codes were unilaterally established by the companies. However, to an increasing extent there is a new generation of codes called "multi-stakeholder" initiatives.[10] Companies, trade unions, human rights groups, community and development organisations participate in formulating such codes of conduct. These "multi-stakeholder codes" contain also provisions on monitoring, verification, certification of supplier factories, enforcement mechanisms and transparency. Among the most prominent actors in this activity of monitoring codes of conduct are the "Fair Labour Association", the "Workers Rights Consortium", the "Social Accountability International", the "Ethical Trading Initiative", the "Clean Clothing Campaign" and "Worldwide Responsible Apparel Production", to just give you some examples of an almost endless list.

Many of the codes only cover the relationship between the MNE and their employees. However, to an increasing extent sub-contractors as well as the whole supply chain and some times even clients are included. Normally such codes require that in case of violations these either have to be corrected or the business relationship has to be stopped. The latter, of course, is a very ambiguous sanction since it may lead the employees of the sub-contractor or the client to the loss of the job and, thereby, to a further worsening of their situation.

All these codes are, of course, legally non-binding. They are "light touch" regulations or "soft law". There is only a moral obligation of the MNE to respect them. Unfortunately, it happens quite often that the content of the codes is unknown to the employees as well as to those persons who are responsible for implementing them. Then, of course, there is no awareness of violation. In case of unilaterally developed codes the companies are very much interested in internal conflict-resolution. Therefore, in these cases the outside observers do not learn anything about possible violations. However, many companies that want to make it

---

[9] For an illustration of the big variety of codes see Scherrer, C., and T. Greven. 2001. *Global Rules for Trade: Codes of Conduct, Social Labeling Workers' Rights Clauses.* Muenster: Westphalisches Dampfboot; and Webb, K., ed. 2004. *Voluntary Codes: Private Governance in the Public Interest and Innovation.* Ottawa: Carleton Research Unit for Innovation, Science and Environment.

[10] For details of this development see Compa, L. 2008. "Corporate Social Responsibility and Workers' Rights," *Comparative Labor Law and Policy Journal,* 5 et seq.

perfectly clear that they are not interested in hiding violations have decided to be exposed in regular intervals to so called "external monitoring". As already mentioned, this applies of course to all "multi-stakeholder codes" of the new generation. Such monitoring procedures prove to be quite efficient. In case of negotiated codes, it depends on the strength and vigilance of the partner with whom the code was established whether and in how far the public can be mobilised and thereby put pressure on the company's management. In this respect up to now NGO have proved to be much more efficient than trade unions. For example, the NGO "clean clothing campaign" has succeeded in provoking immediate reactions of multinationals in case of violations which happened in developing countries. In short and to make the point: even if the codes are not legally binding and even if there are still deficiencies in implementing them, to a bigger and bigger extent the external pressure in case of violation can no longer be ignored.

In the meantime, quite a few MNEs use the standards of their employment relationships as marketing strategy and therefore initiate competition for the better in this area. In this context, and to a significant extent "social labelling" plays an important role. Products of companies fabricated according to the rules of the game get a label in a so called certification procedure. It is not surprising that those who get such labels use them in their marketing strategy.

The most recent development in this context consists in agreements which are concluded between global union federations and a growing number of MNE.[11] The difference compared to the codes of conduct as sketched above is not so much the content of these agreements but the fact that on the workers' side there is a strong actor which may even better guarantee the factual implementation of these agreements.

These international framework agreements contain in particular sophisticated monitoring procedures. In many MNEs, this has led to a restructuring of management systems in order to make sure that the commitments resulting from these agreements are upheld. Nevertheless, enforcement still remains to be a problem and has to be improved.

Even if the development of codes of conduct – and in particular international framework agreements – gives rise to hope, it should not be overlooked that it is only a first step in the direction of CSR. The challenge of CSR is a much more far-reaching one, implying measures

---

[11] For an interesting account of this development see Drouin, R.-C. 2010. "Promoting Fundamental Labor Rights through International Framework Agreements: Practical Outcomes and Present Challenges," *Comparative Labor Law and Policy Journal*, 591 et seq.

significantly beyond the legal minimum. Of course, there are countries where the legal platform exceeds by far the level of minimum standards as envisaged by the ILO and by the codes of conduct. There the requirements of CSR already may be met by the law. This, however, is rather the exception than the rule.

4. Living up to Corporate Social Responsibility

Before discussing the implications of CSR for strategies to be developed beyond the legal minimum it might be helpful to keep in mind the effects of the already mentioned financial and economic crisis for the employees and, of course, also for job seekers. As indicated above, there is the fear of losing the job. But there is much more. There is particularly a loss of trust and confidence in management's operations. There is a loss of trust and confidence in the functioning of the economic system as a whole. And there is an increasing and unspecified fear of the impact of globalisation. Therefore, the main task for all companies in this situation and further on throughout the 21st century is to re-establish trust and confidence and to cope with the fears just indicated.

In such a context, CSR requires first of all making sure that lay-offs, collective redundancies, mass dismissals or whatever these phenomena may be called are understood as a last resort. It should always be kept in mind what Louis Uchitelle[12] reports on the psychological effects of mass lay-offs. He shows that lay-offs have serious economic and psychological consequences for the affected individuals. According to him, "a lay-off is an emotional blow from which very few fully recover". Therefore, keeping people employed as long as possible should be a key priority for all employers who regard themselves as socially responsible. The implication of this insight is that all possible alternatives are to be checked before. This, by the way, is already contained in the mentioned Recommendation No. 166 on termination of employment according to which "measures ....should be considered with a view to averting or minimising" mass lay-offs. These

> might include, inter alia, restriction of hiring, spreading the workforce reduction over a certain period of time to permit natural reduction of the workforce, internal transfers, training and retraining, voluntary early retirement with appropriate income protection, restriction of overtime and reduction of normal hours of work (section 21).

---

[12] Uchitelle, L. 2006. *The Disposable American: Layoffs and their Consequences.* New York: Knopf.

This, of course, applies also to items not explicitly mentioned in the text of the recommendation, as are extended vacations—paid or unpaid, transfer companies, sabbaticals, outplacement, salary reductions and so on. Undoubtedly, all these options are at least to be considered as mechanisms to prevent lay-offs. It goes without saying that the consequences of such options have to be carefully checked and evaluated in each individual case. But whether and in what way these options can be used depends to a great extent on the legal and institutional context of the respective country. The same may be true for something which exceeds the preventive set of measures and refers to the period after a mass lay-off. The already quoted ILO recommendation includes a passage according to which "workers whose employment has been terminated" by mass lay-offs

> should be given a priority of rehiring if the employer again hires workers with comparable qualifications....within a given period from the time of their leaving (section 24).

Coming back to the preventive measures, it is evident that, for example, the possibility of short-time work over a longer period depends very much on the wage subsidies by external institutions or by the State. Whether and in what way salary reductions or alternative working time arrangements are a useful tool to overcome situations of crisis depends on the available instruments in the respective system, as well as on other factors. The problem is not which of these options are to be chosen and whether perhaps they are to be cumulated. The focus rather has to be on the question whether the use of such preventive measures helps to rebuild trust and confidence in the workforce and whether it helps to destroy the fears indicated above.

This leads me to the first element of the message I would like to express in this sketchy contribution. It is not important which of the available options to prevent lay-offs is chosen, it is important how it is done. It should, first of all, be clear that management has to avoid acting unilaterally. According to the ILO's present decent work agenda as well as to the concept of CSR, it is crucial that all those decisions are to be made in cooperation with the employees or the employees' representatives. Information and consultation are tools to offer the workforce transparency of decision making and get it involved into the decision-making process. There has to be a dialogue with the employees or their representatives on the availability of alternatives as well as on the foreseeable consequences of each of them. The goal has to be to reach a consensus which tremendously increases the legitimacy of such decisions. It promotes confidence, trust and credibility. Employees do have to get the feeling that they are not mere objects of management's decision-making or even victims of a hidden agenda, but rather actors in a joint effort to overcome the effects of the crisis and to restructure the company in a sustainable way.

And here again it might be helpful to come back to Convention No. 158 concerning termination of employment and Recommendation No. 166 supplementing this convention. There provisions on information and consultation of workers' representatives are contained. Such patterns prescribed by law exist in at least some countries not always and not necessarily connected with the ILO's input but as the fruit of domestic developments. Germany, to just give an example, offers a particularly elaborated system of such a system of employee involvement in management's decision making, not only in reference to mass lay-offs but on a much more comprehensive scale. Empirical research on the effect of these systems has proved that they are an excellent tool for companies to adapt in a socially responsible way to changes and new challenges. In addition, they help to absorb conflicts. In particular they promote better and easier implementation of management's decisions compared to unilateral decision-making. The permanent dialogue between management and employees' representatives leads to important changes of attitudes on both sides. Stereotypes of how management behaves and of how employees think tend to fall apart and are replaced by realistic perspectives. This leads to support for pragmatic strategies. And last but not least, such employee involvement tends to produce better decision-making by management because management has to justify towards the workers why it does what it intends to do.

These were the reasons why the European Community (EC) already in 1975 passed a directive on protection of workers in case of collective redundancies[13] according to which information and consultation of workers' representatives in case of collective redundancies is prescribed. This first step has been extended by a Directive of 2002 on a framework of information and consultation in the Member States,[14] covering now many more topics.

This new directive refers to public or private undertakings of at least 50 employees and establishments of at least 20 employees in the Member States. In the original version of the proposal, reference was only made to undertakings. The change is due to the fact that in some Member States the entity which serves as reference point for information and consultation

---

[13] Directive 75/129/EEC of 22 February 1975, OJ 1975, L 48; amended by Directive 98/59/EC of 20 July 1998, OJ 1998, L 225/16.
[14] Directive 2002/14/EC of 11 March 2002, OJ 2002, L 80/29.

predominantly is the establishment (as, for example, in Germany). The purpose of the directive is

> to establish a general framework setting out minimum requirements for the right to information and consultation of employees in undertakings or establishments within the Community.

The directive defines the structure of information and consultation in a very comprehensive way. The definitions contain important procedural requirements. Timing, content and manner of information have to be such that they correspond to the purpose and allow the employees' representatives to examine the information and to prepare for consultation (Art. No. 4 par. 4). Consultation has to meet several requirements (see Art. No. 4 par. 4) : (1) it has to be ensured that the timing, the method and the content are effective; (2) information and consultation have to take place at the appropriate level of management and representation, depending on the subject under discussion; (3) the employees' representatives are entitled to formulate an opinion on the basis of the relevant information to be supplied by the employer; (4) the employees' representatives are entitled to meet with the employer and to obtain a response and the reasons for that response to any opinion they may formulate; and, finally, (5) in case of decisions within the scope of the employer's management powers an attempt has to be made to seek prior agreement on the decisions covered by information and consultation.

Information has to cover the recent and probable development of the undertaking's or the establishment's activities and economic situation in its broadest sense (Art. No. 4 par. 2 lit. a). Information and consultation has to take place on the structure and probable development of employment within the undertaking or establishment and on any anticipatory measures envisaged in particular where there is a threat of unemployment (Art. No. 4 par. 2 lit. b) (which is our case!). Finally information and consultation has to take place on decisions likely to lead to substantial changes in work organisation or in contractual relations (Art. No. 4 par. 2 lit. c).

Since the directive only provides for a minimum framework, it, of course, does not prevent more favourable arrangements in Member States. In addition, the directive cannot be used to justify the reduction or destruction of existing patterns.

More important than the details of the directive is the fact that the EC has taken measures based on the insight that cooperation with workers' representatives has to be promoted. For those outside Europe it may serve as a sign into the right direction. Where law does not yet prescribe such a dialogue, it may be developed voluntarily. And where required by law, there are still many possibilities beyond the legal level.

The second important element in reference to such phenomena as mass lay-offs refers to the criteria used to select those who are included in such measures and those who are kept in the job. In the already mentioned EC-directive on protection of workers in case of collective redundancies such criteria play a dominant role. Of course, the choice of such criteria may be very much restricted by national legislation or by existing collective agreements. But if there is a leeway, it should be made perfectly clear that this selection is not only made in a non discriminatory way—this is self-evident—but in a manner which is compatible with the workers' understanding of justice. This understanding may differ from country to country which is reflected in the respective legislation. In some countries the seniority principle is considered to be a decent expression of justice. Other countries reject it as being too crude and arbitrary and replace it by social considerations, trying to give preference to those for whom the loss of the job would be more difficult to cope with. Therefore, it has to be admitted that there is no universal pattern of generally accepted criteria beyond the prohibition of discrimination. This perception very much depends on the cultural background and the history of each country. But one aspect should be added which is contained in the mentioned ILO recommendation, namely that the criteria for selection have to be "established wherever possible in advance" (section 23) in order to eliminate any suspicion of arbitrariness.

In connection with the selection criteria there is another problem to be observed in the selection process, the differentiation between the categories of qualification. The selection is not to be made between all employees but always between those of the same or similar level of qualification. Thereby, highly qualified employees may perhaps not even be included in such measures of downsizing. In so far mass lay-offs by necessity have an educative effect by demonstrating that investment in qualification pays. And here the crucial and third element of my message is arising: companies have to contribute as much as possible to sustainable development and this means before everything else investment in employability of workers. This implies, first of all, that everything has to be done to bring those who have to be included in mass lay-offs to be put on a track which provides for them a perspective of being reintegrated into the labour market. And this means nothing else but to assist in bringing those people into training programs which offer for them a chance to find a job. This, first of all, implies that the focus on mere financial compensation in cases of mass lay-offs has to be shifted to offering schemes of qualification. In many countries there are programs by government or provided by legislation which are subsidised and can be used by companies under the condition that they financially contribute. In such cases it is easier for companies to just make use of such available structures, even if it still may be an expensive effort for them. If such structures do not exist, the possibility of offering training facilities for those who lose the job, of course, depends on the financial power of the respective company. All possibilities of establishing such programs are to be checked in order to give the workforce the signal that sustainable development of the labour market is the goal to which companies want to contribute.

But if companies want to regain confidence and credibility in the eyes of their employees, they have to significantly invest in the qualification not only of those who lose the job but also of those who remain in the company. The discussion on the necessity of lifelong learning as a precondition of sustainable employment should be kept in mind. Ever changing technological and societal challenges require new and additional skills. This is not only true for those who already are skilled. Those who are unskilled have to get a chance to get qualifications which help them to develop a steady job perspective, within the company and—in case of inevitable job loss—in another company. This implies that training has not only to focus on special skills needed within the respective company but also on general skills valid on the labour market. Of course, this is a giant task which cannot be the exclusive responsibility of companies. The educational system of the respective country as well as the system of vocational training plays an important role in this context. However, the contribution of companies in this context should not be underestimated and promoted as much as possible. To make it perfectly clear: this is not just an activity which helps the employees for their interest, but it will have a sustainable effect for the company's performance. Investment in human resources increases employees' motivation and thereby productivity. And it helps the company to raise the quality of its products and services, a precondition for long-term success in competitive markets. And if employees see that the company invests in order to keep them long term, they build up trust and confidence in management's efforts to build up stable employment relationships. It goes without saying that measures of preventing mass lay-offs for all these reasons should be combined as much as possible with activities of training and further training. This applies to short-time work as well as to extended vacations or sabbaticals to just mention the most evident examples.

The last element to be emphasised refers to the context in which all this has to happen, to the structure of the company. If it is true that confidence and trust in management's activities have to be re-established in order to promote sustainable development of companies, it has to be seen that this is only possible if there is utmost transparency of management's decision-making. Therefore, rules of corporate governance are to be shaped in a way that management's behaviour is becoming transparent for the workforce and that mechanisms of accountability are built in such a system.[15] This definitely is an indispensable precondition for destroying mistrust, for stimulating the motivation of the employees and thereby for sustainable productivity.

5. Conclusion

As indicated at the beginning of my sketchy remarks, my goal was to show in broad terms the implications of the concept of CSR. I purposely did not cope with details. My main message is that the strategies I am suggesting are not a decorative annex to business operations, mainly driven by moral considerations. Just the other way round: it is wrong to perceive social measures merely in moral terms or in terms of labour costs. The strategies I suggest are rather a necessary and indispensable precondition for sustainable business success and, thereby, show the direction not only for overcoming the recent crisis but for acting in the future. Their contribution to sustainable development not only for the companies and their workforce but for the society as a whole can barely be overestimated.

If in the beginning of this contribution the concept of CSR was characterised as a voluntary engagement of the companies, this should not be misunderstood. It is a request to companies to move voluntarily in this direction as long as legal patterns to realise the concept are not or not sufficiently established. But, of course, it does not prevent the establishment of regulation, it merely defines the goal for it. In the long run sufficient and appropriate regulation is a precondition for the well functioning of the concept.

---

[15] See in this context Commission of the European Communities. 2003. *Communication to the Council and to the European Parliament on Modernization of Company Law and on Improvement of Corporate Governance in the EU-Action Plan, COM (2003) 284 final*. Brussels: European Commission.

References

Commission of the European Communities. 2001. *Green Paper—Promoting a European Framework for Corporate Social Responsibility, COM (2001) 366 final.* Brussels: European Commission.

—. 2003. *Communication to the Council and to the European Parliament on Modernization of Company Law and on Improvement of Corporate Governance in the EU-Action Plan, COM (2003) 284 final.* Brussels: European Commission.

Compa, L. 2008. "Corporate Social Responsibility and Workers' Rights," *Comparative Labor Law and Policy Journal*, 5 et seq.

Drouin, R.-C. 2010. "Promoting Fundamental Labor Rights through International Framework Agreements: Practical Outcomes and Present Challenges," *Comparative Labor Law and Policy Journal*, 591 et seq.

Hepple, B. 2005. *Labour Laws and Global Trade.* Oxford/Portland: Cambridge University Press, 35.

Hopkins, M. 2004. "Corporate Social Responsibility: An Issues Paper," ILO Working Paper No. 27, Geneva: ILO.

Murray, J. 2004. "Corporate Social Responsibility: An Overview of Principles and Practice," ILO Working Paper No. 34, Geneva: ILO.

Rubin, N., ed. 2005. *Code of International Labour Law.* 2 volumes, Cambridge: Cambridge University Press.

Scherrer, C., and T. Greven. 2001. *Global Rules for Trade: Codes of Conduct, Social Labeling Workers' Rights Clauses.* Muenster: Westphalisches Dampfboot.

Sengenberger, W. 2002. *Globalization and Social Progress: The Role and Impact of International Labour Standards.* Bonn: Friedrich Ebert Stiftung.

—. 2006. "International Labour Standards in the Globalized Economy: Obstacles and Opportunities for Achieving Progress," in *Globalization and the Future of Labour Law,* eds. Craig, D. R., and S. M. Lynck, (Cambridge: Cambridge University Press), 331 et seq.

Servais, J. M. 2005. *International Labour Law*, The Hague: Kluwer Law International, 24 et seq.

Uchitelle, L. 2006. *The Disposable American: Layoffs and their Consequences.* New York: Knopf.

van Liemt, G. 2000. "Codes of Conduct and International Subcontracting: A 'Private' Road Towards Ensuring Minimum Labour Standards in Export Industries," in *Multinational Enterprises and the Social Challenges of the 21st Century*, ed. Blanpain, R. (The Hague / London / Boston: Kluwer Law International), 167 et seq.

Webb, K., ed. 2004. *Voluntary Codes: Private Governance in the Public Interest and Innovation*. Ottawa: Carleton Research Unit for Innovation, Science and Environment.

FLEXIBILITY AND SECURITY IN THE WORLD BANK'S DOING BUSINESS REPORTS

YARASLAU KRYVOI

1. The Doing Business Report and the Rigidity of Employment Index

Until very recently two major United Nations agencies had very different policies with regard to employment flexibility. The World Bank, by means of its Employing Workers Indicator (EWI) promoted deregulation of labour markets and encouraged fixed-term contracts, easy dismissal procedures and no minimum wages. This approach was recommended for the development of a better business climate. It took a few years of collaboration between the International Labour Organization and the World Bank to fix the situation and to make sure that the employment regulation objectives of the Doing Business report were consistent with the ILO standards.

The World Bank's Doing Business report has become one of the most influential, yet the most controversial instruments which affect labour law reforms around the world. Launched in 2004, it has become the publication with the highest circulation.[1] The report provides a ranking of business regulations and their enforcement across 178 countries.[2] The ranking consists of a number of indexes, dealing with conditions for starting a business, obtaining licenses, registering property and other business regulations.[3] Although the methodology of quantitative analysis

---

[1] See Doing Business report at http://www.doingbusiness.org, (accessed November 11, 2011).

[2] Ibid.

[3] The Doing Business report includes the following indexes: (1) starting a business; (2) dealing with licenses; (3) employing workers; (4) registering property; (5) getting credit; (6) protecting investors; (7) paying taxes; (8) trading across borders; (9) enforcing contracts; and (10) closing a business.

of law used in Doing Business reports has been both praised (mostly by economists),[4] and criticised (predominantly by lawyers),[5] none of its indicators has been more controversial than the one dealing with employing workers.[6]

From a legal point of view, the World Bank does not impose any obligations on states apart from merely ranking them in the Doing Business report. States do not sign any additional treaties or otherwise undertake legal obligations to comply with the Doing Business recommendations. However, the report and its rigidity of the employment index have other important implications. According to a study dealing with international trade unions, almost half of the most recent World Bank Country Assistance Strategies and Country Partnership Strategies included recommendations that the country undertake labour market reforms on the basis of Doing Business scores.[7] The rigidity of employment index has been incorporated into other important policy instruments, such as the World Bank's overall labour market strategy, which encourages countries "to create a more employment-friendly climate for business".[8]

---

[4] See e.g. Besley, T., and R. Burgess. 2004. "Can Labor Regulation Hinder Economic Performance? Evidence From India," *The Quarterly Journal of Economics* 119, No.1:91.
; Caballero, R., E. Engel, K. Cowan, and A. Micco. 2004. "Effective Labor Regulation and Microeconomic Flexibility," NBER Working Paper, No. W10744. Available at SSRN: http://ssrn.com/abstract=590734, (accessed November 11, 2011).

[5] The most common criticisms of quantitative analysis of law generally and labour law in particular includes difficulty of using binary variables to capture graduations of legal rules, growing use of default rules and self-regulation, difference between the law on the books and real enforcement and the importance of non-legal sources of norms. See Deakin, S., P. Lele, and M. Siems. 2007. "The Evolution of Labour Law: Calibrating and Comparing Regulatory Regimes," *International Labour Review* 133, No. 146:141-142; also Davis K., and M. Kruse. 2007. "Taking the Measure of Law: The Case of the Doing Business Project," *Law and Social Inquiry* 1095, No. 32:1104-1105.

[6] See e.g. Davis, B. 2008. "Report on World Bank Sees Deregulation Bias," *The Wall Street Journal,* June 13, No. A6.

[7] See Testimony of Peter Bakvis, Director of Washington Office of the ITUC/Global Unions before the Committee on financial Services, US House of Representatives on "The Fight against Global Poverty and Inequality: the World Bank's Approach to Core Labor Standards and Employment Creation" (October 3, 2007).

[8] World Bank. 2007. *MILES: A Multi-Sector Approach to Foster Job Creation, Poverty Reduction and Growth.* Washington: The World Bank.

The effects of the rigidity of employment index go beyond the World Bank's instruments. The International Monetary Fund recommended labour market deregulation based on the country's Doing Business scores in its loan review documents.[9] The countries themselves strive for better Doing Business scores to send clear and easily available messages to potential investors.[10] According to the ITUC/Global Unions, sixteen countries recently removed employees' protections in response to the rigidity of employment index.[11]

The rigidity of employment index has become the most criticised part of the Doing Business report primarily because employment regulations have a very sensitive political nature often deeply rooted in countries' cultural and historical context. As showed by riots and protests against labour market reforms that took place in France, the review of employment regulations can cause not only peaceful debates, but also serious social unrest.[12]

It is difficult to assert without significant reservations which approach to flexibility of labour regulation is more efficient, because efficiency is understood differently by employers, employees and governments. However, it is possible to examine how the rigidity of employment index fits into existing international labour standards primarily reflected in the ILO conventions and recommendations.

2. The Rigidity of Employment Index and International Labour Standards

Until recently, the rigidity of employment index as a part of Doing Business report reflected the average of three sub-indexes: the difficulty in hiring and firing, and the rigidity of hours index.[13] The difficulty in hiring

---

[9] See e.g. International Monetary Fund. 2007. "Greece: 2006 Article IV Consultation—Staff Report," IMF Country Report, No. 07/26.

[10] See e.g. Belarus Khochet Voiti v Chislo Pervykh 25 Stran v Reitinge Vsemirnogo Banka po Uslovijam Vedenija Biznesa (Belarus Wants to Rank within Top-25 Countries on Doing Business Conditions) Nacionalnaja Ekonomicheskaya Gazeta, 27 November 2007, available at http://news.tut.by/economics/98752.html, (accessed November 11, 2011).

[11] ITUC/Global Unions. 2007. *The IFIs' Use of Doing Business to Eliminate Workers' Protection: Analysis of Doing Business 2008 and New Country Evidence.* Washington: Global Unions.

[12] Bennhold, K. 2006. "French Marchers Protest a Labor Contract Change," *The International Herald Tribune,* February 7.

[13] See methodology of the rigidity of employment index at:

index was calculated on the basis of three measures: (i) whether fixed-term contracts are prohibited for permanent tasks; (ii) the maximum duration of fixed-term contracts; (iii) the ratio of the minimum wage for a trainee or first-time employee to the average value added per worker.[14] There are four main aspects of the Doing Business rigidity of employment index covered by international labour standards, namely employee termination, weekend work, and night work.

Indeed, the rigidity of employment index does not seem to explicitly contradict most of the ILO conventions[15] and does not measure compliance with them in questionnaires.[16] This is consistent with the position of the International Finance Corporation (the IFC), a private sector arm of the World Bank, which is largely responsible for Doing Business reports. In 2006, the IFC implemented new performance and policy standards and demanded its private sector borrowers to comply with requirements based on the ILO fundamental principles and rights at work and other ILO standards with respect to safety and health, conditions of work and termination of employment.[17]

However, a closer look at the full spectrum of international labour standards, which includes not only conventions, but also recommendations[18] and, arguably, case law of the ILO Committee of Experts on the Application of Conventions and Recommendations reveals a number of contradictions.[19] ILO recommendations represent not only the spirit of the ILO, as the World Bank's Independent Evaluation Group pointed out,[20] but also a part of international labour standards and therefore they cannot be ignored.

---

http://www.doingbusiness.org/ MethodologySurveys/Employing Workers.aspx, (accessed November 11, 2011).

[14] World Bank. 2008. *Doing Business 2008*. Washington: The World Bank, 72.

[15] With the exception of Art. No. 2 of Termination of Employment Convention discussed.

[16] See World Bank Group. 2007. *Questionnaire on Labour Laws and Regulations*. Washington: The World Bank.

[17] International Labour Organization. 2007. *World Bank Doing Business Report: The Employing Workers Indicator*. GB.300/4/1. Geneva: ILO, 2.

[18] International Labour Organization. 2005. *Rules of the Game. A Brief Introduction to International Labour Standards*. Geneva: ILO, 12.

[19] The argument that only conventions as binding instruments constitute international labour standards is misleading. Following this logic, because most of the ILO conventions are not ratified even by majority of countries and therefore not binding, they should also be ignored.

[20] World Bank Independent Evaluation Group. 2008. *Doing Business: An Independent Evaluation*. Washington: The World Bank, 33.

Under the Doing Business methodology, a country used to achieve the worst score if fixed-term contracts were prohibited for permanent tasks and the best score if fixed-term contracts could last 5 years or more.[21] Although the difficulty in firing index is also worth exploring from the point of view of international labour standards,[22] this paper will focus only on the hiring index. In other words, the rigidity of employment index effectively penalises those countries, which restrict the use of fixed-term contracts.[23] Art. No. 2 of Termination of Employment Convention No. 158 calls for adequate safeguards against recourse to contracts of employment for a specified period of time.[24] If the countries do not comply with Art. No. 2(3) of Convention No. 158, the ILO usually asks them to change their regulations to ensure that these regulations do not result in avoidance protections resulting from Convention No. 158.[25]

The ILO Termination of Employment Recommendation No. 166 explains that the recourse to contracts for a specified period of time should be limited to cases in which, either due to the nature of work to be performed or to the interests of the worker, the employment relationship cannot be of an indeterminate duration.[26] Thus the ILO treats term

---

[21] Ibid.

[22] The countries with regulations that mandate notification of third parties in case of redundancies or consider retraining or reassignment options and set priority rules for redundancies get lower scores. This may be in conflict with the ILO Recommendation No. 166 on Termination of Employment Recommendation of 1982, which explicitly recommends setting up clear priority rules for redundancy terminations as well as encourages employers to consider training and retraining and other measures to avert or minimise termination. See ILO Recommendation No. 166 on Termination of Employment par. 23-36 (1982), available at http://www.ilo.org/ilolex/cgi-lex/convde.pl?R166, (accessed November 11, 2011).

[23] The countries which answer affirmatively to the question "Are fixed-term contracts prohibited for permanent tasks?" rank lower than those answering negatively. See World Bank Group. 2007. *Questionnaire on Labour Laws and Regulations.* Washington: The World Bank, 3.

[24] Termination of Employment Convention No.158 Art. No. 2(3) (1982), available at www.ilo.org/ilolex/cgi-lex/convde.pl?C158, (accessed November 11, 2011).

[25] See e.g. "[the Committee of Experts on the Application of Conventions and Recommendations] asks the Government [of Finland] to indicate what safeguards have been provided to guarantee fixed-term contracts are not used in practice with the aim of avoiding the protection resulting from the convention...". International Labour Organization. 2008. *Report of the Committee of Experts on the Application of Conventions and Recommendations* 537, 97th *Session*. Geneva: ILO.

[26] ILO Termination of Employment Recommendation No. 166 Art. No. 3(2)(1982), available at http://www.ilo.org/ilolex/cgi-lex/convde.pl?R166, (accessed November 11, 2011).

contracts as an exception which should be allowed only in certain situations.

Consistently with the mentioned instruments, the ILO pointed out that when contracts are concluded for a fixed-term period and then repeatedly renewed, the worker does not acquire the rights and does not obtain the benefits provided for employees by labour legislation or collective bargaining.[27] Moreover, one of the consequences of fixed-term contracts is that workers do not see the benefits of union representation in the context of short-term employment.[28] Thus the use of fixed-term contracts also has an effect on freedom of association.

The rigidity of employment index measures non-unionised employees according to the Doing Business methodology.[29] However, in situations when more than half of workers in a country are covered by collective agreements, unionised workers are considered for the purposes of the rigidity of employment index.[30] As a result, countries with higher union density will be lower in the ranking, because unionised workers usually receive higher levels of protection, especially as far as the termination of employment is concerned.[31] Although this is not explicitly in conflict with the ILO's understanding of freedom of association, this methodology could motivate countries to discourage unionisation.

---

[27] International Labour Organization. 2006. *The Employment Relationship, Report V(1), International Labour Conference,* 95th *Session*. Geneva: ILO, par. 48.

[28] For other possible effects of unlimited use of fixed-term contracts see Kryvoi, Y. 2006. "Discrimination and Security of Employment in a Post-Soviet Context," *International Journal of Comparative Labour Law and Industrial Relations* 5, No. 22.

[29] See Methodology, note 13, for the methodology of the rigidity of employment index.

[30] According to the methodology of the report, employees are considered to be union members only in those cases where union membership is mandatory. However, regulations making union membership mandatory may violate the principle of freedom of association, because workers cannot be forced to join a union in accordance with the ILO Convention No. 87 concerning Freedom of Association and Protection of the Right to Organize. As the author learned from personal conversations with the Doing Business team, in practice they consider unionised workers for countries where more than a half of workforce is unionised.

[31] For example, Art. No. 82 of the Russian Labour Code provides for obligatory participation of a trade union authority in proceeding of termination of a labor agreement on the initiative of an employer. Similar requirements exist in other countries. See International Labour Organization. 2007. *The Termination of Employment Legislation Digest*. Geneva: ILO.

It is therefore not surprising that trade unions vigorously opposed the rigidity of employment ranking.[32] The unions correctly observe that regular violators of fundamental workers' rights such as Belarus, China, Colombia, and Uzbekistan receive better Doing Business rankings for "Employing Workers" than do most countries of Western Europe.[33] In most of the previously listed countries trade unions are harassed, oppressed or otherwise severely restricted. Some of these countries were subject to special measures, such as appointing a Commission of Inquiry under Art. No. 26 of the ILO Constitution.[34] For instance, the ILO made recourse to such special procedures against Belarus, which among other things used fixed-term contracts to eradicate independent trade unions.[35]

From the formal legal point of view, the Doing Business report does not undermine freedom of association, but merely advocates for the employers' interests. However, as a matter of international human rights and development policy, it would not be right to support those few countries regarded as the worst violators of international labour standards by rewarding them with high rankings on the rigidity of employment index.

The section that follows will look into the differences between the Doing Business's and the ILO's perspectives of employment regulation.

---

[32] ITUC/Global Unions. 2007. *The IFIs' Use of Doing Business to Eliminate Workers' Protection: Analysis of Doing Business 2008 and New Country Evidence.* Washington: Global Unions.

[33] Global Unions. "The Role of the International Financial Institutions in Supporting Decent Work and Countering the Risks of Financial Globalization," Statement by Global Unions to the 2007 Annual Meetings of the IMF and the World Bank, Washington, U.S., October 2007. Available at www.whiteband.org/GcapSpecials/ifis-action-2007/statement-by-global-unions-to-the-2007-ifis-annual-meetings, (accessed November 11, 2011).

[34] A Commission of Inquiry is the ILO's highest-level investigative procedure; it is generally set up when a member state is accused of committing persistent and serious violations and has repeatedly refused to address them. To date, 11 Commissions of Inquiry have been established. *See* ILO, Applying and promoting International Labour Standards, available at http://www.ilo.org/public/english/standards/norm/applying/complaints.htm, (accessed November 11, 2011).

[35] See Kryvoi, Y. 2006. "Discrimination and Security of Employment in a Post-Soviet Context," *International Journal of Comparative Labour Law and Industrial Relations* 5, No. 22.

3. Two Visions of Employment Regulation

The ILO, which is the main body within the United Nations system responsible for labour, has criticised the rigidity of employment index in its working papers[36] and the Governing Body documents.[37] According to the ILO

> the methodology of employing workers indicator yields a narrow and misleading view of employment environment for business; results in a ranking in which some countries with a strong and competitive private sector are placed at the lower end; and is being used explicitly and implicitly to determine country lending priorities in the field of labour market reform.[38]

The ILO was also concerned that the rigidity of employment index might discourage countries from ratifying and abiding by international labour Conventions and Recommendations if doing so would push them down the indicator.[39]

Indeed, as the following table shows, the targets of the ILO and the World Bank's Doing Business report were very different.

Table 1-1. Comparison of Selected Doing Business and the ILO Targets

Doing Business target	Factor	ILO target
Right of any party to easily terminate contract	Termination	In a normal employment relationship employees cannot be terminated at will
Right to conclude term contracts without restrictions	Fixed-term contracts	Fixed-term contracts are allowed only in specified cases
Minimum or no restrictions on overtime work	Work hours	Restrictions on maximum daily and weekly overtime work

[36] See e.g. Berg, J., and S. Cazes. 2007. "The Doing Business Indicators: Measurement Issues and Political Implications," Economic and Labour Market Paper, No. 6.
[37] See e.g. International Labour Organization. 2007. *Implementation of the Global Employment Agenda: An Update*. GB.298/ESP/1, Geneva: ILO, 6. International Labour Organization. 2007. *The United Nations and Reform: Developments in the Multilateral System*. GB.300/4/1. Geneva: ILO.
[38] Ibid., 2.
[39] Ibid.

One reason why the ILO targets are so different than those of the Doing Business targets is that the ILO decision-making machinery is based on tripartite dialogue between governments, employers and employees. Not surprisingly, the ILO targets are balanced to harmonise the interests of all three stakeholders—employers, employees and governments, while the Doing Business targets clearly favour the interests of employers.

Another explanation is the ILO's concern about the so-called race to the bottom. According to the Preamble to the ILO Constitution, the failure of any nation to adopt humane conditions of labour is an obstacle in the way of other nations which desire to improve the conditions in their own countries.[40] This is why the ILO from its very inception called for the establishment of a maximum working day and week, provision of an adequate living wage, recognition of the principle of freedom of association and other standards. The organisation emerged in 1919 not long after the 1917 Socialist revolution in Russia and was meant to prevent extreme exploitation of workers, which could have led to more revolutions and instability.

On the other hand, the Doing Business's approach aims at making labour regulations more flexible and more employer-friendly.[41] The background paper on the rigidity of employment index argues that heavier regulation of labour is associated with lower labour force participation and higher unemployment.[42] According to the Doing Business report of 2006, competition from cheaper imports drives jobs away from less productive sectors and into more productive ones, expanding the economy.[43] At the same time, it is argued that where barriers to hiring and firing are high, workers stay in unproductive sectors, which results in less job creation and loss of competitiveness.[44] Moreover, rigid employment legislation has an effect of pushing employees into the grey area and reforms as encouraged by Doing Business reports are meant to expand the reach of regulation by

---

[40] Constitution of the International Labour Organization (Declaration of Philadelphia) (1944).

[41] Not surprisingly, employers' organisations are very supportive of the Doing Business recommendations. See, e.g. International Organization of Employers. 2007. *The World Bank Doing Business Reports*. Statement of 16 November, Geneva: IOE. Available at http://www.ioe-emp.org(accessed November 11, 2011).

[42] See Botero, J., S. Djankov, R. La Porta, F. Lopez-de-Silanes, and A. Shleifer. 2003. "Regulation of Labour," NBER Working Paper 9756 1.

[43] World Bank. 2006. *Doing Business in 2006. Creating Jobs.* Washington: The World Bank, 26.

[44] Ibid.

bringing businesses and employees into the formal sector.[45] The main message of Doing Business reports is to remove rigid employment regulations and to make labour markets more flexible.

The countries' rankings in the Doing Business reports clearly articulate this message. Traditionally, former communist countries of Central/Eastern Europe are considered to be at the one pole of labour market flexibility while the United States is at the other.[46] Consistent with this perception, the United States confidently keeps the first place over the years in the rigidity of employment ranking, which may suggest that countries should use American labour and employment regulations as a model to follow.[47] Most of Eastern European economies are at the bottom of the ranking.[48] To further illustrate this point, the United States ratified only eight out of more than 180 ILO Conventions, while, for instance, Poland ratified eighty-two ILO conventions.[49]

To sum up, the ILO standards being a result of tripartite compromise aim at more security for employees, while Doing Business targets have a clear pro-employer bias in accordance with its business-friendly mission. As a result of cooperation between the World Bank, the International Labour Organization and international trade unions these two visions have been significantly reconciled.

4. Putting Two Visions Together

In response to pressure from the ILO and international trade unions, the World Bank started to gradually change its employment regulation targets.[50] The methodology had been adjusted with the help from a consultative group of relevant experts and stakeholders which included representatives of the International Labour Organization and international unions. In 2007, the Doing Business team modified several indicators,

---

45 Ibid., 6.

46 Fahlbeck, R. 1998. "Flexibility: Potentials and Challenges for Labor Law," *Comparative Labour Law and Policy Journal*, No. 19:515.

47 See World Bank. 2008. *Doing Business in 2007—How to Reform.* Washington: The World Bank.

48 Ibid.

49 Source: International Labour Organization, ILOLEX (2008), available at www.ilo.org/ilolex.

50 World Bank. 2011. *Doing Business 2011 Data Notes*. Washington: The World Bank. Available at http://doingbusiness.org/methodology/methodology-note, (accessed November 11, 2011).

including those dealing with night work and working time, to comply with international labour standards.[51] The report's authors suggested that it was

> possible for an economy to receive the highest score on the ease of employing workers—indicating the most flexible labour regulations—and comply with all 187 ILO conventions.[52]

In 2009, the World Bank modified its methodology even further.[53] In particular, the World Bank changed the calculation of the minimum wage, paid annual leave and a ceiling for working days allowed per week to ensure that no economy benefits in the scoring from excessive flexibility in these areas.[54] Finally, the calculation of the redundancy cost and of the annual leave period for the rigidity of hours were also fixed to comply with the letter and spirit of ILO instruments.

As a result of consultations with relevant stakeholders, the World Bank adjusted its methodology for the Doing Business 2010 report. These adjustments included provisions for fixed-term workers, standards for severance payment, mandatory days of rest and night work and holidays, and minimum wage levels. The goal of these revisions was to encourage worker protection policies which conform to the relevant ILO instruments.[55]

The World Bank also removed the Employing Workers Indicator as a guidepost from the World Bank's regular Country Policy and Institutional Assessments (CPIA). The World Bank's Doing Business report now recognises that "well-designed worker protections are of benefit to the society as a whole".[56]

---

[51] World Bank Group. 2007. *Doing Business. Methodology Changes in 2007.* Washington: The World Bank. Available at http://www.doingbusiness.org/MethodologySurveys/methodologynote.aspx, (accessed November 11, 2011).

[52] Ibid.

[53] World Bank. 2011. *Doing Business 2011 Data Notes*. Washington: The World Bank.

[54] Ibid.

[55] World Bank. 2009. *Revisions to the EWI Indicator*. Washington: The World Bank. http://tinyurl.com/6gljoz8, (accessed April 27, 2009).

[56] Ibid.

5. Conclusions

This article has argued that the World Bank's Doing Business Report progressed from being intentionally skewed in favour of employers and unregulated labour flexibility to a more balanced approach which reflects the spirit of the ILO conventions and recommendations. It shows that cooperation between the ILO and the World Bank resulted in adjustment of the Doing Business report to have a reasonable blend of flexibility and security. The organisations' visions of the proper mixture of flexibility and security seem to be more coherent now.

The Doing Business report no longer includes the employing workers indicator and no longer encourages countries to be as flexible as possible in their employment regulations. That prevents blanket application of the Doing Business targets without becoming aware of what they are trying to achieve.

Finally, as was proposed by the author of this paper in the past,[57] the World Bank committed to develop a new indicator for its Doing Business Reports called the Worker Protection Indicator (WPI).[58] The purpose of such indicator would be to measure countries' adherence to core labour standards—both in terms of law on the books and of real application.

References

Bennhold, K. 2006. "French Marchers Protest a Labor Contract Change," *The International Herald Tribune,* February 7.

Berg, J., and S. Cazes. 2007. "The Doing Business Indicators: Measurement Issues and Political Implications," Economic and Labour Market Paper, No. 6.

Besley, T., and R. Burgess. 2004. "Can Labor Regulation Hinder Economic Performance? Evidence From India," *The Quarterly Journal of Economics* 119, No.1:91.

Botero, J., S. Djankov, R. La Porta, F. Lopez-de-Silanes, and A. Shleifer. 2003. "Regulation of Labour," NBER Working Paper 9756 1.

Caballero, R., E. Engel, K. Cowan, and A. Micco. 2004. "Effective Labor Regulation and Microeconomic Flexibility," NBER Working Paper, No. W10744.

---

57 Kryvoi, Y. 2009. "The World Bank and the ILO: Two Visions of Employment Regulation," in *Fixed-term Employment Contracts,* eds. Blanpain R., and C. Grant, (Bruges: Vanden Broele), 47-59.

58 World Bank. 2009. *Revisions to the EWI Indicator.* Washington: The World Bank.

Davis K., and M. Kruse. 2007. "Taking the Measure of Law: The Case of the Doing Business Project," *Law and Social Inquiry* 1095, No. 32:1104-1105.

Davis, B. 2008. "Report on World Bank Sees Deregulation Bias," *The Wall Street Journal,* June 13, No. A6.

Deakin, S., P. Lele, and M. Siems. 2007. "The Evolution of Labour Law: Calibrating and Comparing Regulatory Regimes," *International Labour Review* 133, No. 146:141-142.

Fahlbeck, R. 1998. "Flexibility: Potentials and Challenges for Labor Law," *Comparative Labour Law and Policy Journal*, No. 19:515.

Global Unions. "The Role of the International Financial Institutions in Supporting Decent Work and Countering the Risks of Financial Globalization," Statement by Global Unions to the 2007 Annual Meetings of the IMF and the World Bank, Washington, U.S., October 2007.

International Labour Organization. 2005. *Rules of the Game. A Brief Introduction to International Labour Standards*. Geneva: ILO.

—. 2006. *The Employment Relationship, Report V(1), International Labour Conference,* 95th *Session*. Geneva: ILO.

—. 2007. *Implementation of the Global Employment Agenda: An Update.* GB.298/ESP/1, Geneva: ILO.

—. 2007. *The Termination of Employment Legislation Digest.* Geneva: ILO.

—. 2007. *The United Nations and Reform: Developments in the Multilateral System*. GB.300/4/1. Geneva: ILO.

—. 2007. *World Bank Doing Business Report: The Employing Workers Indicator.* GB.300/4/1. Geneva: ILO.

—. 2008. *Report of the Committee of Experts on the Application of Conventions and Recommendations* 537, 97th *Session*. Geneva: ILO.

International Monetary Fund. 2007. "Greece: 2006 Article IV Consultation—Staff Report," IMF Country Report, No. 07/26.

International Organization of Employers. 2007. *The World Bank Doing Business Reports*. Statement of 16 November, Geneva: IOE.

ITUC/Global Unions. 2007. *The IFIs' Use of Doing Business to Eliminate Workers' Protection: Analysis of Doing Business 2008 and New Country Evidence.* Washington: Global Unions.

Kryvoi, Y. 2006. "Discrimination and Security of Employment in a Post-Soviet Context," *International Journal of Comparative Labour Law and Industrial Relations* 5, No. 22.

—. 2009. "The World Bank and the ILO: Two Visions of Employment Regulation," in *Fixed-term Employment Contracts,* eds. Blanpain R., and C.Grant (Bruges: Vanden Broele), 47-59.

World Bank Group. 2007. *Doing Business. Methodology Changes in 2007.* Washington: The World Bank.

—. 2007. *Questionnaire on Labour Laws and Regulations.* Washington: The World Bank.

World Bank Independent Evaluation Group. 2008. *Doing Business: An Independent Evaluation.* Washington: The World Bank.

World Bank. 2006. *Doing Business in 2006. Creating Jobs.* Washington: The World Bank.

—. 2007. *MILES: A Multi-Sector Approach to Foster Job Creation, Poverty Reduction and Growth.* Washington: The World Bank.

—. 2008. *Doing Business 2008.* Washington: The World Bank.

—. 2008. *Doing Business in 2007—How to Reform.* Washington: The World Bank.

—. 2009. *Revisions to the EWI Indicator.* Washington: The World Bank.

—. 2011. *Doing Business 2011 Data Notes.* Washington: The World Bank.

FLEXIBILITY—MARKET EXPECTATIONS AND LABOUR LAW DOCTRINE

ARKADIUSZ SOBCZYK

1. Introductory Remarks

Global economic competition and the accompanying labour market competition triggered renewed discussion on labour law development trends in European countries. Here I treat the content of that discussion in the Polish law doctrine, which to a large extent reflects the discussion in other European countries. This discussion refers, among other things, to the development of non-standard forms of employment, though it is not limited exclusively to this sphere. Below I indicate the basic trends in this discussion which requires a general exposition of the specificity of labour law.

2. Development Dynamism as a Special Feature of Labour Law

The discussion on the new, non-standard, atypical or flexible forms of employment and the vast related literature highlight the essential feature of labour law which is its so called development dynamism. Modern times in general seem to be characterised by a rapid evolution of positive law such that the term "legislation inflation" has been coined. However, changes in labour law, sometimes of a fundamental character, and to a large extent in matters of less fundamental significance, justify the thesis that labour law is characterised by development dynamism,[1] though it should be added that this is not the prevailing opinion in the doctrine. On the basis of statements in the literature, we can venture to indicate three groups of

[1] Szubert, W. 1970. *Szczególne właściwości prawa pracy*. Studia Prawno-Ekonomiczne, IV, 56 et seq.

circumstances that are the cause of this state of affairs. They can be systematised as follows: historical circumstances,[2] social and political circumstances, the effects of civilisation and economic circumstances.

I position this recent branch of law as a determinant of the system and history. On the one hand, it causes the need to supplement regulations and, on the other hand, the need to improve their content.[3] If we add to this the very poor regulations concerning rendering labour in Roman law—where labour was based on rights of an ownership nature—and a general delay in the reception of Roman law connected with the regress following the fall of the empire, labour law began its development practically without any tradition which could be the source of stabilisation.

In summary, labour law as a branch of law did not have the privilege of the centuries-old legacy of tradition, which was important for the development of civil or criminal law. Hence, the natural need to improve it. From that perspective, the development dynamism of labour law is not its added value, but rather the sign of its weakness. This is one of the reasons why the codification of this branch of law is still a fairly rare phenomenon, and where codes were introduced, it happened with decades-long delay in relation to other branches of law.

The second group of determinants of the development dynamism has a social and political nature. This is connected both with the object of regulation and its purpose. It is also related to, and at the same time consistent with, the views on the origin of labour law. When making a review of comments on this issue, we may accept the prevailing view that the goal of labour law is to establish harmony in labour relationships and social peace within the framework of the philosophical and social concept of a common good.[4] The above assumptions are not alien to the origins of other legal relationships, however, due to the universality of the employment relationship, as well as its direct influence on a considerable number of concentrated and often organised people, labour law has a special importance.

However, the guarantee of harmony or social peace is also connected

---

[2] The determinants and directions of changes connected with political and economic transformations in Poland are comprehensively described by Zieliński, Z. 1997. "Nowy ład pracy—rzeczywistość i wizja przyszłości," in *Nowy ład pracy w Polsce i Europie*, ed. Matey M. (Warsaw: Fundacja Promocji Prawa Europejskiego), 9 et seq.

[3] Zieliński, Z. 1986. *Prawo pracy—zarys systemu*. Warsaw—Kraków: Panstwowe Wydawn, 35.

[4] Chobot, A. 1977. *Nowe formy zatrudnienia—kierunki rozwoju i nowelizacji*. Warsaw, Prawnicze PWN, 8-11.

with the current system of values or the definition of justice. And this is to a large extent connected with, or perhaps it is described by, the current economic and political doctrine, or maybe more precisely, ideological doctrine. That is why labour law is especially strongly affected by beliefs concerning such inseparable issues as the role of the state in the economy, individualism and solidarity, basic economic, social and political rights, the role of religion, and so on. This was especially observable during the revolutionary and political movements in the 20th century, yet it has always persisted in more subtle forms.

An important group of determinants of intensive transformations in labour law are civilisation and technological elements. In the first half of the 20th century, technological progress and the accompanying economic transformations strongly influenced the ideology underlying the introduction and development of labour law. We are able to observe a close relationship between technological development and changes in social relations, or a joint occurrence of both these groups of causes.[5]

As a rule, however, technological progress means influence on the organisation of work and market processes. A large part of political factors do not find their simple determinants in the evolution of human relations. That is so because they result from people's choices based on recognised values. Not so long ago, the experiment of free market (or, perhaps, of many of its rules) combined with centralisation and ideologisation of public life in China was doomed to failure. Yet, on the global scale, the technological revolution is a spontaneous phenomenon. Deliberate actions can affect the rate of changes. In the long term technological development itself cannot be stopped. This, in turn, means the need to adjust labour law to on the one hand new forms of work and on the other, by facilitating the globalisation of economic transactions, it poses challenges to labour law that result from the dumping of labour markets.

A special determinant of the labour law evolution in Poland is, or rather was, the process of departing from the centrally controlled economy[6] and then the process of its adjustment to EU legislation.

---

[5] Salwa, when assessing the direction of the necessary changes in labour law in the 1980s, emphasised determinants connected with the social and economic system, the determinants of the economy in crisis, and the transformations in the sphere of management and technology, cf. Salwa, Z. 1987. "Podstawowe problemy modelu prawa pracy," in *Przesłanki i kierunki reformy prawa pracy i ubezpieczeń społecznych*, ed. Salwa, Z., (Warsaw: Polska Akademia Nauk and Instytut Państwa i Prawa),14 et seq.

[6] Szurgacz, H. 2007. "Polskie prawo pracy po upadku socjalizmu. Kilka uwag o kierunku rozwoju," in *Człowiek, Obywatel, Pracownik Studia z Zakresu Prawa*

However, I consider this aspect—the one having a special impact on the development of law—to be temporary. More precisely, it temporarily accelerated the evolution of Polish labour law. After the completion of the impulsive implementation which was the result of Poland's accession to the EU, the determinants of the development of Polish law and EU law are the same.

The influence of market factors on labour law can be diverse. The development of factory production in the 19th century which concentrated and carried on in wretched safety conditions, stimulated the development of rigid and restrictive regulations. The technological progress and the increase in production effectiveness, development of employment in services at the expense of the transfer of jobs from industry to services and the globalisation of the market justify the demand for making legal regulations more flexible. I class this latter trend as a demand for the liberalisation or deregulation of labour law, and this is supported by a number of opinions in the literature. I will discuss this trend separately.

As already mentioned, pointing to development dynamism as a special property of labour law is not universally recognised in the doctrine. Nevertheless, the above mentioned determinants and their effects undeniably show a special pressure on the modification of employment-related legal regulations. And even if the basic goals, often called functions, of this branch of law have not changed, the scale of changes in the detailed regulations of labour law is impressive in comparison to other branches of law. Therefore, the defence of this element of description of labour law seems justified.

There is a question about the purpose of highlighting the above feature of labour law, since the descriptive function of the given statement in itself is only of educational benefit. It seems, however, that an analysis of the conditions of the labour law evolution has important interpretative and scholarly value. The former seems to be an important element justifying the functional interpretation. The evolution and richness of the regulated reality is accompanied by a permanent delay in the regulation, and also by quality that does not match its needs. Though that statement cannot justify the predominance of the functional interpretation over the literal one, yet it provides arguments for the wider use of the former in labour relations.

Highlighting development dynamism is also significant in the discourse about the development of labour law. It can be briefly described by saying that every modification in this branch of law is admissible and

---

Pracy Księga Jubileuszowa poświęcona Profesor Urszuli Jackowiak, eds. Stelina, J., and A. Wypych-Żywicka, (Gdańsk: Wydawnictwo Uniwersytetu Gdańskiego), 245 et seq.

imaginable as long as it does not interfere with the basic goals of the modified regulation defined by the protective function or the broadly understood principle of maintenance of social peace (harmonious development, and so on).

In concluding this fragment of my reflections, I will only add that within literature an element of the development dynamism of labour law was considered to be its expansiveness, understood as the process of extending some branches of labour law over legal relationships with outwork employees and over officers of uniformed services.[7] In the seventies, an increase in the number of employees was regarded as signifying an increase in expansiveness.[8]

Today, however, the relevance of those observations is doubtful. The extension of labour law over new employee groups is accompanied by the spread of non-employee employment relationships. Even though more and more safety regulations become applicable to them, the prevailing part of the so called protective function of labour law does not apply here.

The development dynamism manifests itself first of all in the creation of new regulations and modification of those already in existence. It manifests itself also in legislative processes which organise the legal system, e.g. by codification processes. Considering, however, that the general and abstract character of legal norms leaves a specific margin of interpretative freedom, we cannot neglect the opportunities offered by the interpretation of the law. Therefore, the development dynamism of labour law should not be limited exclusively to the evolution of the content of regulations alone. The evolution of the object of regulation can lead to an evolution of the interpretation. This aspect of dynamism will be the object of special attention in further parts of the paper in which I treat flexible forms of employment devised by interpreting the principle of freedom of contract. The above aspect is important because the reaction of the adjudicating bodies is usually quicker than the legislative process.

3. Liberalisation as the Current Trend in Development Dynamism of Labour Law

A concept, or rather a trend in the discussion, defined as "labour law liberalisation" has been appearing in the language of the labour law

---

[7] Zieliński, Z. 1986. *Prawo pracy—zarys systemu.* Warsaw—Kraków: Panstwowe Wydawn, 36.

[8] Szubert, W. 1970. *Szczególne właściwości prawa pracy.* Studia Prawno-Ekonomiczne, 4:59.

doctrine for more than a dozen years. The above expression does not have, of course, its precise referent and it is sometimes understood in different ways, since it is a language from the sphere of opinion and demand and not from the sphere of dogma. A feature of demanding statements, however, is that they reflect the beliefs and opinions of the demanding person. Thus, the demand for liberalisation is based on the assumption that the present legal status is not liberal and, what is more, it is dysfunctional because of that. The above assumption is in turn based on the assumed need to adjust law to changing conditions in which that law is applied. Such examples were mentioned above when analysing the property of labour law called development dynamism.

If there is no definition of a concept, the determination of its meaning has to rely on its common meaning, taking into consideration the context in which such a concept is used. It seems that with such a broad starting point, the concept of liberalisation is used as meaning opposition to excessively strict restrictions, stiffening, State control, and confining the influence of the parties on the rules relating to social relations. Liberalisation in the above meaning seems to be a synonym of the word elasticising, or making flexible.

Next, on the negative side, we may state that liberalisation does not mean liberalism. This latter concept—as a directional element—in its basic meaning of organisation of social life, aims for the restriction of the role of legislation within the scope of the object of regulation. And that would run counter to the historical rationalisation of the labour law entity as a branch aiming at guaranteeing harmony in the social space and at protecting the economically weaker party in an individual relationship. That is why labour law in its essence is a set of norms restricting the freedom of shaping the legal relationship whose object is rendering work. In its orthodox form, liberalism is the obvious opposite of the basic principles and functions of labour law. Absolute liberalisation of law would as a matter of fact mean the liquidation of this branch of law.

The need for a serious debate on whether the degree of restriction has not gone too far was perceived several years ago.[9] Technological development and the globalisation of the economy strongly affects the employer–employee and employer–State relationships. Roger Blanpain has noticed that the position of employer is being strengthened both in relation to employees and to the State. On the other hand, the labour

[9] The need to make working hours more flexible was, however, signalled already in the 1980s in the times of the socialist economy, cf. Pacho, J- 1986. *Czas pracy. Zagadnienia prawne i społeczne*. Warsaw: Instytut Wydawniczy Związków Zawodowych, 103 et seq.

market changes so that jobs are constantly moving from the production sector to the services sector, which has been called de-industrialisation.

The above described determinants of a technological and economic character (although there is no disjunction here) are the achievements of a science dealing with the problem of work efficiency and the latter is related to the daily work schedule, which is an argument for flexible working hours.[10] Similar arguments call for the implementation of work schedules corresponding to so called equivalent working time systems[11]. In this sense inflexible solutions, ones which stabilise both the length of the working time and its schedule, are becoming ineffective, at least for certain types of work. Though, of course, this thesis cannot be generalised.

While exercising some restraint, if only allowing for shift work and strictly cooperated work, we should rather agree that the so called "factory" model of legal employee relations is in many cases unadjusted not only to the expectations of employers, but also to those of employees. Management based exclusively on strict and current subordination and work control maintains its effectiveness only where there is a considerable degree of computability of organisation of work and of demand for it. Not only is such a situation not common, but it simply begins to be an exception. The growing degree of independence of labour—especially in services—begins to cast doubts on its cooperated character. This type of cause is the basis of the development of so called new forms of employment, and in particular telework, work sharing, worker leasing or so called task-based working hours. These solutions try to respond not only to the new demand resulting from organisational and substantive needs, but they are also a reaction to growing competition.[12] Their introduction is no longer only a demand of the doctrine, but it is an object of formal support e.g. in the EU legislation[13] and the legislation of many European countries.[14]

The problem of making regulations more flexible is presented as a

---

[10] Cf. Machol, L. 1975. "*Korzyści z ruchomego czasu pracy*," Polityka Społeczna, No. 1:32.

[11] Cf. Kozioł, L., and R. Kalisz. 1994. "Optymalizacja czasu pracy," *Przegląd Organizacji*, No. 5:19. These authors as optimal indicate the system of up to 12 hours per day, up to 60 per week and 42 hours on average per week.

[12] Cf. Chobot, A. 1977. *Nowe formy zatrudnienia—kierunki rozwoju i nowelizacji*. Warsaw, Prawnicze PWN, 130-171.

[13] Cf. Hajn, Z. 2004. "Nietypowe umowy o pracę," in *Europeizacja polskiego prawa pracy*, ed. Sanetra, W., (Warsaw: Scholar/IPISS), 64.

[14] Cf. Strzemińska, H. 2004. *Zarządzanie zasobami czasu pracy—doświadczenia krajów europejskich*. Warsaw: Karta książki, 72 et seq.

phenomenon that is specific to countries undergoing an evolution in social and economic relations, i.e. as an element of a bigger process of "de-nationalisation of the employer".[15] This circumstance, however, being transitory by nature, should not be treated as an inherent element of the trend that is analysed here.

Another important element of the pressure on the modification of labour law regulations is worth noticing. It is the consequence of the employer's decreasing ability to control the work of workers. While the ability to exercise external control (attendance, working hours) through electronic means is growing, the ability to control effectiveness is decreasing. The above comment refers mainly to highly qualified workers. The ability to control the effectiveness of their work would require the supervisor to possess qualifications even higher than those of the subordinate, which is not possible in the context of growing work specialisation. Increasingly, the employer is content with only organising the workplace and means of work, without influencing or controlling (and without organising control of) the object of the rendered work itself in the process.

The limited ability to exercise real control applies also to less complicated work and it is the consequence of the character of the technical distribution of goods which can be described as direct distribution. This direct character less often concerns final consumers (it applies e.g. to bank and insurance products), but, as a rule, it usually concerns retail outlets. The task of these outlets consists not only in offering a product, but also in its arrangement, collection of unsold product, arrangement of billboards and so on. This in turn requires fragmentation and popularisation of the access network, which as a consequence leads to minimisation of the places of employment. After all, the words "place of employment" is increasingly meaningless e.g. with respect to direct salesmen, sales representatives, consultants or teleworkers. Such fragmentation is accompanied by a change of the control method, i.e. instead of controlling if the work is being done, the supervisor controls the results of the work. Consequently, the employer organises the economic facilities and provides tools for work and in exchange the employer expects the achievement of the anticipated effects.

The above described process of minimisation or of the change in the method of controlling and managing work by employers is bringing employee relations under labour law closer and closer to relations under

---

[15] Cf. Kubot, Z. 1996. "Uelastycznienie stosunków pracy," *Polityka Społeczna* No. 5–6:12.

civil law. It is easier to argue that specific actions do not need to be rendered by an employee, but by a person connected with an entity which commissions work under a civil law contract.[16] For that reason, a discussion is being conducted within European labour law theory about the possibility to extend the institution of labour law over non-employee employment relations, or even on making the construction of the independent work contract legitimate.[17] We should note here the demands to partially include so called civil non-employee employment into the scope of the labour code, which appears in the Polish literature.

I have already mentioned that employers' demands to curb State control are provoked by the process of globalisation of the economy, and consequently, the competition of labour markets. When discussing development dynamism, I also mentioned that there was a close relationship between technological progress and global availability of goods. To this we should add the influence of legal institutions that extend the sphere of free trade. In consequence, costs of labour, which at least partially result from specific legal regulations in the sphere of labour law and social security, are an element of direct competition which, by lowering the protection standards and the costs of labour, takes the form of so called social dumping.[18] Therefore, simplifying the employers' arguments, the line of reasoning of those arguing for the lowering of the protective standards of labour law is as follows: "liberal" labour law means lower costs of labour, these at a later stage generate investments which create a larger labour market. As I have already mentioned, that is a simplified thesis and the author is aware of more complex conditions of the competitiveness in a given economy. In this sense, lowering the protective standards in the sphere of labour law seems to be beneficial also for employees, as it protects jobs, even if they are less attractive. Liberalisation in the form of more flexible regulations has already

---

[16] Salwa, Z. 2002. "Przemiany prawa pracy na początku stulecia a jego funkcja ochronna," in *Prawo pracy a wyzwania XXI wieku—księga jubileuszowa prof. Tadeusza Zielińskiego*, eds. Matey-Tyrowicz, M., L. Nawacki, and B. Wagner, (Warsaw: Biuro Rzecznika Praw Obywatelskich), 297; also in the same book: Kijowski, A. 2002. "Zakres swobody pracodawcy w korzystaniu z zatrudnienia cywilnoprawnego," 217 et seq.

[17] Supiot, A. 1999. "Zatrudnienie pracownicze i zatrudnienie niezależne," in *Referaty na VI Europejski kongres prawa, pracy i zabezpieczenia społecznego*, (Warsaw: Scholar), 169.

[18] Blanpain, R. 1999. "Dialog społeczny. Współzależność gospodarcza i prawo pracy," in *Referaty na VI Europejski kongres prawa pracy i zabezpieczenia społecznego*, (Warsaw: Scholar), 125.

provided verifiable proof of that.

Without elaborating on the social and economic causes we should only note that deliberations concerning the validity and the degree of limitations resulting from labour law regulations are the subject of an already everyday discussion.

In this place we must return to the definition dilemmas. In the first place we should reject the definition of liberalisation as an idea that calls into question all protective institutions. As I mentioned above, this would in fact mean calling into question the being of labour law. Rather, I understand liberalisation as actions in the sphere of lawmaking and law interpreting that contribute to addressing the needs of a reduced stabilisation of the demand for labour and allow for changes in the methods of performing work with a simultaneous increase in the cost of labour. Liberalisation in the sphere of lawmaking means the verification of the current legal status with the resulting abolition or changes in regulations which, while not giving significant results in the sphere of the protective function of labour law, restrict the freedom of economic activity. Liberalisation is thus a demand for a review of legal regulations that realise the protective functions of labour law from the point of view of their effectiveness. In the sphere of interpretation of the law, liberalisation means the adoption of the interpretative directive which says that where regulations do not explicitly define employee rights, interpretation of the law should take into account the need to give the employer a guarantee of the necessary flexibility in the sphere of management as well as the necessary legal instruments. In this sense liberalisation becomes a synonym of a more flexible interpretation, one which emphasises *inter alia* the so called organising function of labour law. However, the limit of that interpretation is its consistency with protective regulations.

To sum up the discussion of liberalisation, in foreign literature we should point to the ambiguity of this term. This term is used to mean deregulation i.e. repealing a part of regulations, or enabling the parties to depart from universally valid regulations to the disadvantage of employees, which is called flexibility. The above concepts are not unambiguous, however, and some give them quite the opposite meaning. For that reason, deregulation will be the subject of a separate discussion. The reason why the concept of deregulation is emphasised is rather the will to give an accurate account of the state of the discourse on this issue.

The formal and substantive limits of possible liberalisation are indicated in the literature. Among recent commentators mention is made of basing employment on the employment relationship, the limitation on freedom of contract, and the principles of labour law. Liberalisation is perceived both in the making of law and in its interpretation.[19]

An in-depth analysis of the notion of liberalisation would be useless for the purpose of this paper. Further in this paper I will use the concepts of liberalisation or flexibility interchangeably.

4. Deregulation of Labour Law

A concept close in meaning to liberalisation is the concept of labour law deregulation. As I mentioned above, in the theory of law, this concept seems to be synonymous with the concept of flexibility or liberalisation. However, the origin of this concept is non-legal. It was developed by social politics as a demand for deregulation of the labour market, and only then it was adopted in the labour law doctrine as a demand for deregulation of labour law.

The demand for deregulation does not at all mean a demand for abandoning the legal regulation of the labour market and for leaving it in a state of chaos. This demand has in mind legal regulations which increase the freedom of the parties concerning the choice of the legal instrument to regulate mutual rights and duties. After all, law is only one of the elements, and not the most effective one, of deregulation.[20]

Deregulation is synonymous to the thesis of "more market on the labour market". This is supported by increasing the freedom of economic entities and decreasing State regulation in the sphere of collective labour law, which in consequence also means a reduction in the role of the public sector.[21] The essence of deregulation is thought to be the reduction in the costs of labour,[22] though when it comes to detailed statements, the unanimity ends. But the difficulty is not only in defining the concept, but also in determining the limits of deregulation. One cannot fail to perceive a fairly unambiguous conclusion that deregulation means weakening of

---

[19] Florek, L. 2003. "Granice liberalizacji prawa pracy," in: *Granice liberalizacji prawa pracy. Problemy zabezpieczenia społecznego, Materiały z XIV Zjazdu Katedr (Zakładów) Prawa Pracy i Ubezpieczeń Społecznych,* Łódź: Wydaw. Uniwersytetu Łódzkiego, 10.

[20] Cf. Frieske, K. 2003. *Deregulacja polskiego rynku pracy.*Warsaw: Instytut Pracy I Spraw Socjalnych, 12.

[21] Cf. Zawadzki, K. 2003. "Deregulacja a koncepcja przejściowych rynków pracy," in *Deregulacja polskiego rynku pracy* ed. Frieske, K., (Warsaw: Instytut Pracy I Spraw Socjalnych Frieske), 84.

[22] Cf. Borkowska, S. 2003. "Regulacja rynku pracy w Polsce a polityka gospodarcza," in *Deregulacja polskiego rynku pracy* ed. Frieske, K., (Warsaw: Instytut Pracy I Spraw Socjalnych Frieske).

employee guarantees, in particular in the sphere of wage-shaping and legal stability of employment.

We must add that the difficulty in defining the optimum model leads to the point that deregulation is more of a process than a one-time event.[23]

When writing here about the deregulation of the labour market and thus about the deregulation of labour law, I do not take an evaluating stance on this issue. I only note that labour law is an element of discussion and an instrument for labour market specialists in this context. A lawyer does not have a suitable research apparatus to evaluate the social effectiveness of a given legal solution on a macro scale. Therefore, the assessment of the idea itself, including the assessment of the flexibility or lack of flexibility of the Polish labour law, is beyond the scope of this paper.

Therefore, and just in case, I only mention that the published research indicates diverse effects of the proposed process which, to a certain degree at least, have already been implemented. If we assume that the purpose of deregulation is reduction in unemployment rates, then this purpose has been reached to some extent. Only in return, we have a growing number of employment relationships characterised by very low wages or very low stability.

To recap, it seems that the concept of deregulation is not significantly different from the concept of liberalisation. Of course, one can describe the relationship between these concepts by saying that the demand for deregulation developed by social politicians results in the demand for liberalisation in labour law doctrine. But such division is not clear. In fact, the difference is in the accents. That is so because, the demand for deregulation has improvement on the labour market as its central element. However, liberalisation concentrates on changes within the protective function. In this sense we can even say that social politicians make demands for changes and give justifications for them, while the labour law doctrine lays down the limits of the possible changes. Nevertheless, the subject of the discussion is the same.

5. The Concept of Flexicurity

In labour law literature, and to a large extent also in the literature and discussions of labour market experts, the concept of flexicurity is present.

---

[23] Cf. Kryńska, E. 2003. "Deregulacja a segmentacja rynku pracy," in *Deregulacja polskiego rynku pracy* ed. Frieske, K., (Warsaw: Instytut Pracy I Spraw Socjalnych Frieske), 98.

The term itself does not have a simple counterpart in Polish. The natural method of translating it would be a reference to its component parts i.e. *flexibility* and *security*. However, an attempt to define this concept by reference to its substantial meaning seems to be correct. In this context, the author defined flexicurity as "flexible safety of employment".[24]

The intensive development and popularity of this concept is connected with the "Green Book on Modernising the Labour Law in order to Cope with the Challenges of the 21st Century", issued by the European Commission in 2006, though the particularisation of the concept was done later. To be precise, we should add that the concept was used in national debates much earlier. The place of birth of the concept itself is believed to be Denmark. One of the reasons why the popularity of the term and the concept was noticed was the fact that the country scored spectacular successes in the fight against unemployment without raising inflation pressure on wages and prices while maintaining a budget surplus. The essence of the Danish system is thus called the golden triangle, which includes a very flexible labour market, active labour market policy and a generous welfare system. It should be added, however, that the Danish concept of flexibility and security is an expensive policy and that it is realised in a country where employment in small and medium enterprises prevails and the public sector employs 30% of workers.

The flexicurity model was the subject of a number of EU documents which I do not mention here. I will only note the Commission's Communiqué to the European Parliament, the Council of the European Economic and Social Committee, and the Committee of the Regions—Common rules of implementing the flexicurity model, which defined the aim of the flexicurity model, which was needed to reach the targets of the renewed Lisbon strategy, in particular an increase in the number of jobs and their quality improvement, and at the same time the modernisation of European social models. This would require strategies which would regulate at the same time the flexibility—of labour markets, organisation of work, and labour relations—and security—including certainty of employment and social security. But certainty of employment is understood as the possibility to quickly get a job at every stage of professional life and chances to pursue occupational development in the quickly changing economy. Based on those assumptions, flexicurity was defined as an integrated strategy of a simultaneous increase in the flexibility and security

[24] Hajn, Z. 2010. "Ochrona trwałości stosunku pracy a flexicurity," in *Ochrona trwałości stosunku pracy w społecznej gospodarce rynkowej*, ed. Goździewicz G., (Warsaw: Wolters Kluwer), 87.

of the labour market. Additionally, labour security does not consist only in keeping the currently held post, but also in providing people with such skills which will enable their professional development and help them in finding a new job.

The answer to the above Commission's Communiqué was the Resolution by the European Parliament of 29th November 2007 on the common principles of implementation of the flexicurity model (2007/2209(INI). And here the Commission's approach was not accepted uncritically. The Parliament's attitude could be summarised by the principle of "flexible organisation of work within the framework of stable contracts of employment". The Parliament speaks about good jobs, and not about simply any jobs.

We should bear in mind that the above differences in the discussion are accompanied by equivocal assessments of the effects of the possible changes. We should also note analyses which indicate that we cannot be sure about the simple interrelation between making labour law more flexible, understood as weakening the solutions that stabilise employment, on the one hand, and an increase in employment, on the other. And the latter is, after all, the flagship argument of the advocates of changes. On the other hand, the same research shows that stable employment is the cause of employment segmentation, for the benefit of those already employed, at the expense of those entering the labour market.[25]

The analysed concept is a combination of the concepts of *flexibility* and *security*. As with every doctrinal phrase, this one is understood in different ways. An analysis of the discussion at the Union level leads to a conclusion that flexicurity is an idea from the sphere of labour market policy, and not the sphere of law. This conception is defined as a balance between flexibility and security.[26] That this conception should be treated as a sphere of politics, and not only law, seems indisputable.[27]

The demand for the balance between flexibility and security is

---

[25] On this question I refer the reader to comprehensive and multifaceted considerations of Rycak, A. 2009. *Wpływ prawnej ochrony trwałości stosunków pracy na poziom bezrobocia, zatrudnienia i produktywność przedsiębiorstw w świetle międzynarodowych badań ekonometrycznych*, PiZS No. 3:2 et seq.

[26] Cf.. Kryńska, E. 2007. *Równowaga między elastycznością i bezpieczeństwem na polskim rynku pracy. Jak osiągnąć flexicuritu? Flexicurity—między elastycznością a bezpieczeństwem na rynku pracy*, Warsaw, 8. The same text was also published in MPP 2007, No. 7:340 et seq.

[27] Cf. Seifert, H. 2007. "Flexicurity—nowa koncepcja polityki zatrudnienia pod znakiem zapytania," w *Flexicurity—między elastycznością a bezpieczeństwem na rynku pracy*, ed. Kamińska A. (Warsaw: C. H. Beck), 49.

reached—according to this idea—only when the following four elements are in harmony with one another:

- adequately flexible legal regulations (in the sphere of freedom of contract);
- active labour market policy;
- credible systems of lifelong learning;
- advanced social protection systems.[28]

Comments on the first of those conditions point to the fact that the purpose of flexibility is to increase employment or cause unregistered employment to be exposed. This is quite an interesting observation, since it breaks with emphasising employers' interests, though *de facto* it concerns their interests. However, it is not a new observation. I mentioned it when analysing the content of the Green Book.

Definitions of the concept of flexicurity, though not uniform, include some of the same elements. The authors of the definitions mention equilibrium between the flexibility of the labour market and social protection, to promote the insertion of all groups of unemployed, and in particular women, young people and older people. Of course, we can find different emphasis in individual comments. Thus, commentators point to the fact that flexibility is expected to consist of the ease of taking up a job and in a simplified procedure of dismissing employees, interlinked with high social protections in case of unemployment.[29] When listing the component parts of the conception, commentators point to the ease of taking up a job, availability of offers of career development, motivating the unemployed to take up jobs within the framework of active labour market policy, negotiation by social partners of solutions that are favourable for both sides of the employment relationship, popularisation of non-standard forms of employment, and advanced systems of social protection. At the same time, commentators indicate that this concept opposes the assumption that more flexible rules, are favourable only for employers, while social protection is favourable for employees. However, both these views can complement each other. Then, social policy becomes a tool of development, and not only a social element. A high level of social

---

[28] Cf. Kryńska, E. 2007. *Równowaga między elastycznością i bezpieczeństwem na polskim rynku pracy. Jak osiągnąć flexicuritu? Flexicurity—między elastycznością a bezpieczeństwem na rynku pracy*, Warsaw, 8 and EU sources quoted therein.

[29] Jodkowska, L. 2009. *Państwo opiekuńcze*. Warsaw: Difin, 227.

protection is a condition of high flexibility.[30]

Comments in the doctrine point out the difficulties in clearly understanding the flexicurity concept itself, mostly due to a strong influence of national models. It seems, however, that certain common elements and universal constituents of both component parts (i.e. of security and flexibility) can be assumed. Here they are:

flexibility elements:
a. numerical flexibility—consisting in guaranteeing freedom to dismiss and employ as needed (so called external flexibility);
b. working time flexibility—allowing the use of employees' working time depending on the employer's needs (so called internal numerical flexibility);
c. functional flexibility—consisting in freedom to relocate employees within the company depending on the needs;
d. wage flexibility—consisting in the possibility to adjust wages to the company's capabilities, on the one hand, and to the individual achievements of an employee, on the other.
Security elements:
a. job security—defined by labour legislation;
b. employment security—understood as the ability to be employed in many places owing to the guarantee of the opportunity to acquire new professional qualifications;
c. income security—in case of loss of the job or loss of the ability to earn a living;
d. *combination security* or *work-life balance*—allowing one to reconcile work and family life.[31]

Concluding the reflections on the conception of *flexicurity* we should note an undoubtedly apt observation that making this concept more substantial will continue to be dependent on national autonomies for a long time. This heterogeneity results, for example, from different models of European welfare states and different models and traditions of the development of flexicurity itself. Finally and above all, the concept of social policy as a buffer of the effects of increased flexibility in employing and dismissing employees means that the wealth of the given State comes to the fore, and specifically the resources that can be shifted to social

[30] Czerwińska, K. 2008. "Flexicurity jako koncepcja polityki społecznej i zatrudnienia," *Polityka Społeczna*, No. 3:13.
[31] *Ibid.*, 13.

protection.[32] And though this model assumes an expected return effect in the form of the increase in registered employment, the social protection system must be prepared for increased spending.

6. Flexicurity and Liberalisation of Labour Law

First of all, we must fairly early on state that there is no contradiction between the process of liberalisation and the concept of flexicurity. It seems that what we have here is rather a relation of overlapping. First, because the concept of flexicurity relates not only to labour law, but also to social protection law. And though the authors of the above mentioned comments state that this concept belongs to the sphere of social policy or labour market policy, yet its realisation obviously requires the employment of legal instruments. Apart from that, labour law is only a part of the necessary infrastructure in this model.

The unquestionable common feature of both these concepts, or rather processes, is that they are justified using the same scope of arguments. Moreover, basically all elements of labour law liberalisation are contained in the element of making labour law more flexible within the meaning of the flexicurity. However, it seems that there are two basic differences. The first is that the problem of employee security is perceived differently in the liberalisation process. We can even state that labour law liberalisation consists of a process whose purpose is the rationalisation of the regulation of labour law within the limits of its protective function. In other words, liberalisation consists of the fact that the focus of attention is on whether or not labour law still performs the protective function after the proposed changes. The latter is, of course, connected with continuously defining *in concreto*, what the protective function consists of, what its limits are, and if it has not been excessively or disproportionally realised. However, the concept of flexicurity, by shifting employee protection from labour law to social policy, including social protection, releases—of course only partially—labour law from thinking about the realisation of the protective function within its limits. Thus we can say that the concept of flexicurity is definitely more radical from the point of view of potential changes in labour law. And in this sense it is, so far at the intellectual level, another possible stage in the development of labour law – if it will still be possible to call that law labour law.

---

[32] Cf. Świątkowski, A. 2008. "Ograniczenie swobody zawierania umów o pracę na czas określony jako alternatywa koncepcji flex-security," *MPP* No. 11:569.

7. Final Remarks

The above mentioned trends in the scholarly discussion clearly indicate that there is a common consensus as regards to the analysis of the status of labour law and the directions of the development of those trends. The above described trends indicate various aspects and emphasis of the demanded changes, but as regards to the basic assumptions, we can speak about the existence of the consensus of the labour law doctrine and social politicians. However, the situation is different in the sphere of the execution of the demands for making labour law more flexible. And this is quite understandable, since no matter how strong the arguments from the sphere of macroeconomics are, the realisation of the demands for labour law liberalisation weakens the position of employees. It seems, therefore, that the unavoidable process in the evolution of labour law will be implemented at a slower pace than needed to effectively meet the requirements of international competition.

References

Blanpain, R. 1999. "Dialog społeczny. Współzależność gospodarcza i prawo pracy," in *Referaty na VI Europejski kongres prawa pracy i zabezpieczenia społecznego*, (Warsaw: Scholar).

Borkowska, S. 2003. "Regulacja rynku pracy w Polsce a polityka gospodarcza," in *Deregulacja polskiego rynku pracy* ed. Frieske, K., (Warsaw: Instytut Pracy I Spraw Socjalnych Frieske).

Chobot, A. 1977. *Nowe formy zatrudnienia—kierunki rozwoju i nowelizacji*. Warsaw, Prawnicze PWN.

Czerwińska, K. 2008. "Flexicurity jako koncepcja polityki społecznej i zatrudnienia," *Polityka Społeczna*, No. 3:13.

Florek, L. 2003. "Granice liberalizacji prawa pracy," in: *Granice liberalizacji prawa pracy. Problemy zabezpieczenia społecznego, Materiały z XIV Zjazdu Katedr (Zakładów) Prawa Pracy i Ubezpieczeń Społecznych,* Łódź: Wydaw. Uniwersytetu Łódzkiego, 10.

Frieske, K. 2003. *Deregulacja polskiego rynku pracy*.Warsaw: Instytut Pracy I Spraw Socjalnych.

Hajn, Z. 2004. "Nietypowe umowy o pracę," in *Europeizacja polskiego prawa pracy*, ed. Sanetra, W., (Warszawa: Scholar/IPISS).

—. 2010. "Ochrona trwałości stosunku pracy a flexicurity," in *Ochrona trwałości stosunku pracy w społecznej gospodarce rynkowej*, ed. Goździewicz G., (Warsaw: Wolters Kluwer).

Jodkowska, L. 2009. *Państwo opiekuńcze*. Warsaw: Difin.

Kijowski, A. 2002. "Zakres swobody pracodawcy w korzystaniu z zatrudnienia cywilnoprawnego," in *Prawo pracy a wyzwania XXI wieku—księga jubileuszowa prof. Tadeusza Zielińskiego*, eds. Matey-Tyrowicz, M., L. Nawacki, and B. Wagner, (Warsaw Biuro Rzecznika Praw Obywatelskich).

Kozioł, L., and R. Kalisz. 1994. "Optymalizacja czasu pracy," *Przegląd Organizacji*, No. 5:19.

Kryńska, E. 2003. "Deregulacja a segmentacja rynku pracy," in *Deregulacja polskiego rynku pracy* ed. Frieske, K., (Warsaw: Instytut Pracy I Spraw Socjalnych Frieske).

—. 2007. *Równowaga między elastycznością i bezpieczeństwem na polskim rynku pracy. Jak osiągnąć flexicuritu? Flexicurity—między elastycznością a bezpieczeństwem na rynku pracy*, Warsaw, 8. The same text was also published in MPP 2007, No. 7:340.

Kubot, Z. 1996. "Uelastycznienie stosunków pracy," *Polityka Społeczna* No. 5–6:12.

Machol, L. 1975. "*Korzyści z ruchomego czasu pracy*," Polityka Społeczna, No. 1:32.

Pacho, J- 1986. *Czas pracy. Zagadnienia prawne i społeczne.* Warsaw: Instytut Wydawniczy Związków Zawodowych.

Rycak, A. 2009. *Wpływ prawnej ochrony trwałości stosunków pracy na poziom bezrobocia, zatrudnienia i produktywność przedsiębiorstw w świetle międzynarodowych badań ekonometrycznych*, PiZS No. 3:2.

Salwa, Z. 1987. "Podstawowe problemy modelu prawa pracy," in *Przesłanki i kierunki reformy prawa pracy i ubezpieczeń społecznych*, ed. Salwa, Z., (Warsaw: Polska Akademia Nauk and Instytut Państwa i Prawa).

—. 2002. "Przemiany prawa pracy na początku stulecia a jego funkcja ochronna," in *Prawo pracy a wyzwania XXI wieku—księga jubileuszowa prof. Tadeusza Zielińskiego*, eds. Matey-Tyrowicz, M., L. Nawacki, and B. Wagner, (Warsaw: Biuro Rzecznika Praw Obywatelskich)

Seifert, H. 2007. "Flexicurity—nowa koncepcja polityki zatrudnienia pod znakiem zapytania," w *Flexicurity—między elastycznością a bezpieczeństwem na rynku pracy*, ed. Kamińska A., (Warsaw: C. H. Beck).

Strzemińska, H. 2004. *Zarządzanie zasobami czasu pracy—doświadczenia krajów europejskich.* Warsaw: Karta książki.

Supiot, A. 1999. "Zatrudnienie pracownicze i zatrudnienie niezależne," in *Referaty na VI Europejski kongres prawa, pracy i zabezpieczenia społecznego*, (Warsaw: Scholar).

Szubert, W. 1970. *Szczególne właściwości prawa pracy*. Studia Prawno-Ekonomiczne, IV.

Szurgacz, H. 2007. "Polskie prawo pracy po upadku socjalizmu. Kilka uwag o kierunku rozwoju," in *Człowiek, Obywatel, Pracownik Studia z Zakresu Prawa Pracy Księga Jubileuszowa poświęcona Profesor Urszuli Jackowiak*, eds. Stelina, J., and A. Wypych-Żywicka, (Gdańsk: Wydawnictwo Uniwersytetu Gdańskiego).

Świątkowski, A. 2008. "Ograniczenie swobody zawierania umów o pracę na czas określony jako alternatywa koncepcji flex-security," *MPP* No. 11:569.

Zawadzki, K. 2003. "Deregulacja a koncepcja przejściowych rynków pracy," in *Deregulacja polskiego rynku pracy* ed. Frieske, K., (Warsaw: Instytut Pracy I Spraw Socjalnych Frieske).

Zieliński, Z. 1986. *Prawo pracy—zarys systemu*. Warsaw—Kraków: Panstwowe Wydawn.

—. 1997. "Nowy ład pracy—rzeczywistość i wizja przyszłości," in *Nowy ład pracy w Polsce i Europie*, ed. Matey M. (Warsaw: Fundacja Promocji Prawa Europejskiego).

THE NOTION OF A "LABOUR MARKET" AND ITS LIBERALISATION IN POLAND

WALERIAN SANETRA

The "market" is traditionally defined as a place for concluding purchases and sales agreements and exchanging goods on a regular basis. However, and for a long time now, in addition to this "spatial" definition, other meanings have also been assigned to the term, providing it with a certain degree of abstraction.

European Union law, and more specifically the Treaty on the Functioning of the European Union (O.J. 2008/C 115/01), gives special attention to the concept of an internal market—that is the EU market (also referred to as the free market or single market)—which has also been the major concern of EU institutions and the subject of various EU provisions. Of course the focus of the definition of an internal market implies the existence of an external market, that is a "non-EU market".

In considering the freedom characterising the Treaty on the Functioning of the European Union, one can *inter alia* isolate the capital market, the market of goods, the market of services or the labour market. The term "labour market(s)" appears in Art. No. 145 of the Treaty, though not clearly defined along the text. In addition, and within the specified markets, further market categories can be distinguished, such as markets of the individual Member States (national internal and external markets).

Taking as a starting point the original meaning of the word "market"—i.e. a place for the exchange of goods (the buying and selling of products) on a regular basis—and in considering the working activity, it might be argued that this notion can also encompass the place where labour is performed in exchange of remuneration. The market is therefore regarded as a workplace where an employment relationship is established and work is performed and paid for. However, the market has never been understood as a workplace where work is exchanged for capital. The workplace is not a market in its "spatial" meaning, and the establishment of an employment relationship, as well as its legal consequences—such as the transfer of the work results to the employers and their obligation to remunerate employees—are not treated as the labour market in its abstract meaning, be it economic or legal. In other words, the workplace is not a labour market but a place where one works; the labour market is situated outside the workplace and notionally it is not associated with the conclusion of the employment relationship or generally with its establishment. In most of the cases, the notion of a labour market refers to the preliminary stage of the establishment of an employment relationship, in particular including the employment contract.

In Poland, the conclusion of an employment relationship and the employment relationship itself are the subject of provisions laid down in the Labour Code, a set of rules which is not perceived as regulating the labour market. These provisions can be found in the Law on Employment Promotion and Labour Market Institutions of 20 April 2004 (from now on Law 20/04/2004), that governs a number of relations of different legal natures and facilitates the establishment of employment relationships, along with rules concerning unemployment. Some of these relations give rise to obligations (private law relations), while some fall into the sphere of administrative law, social security law, financial law and criminal law. The complex legal nature of these relations often leads one to argue that they should be included in social security law and treated as a separate branch of law. In the author's view, these relations are shaped with a view to facilitate and encourage the establishment of employment relationships (taking up a job), which means that the reason for their existence and their primary objective is usually that of *establishing* an employment relationship. Hence, even though they are only partly obligations in their nature and give rise to a complex series of various legal relations, they are functionally connected with employment relationships and therefore can be dealt with within the area of labour law.

In previous laws concerning this subject the legislator did not make use of the notion of a labour market, not in the 1989 Law on Employment, nor in the 1991 Law on Employment and Unemployment. The expression "labour market" appeared in 1994 in the Law on Employment and Counteracting Unemployment ("Support for regional and local labour markets", as referred to in one of the titles) and in currently applicable Law 20/04/2004,when speaking of a "labour market category". Neither provisions encompass the definition of a labour market, which means that, on the one hand, the legislator defines it on an intuitive basis, and, on the other hand, the analysis of the wording of the law—the use of such notional categories as labour market policy, labour market institutions, labour market services, support for regional and local labour markets and labour market instruments—as well as the normative context in which it appears, makes it possible to some extent to specify the meaning as provided in Law 20/04/2004.

On the basis of these considerations it is possible to talk about the normative understanding of the labour market. Art. No. 1 of Law 20/04/2004 lays down the government responsibilities with regard to the promotion of employment and vocational training, as well as the measures to reduce the impact of unemployment. A number of relevant bodies have been set up in order to ensure:

1. full and productive employment;
2. human resource development;
3. achievement of the high quality of work;
4. full integration and social solidarity.

Law 20/04/2004 provides that the National Action Plan for Employment envisages labour market policies as those that include principles for the implementation of the European Employment Strategy. Institutions in charge of ensuring the implementation of such measures are public and private employment services, voluntary labour corps, training institutions, social dialogue bodies and partnerships at a local level, while main services provided are job placement, European Employment Services (EURES), vocational guidance and information, active job search support, and training arrangements. In addition, there are a number of other initiatives aimed at supplementing these services, such as the coverage of travel costs for a job interview, accommodation for newly-hired or trainees who operate away from their place of residence, the provision of work equipment for those starting business activity, and the cost of legal advice. Other initiatives of this kind include the coverage of social security contributions to be paid in the event of hiring an unemployed person, and the financing of employment funds.

The development of measures and policies at a local level should take place through the setting up of several projects aimed at combining services and instruments within the labour market, particularly geared towards maintaining and creating jobs, reducing the negative effects of unemployment, supporting any restructuring process in enterprises, developing human resources, and guaranteeing equal opportunities.

Law 20/04/2004 includes all these aspects under the labels of labour market policy, labour market institutions, labour market services or labour market instruments, however failing to explain differences in how and what exactly should be regarded as the labour market in legal terms.

Because of this narrow definition, an attempt could be made to identify the agents and the actors characterising the labour market and contributing to the establishment of the employment relationship, simply equating it to a "job placement market". As a rule, agents establish or maintain, by virtue of law, certain legal relations with future employees, employers and other entities. Thus there is an exchange of specific values (goods and services), which justifies the use of the term "market". However, if adhering to the wording used in Law 20/04/2004, one may also assume that terms such as "labour market policy", "labour market institutions", "labour market services", "labour market instruments", "regional and local labour markets" —which *inter alia* imply a national and more general labour market—are the components of the notion of labour market within the meaning provided by law. In this sense, the labour market is a mechanism which includes a certain policy (laid down by the National Action Plan for Employment), the devising of certain institutions (e.g. public and private employment services), the provision of certain services (e.g. job placement, vocational guidance and information), the use of certain instruments (e.g. bearing the costs for work equipment, the taking-up of business activity) and certain activities to be undertaken at regional level (the devising of local projects).

This is, however, a highly specific and technical understanding of the labour market, since there are no such entities as an employee or employer among the institutions or actors of such markets, nor are there any actions leading to the establishment of the employment relationship—notably the employment contract—among its instruments. In the context of all the provisions characterising Law 20/04/2004 and taking the popular assumption as to the meaning into account, the notion of a labour market should, first and foremost, refer to the establishment of the employment relationship, or be associated with the economic phenomenon of demand and supply of labour. The legal mechanism of labour supply and demand is treated as one of the essential characteristics of the market, which can hardly be found in the proposals envisaged and regulated by Law 20/04/2004. It is difficult to imagine the market as traditionally defined, especially including the market of goods, without the purchase and sale agreements as its essential and indispensable part that enables the operation of the law of demand and supply. It is likewise difficult to assume the existence of the labour market without an employment contract as its main element, if one accepts the economic definition of that market, for which the most important aspect is the exchange of labour and capital (employment performance and remuneration) and where the law of supply and demand applies.

Finally, it should be argued that Law 20/04/2004 ascribes a technical and legal meaning to the term "labour market" that clearly strays from its economic meaning, as the essence of the market is mainly expressed by the conclusion of employment contracts—the arrangement of terms and conditions—and by their subsequent implementation.

This is a matter that is generally regulated by the Labour Code rather than Law 20/04/2004.

In this respect, while Law 20/04/2004 generally shapes legal relations that allow for the establishment of an employment relationship, the Labour Code governs the ways in which the employment relationships are established, together with provisions concerning the submission of offers and the negotiation of the contract, in accordance with rules laid down by the Civil Code. However, it should be stressed that such separation in terms of regulatory power are not fully adhered to, and a certain degree of overlapping is seen.

Accordingly, it might happen that Law 20/04/2004 contains provisions on matters dealing with the establishment of the employment contract, discrimination practices resulting from a refusal to enter into an employment contract and the consequences arising from the breach of an agreement that is usually regulated by Labour Code.

The arguments that have been put forward so far highlight the need to distinguish the economic notion of a "labour market"—that mainly consists in the conclusion of the employment relationship and, more generally, the engagement of people in exchange for remuneration, and the way their working conditions are arranged (as laid down by labour laws, collective agreements, employment contracts)—from the more technical and legal notion of labour market as defined by Law 20/04/2004, that also defines the "job placement market", i.e. the labour market as defined in narrower—technical and legal—terms.

The notion of a market is inherently connected with the freedom of carrying out certain activities (in particular, the freedom of management) on the part of entities operating in it. Therefore, it should come as no surprise that in this era the notion of a market in the People's Republic of Poland is ill-defined in legal terms, if anything, it is stigmatised in doctrinal and ideological writings. In the presence of a centrally planned and controlled economy, the trend to limiting the freedom of activity of lower-performing entities, particularly businesses, in favour of the decision-making is so pronounced that the market and its mechanisms are *de facto* disregarded. However, this does not mean that the market economy lacks restrictions on the operations of the entities that are typical of the market more generally. Certain limitations also apply, but because of their scope they do not erase the essence of this economy, nor question it. There is a qualitative difference between the restrictions on freedom of business activity—particularly the freedom of management, within the centrally planned and controlled economy—and those existing in the market economy, including the social market economy which is one of the pillar activities of the European Union in terms of sustainable development, according to Art. No. 3(3) of the Treaty on the European Union. Not surprisingly, the term "market"—and its derivate "market economy"—has been somehow banished from the legal provisions since "real-socialism", whereas it became and still is a well-established concept in the European Union, despite certain difficulty exists in defining it with regard to differences arising from national markets.

With reference to the economic meaning of a labour market, the restrictions of freedom of the main entities operating in it—i.e. employees and employers—are associated with the origins, the functions and the essence of labour law itself, the result of the willingness to protect the weaker party to the employment relationship, i.e. the employee. These restrictions apply in particular to the freedom to arrange the terms and conditions of the employment contract and the resulting employment relationship by the parties. They also apply to the decision on the establishment of the employment relationship—it might happen that the establishment of such a relationship is of a compulsory kind, e.g. pursuant to criminal law), the selection of the other party to the employment relationship (e.g. employer), the duration of the established relationship and the possibility to terminate it, as well as the legal drafting that certifies the employment relationship. In recent years, a phenomenon often referred to as the liberalisation of labour law has been observed, which has also led to the liberalisation of the labour market in an economic sense. In particular, such liberalisation envisages the possibility to establish an employment relationship under arrangements other than the open-ended employment contract, such as fixed-term and part-time contracts. New employment schemes has been introduced, thus providing better opportunities and more freedom for selecting one type of employment contract rather than another. Recently, Polish labour law has been amended to include provisions on temporary employment and telework, —even though this terminology is not used in labour law—and now these employment schemes can be used within the labour market. The replacement contract introduced in the Labour Code can also be regarded as another sub-type of an employment arrangement—in addition to the employment contract for a definite term. In the context of this paper, it seems also worth pointing out that the draft Labour Code of 2006 provided for the opportunity to conclude special working arrangements, falling within non-standard employment, involving contracts for trainees, outworkers, household workers, family workers.

According to the draft, the practice of concluding relationships other than the employment relationships in a narrow sense would be enhanced by labour provisions aimed at facilitating the hiring of "non-employees", by means of special employment arrangements falling outside the traditional notion of employment contract. Another phenomenon has been observed recently, that is the liberalisation of labour law, tough this will not be the subject of this paper. This aspect is important all the same, as is connected—either directly and indirectly—with the liberalisation of the labour market in economic terms, that presumably provided it with higher levels of freedom.

On close inspection, Law 20/04/2004 provides for further limitations of the activity carried out by certain institutions, thus some doubts arise as to whether it is possible to refer to the labour market at all (in the technical meaning of the expression as defined by law), also considering the way it is regulated.

It should be borne in mind that, under the influence of the regulations of the International Labour Organisation, in the period of real-socialism people strongly adhered to the rule that job placement services could be only provided free of charge by state agencies (employment offices). In such conditions, it was difficult to talk about the existence of any "job placement market"—the labour market in a more technical and narrower meaning. In addition, employment policies was planned on a national scale, and implemented by means of administrative—and often—sanctioning measures. The state monopoly system of employment services was broken by the Law on Employment and Counteracting Unemployment of 1994, though major changes in this respect were introduced by the Law 20/04/2004. Art. No. 18 of Law 20/04/2004 sets forth that placement services at national and international for personnel consultancy, vocational guidance and temporary employment should be regarded as an economic activity falling within the provision of services—regulated by the Law on the Freedom of Economic Activity of 2 July 2004—and therefore need to carried out by employment agencies.

These agencies are recorded in registers maintained by the chairman of the provincial board and they are classed into four groups:

1. job placement agencies;
2. personnel consultancy agencies;
3. vocational guidance agencies;

4. temporary employment agencies.

The placement service may also be conducted by governmental institutions at a local level, bodies providing higher education, associations, foundations, social and professional organisations whose objective to render said services is laid down statutorily, provided that they are enrolled into the relevant registers. However, this opportunity does not include temporary employment agencies, as the placement service may be rendered on a temporary basis only by bodies that are registered by a provincial board as temporary employment agencies, in accordance to the Law on the Freedom of Business Activity. The establishment of employment agencies, which are private institutions, in addition to public employment offices, represents a major liberalisation of the "job placement market", as well as of the labour market in the technical meaning. At the same time, the underlying idea of providing free placement services has been questioned, as employment agencies cannot derive any benefits neither from the user company nor from the job-seekers. However, they may receive some funds to cover the costs resulting from their activity, that is to some extent understandable if one considers that the placement service is regarded as a business activity.

However, constraints laid down by relevant regulation is controversial, as the entitlement to reimbursement clashes with the entrepreneurial nature of the agency, that is mainly profit based.

It is difficult to expect that private employment agencies will carry out their activity on a charitable basis funded from the Government only. In order for such activity to make sense and be successful, it has to be profitable for those agencies and conducted in a competitive manner. In practice, this means that the principle of providing placement services on a gratuitous basis—evidently not considering public employment services—within certain statutory limitations, has been regarded as impracticable.

This is particularly the case of temporary employment agencies, as they have a twofold—and to some extent ill-defined —legal status, as under Law 20/04/2004, these agencies provide temporary employment services and not placement services. Further, according to Law on the Employment of Temporary Workers of 9 July 2003, they conclude employment contracts with temporary workers, thus acting as employers for such workers. One might conclude that these agencies are employers rather than agents assisting in establishing the employment relationship. However, they have a distinct legal status as a special kind of agencies, i.e. employment agencies. What is more, although formally a party to the employment contract, they just provide a form of intermediation, since it is the user company, for which temporary workers perform their work, that assigns them tasks, organises their work, and monitors their performance. Thus, in fact, the activity of a temporary employment agencies consists in providing placement services rather than playing the role typical of the employer. This is also upheld by the ILO Convention on Private Employment Agencies of 19 June 1997 (Convention No. 181), since it provides for the performance of temporary work and associates such work with the activity of private employment agencies, as is evident from its title. This means that in light of the ILO convention, temporary employment agencies are regarded as private employment agencies. In a nutshell, employment agencies as such cannot act as employers. However, domestic legislation does not allow for formally temporary employment agencies to provide placement services and they enter into employment contracts with temporary workers, therefore acting as employers. Therefore, they should not be subject to the provisions on placement bodies in the interest of job-seekers, including restrictions on benefits resulting from such activity. In fact, placement agencies are institutions that act as a go-between in the establishment of employment relationships. However, recent provisions make it possible to partly conceal this role, and thus justify the fact of giving up the restrictions and discipline imposed by the legislator with regard to this activity. Thus, it turns out that provisions concerning temporary employment agencies have become a particularly important and convenient instrument to escape the limits on the freedom of providing placement services, resulting in high levels of liberalisation within the market in terms of placement.

In conclusion, it is worth stressing that the term "labour market" does not have a clear meaning and, what is more, it can also present different facets in the context of individual legal provisions. Thus, the attempt on the part of research should be to provide a more precise notion of this concept in normative terms, as the current one is inconsistent and fragile. In the author's view, it is legitimate to single out the economic notion of labour market characterised by the employment contract (the legal mechanism which leads to the establishment of an employment relationship) as its main instrument and the employers and employees as its main actors. Apart from that, there is the notion of labour market that is associated with a set of legal relations set up prior to the establishment of an employment relationship (engagement relationships), which in Polish labour law are laid down by Law 20/04/2004, and which defines the labour market in more conventional and technical terms—in the form of placement service giving it a narrower and technical meaning. In factual terms, a particularly important and new element of that market is represented by temporary employment agencies which act as a go-between for the establishment of legal relations between user employers and temporary workers. In recent years, the liberalisation of labour law—both in terms of governing the employment relationship and regulating relations prior to the establishment of employment relationships—has been a main feature, and has led to increased levels of freedom of activity of the parties to employment relationships, in particular the employer, thus reducing the functioning of the labour market in economic terms. This has also been accompanied by the expanded freedom of activity of labour market entities and institutions in the technical legal meaning, which mainly consisted in allowing private entities to provide placement services, a limitation in providing such services on a gratuitous basis, and the establishment of a legal framework for temporary employment and temporary employment agencies. This aspect may be regarded as a gauge of the consolidation of the ideology underlying economic liberalism and the free market economy. The conditions, rationale and consequences of these changes—such as more freedom for entities operating on the labour market (in the economic and technical meaning, the development of the labour force)—are diverse and cannot be explained only by reference to this ideology. They require an investigation into the economic and the technical meaning defined by the notion of a labour market, without overlooking the relations and the interdependence existing between them.

AUSTRIAN LABOUR LAW AND LABOUR RELATIONS AS A PATTERN OF FLEXIBILITY

ROBERT REBHAHN

1. Introduction[1]

Over the last two decades, the economic performance of Austria was rather good. The Gross National Product (GNP) increased, at worst, modestly, the rate of unemployment was one of the lowest among the Member States, and the social net was, and still is, densely woven. Five years ago, even many in Germany looked at Austria's "successful story" with envy.[2] The economic recovery was quick after the two recent crises.

However, reality is less glorious than it looks. The employment rate of those over 58 years old is among the lowest in the EU, and low unemployment seems to be the result of high levels of early retirements, largely funded by fiscal subsidies. In the past, the annual public budget was nearly always in the red, and this led to a huge public debt that today officially amounts to 70% of GNP, without taking into account the hidden or implicit debts whose exact sum is uncertain. Investment in public goods is comparatively low, especially with regard to education and research. The demographic trend endangers the widening of the gap between working and retired people even further. Nevertheless, Austria is still seen as a prosperous country whose public bonds are awarded the highest ratings (although this seems to be in danger recently).

---

[1] This is an enlarged version of the original paper presented at the conference "Labour Market of the 21st Century: Looking for Flexibility and Security", on occasion of 370th Anniversary of the Establishment of Vilnius University Faculty of Law, that took place on 12-14 May 2011 in Vilnius, Lithuania.

[2] Cf e.g. Wahl, S., and M. Schulte. 2005. *Arbeitslosigkeit abbauen*. Munich: Olzog. Rebhahn, R. 2006. "Die Sicht der deutschsprachigen Länder," in *Reformdruck auf das Arbeitsrecht in Europa—Wie reagieren nationale Rechtsordnungen?* eds. Ochel, W., S. Evju, I. Asscher-Vonk, D. Brodie, P. Hurka, R. Rebhahn, and V. Rieble, 3. ZAAR-Kongress 2006 (München: Stiftung für Arbeitsbeziehungen und Arbeitsrecht), 98-126.

These statistics lead to the question on how this result was achieved, particularly with regard to employment. The workforce is the main capital of the country, while natural resources are scarce. One factor explaining this seems to be the size of the country, as it is widely held that small countries can adapt to exogenous challenges better than their larger counterparts. Therefore, it is important to investigate the specific features of the socio-economic structure that allowed for good results and quick adaptation. Of significance is the fact that this question is not widely investigated in the country itself,[3] but some main characteristics can be discussed and outlined. In the context of this paper, attention will be given to the main aspects of labour law and labour relations,[4] the result not only of my experience as a labour law scholar, but also of the belief that the framework and the basic structure of labour relations have the same impact on economic performance as short-lived action programs to stimulate employment.

a. Austrian labour law complies with a very traditional notion of the definition of an employee.[5] The main criterion is still the individual subordination of the working person, which is valued primarily according to organisational features. Economic subordination in the contractual relationship does not count for much at the time of establishing the employment contract. "Working for the account of the other" is seen more as a consequence of the employment relationship than as an indicator or a prerequisite. Economic dependency upon the contract does not lead to an employment contract. Further, most labour law rules as well as collective agreements apply to employees exclusively; only very few statutory provisions apply to economically dependent workers as well.[6] There is no special statute for autonomous workers. Thus, the range of personal-work relationships goes beyond that of the employment contract and the application of labour law.

---

[3] See, however, some publications of the Österreichisches Institut für Wirtschaftsforschung (WIFO; www.wifo.ac.at) and the Institut für Höhere Studien (IHS).

[4] Cf for legal issues Risak, M. 2010. "Austria," in *International Encyclopaedia of Labour law and Industrial Relations* (IELL), ed. Blanpain, R. (The Hague: Kluwer Law International). I refrain from citing many references to Austrian law written in German; those who read German will find them anyway, and for others such references seem useless.

[5] Ibid., 35 et seq.

[6] Cf, in a comparative perspective, Rebhahn, R. 2009. "Arbeitnehmerähnliche—Rechtsvergleich und Perspektiven," *Recht der Arbeit* (RdA), 236-253.

Austrian labour law is codified only partly:[7] collective labour law was codified in 1974 in the *Arbeitsverfassungsgesetz*, which was only slightly amended since then. Individual labour law is not codified at all, and there are some provisions of the Civil Code dating back to 1916 that are still relevant today. Besides, there is a bulk of different statutes, which look more like a patchwork set of rules than systematic legislation. Although theses statutes comprise a considerable number of provisions, they regulate some important questions only *en passant*, whereas less important questions often are regulated in a detailed fashion.

b. Reference should be made also to the basic structure of the social security system, which originated from the Bismarckian system.[8] At the beginning, only employees were affiliated. However, since the 1960s, self-employed, who are members of the "Chamber of Commerce" as well as farmers were also included into the system. In 1997, the legislator closed the last gap including self-employed workers who are not members of the Chamber of Commerce, thus integrating all own-account workers (autonomous workers) into social security. In consequence, one can barely avoid paying social contributions by avoiding an employment contract; this also helped to stabilise the scope of labour law. Recently, own-account workers are also entitled to sickness benefits to be paid by the social insurance, and they are even able to insure themselves against unemployment.

c. Labour and social security regulations must always be considered in relation to their real scope of application. In practice, labour laws only apply to those who work legally. Non-official estimations report that the share of shadow economy and informal work in Austria—around 8%—is among the lowest in Western Europe. Notwithstanding the opening of borders, this percentage has decreased even further over the last decades.[9] Official statistics for the formal economy report that about 90% of all people who work (as employees, self-employed or employers) are still regarded as employees, with the number of personal-work contracts outside the scope of labour law—e.g. freelancers—rising slightly during the last decade. The reluctance to resort to such employment arrangements

---

[7] Cf Risak, M. 2010. "Austria," in *International Encyclopaedia of Labour law and Industrial Relations* (IELL), ed. Blanpain, R. (The Hague: Kluwer Law International), 53 et seq.

[8] For a history of the evolution of Welfare in Western Europe after 1945, see Rebhahn, R. 2009. "Wage Labour," in *The Transformation of Labour Law in Europe*, eds. Hepple, B., and B. Veneziani (Oxford: Hart Publishing).

[9] Cf http://www.oekonomenstimme.org/artikel/2011/04/rueckgang-der-schatten wirtschaft-dank-aufschwung/, where the estimations of Schneider F. are presented.

outside the employment contract might be due to several motives. In addition to cultural reasons and to an increase in the costs of such arrangements, there seems to be common consensus in the working world that an undertaking should hire employees rather than freelancers.

With regard to the following, attention should be paid to the differences between the macrostructure of collective bargaining and the microstructure of the employment relationship. Whereas the macrostructure for the former seems to be rather strict, the microstructure allows for much flexibility and in some way demands it from the employees. In other countries, the system seems to work differently, combining a stricter microstructure with a less strict macrostructure.

2. Collective Regulation and Labour Relations

The focus is now on the role played by collective agreements, regarded as one of the most important instruments of the Austrian labour system.[10] Collective agreements mainly regulate the employment relationship in the private sector.[11] There, they cover more than 95% of employment relationships, a density which is among the highest throughout the Union.[12] The background for this peculiarity is a combination of some specific rules with the spirit of social partnership.

a. In most countries, *collective agreements* are concluded by a voluntary employers' association or by a single employer. This is not the case of Austria,[13] as here nearly all undertakings are required to be members of the regional Chamber of Commerce, whether an artisan, a service provider who works on their own, or a biggest enterprise.[14] Compulsory membership also exists in other countries, with the difference lying in the tasks to be carried out. In Austria, the Chambers and their subdivisions, organised mainly by branches, have a wider set of competences than abroad. In particular, they have the legal capacity to

---

[10] Cf Risak, M. 2010. "Austria," in *International Encyclopaedia of Labour law and Industrial Relations* (IELL), ed. Blanpain, R. (The Hague: Kluwer Law International), 669 et seq.

[11] Whereas employment in the public service (public servants and public employees) is regulated mainly by statute.

[12] Cf e.g. Rebhahn, R. 2010. "Tarifautonomie aus vergleichender Sicht," EuZA Heft 1:62-87.

[13] Cf Risak, M. 2010. "Austria," in *International Encyclopaedia of Labour law and Industrial Relations* (IELL), ed. Blanpain, R. (The Hague: Kluwer Law International), 694 et seq.

[14] Cf Ibid., 664 et seq.

conclude collective agreements, whereas single employers normally cannot perform this task, making Austria a unique case in Europe. Thus, Austrian law practically prohibits collective bargaining with trade unions at enterprise level. From a legal point of view, the bargaining capacity of the Chambers of Commerce or its subdivisions would give way if a voluntary association of employers concluded a collective agreement. However, voluntary organisations of employers are rare, and only some of them are involved in the bargaining process.

On the employees' side, the structure is much more centralised,[15] as there is only one trade union (the *ÖGB—Österreichischer Gewerkschaftsbund*), although it is comprised of a number of "unions" as subdivisions of the ÖGB. There are some frictions between the subdivision representing white-collar and the several subdivisions representing blue-collar branch workers. In addition to the trade union, there are also a number of regional Chambers of Labour, which are organised by statute and affiliate all employees.[16] However, the Chambers of Labour do not interfere with collective bargaining actors, as they deal with social policy matters and represent employees in court.

Thus, Austrian law strongly favours collective bargaining that covers at least all undertakings of a specific branch, granting the Chambers of Commerce the *de facto* monopoly to conclude such branch-wide agreements. The attitude of the employers is still the result of this legal framework. The Chambers are prepared to conclude agreements at branch level, perhaps also because this contributes to their legitimacy. However, in some branches, the number of members who do not have employees is greater than those employing workers, with this aspect that will make collective bargaining difficult in the years to come. With regard to blue-collar workers, collective agreements are concluded at branch-level, whereas collective agreements for white-collar workers usually embrace the whole sector of the economy, such as industry, trade, or tourism. Collective agreements are concluded either at national or at a regional level, not at both. Thus, the hierarchy of collective agreements does not give rise to many questions. Disputes about the resolution of cases regarded as falling within the scope of two different branches rarely arise, as the membership to one or another subdivision of the Chamber is usually taken into consideration.

All collective agreements provide for minimum wages, which then

---

[15] Cf Risak, M. 2010. "Austria," in *International Encyclopaedia of Labour law and Industrial Relations* (IELL), ed. Blanpain, R. (The Hague: Kluwer Law International), 643 et seq.

[16] Cf Ibid., 659 et seq.

apply to all undertakings of the branch or the sector. A collective agreement has a binding effect on the employer, because they are members of the relevant section of the Chamber, and applies to all their employees,[17] whether they are members of the trade union or not.

Collective agreements have normative effect, with the employment contract that can deviate from the collective agreement usually only in favour of the employee. However, the statute allows the agreement to also include rules that are binding in both directions, so that the employment contract cannot deviate at all. Although such provisions seldom apply, this possibility enlightens the spirit of Austrian collective labour law.

Collective agreements cover matters such as minimum wages and deal with many other issues, e.g. working time. If one also considers the vast statutory labour law, it can be argued that national labour regulation is very stringent. However, the wage levels set by the collective agreements are lower than in some Western neighbouring countries, especially in Germany and Switzerland. Further, the annual increase of minimum wage was moderate and rarely beyond the medium growth of productivity. Thus, the average labour cost in Austria was, and still is, lower than in Germany, which remained Austria's main export destination.

As collective agreements are only semi-cogent, the employment contracts can include clauses that favour the employee—e.g. they often set higher levels of remuneration. A new collective agreement does not only provide for higher collective minimum wages, but it also sets forth an increase in wages above such minimum. For example, the new collective agreement lays down an increase of minimum wage and factual wage of 3% and 2%, respectively. However, the parties to the employment contract are free to reduce the wage above the national minimum only afterwards, not in advance.[18]

The economic effect of the legal framework with regard to collective bargaining is that labour standards are highly collectivised and similar at branch level. In Austria, employers cannot use labour costs as a prior means of competition. In the past, this lack of competition was more important than today, when a significant number of undertakings could delocalise entire plants.

On the other side, the present situation regarding statutory labour law and collective bargaining causes a legal fragmentation of the workforce, if their general working conditions are considered. At statutory level, the

[17] Cf Ibid., 720.

[18] Cf Risak, M. 2010. "Austria," in *International Encyclopaedia of Labour law and Industrial Relations* (IELL), ed. Blanpain, R. (The Hague: Kluwer Law International), 713.

main difference is the divide between the public sector (with differences between public servants and public employees) and the private sector (with differences within for former public enterprises that had been privatised later on), although its relevance has somewhat diminished lately. Further, statutes and collective bargaining still uphold the divide between white- and blue-collar workers. Collective bargaining at branch or at sectoral level produces different wage levels and other differences in working conditions even for employees in the same occupation working in different branches. Particularly, some collective agreements, for instance in the financial or oil industry, provide much better conditions than others. In some occupations, there are even differences in the statutory rules. Undoubtedly, this fragmentation is more pronounced than in the north of Europe, although it is less accentuated than in Germany or in some southern European countries. As a result, employees may be unwilling to change occupation and to transfer to another branch.

b. With regard to the *collective bargaining process*, Austrian law does not provide for compulsory arbitration. Nevertheless, only rarely are collective negotiations followed by industrial action.[19] I cannot remember any major strike to promote better conditions of a collective agreement, with the regulation of strikes and other collective actions that are thus opaque.[20] Special statutory rules, as well as relevant case law barely exist. The prevailing view in the literature is that most strikes are lawful with regard to their collective nature. The most important restriction is the duty imposed on trade unions to refrain from industrial action that aims at matters already regulated by collective bargaining.[21] More remarkable is that the literature still holds that—in the event of a strike—there is a breach of the employment contract even when the collective action itself is lawful.[22] Presumably, this traditional view will give space to the new rulings of the European Court of Human Rights and the new spirit that shall spring of the Charter of Fundamental Rights (CFR). Nevertheless, the traditional perspective contributed to the shaping of social partnership effectively, as it favoured organised strikes by the large trade union ÖGB, because participants to wildcat strikes are more exposed to dismissal. It also motivated the ÖGB to engage only in strikes that presumably were successful, so that this union could secure that no employee would be

---

[19] Cf Risak, M. 2010. "Austria," in *International Encyclopaedia of Labour law and Industrial Relations* (IELL), ed. Blanpain, R. (The Hague: Kluwer Law International), 863.

[20] Cf Ibid., 860 et seq.

[21] Cf Ibid., 729.

[22] Cf Ibid., 864 et seq.

dismissed afterwards. Nowadays, however, this line of reasoning is not very welcomed.

The present overview of collective negotiations explains why Austria is regarded as the country of social partnership *par excellence*. Large organisations—the trade union and the Chamber of Commerce—cooperate to solve labour issues at different levels, heavily influencing also social legislation, as in this area the Parliament enacts only what has been approved by social partners. In the period 2000—2006, this influence was retrenched by the then Centre-Right Government.

c. One of the main questions in terms of labour relations is the setting up of a *statutory minimum wage*, which today exists in more than 20 Member States, but not in Austria. Here, the statute even limits the possibility of establishing a minimum wage, as this matter can be dealt with only in those areas where no association of employers exists that is able to conclude a collective agreement.[23] Thus, the administrative regulation of wages may include only those few employers that are not members of the Chambers of Commerce.

Some years ago, the Government announced that all employees should receive at least 1,000 Euros a month for working 40 hours a week. Foreign commentators reported that this was the sign that Austria was about to introduce a statutory minimum wage. However, the Government only expressed a political wish, which should have been realised by collective agreements. Only if the collective actors had failed to implement the goal, would the Government have intervened. As the goal was realised through collective bargaining, there is no longer discussion about introducing a statutory minimum wage. This situation stands in stark contrast to what happens in Germany, where the issue is currently the subject of a heated debate.

d. The system of *works councils* is closely connected to the notion of social partnership. The works councils represent all employees of a plant, with the statute regulating the functioning of these bodies in a very detailed way.[24] Only in plants with at least five employees can works councils be elected; although the law does not create any obligation for the establishment of a works council, they exist in the majority of large plants.

The statute recognises the works councils a wide range of rights. Of course employers are obliged to inform and consult it for various matters. For some specified initiatives of the employer, the statute recognises the

---

[23] Cf Risak, M. 2010. "Austria," in *International Encyclopaedia of Labour law and Industrial Relations* (IELL), ed. Blanpain, R. (The Hague: Kluwer Law International), 745 et seq.

[24] Cf Ibid., 750 et seq.

works council stronger rights, e.g. the veto right or the right to ask for compulsory arbitration. However, the statute provides the works councils with this power only with regard to specific social and personal issues, whereas economic decisions remain out of its reach. Further, the statute allows works councils to conclude collective agreements with the employer at plant level (plant-level agreements), although only for issues envisaged by the statute itself.[25] In this sense, plant agreements can regulate performance-based pay, but are not allowed to regulate "time work" (work paid by reference to a period of time). Finally, the statute says implicitly that works councils as such have to refrain from any industrial action. In addition, the employer needs the council's consent to introduce specific surveillance measures. The same applies to specific forms of performance-related pay, whereas the consent of works councils is not needed to raise or alter wages paid in reference to a period of time (e.g. hourly wages). Further, in specified cases the council may ask for compulsory arbitration by an independent body. Significant examples of this concern the schedule of working hours, the internal code of conduct, and social measures in case of restructuring (social plan, e.g. in case of mass dismissals). However, the employer does not need the council's consent to order extra-work, and the arbitration board that devises a welfare plan can impose the obligation on the part of the employer to pay redundancy benefits, although not empowered to decide upon restructuring. Thus, the statute tries to give the works councils some say in the shaping of the employment relationship, yet maintaining the management's prerogative. The basic intention of the legislator and the social partners are further confirmed by some recent developments. Two years ago, the Supreme Court widened the scope of the veto right of the works councils so that to include all performance-related pay. In 2011, the Parliament response was to limit the veto power to the traditional nucleus of performance pay.

3. The Individual Labour Relationship

3.1 General Features

a. Austrian employment law considers the contract of employment as a special arrangement among the contracts of civil law. Some decades or so

[25] Cf Risak, M. 2010. "Austria," in *International Encyclopaedia of Labour law and Industrial Relations* (IELL), ed. Blanpain, R. (The Hague: Kluwer Law International), 817 et seq.

ago, there was some arguing that the general rules of contract law were inappropriate with regard to employment. However, these opinions receded, perhaps because in the meantime, the civil contract law itself has been amended and evolved, with a view to provide more protection to the weaker party. Nowadays, it seems uncontested that the rules of civil law must be taken into account whenever there is a legal issue related to the employment relationship, and that they apply if the labour statutes and their intrinsic values do not give sufficient ground to deviate from civil law.

In Austria, there is a prevailing view that it is up to the legislator to orient the courts, as only the legislator has democratic legitimacy. The legacy of the school of *Kelsen*—the Pure Theory of Law—still holds, although its peculiar impact has diminished. As a rule, legal cases have to be decided in accordance to what is set forth in the statute; prior cases are not legally binding. The courts thus comply with the guidelines for interpretation of written rules. However, the influence of European Union law might diminish such adherence to the statute.

Austria has no special branch of the judiciary dealing with labour cases. However, ordinary courts have special chambers for these cases, which also comprise lay judges appointed by the chambers of commerce and those of employees.[26] The integration of labour courts into ordinary courts allows for changes of judges between civil and labour chambers resulting in strengthening the bonds between labour and civil law, as well as its methodology.

b. Austrian labour law is rather liberal with regard to the conclusion of the employment contract. The parties may conclude a contract for a fixed-term or for part-time work, also on an oral basis. Nevertheless, the proportion of written contracts has risen considerably in the last two decades. A reason might have been the duty to inform on the main rules of the employment relationship in writing. Another reason is that employers increasingly wish to fill some legal "gaps"; although statutes and collective agreements deal with many aspects of the employment relationship, there is much room left to manoeuvre. The rise in the use of written contracts also favoured the introduction of general terms within the employment contracts, which are usually proposed by the employer. Austrian law does not deal with such general terms of employment explicitly, as there are no special statutory rules. Basic provisions of contract law also apply to general terms of employment, but the courts

[26] Cf Risak, M. 2010. "Austria," in *International Encyclopaedia of Labour law and Industrial Relations* (IELL), ed. Blanpain, R. (The Hague: Kluwer Law International), 67 et seq.

have rarely used them in this context so far. Employers do not need the consent or the advice of works councils at the time of hiring, nor to draft an employment contract or to identify the general conditions of employment.

c. Labour statutes create an obligation for the employer to look after the employee's interests, particularly to provide workers with health and safety protection, which in German is called the duty of protection (*Fürsorgepflicht*). According to the doctrine, there is also a corresponding duty on the employees' side, *Treuepflicht*, which might be translated into the duty of loyalty. The employment contract can amend the two duties only partly. They play a major role for the understanding of Austrian labour law as well as of employment relations,[27] as pointing out the binding nature of the employment relationship going beyond what written rules explicitly provide. They correspond as well to the spirit of social partnership that shapes collective labour relations at a national level.

Thus, Austrian law goes further than British law, where the courts only recently detected the duty of mutual trust and confidence as an implied term of any employment contract. On the other side, the Austrian concept is not as fully developed as, for instance, the German one, where both sides are generally obliged to behave as a "good" employer or employee, respectively. As in Germany, this duty to behave appropriately in the capacity of employer or employee, respectively, seem to be very specific. In Austria, however, the two duties are dealt with more restrictive, providing some limits if compared to what occurs in Germany, where the Civil code already obliges every party to a contract to act in good faith (*Treu und Glauben*).

In addition to the duty of protection, there is another encompassing obligation that is incumbent on the employers, that is the duty of equal treatment,[28] although it is applied less strictly than in Germany. Whereas in Germany, employers have to place all comparable employees on equal footing, Austrian law only prohibits the discrimination of minority employees. Accordingly, equal treatment can be regarded more as ban to discriminate a numerical minority than a strict duty of equality, although there is now a trend towards the German approach. Further, Austrian law allows for the employer to provide newly hired workers with less benefits than other employees, thus increasing flexibility over time. Nowadays, the duty to treat workers equally coexists with the principle of non-

[27] Cf Risak, M. 2010. "Austria," in *International Encyclopaedia of Labour law and Industrial Relations* (IELL), ed. Blanpain, R. (The Hague: Kluwer Law International), 205 et seq, 254 et seq.

[28] Cf Ibid., 265 et seq.

discrimination, with the latter seemingly overshadowing the former in terms of clarity and strictness. However, there are not many judicial proceedings resulting from discrimination practices, although there are many referrals to the conciliatory bodies established to deal with discrimination matters.

d. As a rule, only individual employees can file an action to pursue their rights. Neither the trade union nor the works councils can bring an action on behalf of the employee. Works councils, however, are empowered to appeal to the court if the matter concerns several employees, with its ruling that is only "declaratory" in that it is not legally binding, therefore not prejudicing the relationship between employers and employees.[29] Thus, the works councils themselves cannot institute legal proceedings against the employer for arrears of pay. For a long time, the government (the state administration) only ensured that the employers abide by the rules on health and safety and on maximum working time. However, in 2011 the Parliament widened these powers of the Government. From now on, the state administration will be able to ensure that the employers provide the minimum wage and paid holidays as laid down in the collective agreement. In the event of failing to comply with these obligations, the employers might be fined. This marks an important shift in Austrian labour law as for the first time, the state administration also considers some rights of employees other than simply health and safety, which results into employment law moving from the sphere of private law to that of public law. The reason for this innovation was the full application of the freedom of workers within the new Member States, and the fear of a non-compliance of foreign employers with domestic labour law with regard to the posting of workers.

e. The Austrian economy heavily relies on a trained workforce, with a well-established system of apprenticeship that has contributed to instruct a significant number of workers for decades. Undertakings employ young people, who complete compulsory education and enter into special employment contracts allowing them to receive vocational training at the workplace, while also attending special schools. In the past, and unlike a number of other countries, very few young people entered adulthood without having received the one or other form of training. However, the share of young people opting for an apprenticeship programme has decreased, and many employers now complain that basic knowledge of many school-leavers diminished over time. In addition, the fact that those

---

[29] Cf Risak, M. 2010. "Austria," in *International Encyclopaedia of Labour law and Industrial Relations* (IELL), ed. Blanpain, R. (The Hague: Kluwer Law International), 70.

who complete higher education in one of its different forms have the skills reported in their final certificate is far from being obvious; intense vocational training during their lifetime could perhaps fill the gap. However, labour law does not yet really demand for or encourage such training on the job. In this sense, the obligations of both the employer and the employee in terms of retraining are not specified. Accordingly, the skills needed to promote economic prosperity are less secure than in the past.

3.2 External Flexibility

Within the employment relationship, one can distinguish between external and internal flexibility. As for external flexibility, it mainly deals with the levels of protection against dismissal, the use of fixed-term arrangements, and—as seen above—the fragmentation of the labour market. Unfortunately, no data has been found about the average duration of the employment relationship in Austria. In the largest countries of Western Europe, such duration has increased since 1990.[30]

a. According to the general rules, the employer can terminate a contract for an indefinite period by giving notice. Austrian law does not provide a general duty to justify dismissal. Only if a works council is present at the plant, does the employer have to inform this council before dismissing the employee. However—and contrary to what is laid down by German law—the employer is not obliged to provide much information, apart from the name of the employees and the date of dismissal. Further, the employer has to provide the worker with a period of notice, corresponding by statute to two weeks for blue-collar workers. Collective agreements seldom prolong it, if anything, they shorten it to one week. As for white-collar workers, the statute provides for longer periods of notice, based on the length of service of the employee. However, if the employer dismisses a worker and fails to respect the appropriate period of notice in advance, the dismissal is valid and terminates the contract at the date pronounced by the employer. The employee then is entitled to the wages they would have earned during the appropriate period of notice (back pay), but this amount is reduced after three months by the amount they have earned or could have earned over the period if in employment.

As a result, the forms of protection against dismissal depend upon

---

[30] See Rhein, T. 2010. "Ist Europa auf dem Weg zum Turbo-Arbeitsmarkt?" *IAB-Kurzbericht*, No. 19. E.g., the figures are about the following: 7 years in Denmark; 10 years in Germany; 9 years in Spain.

specific legislation. A general regime safeguarding the worker against dismissal exists, as well as some special regimes. The general regime allows the dismissed worker to apply to the court to have an unwarranted dismissal made invalid. If this is the case, the employment relationship is deemed uninterrupted. On the contrary, in case of such an unwarranted dismissal, Austrian law gives neither the employer nor the employee the right to evade the continuation of the employment relationship by offering or demanding compensation. Of course, the two parties have the possibility to negotiate such compensation. Employees often prefer a lump sum over reinstatement, the amount of which is not possible to assess, as the result of the foregoing negotiation.

This general regime of dismissal protection has, however, some important limitations in terms of application,[31] that are relevant to understand the way the Austrian legislator shapes labour law. The general regime only applies to employees working in a plant with five or more employees, who have more than six months of service, if the dismissal encroaches upon the interests of the dismissed worker. In addition, employees cannot challenge a dismissal for economic reasons if the works council explicitly approved it. These four elements of applicability of the general regime show that Austrian legislation aims at hindering the deliberate dismissal of employees rather than at securing their employment. In particular very small employers can dismiss their employees without justification, as they only have to abide by anti-discrimination rules. The waiting period of six months corresponds to a statutory probation period. The courts construe the pre-requisite that the dismissal encroaches upon the interests of the dismissed worker requiring that the dismissal affects the dismissed in a specific way. As a result, for instance those who could easily find a similar occupation cannot challenge the dismissal. The practical importance of the said pre-requisite might depend upon the situation of the labour market, though usually affecting younger more than older workers. Finally, the consent of the works councils is taken into consideration especially in cases of mass redundancy, where its consent can be relevant in deciding the number of workers and who to be dismissed. One might ask whether some of these traditional restrictions would be in line with Art. No. 30 of Charter of Fundamental Rights and whether this provision would be binding for national regulation.

If a dismissal can be challenged in court, the judicial review follows

---

[31] Cf Risak, M. 2010. "Austria," in *International Encyclopaedia of Labour law and Industrial Relations* (IELL), ed. Blanpain, R. (The Hague: Kluwer Law International), 503 ff.

the general spirit mentioned before.[32] Apart from the case of illness, the employer can easily justify a dismissal for personal reasons. In addition, dismissals on economic grounds are not investigated in detail, although the wording of the rulings of the Supreme Court in some cases could indicate the use of more severe criteria to justify such dismissals. The courts, however, will not review the economic decision of the employer itself, e.g. to close the plant or stop manufacturing a product. The rather few number of actions against dismissals that came to the Supreme Court have not yet allowed this Court to clarify its position in every direction. However, in the recent past, the number of such claims has risen sharply due to the economic crisis.

Some other clues reveal that the legislator does not particularly focus on the forms of protection provided against dismissal. The possibility to dismiss without justifying the dismissal before litigation has already been mentioned. In addition to this, the period to appeal to the Court was for a long time set at only one week after the dismissal. Only in 2011, it was prolonged to two weeks.

b. In addition to the general regime of dismissal protection, there are special rules for specific categories of employees, such as pregnant women and disabled persons, for which the conditions for dismissals are stricter and a previous authorisation by a national authority is needed. The share of employees covered under the special protection regime has been rather limited for a long time. However, some years ago, a new regulatory regime was introduced to safeguard employees on parental leave—also on a part-time basis—which considerably increased this proportion of employees. Since then, the legislator seems to have realised that these special regimes might give rise to certain problems. Recently, special protection for disabled persons against dismissals during the first three years of service has been abolished. This change has been adopted in accordance with representatives of this category of workers, in order to increase their employability. Needless to say, rules prohibiting discrimination on the grounds of disability apply.

c. Another form of external flexibility is the recourse to fixed-term contracts.[33] Significantly, the Austrian legislator has refrained from explicitly regulating renewed fixed-term contracts. It is surprising that the European Commission has not yet initiated an infringement procedure.

According to the rulings of the labour courts, the fixed-term contract

---

[32] Cf Ibid., 521 et seq.

[33] Cf Risak, M. 2010. "Austria," in *International Encyclopaedia of Labour law and Industrial Relations* (IELL), ed. Blanpain, R. (The Hague: Kluwer Law International), 181.

entered into by the worker for the first time is lawful without further scrutiny or restriction. On the other hand, if the same parties conclude another fixed-term contract, the renewal of the fixed-term contract is lawful only if it can be factually justified, if not much time has elapsed since the previous one. The burden of justification rises with every renewal and—if lacking—the contract of employment is converted into an open-ended employment contract.

In Austria, the percentage of fixed-term contracts is not very high compared to other countries (e.g. Spain) as—if we exclude the apprentices—about 5 % of the workforce is employed under a fixed-term contract. The comparatively low use of fixed-term employment might also depend on the fact that it is relatively easier to dismiss employees with an open-ended employment contract. In any case, it seems that Austrian employers did not need a great share of fixed-term contracts to implement external flexibility. However, labour representatives complain that today a growing number of employment relationships—particularly involving young people—start with a fixed-term contract, and often end therewith. In this sense, the percentage of fixed-term contracts is on the rise, but there is no willingness to limit their implementation, for example, by setting a ceiling on the use of this contractual scheme.

d. In 2003, Austria reviewed the national *severance payment* system,[34] and the EU Commission widely praised the reform as a pivotal measure to improve flexicurity. Such enthusiasm seems exaggerated, considering that the reform of 2003 mainly regarded severance benefits, and no other major changes were introduced.

Further, the old system is still in force for contracts concluded before the year 2003. According to this system, the employer has to pay a lump sum if the dismissal takes place after three or more years of service (except for termination without notice for substantial reasons). Thus, dismissals for economic and personal reasons triggers a duty to severance pay, the amount of which corresponds to two monthly wages and rises in accordance with seniority up to twelve monthly wages after 25 years of service. This system might lead employees to neglect other job opportunities, as they would not be entitled to redundancy benefits if they give notice when they wish to terminate their employment. In addition, it might motivate employers to postpone dismissal if a recovery seems likely, inducing some to consider the earlier system as hindering flexibility. On the other side, trade unions demanded that the old form of

---

[34] Cf Risak, M. 2010. "Austria," in *International Encyclopaedia of Labour law and Industrial Relations* (IELL), ed. Blanpain, R. (The Hague: Kluwer Law International), 347 et seq.

severance pay be extended also in case the employees are the ones giving notice. Thus, it was the employers in particular that demanded for reforms, also to prevent the realisation of the unions' claims. Further, in industries where a change of job takes place frequently—e.g. tourism and construction—most employees did not have the opportunity to receive severance pay.

According to the new system introduced in 2003, the employer has to pay monthly contributions to a special fund, amounting to 1.53% of the monthly salary. These funds are managed by private bodies that invest contributions in the capital market. Employees are entitled to withdraw the capital—and possible gains—from their account if dismissed. Alternatively, money can be left in the fund until retirement. Employees are not satisfied with these financial schemes because of their low performance, which is due partly to the trend of the capital markets, and partly to the fact that the capital is not bound to a specific period and cannot be invested for longer terms. Further, employers are now less reluctant to dismiss quickly, with this aspect perhaps having contributed to the increasing number of dismissal claims. Employers are not happy with the reform either, as they have to look for other measures to motivate employees to remain with their company. As a result, the widely-acclaimed reform of severance payment cannot be really regarded as successful, but rather as a failure.

One of the main indicators of external flexibility is the costs to be borne by the employer to dismiss a worker. From a legal point of view, the answer for the Austrian case is clear: statutory law no longer prescribes such payment of redundancy benefits at the end of the employment relationship, neither in cases of fair nor unfair dismissals. However, the employer might pay a lump sum in order to avoid litigation against dismissal or to prevent the reinstatement of the employee in the event of unfair dismissal. The situation is different when mass dismissal takes place. A redundancy programme (social plan) may provide employees with severance pay, though such a programme can be the result of negotiation with the works council, or can be imposed by an arbitration board. In this latter case, severance pay is calculated on the monthly wage and the period of service. Unfortunately, no data has been found indicating the average amount of money paid by Austrian employers. Unemployment benefits provided by social security will be treated later on in this paper.

Comparatively, the levels of protection against dismissal in Austria are undoubtedly lower than those in France, Germany, Italy or some of the new Member States, but higher than those in Belgium, the UK, and some other countries which have just joined the EU.

3.3 Internal Flexibility

From a legal point of view, assessing the level of internal flexibility is a difficult task. As a starting point, one should distinguish between the degree of flexibility provided within the contract and how to amend contractual terms already agreed upon.

a. With regard to the first point, flexibility demanded from the worker depends partly on statutory rules on specific topics, particularly on working time, and partly on the wording and the drafting of the contract. Most employment contracts do not restrict the employees' obligations in a specific way, because they are either concluded orally or drafted in a rather generic manner, or because of the employers' attempt to meet their needs. As noted earlier, Austrian courts rarely go through general conditions laid down by an employment contract, seemingly favouring a common assumption that the employee's duty to be flexible is somehow implied in the contractual arrangements. To some extent, the doctrine sustains the dynamic nature of the duty to work which obliges one to adapt to changing demands at the workplace and to accept transfer whereas necessary. Normally, a worker has to comply with what a "reasonable" employer might expect from a "reasonable" employee.

b. A major concern for internal flexibility is the regulation of working time. The statute requires that the employment contract fixes the length of the working time of the employee normally due (full or part-time work), as well as the time-schedule regarding this working time. However, this time-schedule may alternatively also be provided for by a plant-agreement. The employers can change the working time schedule unilaterally only if the schedule has not been enclosed in the plant-level agreement, and if the employment contract or the collective agreement empowers them to do so.

This regime limits the managerial prerogative more than the traditional definition of employee. The employee is obliged to additional work over the normal working hours only if such an obligation is stated either in the employment contract or in the collective agreement;

In addition, the employer has to comply with the regulation of maximum working hours. The Austrian statute insofar seems restrictive at a first glance. Since 1975, the statute sets the limit for the traditional weekly and daily working time at 40 hours and at 8 hours, respectively.[35] All work done in addition to these time arrangements is regarded as overtime work. However, the statute itself allows broadly for overtime

[35] Cf Risak, M. 2010. "Austria," in *International Encyclopaedia of Labour law and Industrial Relations* (IELL), ed. Blanpain, R. (The Hague: Kluwer Law International), 181.

work (e.g. 5 hours a week if there are additional tasks to perform, a prerequisite that is difficult to assess). On the other hand, the statute tries to deter employers from using overtime work, making it expensive for the employer. It prescribes a wage supplement amounting to 50% of the hourly wage; instead, if the employee agrees, the employer may reduce the working time by the 150% of the rendered overtime work. Thus, according to these general provisions, overtime work and flexible working time arrangements are costly to the employer, particularly when involving full-time workers. In a similar vein, the wage for overtime work makes it very appealing to many employees.

However, the foregoing provisions do not reflect the current reality. Over the last twenty years, the legislator attempted to smooth such a set of rules, causing it to become more complicated. In several cases, the statute empowers collective agreements to manage the working time regime by resorting to calculating the maximum working time over a set period of calculation/reference. Thereby, the traditional weekly working time may be extended up to 50 hours if not exceeding 40 hours over a period of one year. Then the working time beyond the 40-hours limit is not considered overtime work so employers are not under the obligation to pay the wage supplement. Thus, over the year, employees may have their work time divided over a period, so, for instance, an employee may work for 50 hours one week, 40 hours the following week, and then 30 hours the week after and be entitled to the same salary. Employers still demand for more flexibility, especially in extending the calculation period up to two years and the effective maximum weekly working hours to 60.

A significant number of collective agreements shorten the traditional working week time below statutory 40 hours, mostly to 38 hours. However, statistics show that Austrian employees rank second in Europe in weekly hours worked, and most full-time employees regularly work more than 40 hours a week, making them busy, but only until the factual retirement age of 58.

c. From a gender perspective, the share of part-time work—which relates to external as well as to internal flexibility—differs considerably, as it stands at 7% and 42% for women and men, respectively. The percentage reports ongoing increases, though far from that of North European countries. The general provisions regulating overtime pay encourage employers to use part-time employment, as they have to pay the wage supplement only if exceeding the limit of 40 weekly hours (8 daily hours). Thus, if the contract empowers one to do so, many employers hire workers on a part-time basis, and demand for additional work without having to pay them extra money. Some years ago, the Parliament approved the payment of a wage supplement for part-timers as well, though only corresponding to 25% of their wage. In addition, the regulation is highly complex and allows the employer to find loopholes to avoid paying even this lower amount of money.

Accordingly, national legislation still favours the flexibility that part-time work may offer to the employer, promoting these contractual arrangements. In addition, it does not provide any limitation to the share of the workforce to be employed under part-time contracts. On the contrary, the statute promotes the so-called "small employment", through an exemption from employer social security contributions. At present, the statutory maximum wage for this particular working arrangement stands at 374 Euros a month

d. In the event of *job shortage*, the Civil Code provides that employees are entitled to remuneration, even though they are not performing their working tasks. The contract, however, may derogate from this rule to a certain extent. Such derogation seldom occurs with regard to work time wages, whereas the stipulation of performance-related pay is often held to imply a modification of the said rule.

Over the last crisis, employers had often to deal with the dilemma of guaranteeing their employees full remuneration—although they only needed workers on a part-time basis—or to resort to dismissal. In this sense, employment levels in bigger undertakings were maintained by a reduction of working time that was heavily subsidised by state-funded unemployment benefits, so that the number of dismissals resulting from the crisis was not significant. Moreover, these subsidies for part-time work were needed for a relatively short period of time; in most enterprises, these measures were only in use for a number of months.

e. In relation to *changes to contractual terms*, Austrian law requires the employee's consent that is it does not empower the employer to unilaterally change the terms of a contract. However, domestic labour law facilitates such amendments in a number of ways. Firstly, it allows that the contract empowers the employer to change specified terms unilaterally, with the courts that show reluctance to go through such clauses in depth. They only take into account the concrete exercise of the right of variation according to a vague standard of equity, without fully considering the empowerment to variation itself. Further, the law eases the process to obtain employees' consent for altering terms, insofar as they are not covered by a special regime of dismissal-protection discussed earlier. The employer then may combine the proposal of a variation of contractual terms with threat of a real dismissal. Employees who are covered by the general regime of dismissal protection cannot challenge the variations of the contract terms as such in court. They can either accept the changes—which bars them from challenging them in court—or reject such variations, face the dismissal, and then challenge the dismissal. In reviewing such, the court will weigh the variations proposed to the detriment effect of the dismissed worker, considering the extent to which the variations have been put forward to maintain the employment relationship. As a result, employees have no possibility to keep the job and have the variations in their employment conditions as such examined by the court.

3.4 Labour and Internal Market

Austria joined the EC in 1995. Until 2004, the inflow of foreign workers has been rather irrelevant, be they employees or self-employed workers. After the accession of the EU12, Austria did not apply the freedom of workers principle to citizens of the EU12 countries. Many of them moved to Austria to work all the same, under the label of self-employed or posted workers, with a significant number involved in bogus self-employment, especially in the construction sector. In addition, the number of German workers—particularly from its eastern provinces—rose constantly over the last years. The freedom of workers includes citizens of the EU-10 starting from May 2011, although it is difficult to evaluate the effect of this measure. Some presume that most of these workers already work in Austria, either as truly or bogus self-employed.

In Austria, a number of core rules of statutory labour law and collective agreements also apply to posted workers,[36] in an attempt to secure a level playing field regarding labour costs for subordinated work done in Austria. Austria requires posted workers to receive the full minimum wage set by collective bargaining, and not only the minimum wage set for the specific occupations. Further, Parliament has recently set forth that the state administration has to look after some additional employee's entitlements, especially the payment of minimum wage. Previously, it was left to the initiative of the employee to bring the case to court. However, the practical effect of these recent legal efforts remains doubtful, as the monitoring of bogus self-employment and the fulfilment of the entitlements are seldom effective.

---

[36] Cf Risak, M. 2010. "Austria," in *International Encyclopaedia of Labour law and Industrial Relations* (IELL), ed. Blanpain, R. (The Hague: Kluwer Law International), 112.

4. Labour Market Policy (LMP)

The unemployment rate in Austria is lower than in most other countries, though being supported by widespread early retirement. Labour Market Policy comprises passive measures in the form of cash benefits for the unemployed as well as active measures, such as training programmes and government subsidies. Austria spends nearly 2% of GNP for LMP. Passive measures are still given priority, particularly because they cost more: expenses for passive measures double those for active measures, and their of GNP rose quicker than that of active measures. As the German experience of Hartz IV shows, equally important is the planning of unemployment benefits (the reservation wage is already set), for the details heavily influence the attitude towards work.

Unemployment benefits have existed in Austria for a long time, and their general features have not changed considerably. Benefits for those who have fulfilled the waiting period, which is rather short, are paid in relation to their former income, not to a flat rate. The Department of Labour pays these income-related benefits to both short-term and long-term unemployed, in some cases until retirement age is reached. In this sense, the Austrian welfare system is rather generous, although demanding with regard to the willingness to accept a new job. An unemployed person may refuse a job that does not correspond to the previous kind of occupation (and thus is not deemed to be suitable) only during the first hundred days of the unemployed period. Thereafter, the benefit will be withdrawn at least temporarily if the unemployed refuses any job that can be performed allowing him/her to earn at least 80%—later decreasing to 70%—of their previous income. Moreover, the net replacement rate is set at 55% of the previous net income; small supplements are due if the recipient has to take care other of other persons. In 2011, the net maximum benefit amounted to 1,400 Euro for single workers and to 1,500 Euro for workers with a spouse and two children. The net replacement rate diminishes only slightly in cases of long-term unemployment. However, if the amount of the unemployment benefit is below the amount of the one provided by social welfare, the jobseeker is entitled to an additional benefit that brings his allowance into line with the one provided by social assistance.

In 2011, the system of social assistance was reviewed, and the monthly allowance delivered as social assistance (in form of cash benefits) increased from about 400 Euro to 558 Euros a month without housing benefit, and to 744 Euros if the latter was included. However, now the recipients have to pay some goods themselves that were formerly delivered as specific allowance, aside from cash benefit. Nevertheless, the reform further increased the benefits for the unemployed. Today, the minimum reservation wage amounts to 744 Euros, while the overall effects of the reform on the willingness to work remain to be seen.

National unemployment benefits provide an income that is related to the former income for a long time, but only if there are no other jobs available, and—especially before the reform of 2011—at a lower level. This state of affairs expresses the public opinion that people should earn their living themselves until the day they decide to retire. However, the majority of Austrians think that the golden age for retirement should be between 55 and 60, yet this perspective is far from being sustainable in the long run. With regard to the notion of flexicurity, Austria provides a medium level of protection against dismissal with a mixed system of benefits.

According to statistics, Austria spends less than the European average for Active Labour Market Policies (ALMPs), although this difference might be partly explained by the fact that the basic training of the workforce is delivered in different ways. Another reason might also be that in Austria the share of long-time unemployed was lower than in other countries. In this connection, to administer ALMPs the Government appointed a special agency (*Arbeitsmarktservice*). The main aim of active measures is to provide training to unemployed or to employees who are (only) partly redundant/on short-time work. Special measures are often implemented if large undertakings dismiss a significant number of employees and/or many unemployed come from the same industry. In this case the agency funds a training programme (*Arbeitsstiftung*) that organises the retraining and also pays additional benefits. The agency also subsidises employment, providing financial support to the undertaking, on the condition that the undertaking employs people who are not or not yet fully able to perform in the labour market—such as people with disabilities—or employs people who have particular difficulty entering the labour market—e.g. those over 50. In some cases, the agency pays assistance subsidies directly to the employee, but the legal basis for all these measures is rather unspecific, and much discretion is left to the agency. Such discretionary power allows the actors involved to manage the entitlement of these benefits at their will—especially considering that social partners heavily influence the agency—yet enabling a more flexible and proper handling of such benefits.

5. Conclusions

To sum up, it can be argued that Austrian labour law shows a peculiar and interesting mixture of rigidity and flexibility. The main framework—the macro-structure—is rigid, as collective agreements cover nearly all undertakings, also considering a vast bulk of statutory regulation. However, the microstructure allows for higher levels of flexibility. Protection against dismissal is usually weaker than in many other countries, and the implied terms in an employment contract oblige the employees to be quite flexible. Labour Market Policy fits well into this structure, as it secures a stable, albeit comparatively low social income in combination with a strong inducement to work. Perhaps, the combination itself of a rather strict macrostructure and a more flexible microstructure was the contribution the labour law system gave to the country's comparatively good economic performance. Presumably, the stable legal background characterising Austria was an important catalyst for economic performance, as short-time measures were only needed to tackle the crisis.

References

Rebhahn, R. 2006. "Die Sicht der deutschsprachigen Länder," in *Reformdruck auf das Arbeitsrecht in Europa—Wie reagieren nationale Rechtsordnungen?* eds. Ochel, W., S. Evju, I. Asscher-Vonk, D. Brodie, P. Hurka, R. Rebhahn, and V. Rieble, 3. ZAAR-Kongress 2006 (München: Stiftung für Arbeitsbeziehungen und Arbeitsrecht), 98-126.

—. 2009. "Arbeitnehmerähnliche—Rechtsvergleich und Perspektiven," *Recht der Arbeit* (RdA), 236-253.

—. 2009. "Wage Labour," in *The Transformation of Labour Law in Europe,* eds. Hepple, B., and B. Veneziani (Oxford: Hart Publishing).

Rhein, T. 2010. "Ist Europa auf dem Weg zum Turbo-Arbeitsmarkt?" *IAB-Kurzbericht*, No. 19.

Risak, M. 2010. "Austria," in *International Encyclopaedia of Labour law and Industrial Relations* (IELL), ed. Blanpain, R. (The Hague: Kluwer Law International).

Wahl, S., and M. Schulte. 2005. *Arbeitslosigkeit abbauen*. Munich: Olzog.

From Labour Market Crisis to Labour Market Reform: Lessons from and for a Divided European Union

Marc De Vos

1. Introduction

The economic turmoil triggered by the 2007 Subprime Crisis and the 2008-09 Great Recession keeps rocking the European Union boat. The global crisis has clearly revealed underlying European structural problems, particularly in fiscal policy (national public debt), in monetary policy (the Euro turbulence), and in labour market policy (unemployment). Indeed, one of the many challenges of what is rapidly becoming a crisis epoch is its differing labour market fallout among core European countries.[1] This is another illustration of how the European Union—notwithstanding such grand projects as the Lisbon Strategy and the hyped "Flexicurity"—has patently failed to effectively streamline labour market performance among its member states.

This varying national context obviously makes any coordinated European labour market strategy even more difficult than prior to the crisis. However, there can be little doubt that the European Union should take the current crisis as an opportunity to reconsider and improve its policies in both the economic and the social realm. This will not be an easy task, as the crisis has heavily damaged whatever feeble consensus on the need and the direction of labour market reforms, while persisting unemployment always tends to promote quick political fixes over fundamental reforms. Against this overall backdrop, this brief article sets its sights on the legal framework for EU labour market policy coordination, with particular attention to Active Labour Market Policy (ALMP).

---

[1] See, inter alia, Kiiver H., and R. Hijman. 2010. *Eurostat Statistics in Focus, 20/2010*. Brussels: European Commission.

2. From European Employment Strategy to "Flexicurity"

The European Union's labour market policies rest upon two pillars: "social policy" and "employment policy". The former refers to the traditional mechanism of EU coordination through legislation (directives in the field of labour regulation), while the latter consists of the open method of coordinating national labour market policies through European targets, without resorting to formal EU legislation.

The European drive—supported by the necessary Green Paper and White Paper—towards a more conscious European *employment* policy, irrespective of the EU's *social* policy, is well documented.[2] An Employment Title was inserted into the foundational treaty through the Amsterdam Treaty, the essence of which—currently set out in Art. No. 145 to 150 TFEU—is the development of a

> coordinated strategy for employment and particularly for promoting a skilled, trained and adaptable workforce and labour markets responsive to economic change (Art. No. 145): the European Employment Strategy (EES).

The coordination rests upon the broad framework of employment policy guidelines promulgated by the Union and designed for national implementation.

Under the aegis of the European Commission, the EES has become closely identified with the agenda of "Flexicurity". The European Commission, reflecting on a wide and recent body of research, defines Flexicurity as "an integrated strategy to enhance, at the same time, flexibility and security in the labour market".

> Flexicurity is about striking the right balance between flexible job arrangements and secure transitions between jobs so that more and better jobs can be created. *Flexibility* is about developing flexible work organisations where people can combine their work and private responsibilities, where they can keep their training up-to-date and potentially have flexible working hours. It is also about giving both employers and employees a more flexible environment for changing jobs. *Security* means 'employment security'—to provide people with the training they need to keep their skills up-to-date and to develop their talent

[2] See Ashiagbor, D. 2005. *The European Employment Strategy*. Oxford University Press, 127 et seq.

> as well as providing them with adequate unemployment benefits if they were to lose their job for a period of time.[3]

The "security" advocated by Flexicurity is of a dynamic type, seeking to obtain *general employment security in the labour market* by preparing, assisting and pushing individuals in and for the job transitions that follow from our flexible economy. Traditional labour law, on the other hand, has sought to realise security in a more static way by shielding the individual from transitions and thus protecting *specific job security at a particular employer.* Flexicurity, therefore, requires a shift from static "job security" and protection to dynamic "employment security" protection on the labour market. Whoever wants to make that switch within the confines of old school rigid labour market organisation embarks upon a broad reform platform that mobilises just about every actor of labour market organisation.[4]

What Flexicurity wants, therefore, is the partial dismantling of static labour law protection that counters flexibility, and its replacement with dynamic protection that embraces flexibility but offers a new kind of security in return. This is particularly difficult with regard to the vested interests in static labour market protection, namely the 'insiders' of the labour market with relatively stable employment positions and their unions. These vested interests know what they stand to lose but often remain to be convinced of the benefits. The flexibility part of Flexicurity is indeed certain, whereas the security part is uncertain. Moreover, to become effective in its quest for dynamic employment security, Flexicurity requires labour law to focus more on particular individuals and their labour market position. Here too lies an obstacle, to the extent that the traditional labour law of the static kind is often also collective and standardised in its approach, with unions as the agents for a supposedly uniform and unison labour force. Flexicurity thus interferes with the traditional role model for unions, further complicating its reception at the level of Member States with powerful unions.

---

[3] European Commission. 2007. *Towards Common Principles of Flexicurity: More and Better Jobs Through Flexibility and Security.* Brussels: European Commission.

[4] For an example, see De Vos M., and J. Konings. 2007. *Van baanzekerheid naar werkzekerheid op de Belgische arbeidsmarkt. Ideeënvooreen New Deal voorarbeid in België.* Antwerp: Intersentia, 120; - *D'une sécurité de l'emploi vers une sécurité du travail sur le marché du travail belge. Idées en faveur d'un New Deal sur le marché du travail belge.* Louvain-la-Neuve: Anthémis, 130.

All this was prior to the crisis. The crisis has undermined the European Flexicurity agenda even more. Two factors have further complicated the picture. *First*, labour market performance in the heat of the crisis has not particularly strengthened the superiority of the Flexicurity model. *Second*, it is harder to make Flexicurity policies a working reality when there are not enough jobs. We will briefly address these obstacles in turn.

3. Flexicurity Challenged by the Crisis

There is something stirring in the world of labour market punditry. The Great Recession is showing some unexpected results on the unemployment front. The irresistible job machine that used to be the US labour market continues to sputter. Job creation remains disappointing. A decidedly un-American unemployment rate of close to 10% keeps almost 15 million Americans unemployed. And that is not counting the millions more who have simply given up or are underemployed, or the equally numerous jobs that are officially and artificially "saved or created" by stimulus spending.

Across the pond, on the European continent traditionally lambasted for its outdated and stifling labour rigidities, the picture is surprisingly less bleak. For sure, European countries have had their fair share of the massive employment haemorrhaging and the frosty hiring slump that has been the crisis fallout throughout most of the developed world's labour markets. But in relation to their economic contraction, many European countries have registered less unemployment increase than the US. The list covers almost the entire Old Europe, including otherwise notorious labour market underperformers such as Italy, France, and Belgium.[5]

It used to be different. For decades, Europeans have been told that they need to become more American if they want more growth and more jobs. That conviction eventually morphed into the official European Union agenda for "Flexicurity", seeking to combine flexible labour markets with supportive policies for personal employability. Whatever its merits, *Flexicurity* was always more a hype among policy wonks than a reality on the European work floor. The recent change in labour market fortunes has now brought a number of observers to question the mantra altogether. European politicians did not go on a Keynesian spending spree and instead claim credit for their country's built-in protections. Union experts have joined the chorus, labelling Flexicurity a fair-weather friend and

[5] Gregg P., and J. Wadsworth. 2010. "Jobs in the Recession," London School of Economics. *CentrePiece* 15, No. 1.

reclaiming old-fashioned employment restrictions and protections as the guarantors of stability.[6]

This particular observer finds the transatlantic labour market comparison premature. There is simply no quick labour market fix for an economic recession, whatever your policy persuasion may be. Economic differences come a long way in explaining today's differences in labour market outcomes among countries. Some countries have been hit more by the Great Recession than others, some have had a major domestic real estate crisis to add to the global contraction, and some have been able to take better advantage of the rebounding economy in the developing world. Germany's ability as an export economy towards Asia helps its domestic employment. A real estate crisis weighs heavily on unemployment in Ireland and Spain alike, notwithstanding big differences in their respective labour market models. Beyond the economy there is demography. Aging and immigration affect different countries differently, with ramifications for their respective labour force and—consequently—unemployment figures. Persistent US unemployment for a large part is the symptom of structural problems in the US economy: the gradual reduction of excessive consumption, the continuing crisis in the housing sector, the shrinking of financial sector employment, the downsizing of domestic car giants, and the wide business uncertainty which has led US companies to horde cash while squeezing their workforces.

Nothing of the above relates to labour market policies per se, but all of it heavily impacts labour market outcomes. Moreover, the traditional assumption of inflexible European labour markets is really outdated. Virtually all of the European countries that typically have rigid and inflexible labour regulations at their core have also grown a wide penumbra of often extremely flexible a-typical work. Companies in Europe thus have layers of flexible temporary workers that can be employed, re-employed, and laid off as a matter of course. Such is the legacy of rigid labour markets whose beneficiaries have never accepted overall modernisation: a multitier market where insiders enjoy cushy stability for most of their careers, at the expense of incoming outsiders. Predictably, the brunt of any labour market contraction then falls on the outsiders, who either lose temporary work or enter the labour market with very limited job perspectives. Spain has seen its unemployment rate skyrocket to 20% because of the prevalence of temporary work that was quickly shed as the crisis set in. Stricter employment protection might

[6] Tangian, A. 2010. "Not for Bad Weather: Flexicurity Challenged by the Crisis," ETUI Policy Brief 3/2010.

have substantially reduced the unemployment effects of the crisis, even though it would have hindered employment creation in the first place.[7]

Therefore, the labour market lesson of the Great Recession so far lies not in the vagaries of unemployment statistics, but in the worsening of the divide between insiders and outsiders. For the responses of virtually all European governments to the current jobs crisis have primarily been aimed at protecting existing jobs even more. Across the continent, subsidy mechanisms and regulatory measures have sought to avoid redundancies through working time reduction, temporary unemployment systems, cash-for-clunkers programmes, and the like. As a result, the chasm between the haves and the have-nots on the labour market has only deepened further.[8]

By entrenching existing employment, European politicians and employers have not demonstrated the uselessness of flexible labour markets in times of crisis. They have instead undermined the potential of job transitions in a period of profound economic change. Europe's internal market rules did prevent the repeat of wholesale state support as a crisis policy. But its light version on the labour market has similar consequences. Time will tell whether Europe is—once again—only slowing inevitable transitions and therefore undermining future growth and productivity to the detriment of all, or whether its job shielding will be a jump board and allow companies to grow anew with lower redundancy and recruitment costs.

Whatever the outcome, the bottom line is a labour market preference for the incumbent at the expense of the newcomer. This goes beyond reduced job opportunities to the price tag as such. The niceties of increased employment protection and automatic stabilisers translate into deficits that will have to be paid by future workers. The same generational arithmetic obviously holds for deficit spending on expanded unemployment insurance and Keynesian job creation in the US. Labour market realities on both sides of the Atlantic thus share what is becoming an overall tendency of our crisis epoch: our generation's unwillingness or inability to pay for its collective mistakes.

The Great Recession does not demonstrate the failings of any particular labour market model, at least not yet. But the recuperation of the

---

[7] See Bentolila, S., P. Cahuc, J. J. Dolado, and T. Le Barbanchon. 2010. "Two-Tier Labor Markets in the Great Recession: France vs. Spain," Bonn: IZA Discussion Paper No. 5340.

[8] See Eichhorst W., M., Feil, and P. Marx. 2010. "Crisis, What Crisis? Patterns of Adaptation in European Labour Markets," Bonn: IZA Discussion Paper 5045; European Commission. 2010. "Labour Market and Wage Developments in 2009," European Economy, 5/2010.

crisis for political purposes is clearly spilling over into labour market territory. The renewed foundational EU-Treaty (the infamous Lisbon Treaty) already advocates a "social market economy" aimed at "full employment" (Art. No. 3 TEU). Europe 2020, the EU's new flagship programme, similarly seeks to steer economic development towards "smart, sustainable, and inclusive growth", including an industrial strategy for "green jobs". This overarching agenda has recently spawned a fully-fledged "industrial policy for the globalisation era".[9] Keynesian dreams of a more politically managed labour market are thus gaining political traction. If this tendency becomes a trend, it will be the Great Recession's real labour market legacy. The new EU social policy may thus influence the future course of the EU employment policy.

4. Active Labour Market Policy in Times of Crisis

In its official description, the Flexicurity agenda is seen to contain four essential components: Flexible and reliable contractual arrangements, comprehensive lifelong learning, modern social security systems, and effective active labour market policies (ALMP).[10] The latter are the focus of our attention as they are supposed to "help people cope with rapid change, reduce unemployment spells and ease transitions to new jobs." So called "active" labour market policy is a container notion that covers a wide and varied range of

> policies aimed at improving the access of actual or potential job seekers—whether unemployed, inactive, underemployed or in employment transition—to the labour market, to jobs and to job related skills.

These policies can be aimed at both the demand side and the supply side of the labour market and its labour relations. What binds the various policies together is that they do not constitute pure and passive income transfers such as unemployment benefits or early retirement benefits.

The boom and bust of economic cycles and the economic progress of perennial "creative destruction", further fuelled by globalised markets, technological change and international competition, generate tremendous and continuous change in the labour market. In this high velocity market,

[9] See European Commission. 2010. *An Integrated Industrial Policy for the Globalisation Era. Putting Competitiveness and Sustainability at Centre Stage*, COM(2010) 614. Brussels: European Commission.

[10] European Commission. 2007. *Towards Common Principles of Flexicurity: More and Better Jobs through Flexibility and Security*. Brussels: European Commission.

labour is constantly shifting and evolving, whether through internal reallocation, through voluntary mobility or through hiring and firing. ALMP facilitate the matching process in this shifting labour market, whether through job brokering in specific cases or through general employability policies. Left to their own devices, the economy and the labour market would suffer from information asymmetries between job seekers and job providers, from skills shortages or productivity gaps, and generally from an underdevelopment in human capital that is perhaps typical of free markets.[11] Resulting qualitative and quantitative mismatches cause frictional and eventually structural unemployment. ALMP and government intervention can help to correct these market imperfections, thereby smoothing labour transition for the benefit of workers, businesses, and the overall economy alike. This may occur through a wide variety of mechanisms, instruments and policies, but all of these will ultimately share the same finality and rationale.

In the context of job losses—the background to our reflection—ALMP can be regarded as the policy instrument that serves most directly to enhance the re-employment prospects of displaced workers. From the perspective of the worker, employment or re-employment may then be actively promoted by providing access to information on job opportunities, by supporting geographical mobility, by helping vocational retraining, by offering various counselling and outplacement services, or by providing financial support towards re-employment. The reintegration of displaced workers possessing obsolete skills, for example, can be facilitated if adequate retraining programmes can qualify these workers for new jobs. From the employer's perspective, assistance in recruitment and outreach, or reductions in wage or training cost may serve the same goal of efficient transition and re-employment.

All of this sounds great on paper but faces the inescapable contemporary difficulty of a major jobs crisis. Overall economic background and labour market reality indeed play a major role. Hence the varying impact of identical ALMPs across various country groups at any time. Moreover, ALMP cannot realise labour market transitions when there are no jobs to transit to. If ALMPs are designed to be the bridge between jobs, they risk being a bridge to nowhere without an appropriate general macroeconomic

---

[11] In a free capital market, investment decisions are less likely to go towards human capital than towards real capital investments that are less risky. Consequently, government intervention can make it possible to correct the imperfections of the capital market and rectify the divergence between the private cost and the social benefit of human capital investment: see Friedman, M. 1962. *Capitalism and Freedom*. Chicago: University of Chicago Press, 102-105.

and structural policy that creates and supports labour demand. The ongoing labour market crisis is no fertile context for quick transitions, no matter how well designed the ALMP may be. The Great Recession and its aftermath have exposed structural economic problems. The transition challenge is harder, bigger and will take more time. ALMPs are no miracle cure and their relative impotence may further erode its status as the desired end of labour market policy in general.

However, the difficulty of successful ALMP should not undermine the legitimacy of its key policy tenet: when transition is economically necessary, effective labour market policy will seek to accommodate and organise it, rather than to block or to ignore it. Unemployment levels and unemployment duration will indeed be higher than average because of an exceptional crisis. But we should not lose hope for new employment. ALMP should not be given up. Rather, it should be targeted so as to make sure that the unemployed stay employable notwithstanding their unemployment. It should be directed at those sectors of activity that do well and have shortages notwithstanding the crisis. It should accelerate labour mobility, not abandon it. In short: ALMP in times of crisis should focus policy attention on the outsiders finding new jobs or staying employable, away from the early focus on keeping insiders in their current jobs no matter what.

Empirical studies offer broad guidance for the selection of active policies in order to maximise their effectiveness:[12]

1) Rely as much as possible on in-depth counselling, job-finding incentives (*e.g.* re-employment bonuses) and job-search assistance programmes. But it is vital to ensure that such measures are combined with increased monitoring of the job search activity of the unemployed and enforcement of the work test.

2) Keep public training programmes small in scale and well targeted to the specific needs of both job seekers and local employers.

---

[12] What follows draws essentially on Betcherman, G., K. Olivas, and A. Dar. 2004. "Impacts of Active Labour Market Programs: New Evidence from Evaluations with Particular Attention to Developing and Transition Countries," Social Protection Discussion Paper Series 402. The World Bank; Calmfors, L. 1994. *Active Labour Market Policy and Unemployment—A Framework for the Analysis of Crucial Design Features*. OECD Economic Studies No. 22:7-47; Card, D., J. Kluve, and A. Weber. 2009. "Active Labour Market Policy Evaluations: A Meta-analysis," CESIfo Working Paper No. 2570; Estevão, M. 2000. "Do Active Labour Market Policies Increase Employment?" IMF Working paper 03/234; Martin, L. 2000. *What Works Among Active Labour Market Policies: Evidence from OECD Countries' Experience*. OECD Economic Studies No. 30, 2000/1.

3) Early interventions, reaching back to pre-school, can pay dividends for disadvantaged youths, but they must be sustained and combined with appropriate schooling and effective attitude policies.

4) As the duration of unemployment spells lengthens, various forms of employment subsidies may serve to maintain workers' attachment to the labour force. However, employment subsidies should be of short duration, targeted and closely monitored. Subsidised public sector job programmes are generally suboptimal.

5) Use subsidised business start-ups for the minority among the unemployed who have entrepreneurial skills and the motivation to survive in a competitive environment.

This is a time to strengthen and target ALMP so that we get the best out of the existing opportunities and avoid the spectre of a lost generation all together. ALMPs are not *the* solution to our crisis, but they can be part of the solution. We should simply realise that ALMP in times of crisis requires careful redirection and concentration, with the creativity of using available budgets where possible.

5. Can a Divided European Union Turn Crisis into Opportunity?

The ongoing crisis has exposed major shortcomings in EU policy. The Stability Pact which was supposed to ensure fiscal discipline throughout the euro-zone has brought indiscipline and instability instead, further deepening the fiscal woes and economic outlooks in several indebted Member States. The Lisbon Strategy which was supposed to turn the EU into a paragon of competitiveness has failed miserably, further exacerbating the inevitable toll of a major financial crisis on the real economy.[13] Both these structural failures contribute heavily to the labour market impact of the crisis in Europe. This is not the time to question the validity of these failed strategies. Rather, we need to question the reasons of their failure.

At the time of writing, the EU embarked upon an exercise of improved economic and fiscal management for the euro-zone. A so-called "competitiveness pact" is in the making. We also need to improve the mechanism for policy reform on the labour market. The European Union has spent too many years preaching without being able to practice. Whether it will be able to practice what it preaches in the future, will depend on whether it can use the crisis as an opportunity for more

[13] A noted exception is obviously Germany, which is now reaping the benefits of its "Agenda 2010" reforms under the Schröder administration.

European coordination. Separately, Member States and their national interest groups can but offer a patchwork of partial and incomplete labour market reforms. Together, the European Union may just be able to coordinate and steer effective and comprehensive reforms that will serve all its Member States as they move from job crisis to ageing crisis in the blink of an eye.

However, this will require conviction and determination, both of which have been conspicuously lacking during the recent years of crisis improvisation and economic nationalism. The Lisbon Treaty itself is not particularly helpful: the social aim of "full employment" (Art. No. 3 TEU) is indeed difficult to square with the employment aim of an "adaptable workforce and labour markets responsive to economic change" (Art. No. 145). The former requires activist state intervention in the old Keynesian mould. The latter leaves the economy alone while investing in personal employability. We can have flexible labour markets that offer high employability, but not by making the Keynesian artificial demand policies of our crisis epoch permanent. This is the crucial choice before us as the acuteness of the crisis has given way to an uncomfortably slow recovery.

The foundational EU treaty no longer speaks in one voice on the orientation of labour market organisation. The European Employment Strategy stands for a different labour market model than the EU's overall Keynesian dream—inserted through the recent Lisbon Treaty—of "full employment" in a "social market economy". The European Union therefore faces a historic challenge without a clear constitutional orientation. Power politics are likely to determine the outcome. Under the pressure of Germany, economic competitiveness in some form or another will become the norm. For the first time in its existence, the European Union will actively impose fundamental changes upon the welfare states of its members. The process will be difficult and contentious, the outcome uncertain. If the EU succeeds in turning crisis into opportunity, we may well be on the threshold of a new age for labour law reforms. If it does not, the European impetus for labour market modernisation will peter out. The European Union has always been a paper tiger for labour market reform. It can either start roaring now, or shut up forever.

References

Ashiagbor, D. 2005. *The European Employment Strategy*. Oxford: University Press.

Bentolila, S., P. Cahuc, J. J. Dolado, and T. Le Barbanchon. 2010. "Two-Tier Labor Markets in the Great Recession: France vs. Spain," Bonn: IZA Discussion Paper No. 5340.

Betcherman, G., K. Olivas, and A. Dar. 2004. "Impacts of Active Labour Market Programs: New Evidence from Evaluations with Particular Attention to Developing and Transition Countries," Social Protection Discussion Paper Series 402. The World Bank.

Calmfors, L. 1994. *Active Labour Market Policy and Unemployment—A Framework for the Analysis of Crucial Design Features*. OECD Economic Studies No. 22:7-47.

Card, D., J. Kluve, and A. Weber. 2009. "Active Labour Market Policy Evaluations: A Meta-analysis," CESIfo Working Paper No. 2570.

De Vos M., and J. Konings. 2007. *D'une sécurité de l'emploi vers une sécurité du travail sur le marché du travail belge. Idées en faveur d'un New Deal sur le marché du travail belge*. Louvain-la-Neuve: Anthémis.

De Vos M., and J. Konings. 2007. *Van baanzekerheid naar werkzekerheid op de Belgische arbeidsmarkt. Ideeënvooreen New Deal voorarbeid in België*. Antwerp: Intersentia.

Eichhorst W., M., Feil, and P. Marx. 2010. "Crisis, What Crisis? Patterns of Adaptation in European Labour Markets," Bonn: IZA Discussion Paper 5045.

Estevão, M. 2000. "Do Active Labour Market Policies Increase Employment?" IMF Working paper 03/234.

European Commission. 2007. *Towards Common Principles of Flexicurity: More and Better Jobs Through Flexibility and Security*. Brussels: European Commission.

—. 2010. "Labour Market and Wage Developments in 2009," European Economy, 5/2010.

—. 2010. *An Integrated Industrial Policy for the Globalisation Era. Putting Competitiveness and Sustainability at Centre Stage*, COM(2010) 614. Brussels: European Commission.

Friedman, M. 1962. *Capitalism and Freedom*. Chicago: University of Chicago Press.

Gregg P., and J. Wadsworth. 2010. "Jobs in the Recession," London School of Economics. *CentrePiece* 15, No. 1.

Kiiver H., and R. Hijman. 2010. *Eurostat Statistics in Focus, 20/2010.* Brussels: European Commission.

Martin, L. 2000. *What Works Among Active Labour Market Policies: Evidence from OECD Countries' Experience.* OECD Economic Studies No. 30, 2000/1.

Tangian, A. 2010. "Not for Bad Weather: Flexicurity Challenged by the Crisis," ETUI Policy Brief 3/2010.

LEGAL NOTIONS OF STABILITY AND FLEXIBILITY IN LABOUR AND SOCIAL SECURITY AT THE TURN OF THE CENTURY: A FRAGILE JURIDICAL EFFECT. THE CASE OF TELEWORK

ANDRZEJ MARIAN ŚWIĄTKOWSKI AND MARCIN WUJCZYK

1. Introduction

The experience gained by the European labour law and social security doctrine of the last 20 years resulted in a need for research to simultaneously increase the flexibility of protective labour laws as well as ensuring social stability for workers, which in turn has led to the generally applicable provisions of labour laws (labour codes) in European countries of atypical forms of employment. The most "progressive" of these forms is telework. It allows management of working time of the concerned employees and it requires telework employees in individual employment relationships to communicate via electronic means. We believe that the idea of *flex-security*,[1] which is based on a relationship between flexibility in labour relations and social stability of people who have lost their jobs, despite becoming popular at the turn of the new century, has not been fully made use of in Europe. In this paper we show the reasons why telework could not be realised in Europe and analyse telecommuting as a basic form of flexible employment, recognising it as a "weak" surrogate of an attractive idea which connects two extreme labour law trends: flexibility and social security.

[1] Cf. Krynska, E., A. Ambroziak, and B. Grzybowski. 2008. *Flexicurity—Between Flexibility and Security on the Labour Market*. Warsaw: C.H. Beck.

2. Flexibility of Employment

Labour law has two basic functions: protective and organisational, with the former that is more important than the latter. Labour law is the branch of law which became distinct from civil law in order to ensure legal protection for the employee, who was seen as the "weaker" party to a contract of employment. Formally, however, parties to the individual employment contract have their relationship based on mutual reciprocity. For performance of work, the employee is entitled to remuneration for the work rendered.[2] However, there are fundamental differences between the parties in a contract of employment. Employees are primarily interested in reducing the daily and weekly working times and increasing their hourly rates and monthly wages. They want to work less and earn more. Employers, of course, have different interests. They are primarily concerned to increase productivity and reducing labour costs.

In the early days of labour law, in order to appease the interests of the employer, labour law served by extend the duration of working hours and maximum salary reductions. The progressive humanisation of industrial relations meant that employers began to give greater importance to involving employees in managing workplace and the use of more sophisticated measures to encourage economic activity, *inter alia* by increasing interest in the effects of economic activity and thereby stimulating motivation to achieve work efficiency. This is done through joining remuneration for the work rendered to the effects of individual and team work results. Such changes in management techniques could only take place under existing labour laws. However, such laws are in almost all countries on guard to protect the rights of workers. A more flexible approach to protective labour legislation, concerning the process of loosening the legal procedures and requirements established by the state legislature, can only truly be taken into account when state authorities permit employers through universally applicable labour legislation to extend daily, weekly, monthly and annual working hours standards, lengthen the periods of paying remuneration, permit the termination of contracts of employment with notice without providing reasons, and to allow for the temporary closure of the workplace without the obligation to pay workers who are willing to render services. Such cases, however, have been rare and have not been reported in labour laws of any of the European countries. Classic U.S. law, which is no longer valid, allowed for

[2] Swiatkowski, A. M. 2010. *Polish Labour Law.* Warsaw: LexisNexis, 24 et seq.

the structure of the employment relationship to be based on the freedom of each party, and was termed the "employment at will". It enabled employers to dismiss employees with or without notice after paying the employee a certain amount of monetary damages for the loss of employment, without providing any reasons for the termination decision. This U.S. legal concept, which is now extinct, was always foreign to European labour laws. The above freedom of employers deciding to terminate contracts of employment with notice is—to a greater or lesser extent—referred to by regulations specifying the reasons and procedures for group and individual redundancies for economic reasons. After payment of remuneration for the period of notice or compensation for shortening the notice period as well as severance pay, thus compensating the loss of employment for reasons beyond the worker's control, employers are entitled to terminate contracts with workers seen as least useful. The suitability criteria are stipulated in the work regulations concerning collective redundancies, which are agreed upon by employers and employees' representatives.

The corset of protective labour laws is relaxed by the state issuing such legislation during times of economic crises.[3] Therefore the overriding interest, which requires the economic action to be taken, justifies shortening of working hours, limiting part-time employee wages, managing economic downtime, justifying the withholding of salary of workers who are not performing work, compensating for work of a certain type carried out during extended working hours of some days, weeks and months by days off in a 1:1 ratio (despite the fact that employees rendering overtime hours should be rewarded with additional overtime rates and not with an equivalent remuneration rate).

The flexibility of labour law enacted by the state legislature is only dependent on the level of protection of workers' rights assured by minimum labour laws issued by state authorities. The concept of "flexible" labour laws is[4] used to determine a certain process, accentuating the amendment of certain occurrences. It is thus used to determine the legislative policy of the state authorities seeking to adapt the standards of this branch of law to the changing economic situation.[5] In times of

---

[3] Swiatkowski, A. M. 2010. *Anti-Crisis Act with Commentary. The Monitor's labour Law.* Warsaw: CH Beck, passim.

[4] Swiatkowski, A. M. 2009. "Poland," in *Fixed-Term Employment Contracts. A Comparative Study,* eds. Blanpain, R., and C. Grant (Bruges: Vanden Broel Publishers), 377 et seq.

[5] See Blanpain, R., ed. 1990. "Flexibility and Wages, a Comparative Treatment," Bulletin of Comparative Labour Relations, Catholic University of Leuven, No.

economic crisis, the flexibility of labour law amounts to a partial liberalisation of standards for the protection of workers' rights to the following: maintaining existing wages and employment in accordance to the working hours as stipulated in the employment regulations, and keep the current level of sustainability of the employment relationship.

A special method for more flexible labour law is to regulate the freedom of the parties to establish individual employment relationships for fixed periods of time. Such agreements, in particular fixed-term contracts, expire by law after a period of time for which they are entered into, or as a result of the objective pursued by the parties to such agreements. The function of labour law, which protects the stability of the employment relationship, is significantly reduced, since such agreements are automatically solved at the time of the reached effect as intended by the parties. In accordance with the concept of labour law of protecting employment stability, it only applies to cases of terminating of employment contracts through legal actions carried out by the employer. In the event of an expiration of a work contract entered into on a fixed-term agreement, employees who have had their work contract terminated in such a manner shall have no claim. Even in cases where the parties to a fixed-term contract allow for the possibility of the termination of the agreement before the period of the contract ceases, in some labour law systems a statement issued by the employer to terminate the contract is not conceded by the legislature to be a causal action.[6]

European Union Member States control the parties' freedom to enter into period specified employment contracts. They allow, however, for an unlimited amount of such contracts to be entered into for several years preceding retirement.[7] In Poland, the principle of freedom of parties to

---

18/1990; Blanpain, R., A. Galin, and O. Cani, eds. 1991. "Flexible Work Patterns and their Impact on Industrial Relations," Bulletin of Comparative Labour Relations, No. 22/1991; Fahlbeck, R. 1998. *Flexibilisation of Working Life: Potentials and Pitfalls for Labour Law. An International Analysis*. Lund: Lund University Faculty of Law Press, 21 et seq.

[6] See Art. No. 33 of the Polish Labour Code, which allows the parties to an employment contract for a non-fixed period (of at least 6 months) to introduce into the contract a clause allowing either party to terminate the contract with a two week period notice. An employer is exempted from giving an employee whose contract is being terminated, a reason for the termination. Fixed-term contracts with such a clause included are typical contracts of employment, which each party to the employment relationship is bound by before the expiry of the period for which this arrangement has been made as long as both parties want to remain in the employment relationship.

[7] As in the case of Germany.

choose the type of employment contract prevails. In the case where the parties intend to conclude a contract for a specified period, this intention must be underpinned by circumstances providing that the selection of such an agreement was not only consistent with the will of both sides, but that there was an objective justification for it. Lack of evidence in such a scenario, however, has no legal effect in the case of two consecutive contracts for a specified period entered into in less than a month. However, with a third such agreement a contract shall be deemed under the law to be concluded for an indefinite period.[8] *De lege lata*, limiting the parties' freedom to choose the type of employment contract can be regarded as one of the main obstacles to a more flexible labour law system. This claim does not relate to any non-typical employment contracts. In particular, it does not apply to employment contracts under which an employee is employed in the form of telework. Such an agreement is not regarded as "non-typical", if the employee is employed in a permanent, full-time position.[9]

3. Social Stability

Stability in labour relations is seen to be the opposite of flexibility.[10] Stability is synonymous with the inability to alter unilaterally by the employer the terms of employment laid down by the parties in the employment contract. The legislature generally forces the parties to individual employment relationships to agree to the following terms of the contract: the type of work, workplace, working time and salary. The unilateral amendment to these conditions is possible only in exceptional circumstances, accepted by the legislature. Amending the conditions of

---

[8] Art. No. 25 [1], par. 1 L.C.

[9] The reference point for employment under an unusual contract of employment is a "typical" contract, under which the concept is understood to be full-time work for an indefinite period. If we are going to use the two basic categories of employment contract (typical and atypical) as a benchmark, then telework must also be considered, depending on the nature of the contract (for an indefinite period or for a fixed period) as either a typical or a atypical contract. It follows that the electronic means of communication with an employer is not to be regarded as a feature distinguishing between a "typical" and a "atypical" employment contract.

[10] Rymsza, M., ed. 2005. *A Flexible Labour Market and Social Security. Flexicurity in Polish* [in Polish].Warsaw: Instytut Spraw Publicznych; Grotkowska, G., M. W. Socha, and U. Sztanderska. 2005. *Flexibility of Employment and Social Security on the Labour Market. The Polish Experience* [in Polish]. Budapest: ILO.

employment specified in the contract is limited in time. Art. No. 42, par. 4 of the Labour Code allows employers to amend the type of work, while retaining the right to the existing remuneration for a period not exceeding three months in a calendar year. The Anti-Crisis Act of 1 July 2009, which is valid until 31 December 2011,[11] authorises employers to extend the accounting standard period of time up to 12 months. The Act suspended the validity of the provision Art. No. 25,[1] par. 1 of the Labour Code, which considers third consecutive non-fixed employment contracts (entered into within a month from one another) to be automatically declared as permanent, indefinite period employment contracts. Because of the need to protect the interests of workers and employers against the negative effects of the recent economic crisis, the Anti-Crisis Act temporarily made Polish labour law more flexible. At the same time, it resulted in a reduced sense of stability for employees in individual employment relations.

Experts in the field of social policy, who during the last twenty years tried to reconcile two opposing tendencies—flexibility and social stability—seemed to believe that flexibility should be the domain of employment law, whilst social security law should ensure that individuals who have temporarily lost their jobs receive social insurance coverage in the form of short or long-term social security benefits to reimburse lost wages. Monetary benefits paid to insured individuals compensate the loss of earnings as the result of one or more occurrence as defined in the social security law.[12] However, few social security benefits (pension, permanent disability pension, survivor's pension) permanently compensate for loss of earnings due to the reduction or loss of employment based on age, reduced efficiency of the body, or loss of the breadwinner. Given the serious disparities in relation to a loss of permanent salary, long-term social benefits do not guarantee full social stability. The differences between the amount of such benefits and lost income during the professional activity of the insured, should be made up by benefits from a supplementary, voluntary social insurance or by savings of the persons concerned.

From the above, it is obvious that the condition *sine qua non* in social relations regulated by labour law and social security law, in order to achieve a balance between the two opposing tendencies (flexibility of employment and social stability) there must be adequate regulations of the relationship between freedom of decision-making by employers in matters

[11] Act of 01.07.2009 on mitigating the effects of economic crisis for workers and employers, OJ No. 125, item. 1035.

[12] Swiatkowski, A. M. 2007. "Flex-Security (Interactions Between Employment and Flexible Policies of Stable Social Security Measures)," in *The Right to Social Security*, ed. Van Langendonck, J., (Antwerpen-Oxford: Intersentia), 271 et seq.

concerning the termination of contracts of employment with notice, unrestricted power to enter into non-specified period employment contracts and reducing the duration of working time without assuring workers' compensation. These scenarios must be covered by the general social security scheme for all persons of working age and to guarantee them the right to receive social security benefits to reimburse a substantial portion of lost wages or to develop their professional skills, or gain additional qualifications to enable re-entry into the labour market.

According to the studies previously conducted in the field of employment flexibility and social stability, the above goals have yet not been reached. The obstacles standing in the way are a lack of general social security systems and/or limited funds, which are financed by social security benefits. In Poland and some other European countries, an additional hurdle is the defectively drafted concept of the relationship between rights to social benefits in guaranteeing stability, i.e. the remuneration for work and adequate social security benefits. For these reasons, in considering the use of atypical forms of employment on the parts of employers, telework must be seen mainly as a substitute, which to some extent can reconcile the contrast between the two tendencies, the flexibility of employment and social stability.

4. Flexibility of Employment and Social Stability

Under labour and social security law in the previous political and economic system in Poland, the relationship between work and welfare benefits was one-sided.[13] All employees entering into an employment relationship were automatically subject to a universal, compulsory social security system. They attained social benefits rights in all contingencies, with the exception of job loss. The official social policy, whereby the most important achievement of the socialist system was the lack of unemployment, guaranteed all persons who were able to work (and were at a socially active age), the right to take up employment. People who were physically unable to engage in a contract of employment could apply for short-term support from social assistance. These people, therefore, operated outside the system of state social insurance. In order to minimise the number of people forced to apply for support to national institutions of social welfare, authorities introduced the obligation to take up employment.

---

[13] Pennings, F., and A. M. Swiatkowski. 1993. "The Right to Work and the Changing Relationship with Social Security," *Yearbook of Polish Labour Law and Social Policy,* No. 4:55 et seq.

It would apply to certain categories of people, that is men aged 18 to 45 years. The phenomenon of social employment, which was then quite a common occurrence, was an argument for the authorities and institutions to promote the hypothesis of complete eradication of unemployment and the achievement of full employment.[14] Achieving a fictitious state of full employment was made possible by ignoring the objective need to maintain the labour market phenomenon of rational employment. The socialist labour and social security system was based on legal, administrative and moral obligations. In this regime, citizens had the legal and/or moral obligation to attain employment, whereas the state administration had the political duty to guarantee such employment. Hence there were no unemployed. Almost all citizens of working age were subject to a system of universal, compulsory social security. In the event of temporary or permanent inability to perform work they benefited from social benefits. The labour law system exhibited the need to protect the employee as a "weaker" part of the employment relationship. Limitation of the powers of state employers in matters relating to the termination of contracts of employment meant that the work was not in short supply. Employment was also not overly valued due to low wages. The social benefits which temporarily replaced lost earnings were even lower. For more than four decades of the second half of the twentieth century the socialist countries of Central and Eastern Europe achieved relative social stability. The socialist state did not give citizens the chance to enrich themselves, but also did not allow them to die as a result of sustaining minimum living standards.

The situation in this part of Europe changed dramatically after the political developments that took place more than twenty years ago. The introduction of a market economy, and the abolition of the domination of state employers meant that there was an introduction of rational employment policies.[15] Laws were enacted on collective redundancies and on benefits for the unemployed. People of working age, who are able to work but are not seeking employment are not covered by compulsory social insurance. They are not under the obligation to take up employment.

---

[14]Swiatkowski, A. M. 1992. "Policy of Full and/or Productive Employment," *Yearbook of Polish Labour Law and Social Policy,* No. 3:209 et seq.

[15] Swiatkowski, A. M. 1994. *Towards a More Flexible Labour Legislation, Studies of the Labour Law and Social Policy* [in Polish]. Krakow: Musica Iagiellonica, 65 et seq.; Swiatkowski, A. M. 2009. "New Design for Promotion of Labour Flexibility and Social Protection in Eastern and Central Europe," in *Search for Flexibility, Fairness and Prosperity: Alternative Employment Policies in the Twenty-First Century,* 12th IIRA Congress, Tokyo, No. 4:173 et seq.

Such people have been excluded from the state universal compulsory social security system. The equivalent to the right to employment, a concept which began to be understood as the freedom to make decisions to enter employment relationships, has now become the freedom to work. Workers who have lost their jobs are covered by unemployment insurance. They have acquired the right to social benefits and unemployment benefits. A necessary condition to make use of such benefits is to be registered as unemployed, agreeing to participate in employment programs without rejecting job offers provided by the employment office without good reason. The right to unemployment benefit has also been made conditional on the obligation to take up alternative employment.[16] A new concept was initiated concerning the relationship between labour laws and the right to social security regulations. Employers have obtained the right to freely make either group or individual decisions about the termination of contracts of employment, firstly, due to company reasons, and, secondly, for reasons not related to employees. Employers have been obliged to provide severance pay to compensate laid off workers who have lost their jobs. The authorities administering the affairs of employment in local labour markets, however, have undertaken the registration of the unemployed and are responsible for organising training courses to enable the unemployed to re-obtain the opportunity to work in another profession, and are responsible for the payment of unemployment benefits. Linking active employment policy measures under the rules of the promotion of employment with the increased freedom of employers in matters relating to termination of contracts of employment decisions for reasons not related to employees, has been seen as a social policy of the state.[17] The state authorities, on the one hand, allow businesses benefiting from the freedom of establishment in the new management system based on rules of economic freedom to make collective redundancies and, on the other hand, offer the possibility to re-enter the job market for those persons who have lost their jobs and provide social benefits partially compensating for lost wages. From a theoretical point of view, this vision could be regarded as the greatest discovery in socio-economic policy. It would allow for employers to take—on a limited basis for collective redundancies—discretionary power on matters relating to the termination of contracts of employment for reasons not related to employees, whilst redundant

---

[16] Swiatkowski, A. M. 1995/1996. "Legal Nature and Jurisdictional Principles of the Polish Unemployment Law of December 14, 1994," *East-West Review of Social Policy* 1, No. 2:149 et seq., eds. Pennings, F., and A. M. Swiatkowski.

[17] Swiatkowski, A. M. 2002. "Social Policy and Employment Law Against Unemployment," *The State and Law*, No. 8:15 et seq.

workers would be able to obtain alternative employment. The concept of flexible management on the part of the employers in matters of collective redundancy and social stability (*flexicurity*) has had limited coverage. It related solely to redundancies for reasons not related to employees. In the other categories of cases concerning the freedom of choice in the type of employment contract, the concept of working hour arrangements and termination of employment for reasons related to workers (which sought to reconcile the opposing tendencies in social policy, flexibility of employment and social stability) was not or could not be applied. Therefore, it was necessary to find an alternative solution. In individual labour relations, the alternative to the failed, and impossible to carry out in practice concept of *flexicurity* has been replaced by non-typical forms of employment, such as teleworking and agency work. In the following and concluding part of this paper, we present telework as a substitute for flexible forms of employment, which guarantees social stability for workers. We warn, however, that the legal argument about teleworking is treated only as an illustration of the thesis of the impossibility to merge the two opposing tendencies, the flexibility of employment and social stability.

5. Telework

Telework[18] as a form of rendering work appeared for the first time in the '60s in the UK.[19] The concept was developed by J. M. Nilles, who saw it as a way of fighting against the fuel crisis (he emphasised that with this form of employment workers did not have to commute to work).[20] The literature suggests three elements, which characterise teleworking:

1) information and communications technology;
2) work performed in your chosen location other than the standard

[18] Cf. Mitrus, L. 2001. "Telework as a New Form of Employment," *Transformations of Private Law* [in Polish], No. 3:14; Sobczyk, A. 2006. *Telework in the Polish Law* [in Polish]. Warsaw: Wolters Kluwer Polska; Swiatkowski, A. M. 2006. "Telework—The Specificity of Employing at a Distance," MPP No. 7:347; Pisarczyk, L. 2003. *Various Forms of Employment* [in Polish]. Warsaw: Dom Wydawniczy ABC, 77-79.
[19] Cf. Kordey, N. 1996. *Telearbeit erfolgreich realisieren—das umfassende, aktuelle und Handbuch für Entscheidungsträger Projektverantwortliche*. Braunschweig/Wiesbaden: Vieweg Verlag, 20.
[20] Chobot, A. 1997. *New Forms of Employment. Development and Revision*. Warsaw: Wydawnictwa Prawnicze PWN, 155.

workplace;
3) the regularity and repetition of such activities.[21]

Telework certainly does not completely fulfil the idea of *flexicurity*. It should be noted, however, that it is characterised by features that allow to conclude that it is a substitute for the concept. On the one hand, teleworking encourages flexibility in the labour market, on the other hand, it provides the safeguards typical of standard employment. In this context, therefore, we can talk about social sustainability of teleworking.[22]

The elements of telework qualify it as being responsible for increasing labour market flexibility and facilitating the functioning of the employer in the economy, indicating a reduction in business operating costs by reducing the rental cost of office space. In addition, telework eases the elimination of the effects of headquarter changes on the change of staff.

Telework can also increase efficiency because of the personal factor, helping to increment employees' productivity—as limiting absenteeism and workplace delays. It also provides the opportunity to hire workers in areas where labour costs are lower, with those who are highly-skilled who do not to move to the headquarters where the employer operates.[23] From the perspective of the employee, telework allows to work flexible hours using them in a more efficient way.[24] Undoubtedly, the idea of increasing labour market flexibility is realised through higher levels of business efficiency. As pointed out by E. Bak, this is made possible by way of a more flexible distribution of teams, increased access to customers or business operations.[25] Finally, telework promotes a reduction in unemployment (through the creation of new jobs in regions affected by high unemployment rates), and reduced state spending on benefits for unemployed people (as a result of activation of those who are in permanent unemployment).

As previously pointed out by J. M. Nilles when assessing the prospects of development of telework,

---

[21] Bak, E. 2006. *Flexible Forms of Employment* [in Polish]. Warsaw: C.H. Beck, 55.

[22] Patulski, A. 2008. "Non-typical Forms of Employment. Flexibility or Stability? Part 2," *Employment Law Monitor* [in Polish], No. 3:130.

[23] Bak, E. 2006. *Flexible Forms of Employment* [in Polish]. Warsaw: PC.H.Beck, 63.

[24] Sobczyk, A. 2006. *Telework in the Polish Law* [in Polish]. Warsaw: Wolters Kluwer Polska, 21.

[25] Bak, E. 2006. *Flexible Forms of Employment* [in Polish]. Warsaw: C. H. Beck, 63.

> greater flexibility of new work arrangements —along with the decreasing prices for telecommunications services—stimulates the development of new organisational forms (...). The ultimate result will be the rapid expansion of a global, multilingual, and multicultural market with greater opportunities.[26]

On the other hand, telework done in the form of a contract of employment offers traditional social security and employment stability. An employee may only be dismissed in situations stipulated by law. An employee has guaranteed rights to remuneration and social security benefits in the event of inability to work. A person employed under an employment relationship may not receive a wage that is below the minimum wage provided by law. Additionally, if such an employee has his/her employment contract terminated, then he or she is given the same assistance that is provided for the unemployed.

It is worth noting that, although much greater protection is available for an employee entering into a contract for an indefinite period,[27] fixed-term employment contracts are nonetheless closer to the idea of flexicurity. In principle, this type of employment contract, provides for an employer a less complicated form of dismissal. Finally, it is worth stressing that social assistance is more often directed and available to people who were previously in employment relationships than to those workers who provided their services on the basis of civil contracts or were self-employed. For example, the Polish Promotion of Employment and Labour Market Institutions Act[28] provides that training can only be given to persons who have been given notice of termination of employment or service for workplace related reasons (Art. No. 43 of the PELMI Act).

However, it must be argued at the outset that, contrary to the unemployed, a worker is not entitled, while performing the training, to receive monetary assistance. Also, only employers and employees may make use of these labour market instruments. Those who render services under civil contracts are deprived of such possibilities. As an example, Art. No. 53 of the PELMI Act provides for the financing of travel costs, either

[26] Nilles, J. M. Telework. 2003. *Strategies in Managing a Virtual Team.* Warsaw: Wydawnictwa Naukowo-Techniczne, 337.

[27] The employer is obliged to give a reason for the termination of employment, and if the employee benefits from the protection of the union, the employer is obliged to conduct consultations with the trade union organisation. Moreover, the contract for an indefinite period is traditionally regarded as a more stable form of employment than the fixed-term contract, which is binding only for a limited time.

[28] The Act of 20 April 2004 on the Promotion of Employment and Labour Market Institutions (i.e. O.J. of Laws of 2008, No. 69, 415).

to the employer who has advertised a vacant position, or to a place of employment, to undertaking an apprenticeship, or to an adult vocational training course or vocational guidance, also offering assistance in the active search for work in connection with the referral given by the district employment office.[29]

In the Polish system of labour law, until recently there were no provisions explicitly governing the implementation of telework, that was performed under general freedom in forming an employment relationship.[30] The amending Act of 24 August 2007 of the Polish Labour Code introduced Chapter IIb "Employment of workers in the form of telework" regulating this form of employment. One of the main reasons for this form of labour legislation in the Labour Code was to make it a more flexible working practice, a known feature of flexicurity. As stated in the explanatory memorandum to the draft of the Labour Code amendment

> This form of flexible employment will enable the employee to primarily reconcile work and family life. Flexible ways of organising work are a very important determinant of economic activity for people who have family responsibilities, are disabled, combine work with study, work in more than one place or live in remote regions away from the workplace. (...) The draft law will also affect employers employing workers. Telework as incorporated by the employers can have an impact on reducing the costs of employing workers, above all reducing the costs associated with maintenance of workplaces and the absenteeism of employees. Telework will also encourage a more flexible organisational structure, as well as increase efficiency and productivity of employees. The use of telework is influential in improving the quality and productivity of workers who make better use of time.[31]

These trends can be clearly seen by analysing each new regulation of the Labour Code relating to telework.[32]

In the Labour Code, telework has been defined as the exercise of work on a regular basis outside the workplace, using electronic means of

[29] Cf. more at Hofmanska, E. 2009. "The Prevention of Unregistered Work and its Eradication," *Employment Law Monitor* [in Polish], No. 10.
[30] Cf. Gersdorf, M. 2008. "Employing Teleworkers," *Work and Social Security* [in Polish], No. 5:9.
[31] Cf. The draft law amending the Labour Code can be found on the website of the Ministry of Labour and Social Policy. (project aimed at the Council of Ministers).
[32] Cf. Latos-Milkowska, M. 2003. "Telework as a Means of Promoting Employment," in *Labour Law and Unemployment*, ed. Florek L., (Warsaw: Dom Wydawniczy ABC).

communication within the meaning of the provision of services by electronic means (Art. No. 67^{5} L. C.). Ensuring flexibility to carry out work is to be able to provide it in an alternative place than the workplace. The Labour Code does not name the place in which telework is intended to be carried out. Undoubtedly, this may be the house of the employee. However, it can also be telecentres or special centres set up by the employer.[33] It is noted that the regulations do not require that all responsibilities of an employee must be carried out in the form of telework. Depending on current needs, the employee and the employer may determine that only some of the activities entrusted to the employee will be performed in the form of telework.

Telework is introduced either by agreement to be concluded between the employer and the local trade union (or with the trade union organisations, if the workplace has more than one union) or, in the absence of company trade union organisations, in the form of regulations set by the employer after consultation with representatives of employees appointed by the procedure adopted by a particular employer (Art. No. 67^{6} L. C.). The work agreement or regulation concerning telework should be considered as the source of employment law. They should set conditions for the use of telework. The legislation does not specify what is meant by the terms which are to determine the rules or agreement on the introduction of telework. As an example of the matters governed by the above legislation, one can indicate the job position that is to be performed through telework, the rights and obligations of teleworkers, and the technical rules for rendering teleworking. Undoubtedly, this method of shaping the rules for providing telework allows to adapt the conditions of this form of work to the needs of both employers and employees. The same purpose is served when establishing between the parties to an employment relationship the extent of the equipment that will be used to perform telework, how such work will be monitored and how the teleworker will confirm his or her presence at the workplace (Art. No. 67^{11}, par. 2 of the L.C.). It is also possible to shift the cost of employee insurance, installation and operation costs of the equipment used by the teleworker in rendering the work (the legislation, however, presumes that these obligations are carried out by the employer, Art. No. $67,^{11}$ par. 1 L.C.) in the form of compensation for an employee who uses their own equipment, thus an employer reimburses this cost.

---

[33] Mitrus L. 2011. “Glossary [in Polish],” in *Labour Code 2011*, eds. Baran, K.W., E. Chmielak-Lubinska, D. Dorre-Nowak, L. Mitrus, T. M. Nycz, A. Sobczyk, and B. Wagner, (Gdańsk: ODDK).

The provisions introduced into the Labour Code give particular attention to the monitoring rules of the teleworker rendering services at home. Such control cannot affect the privacy of the teleworker and his or her family or impede the use of domestic space in a manner consistent with their use. The guarantee of the principle of respect for private life is limiting the ability to control the work carried out in the house of an employee, for the purpose of inventory, maintenance, servicing or repairing of the equipment entrusted, and its installation or the health and safety at work, solely to the situation whereby consent has been granted by the worker or by means of an agreement between the parties at a distance.

However, as mentioned earlier, teleworking can only be regarded as substituting the idea of *flexicurity*, not implementing it. Telework, even that performed on the basis of a fixed-term employment agreement, does not give employers the opportunity of adapting the level of employment to the often rapidly changing needs. Entering into telework may occur either at the conclusion of a contract or during employment. In the latter case, it is necessary for the employee to agree to the changes. Therefore, the employer cannot implement teleworking by way of notice, or to delegate this form of employment under Art. No. 42 par. 4 L.C (as clearly stated in Art. No. 67^{7} par. 4 of the L.C.). In general, this state of affairs restricts the freedom of employers using this form of work. In addition, the teleworker should be treated according to the same standards of employment as a regular worker, including entering into a work agreement and termination of employment, conditions of employment, promotion and access to training. Although it can be said that telework eases the functioning of employment for the employees and the employers, we cannot view it as a way to provide considerable flexibility in the labour market, following its entry into the labour law system.

Finally, it must be indicated that, in terms of social protection, in the event of employment termination, the rights of teleworkers are no different than those of employees performing work in a standard working environment. Accordingly, it cannot be concluded that the introduction of telework into the Polish Labour Code increased the social protection of employees.

6. Concluding Remarks

An overview of the relationship between protective labour law regulations in Poland and other former socialist countries of Central and Eastern Europe—which for more than twenty years comply with the rules of market economy—shows a characteristic trend. In the first years of democratisation of political, economic and social development, attempts were made to reconcile the two opposing trends in socio-economic policy, the flexibility of employment and social stability. It was widely believed that with the return to democracy, citizens' social security would be under increased threat.[34] This can be interpreted as an effort to explain to the public who subjected to system changes (from a central management to the social market economy) of having to bear the necessary costs of transition. Strengthening democratic governance of the political system promotes the pursuit of new non-typical forms of employment. After twenty years of systemic transformation citizens are demanding a minimum guarantee of social stability. As a consequence, state authorities replace the previous social programmes initiated in order to satisfy the divergent interests of social partners by adopting rules to promote the non-typical forms of employment. Therefore, at the end of the first decade of the 21st century, the original ambitious attempts to reconcile the two opposing tendencies in social and economic policy, the flexibility of employment and social stability, were abandoned.

References

Bak, E. 2006. *Flexible Forms of Employment* [in Polish]. Warsaw: C.H. Beck.

Blanpain, R., A. Galin, and O. Cani, eds. 1991. "Flexible Work Patterns and their Impact on Industrial Relations," Bulletin of Comparative Labour Relations, No. 22/1991.

Blanpain, R., ed. 1990. "Flexibility and Wages, a Comparative Treatment," Bulletin of Comparative Labour Relations, Catholic University of Leuven, No. 18/1990.

Chobot, A. 1997. *New Forms of Employment. Development and Revision.* Warsaw: Publishing HouseWydawnictwa Prawnicze PWN.

Fahlbeck, R. 1998. *Flexibilisation of Working Life: Potentials and Pitfalls for Labour Law. An International Analysis.* Lund: Lund University Faculty of Law Press.

Gersdorf, M. 2008. "Employing Teleworkers," *Work and Social Security* [in Polish], No. 5:9.

Grotkowska, G., M. W. Socha, and U. Sztanderska. 2005. *Flexibility of Employment and Social Security on the Labour Market. The Polish Experience* [in Polish]. Budapest: ILO.

---

[34] Swiatkowski, A. M. 1993. "Democracy and [In] Security," *The International Journal of Comparative Labour Law and Industrial Relations*, No. 9:164 et seq.

Hofmanska, E. 2009. "The Prevention of Unregistered Work and its Eradication," *Employment Law Monitor* [in Polish], No. 10.

Kordey, N. 1996. *Telearbeit erfolgreich realisieren—das umfassende, aktuelle und Handbuch für Entscheidungsträger Projektverantwortliche.* Braunschweig/Wiesbaden: Vieweg Verlag.

Krynska, E., A. Ambroziak, and B. A., Grzybowski. 2008. *Flexicurity—Between Flexibility and Security on the Labour Market*. Warsaw: C.H. Beck.

Latos-Milkowska, M. 2003. "Telework as a Means of Promoting Employment," in *Labour Law and Unemployment*, ed. Florek L., (Warsaw: Dom Wydawniczy ABC).

Mitrus, L. 2001. "Telework as a New Form of Employment," *Transformations of Private Law* [in Polish], No. 3:14.

—. 2011. "Glossary [in Polish]," in *Labour Code 2011*, eds. Baran, K.W., E. Chmielak-Lubinska, D. Dorre-Nowak, L. Mitrus, T. M. Nycz, A. Sobczyk, and B. Wagner, (Gdańsk: ODDK).

Nilles, J. M. Telework. 2003. *Strategies in Managing a Virtual Team.* Warsaw: Wydawnictwa Naukowo-Techniczne.

Patulski, A. 2008. "Non-typical Forms of Employment. Flexibility or Stability? Part 2," *Employment Law Monitor* [in Polish], No. 3:130.

Pennings, F., and A. M. Swiatkowski. 1993. "The Right to Work and the Changing Relationship with Social Security," *Yearbook of Polish Labour Law and Social Policy,* No. 4:55.

Pisarczyk, L. 2003. *Various Forms of Employment* [in Polish]. Warsaw: Dom Wydawniczy ABC.

Rymsza, M., ed. 2005. *A Flexible Labour Market and Social Security. Flexicurity in Polish* [in Polish]. Warsaw: Instytut Spraw Publicznych.

Sobczyk, A. 2006. *Telework in the Polish Law* [in Polish]. Warsaw: Wolters Kluwer Polska.

Swiatkowski, A. M. 1992. "Policy of Full and/or Productive Employment," *Yearbook of Polish Labour Law and Social Policy,* No. 3:209.

—. 1993. "Democracy and [In] Security," *The International Journal of Comparative Labour Law and Industrial Relations*, No. 9:164.

—. 1994. *Towards a More Flexible Labour Legislation, Studies of the Labour Law and Social Policy* [in Polish]. Krakow: Musica Iagiellonica,

—. 1995/1996. "Legal Nature and Jurisdictional Principles of the Polish Unemployment Law of December 14, 1994," *East-West Review of Social Policy* 1, No. 2, eds. Pennings, F., and A. M. Swiatkowski.

—. 2002. "Social Policy and Employment Law Against Unemployment,"

The State and Law, No. 8:15.
—. 2006. "Telework—The Specificity of Employing at a Distance," MPP No. 7.
—. 2007. "Flex-Security (Interactions Between Employment and Flexible Policies of Stable Social Security Measures)," in *The Right to Social Security*, ed. Van Langendonck, J., (Antwerpen-Oxford: Intersentia).
—. 2009. "New Design for Promotion of Labour Flexibility and Social Protection in Eastern and Central Europe," in *Search for Flexibility, Fairness and Prosperity: Alternative Employment Policies in the Twenty-First Century,* 12th IIRA Congress, Tokyo, No. 4:173.
—. 2009. "Poland," in *Fixed-Term Employment Contracts. A Comparative Study,* eds. Blanpain, R., and C. Grant, (Bruges: Vanden Broel Publishers).
—. 2010. *Polish Labour Law.* Warsaw: LexisNexis.
—. 2010. *Anti-Crisis Act with Commentary. The Monitor's labour Law.* Warsaw: CH Beck.

WHO IS ALLOWED TO REPRESENT EMPLOYEES? THE CAPACITY OF TRADE UNIONS TO BARGAIN COLLECTIVELY IN GERMAN LAW

BERND WAAS

1. Introduction

Art. No. 9(3) of the Basic Law (*Grundgesetz—GG*) sets forth the fundamental right of freedom of association. According to this provision, the "right to form associations to safeguard and improve working and economic conditions shall be guaranteed to every individual and to every occupation". In principle, freedom of association as laid down in Art. No. 9(3) GG encompasses the right to bargain collectively as well as the right to take industrial action, with the latter being regarded as an essential tool in ensuring that collective bargaining takes place in practice.[1] According to section 2(1) of the Act on Collective Bargaining Agreements (*Tarifvertragsgesetz—TVG*) "trade unions, employers' associations and single employers enjoy the right to conclude collective bargaining agreements". This paper is only concerned with the collective bargaining capacity of trade unions. It will be argued that there are important requirements to be met in order to qualify as a "trade union" within the meaning of section 2(1) TVG.

Under German law, only some entities are entitled to conclude collective bargaining agreements and two conditions must be satisfied. The rationale for the legislator to limit access to collective bargaining lies in the vast regulatory powers granted to the bargaining parties. Not only are they entitled to enter into agreements which are directly binding for

[1] Federal Labour Court of 12 March 1985—1 AZR 636/82, in Arbeitsrechtliche Praxis, Art. No. 9 GG Arbeitskampf No. 84 according to which collective bargaining would be mere "collective begging" (*kollektives Betteln*) without the right to take industrial action.

those employers and employees who—due to their membership in an employers' association or trade union—are subjected to a collective bargaining agreement,[2] but collective bargaining agreements also play a strong role with regard to employment relationships whose parties are not bound to such agreements. The reason for the latter consists in the fact that employment contracts between parties, which are not subject to collective bargaining agreements, are commonly modelled along the lines of the relevant collective bargaining agreements by way of referring, at least to some extent, to such collective agreements.[3] Against this background it becomes plausible to view the collective bargaining capacity as conditional on compliance with a number of pre-conditions of an objective nature, the meeting of which ensures that the freedom to conclude collective bargaining agreements is transferred into "safe hands". There is a downside, however, in that the system of collective bargaining is at peril of being monopolised. If the power of concluding collective bargaining agreements is exclusive to certain trade unions, this, in turn, excludes other trade unions from the process and thus deprives them of the opportunity to commend themselves to potential members by negotiating specific collective bargaining regulations.

This paper will try to shed some light on the requirements of collective bargaining capacity of trade unions. Two sets of requirements must be examined in this regard: firstly, the requirements of an "association" within the meaning of Art. No. 9(3) GG and, secondly, the specific conditions which must be derived from section 2(1) TVG.

---

[2] See section 3(1) TVG: "Tarifgebunden sind die Mitglieder der Tarifvertragsparteien und der Arbeitgeber, der selbst Partei des Tarifvertrages ist". According to section 4(1) sentence 1 TVG the provisions of collective bargaining agreements are immediately binding and coercive with regard to these persons: "Die Rechtsnormen des Tarifvertrages, die den Inhalt, den Abschluß oder die Beendigung von Arbeitsverhältnissen ordnen, gelten unmittelbar und zwingend zwischen den beiderseits Tarifgebundenen, die unter den Geltungsbereich des Tarifvertrages fallen". It must be stressed that in the German system employers are also bound to a collective bargaining agreement if they have concluded such agreement themselves. In other words, individual employers also enjoy the legal capacity to bargain collectively

[3] The so-called *Inbezugnahme* of the collective bargaining agreement causes, as far as it goes, the provisions of the agreement to become implied terms of the individual employment contract according to which – in contrast to what applies with regard to the so-called normative effect (section 4(1) TVG) – the parties to the contract may later dispose of.

2. "Associations" within the Meaning of Art. No. 9(3) GG

Only "associations" within the meaning of Art. No. 9(3) GG may qualify as trade unions enjoying collective bargaining capacity. What are these requirements?

2.1 Organisational Requirements

According to the prevailing view, freedom of association (*Koalitionsfreiheit*) as guaranteed by Art. No. 9(3) GG is nothing more than a special manifestation of the general freedom of organisation (*Vereinigungsfreiheit*), as protected by Art. No. 9(1) GG. As a consequence, a confraternity of employees must, first of all, qualify as an association under Art. No. 9(1) GG.[4] A corresponding legal definition is provided for by section 2(1) of the Law of Organisations (*Vereinsgesetz – VereinsG*). It may not be evident why a definition of a constitutional term can be derived by a provision of mere statutory law. It is, however, generally accepted that in creating section 2 (1) VereinsG, the legislator has given the constitutional term of "organisation" concretisation in a constitutionally permissible manner.[5]

According to section 2(1) VereinsG, the existence of a legally recognised organisation, therefore also applying to an association within the meaning of Art. No. 9(3) GG, is conditional on three requirements: first, the organisation must be entered into deliberately and be governed by the rules of civil law; secondly, the organisation must be intended to be of an enduring nature in the sense that there must be at least some levels of stability;[6] thirdly, the organisation must have a corporate nature with the ability, in particular, of forming a joint will.

The requirement of deliberateness follows directly from the fact that an organisation in the sense of Art. No. 9(1) GG is formed by way of individuals exercising their individual fundamental freedom of forming such an organisation. As a result, public law organisations with obligatory membership do not qualify as "associations" within the meaning of Art.

---

[4] Dieterich, T. 2011. *Erfurter Kommentar zum Arbeitsrecht*. München: Beck Juristischer Verlag, Art. No. 9 GG note 22; Waas, B. 2011. *Beck'scher Online-Kommentar Arbeitsrecht*. Beck-online, par. 2 TVG note 2.

[5] Löwisch, M. and V. Rieble. 2009. *Münchener Handbuch zum Arbeitsrecht*. München: Beck Juristischer Verlag, par. 155 note 57.

[6] Ibid.

No. 9(3) GG.[7] The idea that associations should be undisturbed from state influence is expressed in the condition that organisations need to be governed by civil law. Such independence would not be guaranteed in the case of public law associations, because they depend on recognition by public authorities and, besides, are subject to state control up to a certain extent.

In addition, the organisation must be intended to be of an enduring nature.[8] This requirement must be understood against the background of the associations' far reaching entitlement to industrial action in order to pursue their aims. Since industrial action *per definitionem* inflicts damage on the opposite side (and possibly as well on third parties), there is a need to ensure access to certain liability assets for the damaged party. This access would not be secured if entirely unstable mergers qualified as "coalitions".[9]

Finally, both the existence of a corporative nature and the ability of forming an overall will are required.[10] Corporative nature is to be understood in the sense that the organisation is independent from the joining or leaving of individual members and furthermore employs an integrated company structure, i.e. a structure which allows for bodies capable of representing the members. This requirement, too, arises from the coalition's need to prove a certain degree of stability.[11]

2.2 Specific Purpose of Trade Unions

2.2.1 Trade Union Freedom and Independence

The aim of the "associations" within the meaning of Art. No. 9(3) GG must be the attempt "to safeguard and improve working and economic

---

[7] Federal Constitutional Court of 10 March1992, in Arbeitsrechtliche Praxis, Art. No. 38. Einigungsvertrag No. 1.

[8] Federal Constitutional Court of 26 June 1991, in Arbeitsrechtliche Praxis Art. No. 9 GG Arbeitskampf No. 117.

[9] Waas, B. 2011. *Beck'scher Online-Kommentar Arbeitsrecht.* Beck-online, par. 2 TVG note 5.

[10] Waas, B. 2011. *Beck'scher Online-Kommentar Arbeitsrecht.* Beck-online, par. 2 TVG note 2 et seq.

[11] Waas, B. 2011. *Beck'scher Online-Kommentar Arbeitsrecht.* Beck-online, par. 2 TVG note 9.

conditions". This requires a certain freedom and independence with regard to the relevant "social counterpart".[12]

"Freedom" in that sense means that an association consisting of both employees and employers—in German terms often referred to as a so-called *Harmonieverband*[13]—would not qualify as an "association" within the meaning of Art. No. 9(3) GG. "Independence" in that sense means that a trade union must, for instance, not rely on financial contributions of employers. The rationale of the requirement of trade union freedom and independence lies in the assessment that only independent trade unions can be true representatives of employees' interests. In the past, so-called "yellow trade unions" (*gelbe Gewerkschaften*) existed that were mere puppets of the employers. Today, normally, employers are far from being able to exert such influence. As far as employees' co-determination on board or at plant level and the collaboration of trade unions and employers within the corresponding legal frameworks is concerned, it is generally acknowledged that neither the former nor the latter causes trade unions to depend on employers.[14] In general it can be said that the requirement must be applied reluctantly. In any event, a certain amount of cooperation between employers and trade unions is part and parcel of "social partnership".

Trade unions being dependant on employers may be rare given the fact that most unions in Germany are relatively strong and powerful both in terms of membership and financially. However, the more recent past has seen new trade unions emerging, some of which are ostensibly in danger of employers' interference. According to a decision of the State Labour Court Cologne,[15] one of those "young" trade unions, the *Gewerkschaft der Neuen Brief- und Zustelldienste (GNBZ)*, lacked collective bargaining capacity. The court based its judgment on the fact that—in accordance to its findings—some of the persons worked for both the trade union and the employers. In addition, the union seemed to be dependent on "organisational assistance" offered by the employers. Seemingly, the court may have noticed that employers in this specific case had a particular interest in the existence of a union willing to conclude a collective bargaining agreement, as on the basis of the so-called principle of

[12] Federal Constitutional Court of 18 November1954, in Arbeitsrechtliche Praxis, Art. No. 9 GG No. 1.

[13] Waas, B. 2011. *Beck'scher Online-Kommentar Arbeitsrecht.* Beck-online, par. 2 TVG note 10.

[14] See, for instance, Federal Constitutional Court of 10 December 1985, in Arbeitsrechtliche Praxis, par. 40 BetrVG 1972 No. 20a.

[15] Landesarbeitsgericht Köln of 20 May 2009—9 TaBV 105/08.

speciality (*Spezialitätsgrundsatz*),[16] such an agreement could "put aside" an already existing collective agreement that was declared generally binding by the state and contained less attractive conditions from the perspective of employers[17].

In legal literature, many scholars argued that collective bargaining capacity calls for a trade union to exceed the borders of a single undertaking or enterprise (*Überbetrieblichkeit*). Some others maintained that *Überbetrieblichkeit* as such is legally irrelevant but that a lack of it may indicate a lack of independence.[18] In a recent judgment regarding a small syndicalist trade union operating in Berlin and comprising not more than approximately 100 members, the State Labour Court Berlin Brandenburg held that the trade unions' focus on an individual undertaking prevented the forming of a strong will exceeding the boundaries of a single undertaking and, as a consequence, did not have sufficient "organisational stability" leading at the end of the day to a missing capacity to bargain collectively[19].

In addition to independence from employers, trade unions must be independent from third parties—such as churches, political parties and, in particular,[20] the state. The rationale is, again, that trade unions should represent the interests of employees and employees only. Independence in this sense only requires that trade unions be clearly separated from third party interests. It does not require strict neutrality. Adherence to a certain belief, for instance, is irrelevant[21]. In fact, there is a relatively strong movement of Christian trade unions (*Christliche Gewerkschaften*) in Germany. The collective bargaining capacity of some of the corresponding

---

[16] See in Löwisch, M. and V. Rieble. 2009. *Münchener Handbuch zum Arbeitsrecht*. München: Beck Juristischer Verlag, par. 185.

[17] See Hohenstatt, K-S, and N. Schramm. 2008. "Tarifliche Mindestlöhne: Ihre Wirkungsweise und ihre Vermeidung am Beispiel des Tarifvertrags zum Post-Mindestlohn," *Neue Zeitschrift für Arbeitsrecht*, 433-437.

[18] See Dieterich, T. 2011. *Erfurter Kommentar zum Arbeitsrecht*. München: Beck Juristischer Verlag, Art. No. 9 GG note 25.

[19] State Labour Court Berlin-Brandenburg of 16 February 2010—19 SaGa 2480/09: "Die organisationspolitische Konzentration der Beklagten auf den jeweiligen Betrieb und die jeweilige Betriebsgruppe mag als syndikalistisches Prinzip gewollt sein, verhindert jedoch die stabile Organisation eines überbetrieblich erforderlichen tarifpolitischen Willens. Mithin fehlt es an einer ausreichenden Organisation hinsichtlich der Tarifpolitik ....".

[20] Federal Constitutional Court of 01 March 1979, in Arbeitsrechtliche Praxis par. 1 MitbestG No. 1.

[21] Löwisch, M. and V. Rieble. 2009. *Münchener Handbuch zum Arbeitsrecht*. München: Beck Juristischer Verlag, par. 155 note 64.

unions is in doubt. The doubts, however, do not originate from their religious orientation, but are due to other features to be dealt with later.

In practice, the requirement of third party independence does not play a major role because the majority of the powerful trade unions, almost all of which belong to the German Federation of Trade Unions (*Deutscher Gewerkschaftsbund*), represents the interests of employees in a given branch regardless of, for instance, certain religious beliefs. In German terms: these trade unions are *Einheitsgewerkschaften* ("unitary trade unions"), not *Richtungsgewerkschaften* ("tendency trade unions").

3. Additional Requirements of Collective Bargaining Capacity

A confraternity of employees must qualify as an association within the meaning of Art. No. 9(3) GG. However, in order to enjoy the capacity to bargain collectively further conditions must be met.

3.1 Willingness to Conclude Collective Agreements

At a jurisdictional level, the collective bargaining capacity depends on a willingness to conclude collective agreements (*Tarifwilligkeit*). This means that the statutes of an association claiming collective bargaining capacity need to demonstrate the will to enter into such agreements. Section 2(3) TVG explicitly demands the willingness to conclude collective bargaining agreements in the case of so-called "*Spitzenorganisationen*" (umbrella organisations) which in the German system also enjoy the capacity to bargain collectively (though that capacity is almost irrelevant in practical terms).[22] Equally necessary is the willingness to conclude collective bargaining agreements for all other associations. The rationale behind the requirement of collective bargaining willingness, again, is to be found in considerations concerning democratic legitimisation. The members of an association must be able to foresee at

[22] However, in Federal Labour Court of 14 December 2010, BeckRS 2011, 68969 the court denied an umbrella organisation of Christian trade unions (*Tarifgemeinschaft Christlicher Gewerkschaften für Zeitarbeit und Personalserviceagenturen*) the capacity to conclude collective bargaining agreements in the area of temporary agency work.

the moment of joining, whether or not they will be subject to the association's quasi-legislative power.[23]

Further, what is still subject to some doubts is whether collective bargaining capacity requires a trade union to be prepared to take up industrial action. In a decision dating back to 1964, The Federal Constitutional Court held that associations enjoy freedom with regard to their choice of means, and that, consequently, they are not under a "duty to be prepared to fight".[24] Nevertheless, many argue that the capacity to conclude collective bargaining agreements must be attached to a general preparedness to engage in industrial action. The content of a collective bargaining agreement, the argument goes, is, by the very nature of it, not purely limited to the parties' ability to negotiate but just as much depends on their potential to exert pressure on the opposite side, at least as a means of last resort. Consequently, across the legal literature the call for the criterion of preparedness to enter into industrial action is presented.[25]

3.2 Acknowledgement of Collective Bargaining and Industrial Action Systems

According to the Federal Constitutional Court, an association claiming collective bargaining capacity must acknowledge the existing collective bargaining and industrial action system.[26] The rationale of this requirement is that the right to participate in the collective bargaining process can only be granted on the condition that the "rules of the game" are being recognised.

3.3 Adherence to Democratic Principles

In addition, trade unions must subscribe to at least the basic democratic principles. It would be unacceptable if associations were granted permission to exercise quasi-legislative power over their members, without being sufficiently democratically legitimised. In this sense, a democratic legitimisation calls for members being able to influence the

---

[23] Federal Labour Court of 10 November 1993, in Arbeitsrechtliche Praxis, par. 3 TVG Verbandszugehörigkeit No. 13.

[24] Federal Constitutional Court of 06 May 1964, in Arbeitsrechtliche Praxis, par. 2 TVG No. 15.

[25] Löwisch, M. and V. Rieble. 2009. *Münchener Handbuch zum Arbeitsrecht*. München: Beck Juristischer Verlag, par. 164 note 23 with further references.

[26] Federal Constitutional Court of 20 October 1981, in Arbeitsrechtliche Praxis, par. 2 TVG No. 31.

process of intra-association opinion-building by way of participating in elections which are held in accordance with democratic principles. The requirement of a sufficient form of democratic organisation has another, quasi-horizontal dimension. This follows from the necessity of members being in principle entitled to equal voting rights. It should be noted, however, that the courts apply the requirement of democratic organisation reluctantly to ensure that they do not interfere with the autonomy of trade unions and employers' associations as laid down in Art. No. 9(3) GG.[27] If, according to the by-laws of a trade union, all members are treated as equals and if, in particular, all members can equally influence decision-making, the courts do not usually entertain doubts with regard to collective bargaining capacity on the ground of a possible lack of a democratic organisation.[28]

3.4 Social Power and Effectiveness

It is generally accepted that trade unions must have a capacity to perform and to enforce their objectives. This is commonly referred to as the trade union's social power (*Mächtigkeit*) or effectiveness (*Leistungsfähigkeit*).[29] This means that trade unions must be capable of exerting pressure on the opposite side in order to encourage it to conclude a collective bargaining agreement. If no such power were needed, the courts would have to ensure that collective agreements are fair. Such judicial control, however, could not easily be reconciled with the idea of employers and trade unions regulating their affairs themselves.[30] Or, in the words of the Federal Labour Court: "The right to bargain collectively is constitutionally due to only those coalitions that are in a position to make sensible use of the area left open by the state by entering into collective agreements. This demands from a trade union the ability to exert at least so much pressure on the other side that the counterpart sees fit to set to embark on negotiations for a collective agreement".[31]

---

[27] Waas, B. 2011. *Beck'scher Online-Kommentar Arbeitsrecht.* Beck-online, par. 2 TVG note 17.

[28] Federal Labour Court of 28 March 2006, in Arbeitsrechtliche Praxis, par. 2 TVG Tariffähigkeit No. 4.

[29] See, for instance, Federal Labour Court of 10 September 1985 and 25 November 1986, in Arbeitsrechtliche Praxis, par. 2 TVG No. 34 and 36.

[30] Löwisch, M. and V. Rieble. 2009. *Münchener Handbuch zum Arbeitsrecht.* München: Beck Juristischer Verlag, par. 164 note 11.

[31] Federal Labour Court of 05.10.2010—1 ABR 88/09.

Whether a certain union is regarded to possess such social power can only be determined on a case-by-case basis. Possible factors can be the number of members, the existence of a satisfactory permanent structure of organisation, and sufficient financial funds.[32] Another important factor is whether or not in the past an association has succeeded in regularly enticing the other side to enter into collective bargaining agreements. Problems arise, however, if the relevant collective agreement is nothing more than a so-called "follow-up agreement" (*Anschlusstarifvertrag*), which merely repeats the content of an existing collective bargaining agreement, concluded by another association. It could be argued that in such case, the corresponding trade union lacks the effort of developing an independent position over the course of the collective bargaining process. It could also be maintained that the conclusion of a mere "follow-up agreement" may indicate an intention on the part of the employer to deliberately generate a collective bargaining partner according to the likings of the opposite side.

The Federal Labour Court some time ago seemed to be prepared to fully acknowledge a "follow-up agreement" as indicating collective bargaining capacity without feeling the need of further looking into the circumstances surrounding the conclusion of such an agreement. In the past, in cases where a collective agreement was concluded by way of obligation (*Gefälligkeitstarifvertrag*), through a mere sham (*Scheintarifvertrag*) or "dictated" by the employer, the court rejected the idea of "collective bargaining history" indicating collective bargaining capacity. Nevertheless, according to the Federal Labour Court the latter is an exception to the rule, which means that specific circumstances must exist indicating that no "real" collective agreements were concluded between the parties.[33] More recently, the Federal Labour Court may have changed its view with regard to "follow up-agreements". In a judgment delivered in 2010 the court held that in any event, collective agreements may prove the existence of collective bargaining capacity (only) if they were "originally negotiated" and formed "independent" collective agreements. It seems that mere "follow up-agreements" do not qualify as such agreements.[34]

What if there is no collective bargaining history? In that case the Federal Labour Court determines collective bargaining capacity on the

[32] Löwisch, M. and V. Rieble. 2009. *Münchener Handbuch zum Arbeitsrecht*. München: Beck Juristischer Verlag, par. 164 note 14 with further references.
[33] Federal Labour Court of 28 March 2006, in Arbeitsrechtliche Praxis, par. 2 TVG Tariffähigkeit No. 4.
[34] Federal Labour Court of 05 October 2010—1 ABR 88/09.

basis of a prognosis decision. To successfully arrive at such prognosis, facts must be shown that make it likely that the "social counterpart" will not be able to ignore the trade union in the future. In this connection, the courts examine the "organisational strength" of the trade union as well as its ability to exert pressure on the other side.[35] If, however, a "young" trade union is involved in the conclusion of collective agreements in the context of its coming into existence, the mere number of collective agreements being concluded is not an indicator of its collective bargaining capacity without further information provided by the trade union on both members and organisational resources.[36]

According to the Federal Labour Court, in order to assess social power and effectiveness, the membership base of a trade union is of paramount importance.[37] However, the organisational strength of a trade union must be evaluated by taking into account the area of competence which, in the case of trade unions representing certain professions only, may be fairly limited. Even if the number of members is small, there may be sufficient social power and effectiveness if these members are specialists in key positions, who in the event of industrial action cannot (easily) be replaced by the employer. According to the Federal Labour Court, it is equally dependant on the area of competence chosen by a trade union whether its organisational structure is sufficient to fulfil the tasks of a trade union. As a consequence, a relatively small, centralised apparatus may be sufficient in this sense if a trade union only represents members of a certain occupation instead of employees in a certain branch.[38] The upshot of this reasoning is that one cannot (easily) deny the collective bargaining capacity of (often small) "specialist trade unions"—like the German train drivers' union (*Gewerkschaft Deutscher Lokomotivführer—GDL*). On the contrary: the requirements that apply to such unions are (rightly)[39] less rigid than the requirements applying to (large) industry unions.

As a matter of fact, trade unions representing members of a certain occupation (*Berufsverbandsprinzip*) instead of employees working in a certain industry (*Industrieverbandsprinzip*) have been clearly on the rise in

---

[35] Federal Labour Court of 28.03.2006, in Arbeitsrechtliche Praxis par. 2 TVG Tariffähigkeit No. 4.

[36] Federal Labour Court of 05 October 2010—1 ABR 88/09.

[37] Federal Labour Court of 05 October 2010—1 ABR 88/09.

[38] Federal Labour Court of 14 December 2004, in Arbeitsrechtliche Praxis, par. 2 TVG Tariffähigkeit No. 1.

[39] See Preis, U., and S. Greiner. 2009. "Die staatliche Geltungserstreckung nach dem alten und neu gefassten AEntG, insbesondere bei Vorliegen konkurrierender Tarifverträge," in *Zeitschrift für Arbeitsrecht*, 825.

Germany in the more recent past.[40] This trend may continue due to the fact that recently, the Federal Labour Court has given up the so-called "principle of unity of collective bargaining agreements" (*Grundsatz der Tarifeinheit*)[41] and it will, in general, become easier for trade unions consisting of members of a certain profession to arrive at collective bargaining agreements being effectively applied in a given undertaking.

In the last couple of years considerable problems with regard to collective bargaining capacity can be attributed to a specific legal set-up in the area of temporary agency work. According to section 9 No. 2 of the Act on Temporary Agency Work (*Arbeitnehmerüberlassungsgesetz – AÜG*) the principle of equal treatment applies to temporary agency workers. That means that their basic working and employment conditions must be, for the duration of their assignment at a user undertaking, at least those that would apply if they had been recruited directly by that undertaking to perform the same job.[42] The principle of equal treatment can be disposed of by the parties of a collective agreement.[43] In fact, some trade unions were prepared to enter into such agreements resulting in the pay and other working conditions of temporary agency workers predominantly being far worse than those of ordinary staff. This is because under the existing rules parties who are not bound to the disposing collective agreement can still refer to it and, by doing so, also dispose of the statutory principle.[44] In legal literature it is argued that in any event such agreements cannot be regarded as indicating collective bargaining capacity on the part of trade unions because it is the employer, not the

---

[40] Waas, B. 2008. "Die Tariflandschaft im Umbruch—eine Betrachtung aus der Perspektive des Arbeitsrechts," *in Sozialer Fortschritt—German Review of Social Policy*, 16.

[41] Federal Labour Court of 07 July 2010, in Arbeitsrechtliche Praxis, Art. No. 9 GG No. 140.

[42] Section 9 No. 2 AÜG: "Vereinbarungen, die für den Leiharbeitnehmer für die Zeit der Überlassung an einen Entleiher schlechtere als die im Betrieb des Entleihers für einen vergleichbaren Arbeitnehmer des Entleihers geltenden wesentlichen Arbeitsbedingungen einschließlich des Arbeitsentgelts vorsehen (…)" are void.

[43] Section 9 No. 2 AÜG: "(…) ein Tarifvertrag kann abweichende Regelungen zulassen; im Geltungsbereich eines solchen Tarifvertrages können nicht tarifgebundene Arbeitgeber und Arbeitnehmer die Anwendung der tariflichen Regelungen vereinbaren".

[44] See Waltermann, R. 2010. "Fehlentwicklungen in der Leiharbeit," *Neue Zeitschrift für Arbeitsrecht*, 482.

employee, who is essentially interested in them coming into existence.[45] It must also be seen against this legal context that many experts currently warn against the danger of "yellow trade" unions emerging again in Germany.[46]

4. Conclusion

The capacity of trade unions to bargain collectively is dependent on a set of requirements to be met. Recently, these requirements have been set in motion, essentially as the result of two factors: first, "specialist trade unions" have been on the rise in Germany in the more recent past, a condition which poses specific problems of "measuring" their collective bargaining capacity; secondly, a specific legal set-up in the area of temporary agency work, in particular, has proved to be a strong incentive to form trade unions willing to dispose of workers' protection provided in statutory law.

References

Deinert, O. 2010. "Arbeitsrechtliche Herausforderungen einer veränderten Gewerkschaftslandschaft," *Neue Zeitschrift für Arbeitsrecht*, 1176.

Dieterich, T. 2011. *Erfurter Kommentar zum Arbeitsrecht*. München: Beck Juristischer Verlag.

Hohenstatt, K-S, and N. Schramm. 2008. "Tarifliche Mindestlöhne: Ihre Wirkungsweise und ihre Vermeidung am Beispiel des Tarifvertrags zum Post-Mindestlohn," *Neue Zeitschrift für Arbeitsrecht*, 433-437.

Löwisch, M. and V. Rieble. 2009. *Münchener Handbuch zum Arbeitsrecht*. München: Beck Juristischer Verlag.

Preis, U., and S. Greiner. 2009. "Die staatliche Geltungserstreckung nach dem alten und neu gefassten AEntG, insbesondere bei Vorliegen konkurrierender Tarifverträge," in *Zeitschrift für Arbeitsrecht*, 825.

Schüren, P, and R. Wank. 2001. "Die neue Leiharbeitsrichtlinie und ihre Umsetzung in deutsches Recht," *Recht der Arbeit*, 1-8.

45 See Deinert, O. 2010. "Arbeitsrechtliche Herausforderungen einer veränderten Gewerkschaftslandschaft," *Neue Zeitschrift für Arbeitsrecht*, 1176.

46 See, for instance, Schüren, P, and R. Wank. 2001. "Die neue Leiharbeitsrichtlinie und ihre Umsetzung in deutsches Recht," *Recht der Arbeit*, 1-8.

Waas, B. 2008. "Die Tariflandschaft im Umbruch—eine Betrachtung aus der Perspektive des Arbeitsrechts," *in Sozialer Fortschritt—German Review of Social Policy*, 16.

—. 2011. *Beck'scher Online-Kommentar Arbeitsrecht.* Beck-online.

Waltermann, R. 2010. "Fehlentwicklungen in der Leiharbeit," *Neue Zeitschrift für Arbeitsrecht*, 482.

ANTI-CRISIS LABOUR MARKET MEASURES AND THEIR EFFECTIVENESS BETWEEN FLEXIBILITY AND SECURITY

MICHELE TIRABOSCHI AND SILVIA SPATTINI

1. Introduction

Following the GDP decrease resulting from the economic crisis, the EU Member States experienced a higher level of unemployment and a decline in terms of employment rate. However, the implementation of so-called anti-crisis measures limited such increase—in some cases not to be as high as expected—in the majority of the EU Member States.

With the view to minimise the impact of the downturn in social terms and support both companies and employees, the European Union took a number of actions to drive the economic recovery and coordinate EU Member States public interventions,[1] with Member States adapting existing labour market policies and/or introducing new ones. In this connection, the majority of Member States launched *ad-hoc* and comprehensive "anti-crisis packages" consisting in a variety of measures to cope with the recession and resulting in a wide range of public policy tools aiming at reducing the impact of the crisis on the labour market.

The aim of this paper is to analyse the relation between different labour market policy combinations issued by Member States and their social protection system and employment protection legislation, also considered as a combination of flexibility and security tools, and try to assess their effectiveness in tackling the crisis. Results could be useful when considering possible changes of social protection systems or social models with the purposes of balancing flexibility and security.

---

[1] European Commission. 2008. *A European Economic Recovery Plan*, COM (2008) 800. Brussels: European Commission.

2. The Crisis in Figures

The starting point of the analysis is the set of figures describing the changes in the European labour market during the crisis.

Between the second quarter of 2008 and the second quarter of 2009, the real GDP in the EU (27 Member States) fell by almost 5%.

Fig. 1-1. GDP—Percentage Change on Previous Period

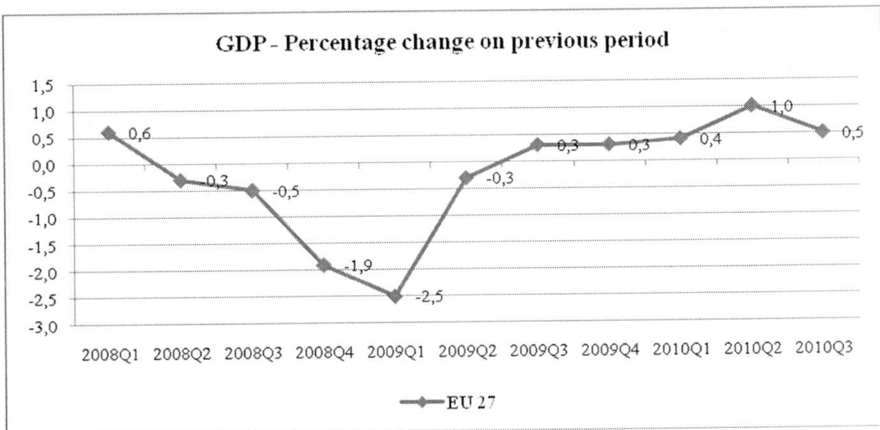

Source: Eurostat, seasonally adjusted and adjusted data by working days.

The fall in GDP caused a reduction of labour demand and, accordingly, an increase in unemployment and the decrease in employment.

The figures show a considerable difference in the impact of the crisis on the 27 EU Member States, particularly if we compare unemployment rates in July 2008—that is before the crisis—and July 2010.

Although being regarded as emerging economies before the downturn, countries such as Spain and Ireland reported a significant increase in unemployment. More specifically, the levels of unemployment almost doubled in a two-year span, with this issue that has became a matter of serious concern.

The same happened to the Baltic States (Estonia, Lithuania and Latvia), which experienced the highest rates of unemployment in Europe (Fig. 1-2).

Fig. 1-2. Unemployment Rate Change and Unemployment Rate 2010/07

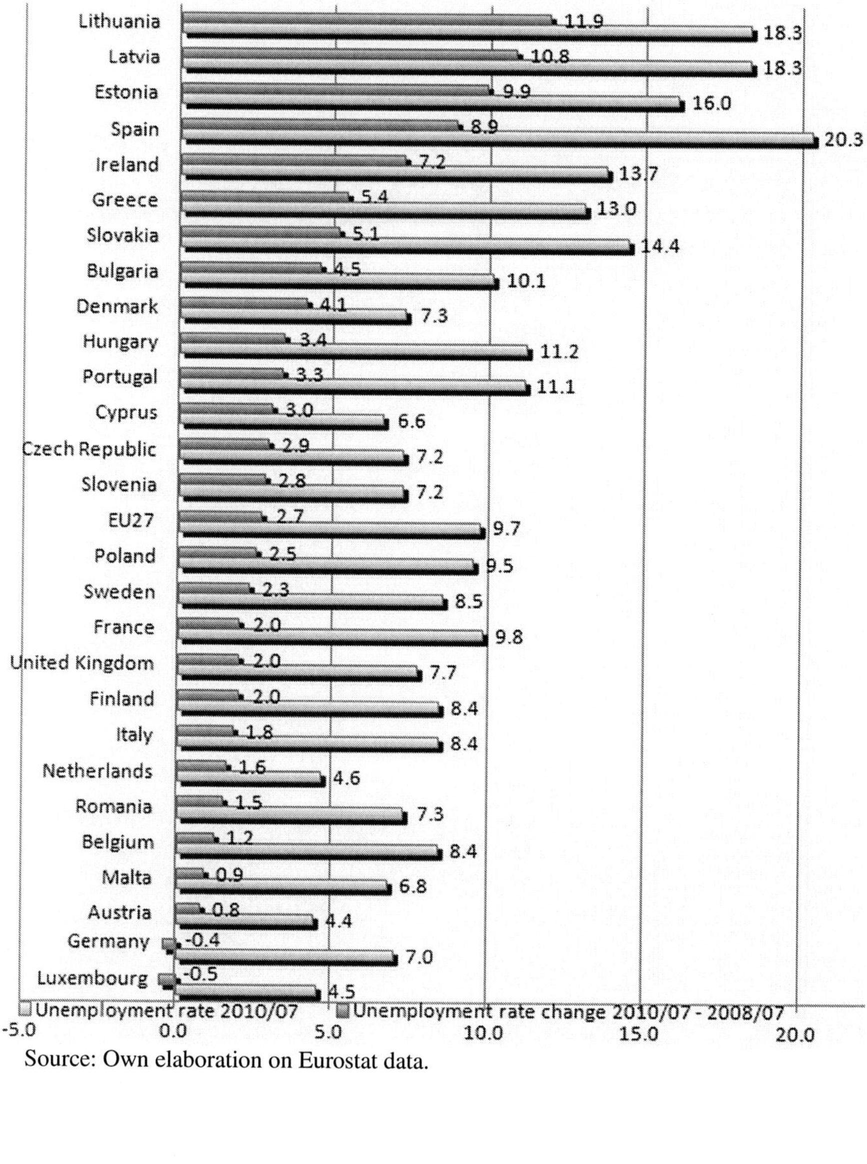

Source: Own elaboration on Eurostat data.

Fig. 1-3. Change in Employment Rate 2010Q2-2008Q2

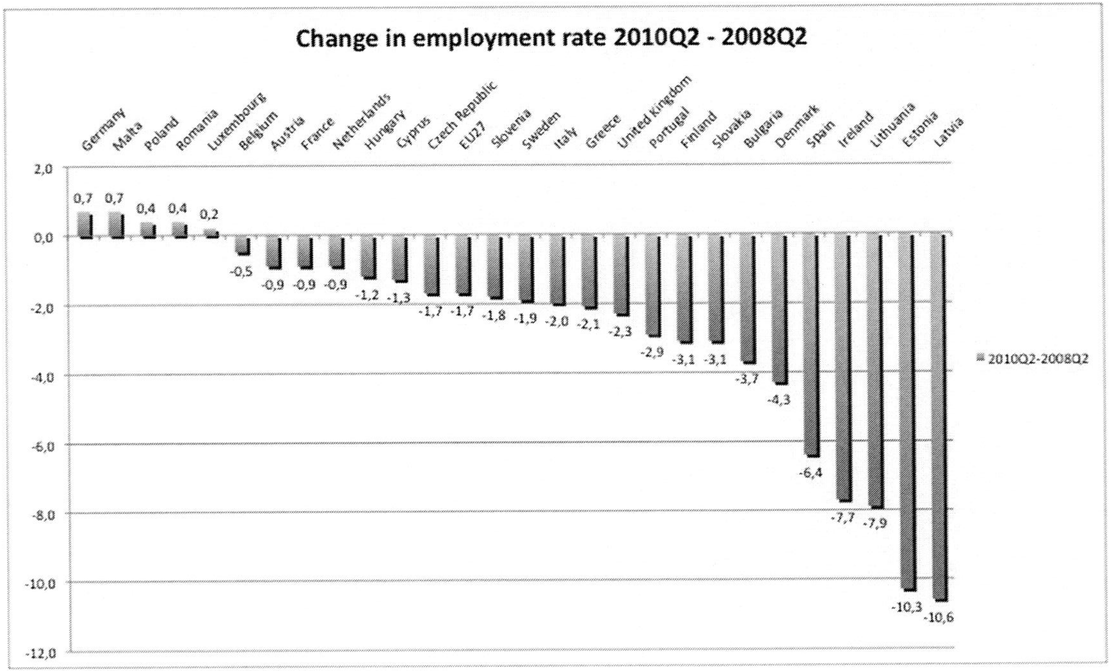

Source: Own elaboration on Eurostat data.

Looking at the trends in Fig. 3, Latvia, Estonia, Lithuania, Ireland and Spain also had the highest decrease in terms of employment rate.

A case in point was Denmark, which, before the crisis had a low level of unemployment, and during the economic downturn has experienced a worsening of labour market situation. Here, despite the unemployment levels (7.3% in July 2010) were not very high and lower than the EU average (9.6%), such levels experienced a critical increase and doubled in a two-year period. At the same time, the employment rate dropped by 2%, which was more than the EU average.

The situation of the labour market is less worrying in countries like Germany, Austria, Belgium, the Netherlands and Italy, where the rise in unemployment rates was in no case higher than 1.7%, with the decrease in employment rates not being as significant as in the countries mentioned above.

Indeed, Germany represents a unique case: after a very limited increase in unemployment (0.4% in July 2009 compared to July 2008), an unexpected reduction was reported in 2010, with the levels of employment experiencing a growth.

Such variability among European countries and the little impact of the recession on some of them is not coincidental.

Although it is "too early to draw final conclusions",[2] there is evidence that the different performance levels within national labour markets result from the diversified nature of labour regulation and existing labour market policies, along with new measures taken by governments to combat the crisis.

3. Anti-crisis Measures across Europe

The combination of several factors at a national level actually produced 27 different ways in which the economic downturn hit the EU Member States. In addition, there were 27 different responses to the crisis. Each country has adopted a set of measure—therefore not a single action—among which it is possible to identify most frequently implemented ones.[3]

In order to assess the effectiveness of these policies, it is necessary to review existing legislation and classify measures implemented by every European country, in accordance with a simple scheme.

---

[2] European Commission. 2010a. "Short Time Working Arrangements as Response to Cyclical Fluctuation," European Economy, Occasional Papers 64. Luxembourg: European Commission.

[3] European Commission. 2009. *Recovering from the Crisis—27 Ways of Tackling the Employment Challenge*. Luxembourg: European Commission.

Moreover, it is necessary to take into consideration that labour market policies adopted by national governments vary considerably especially in terms of issues concerning the role played by social partners in each country.

Their participation to the development and implementation of anti-crisis measures and to the adjustment of existing labour market tools differs across Europe also if one considers the level and the extent of their involvement in public policy design. This depends on the diversity of functions performed by social dialogue over the time, and the power of each government to operate in the present situation.

In Austria, Belgium, Italy, Germany and the Netherlands—countries with a well-established social partnership—agreements between social partners contributed to the drawing up of stimulus packages considerably.

As regards collective bargaining, opening clauses allow company-level agreements to derogate from sectoral collective agreements in order to cut costs and safeguard employment (i.e. derogation to the general framework). These agreements usually envisage the extension of working time without full compensation in pay or cuts in working time, cuts in benefits or delays in agreed pay increases.

The classification of policy measures is a preliminary step to verify whether—at least intuitively and while waiting for empirical evidence—there is a relation between patterns of labour market policies adopted by Member States and the trends of the national labour market during the crisis.

To date, key reports from the European Commission, OECD and EU institutions have analysed public interventions in the labour market. In particular the European Foundation for the Improvement of Living and Working Conditions (from now on Eurofound) has provided a useful classification of crisis-related measures implemented in the EU Member States.[4] This classification is based on three different types of interventions: 1) measures to create employment or to promote reintegration, 2) measures to maintain employment, 3) income support measures for the unemployed.

[4] Mandl, I., and L. Salvatore. 2009. *Tackling the Recession: Employment-related Public Initiatives in the EU Member States and Norway.* Dublin: European Foundation for the Improvement of Living and Working Conditions. Hurley, J., I. Mandl, D. Storrie, and T. Ward. 2009. "Restructuring in Recession," ERM Report 2009. Dublin: European Foundation for the Improvement of Living and Working Conditions.

3.1 Measures to Create Employment and to Promote Reintegration

Measures to create employment aim at promoting the hiring of employees by means of economic incentives, mainly consisting in a reduction of non-wage labour costs and wage subsidies, or public sector job creation. In some countries (France, Germany, Italy, Portugal, Slovenia, Sweden), the economic incentives for companies are provided to hire special target groups. Support measures for self-employment, based on the provision of consultancy and training (Bulgaria, the UK) or the reduction/defer of social security payments also falls within this category. Several Member States (Austria, Italy, Lithuania, Portugal, the UK) have introduced or extended subsidies for business start-ups.

Measures to promote reintegration into employment, put into action by employment services, try to enhance the transition from unemployment to employment by addressing job mismatch, supporting job matching by means of counselling, career guidance, search assistance, activation measures and by increasing employability through training. Efforts have been made to improve and adapt public employment services in order to manage the higher number of "client" (for example hiring additional staff, as in Germany, Norway, Spain, the UK) and to economically support private employment agencies through economic and/or normative incentives (the Netherlands, Italy). In the same vein, and with the view to make workers more willing to accept a new job, mobility grants are envisaged (Czech Republic, Lithuania, Slovakia). In Belgium, for instance, employees that agree to move their residence in order to accept a job offer obtain tax benefits.

3.2 Income Support for Unemployed People

Income support for unemployed people mainly comprises unemployment benefits, provided to reduce the socio-economic consequences of job loss.

Unemployment benefit systems exist in every EU Member State, even though amendments (in some cases temporary) have been made at a national level to their regulation in order to respond to the increased number of unemployed people resulting from the crisis. Relevant changes particularly concerned the following aspects: eligibility criteria, amount, duration of entitlement, beneficiaries. More specifically, some countries relaxed the rules for entitlement to unemployment benefits (Finland, France, Sweden), while others extended the duration: Romania has envisaged an extension of 3 months, Latvia extended such period to 9 months and in Poland it passed from 12 to 18 months. In the Czech Republic, the Government has opted for an increase in the amount of funds, while Italy introduced special benefits for quasi-subordinate workers, yet to be provided on a temporary basis.

3.3 Measures to Maintain Employment

Measures to maintain employment have the purpose to prevent dismissals and preserve existing jobs. Among these instruments, the main ones are short-time work arrangements and compensations.

4. Short-Time Work Schemes

Short-time work may take the form of a temporary reduction in working time or a temporary lay-off. In both cases, the employment relationship between employer and employee persists and the arrangements have a limited duration.[5]

Compensations for income loss are usually envisaged in case of short-time work, in the form of social security payments, to be either publicly-funded—by means of taxes—or based on social security contributions.

Nevertheless, short-time work compensation systems across Europe differ considerably from each other in terms of: procedures, degree of involvement of trade unions, "back-to-normal" plans, coverage, compensations amount, eligibility criteria. Moreover, it is possible to distinguish between well-established systems and innovative schemes introduced to face the crisis.

In the first case (which includes Germany, Austria, Belgium, France, Italy, and so on), the compensation system is part of the unemployment benefit (insurance) system, in that employers and employees pay social contributions to a fund or to the unemployment insurance system so that in the event of short-time working or temporary lay-off, employees are covered by these funds for the lost income as a consequence of a working hours reduction.

Conversely, in Member States (e.g. the Netherlands, Poland, Hungary, Slovakia, and so on) that introduced, whether temporary or not, short-time work compensations as a new measure during the crisis, such new arrangements are not part of the unemployment insurance system and

[5] European Commission. 2010a. "Short Time Working Arrangements as Response to Cyclical Fluctuation," European Economy, Occasional Papers 64. Luxembourg: European Commission.

therefore they are funded by the State through taxes.

Short-time work compensations may be classified also on the basis of their function. In some national systems, they are part-time unemployment benefits.[6] This means that employees in working hours reduction or in temporary lay-off are regarded as people working on part-time basis seeking full-time employment and, in some cases, they have to be available for a new job despite the employment contract with their employer is still in force.

In the majority of EU Member States, even if short-time work schemes envisage lost income compensation within the unemployment insurance system, they represent indeed a form of job protection against dismissal.

With reference to this measure, it is possible to point out that it might be of benefit to different actors involved in the national economic arena. Needless to say, employees benefit from short-time work schemes since measures of this kind avoid dismissal and help maintaining existing jobs, at the same time ensuring income support by compensating lost income.

However, short-time work schemes have many pros for employers. First of all, these arrangements allow companies to preserve human capital and skills that will be necessary in the recovery phase. Further, this means to save potential costs related to personnel turnover, dismissal, recruitment process, and training.

Short-time work compensations are convenient measures also from the viewpoint of governments, as they help maintain social peace and cohesion in that employers and employees share the impact of downturn. Finally, such arrangements represent a flexible tool for governments that are able to control somehow the adjustment of the labour market.

5. Policies Mix Adapted or Adopted by the EU Member States

In order to analyse the relation between different combinations of labour market measures implemented by Member States and their social models, it is necessary to consider *in toto* the set of labour market policies—both new or amended ones—that the EU Member States put into action to face the crisis.

Table 1-2 represents the measures adopted or adapted (if already existing) by each EU Member States against this background. The EU

---

[6] European Commission. 2010a. "Short Time Working Arrangements as Response to Cyclical Fluctuation," European Economy, Occasional Papers 64. Luxembourg: European Commission.

countries have been singled out by increasing unemployment rate growth (considering the difference between July 2010 and July 2008), ranked from the best to the worst in terms of performance.

Although at the early stages of the analysis, it is possible to point out that those countries with the most significant increase in unemployment rates are those that did not envisage or did not amend existing short-time work schemes.

On the contrary, EU Member States with good labour market performance, such as Austria, Belgium, Germany, Italy, and Luxembourg, had already issued measures of this kind in their system, yet making them more flexible in the last years, in consideration of the needs of the moment, and improved or adapted by combining them to training and/or to activation measures. Other countries, such as the Netherlands and Romania have introduced (even on a temporary basis like the Netherlands) short-time work schemes to face the recession.

The next step is to contextualise such different combinations of policies in the wider regulatory framework of the national labour markets, taking into consideration the relevant social model.

There are two main social models in Europe: the new welfare system model and the flexicurity model.

The first one is characterised by a rigid employment protection legislation (particularly in the event of dismissal), an ungenerous unemployment benefit system, a minimum level of implementation of active labour market policies and activation policies through public employment services. We decided to term this model "new" welfare system, as a way to distinguish it from the traditional welfare system, in which active labour market policies and activation policies were usually very limited.

On the other hand, the flexicurity model is based on a generous unemployment benefit system, high levels of implementation of active labour market policies and activation policies, and efficient public employment services.

Examples of the first model can be found in countries like Germany, Austria, Belgium, Italy, while Denmark has always been the model for flexicurity, together with Finland, Sweden, Norway and the Netherlands.

Even in this case, by looking at the labour market performance of these countries, and also by considering their social model, it clearly emerges that countries resorting to the new welfare system model had a lower increase in unemployment rates, while flexicurity countries, especially Denmark, experienced a higher rise.

Table 1-2. Measures Adopted by EU Member States

	STW Compen-ations	**Training activities during the time off/ Training support for employees**	**Reduction/ deferral of non-wage labor costs**	**Public expen-diture**	**Income tax cut**	**Incentives to employ additional workers**	**Direct Enterprise support** (loan guarantees, low interest loans)	**Mobility grants**	**(Re-) Training of unemplo-yed people**	**Improving employment services**	**Unemploy-ment benefits** (amend-ments)
Germany	+	+	+			+	+			+	
Austria	+	+							+		
Belgium	+	+	+					+			
Netherlands	new	compulsory	+			+	+		+	+	
Italy	+	+							+		
Finland									+	+	+
UK		+				+				+	+
France	+	+		+		+	+		+		+
Sweden			+			+				+	+
Poland	new				+		+		+		+
EU 27											
Czech Rep.	new	compulsory	+					+			+
Portugal	+	+	+			+					
Hungary	new	compulsory	+			+	+				
Denmark											+
Bulgaria	new		+			+				+	
Greece		+				+					
Ireland		+							+		+
Spain				+					+	+	
Estonia					+		+		+		+
Lithuania		+			+		+	+			
Latvia		+			+		+		+		+

6. The Effectiveness of Labour Market Measures

This analysis tries to identify which system and policies seem to provide a higher level of effectiveness in tackling the crisis and collect information that could be useful on a general basis while deciding which labour market policies to implement.

It is generally acknowledged that it takes time to evaluate the effectiveness of labour market measures. Indeed, and with specific reference to the crisis-related measures, the European Commission itself points out that it is too early to draw final conclusion or to provide an overall assessment.[7]

However, the European Commission and the Employment Committee try to provide in a joint paper some evidence on the effectiveness of the main labour market policies adopted and implemented by EU Member States during the crisis and, more generally, they review evaluations of the effectiveness of similar measures implemented in the past.[8] The OECD, on the other hand, gives evidence of the effectiveness particularly of short-time work schemes applied during this recession.[9]

Considering the three different types of labour market policies taken into consideration in this paper (measures to create employment or to promote reintegration; measures to maintain employment and income support for unemployed), measures to maintain employment in the form of short-time working arrangements, wage subsidies, non-wage cost reductions are deemed to have been successfully limited the decrease in employment rates[10] and the rise of unemployment, by preventing lay-offs.

Among measures of this kind implemented by the Member States, some of them—particularly short-time work schemes—have been crucial in preserving jobs[11] proving more effective than others.[12]

---

[7] European Commission. 2010a. "Short Time Working Arrangements as Response to Cyclical Fluctuation," European Economy, Occasional Papers 64. Luxembourg: European Commission, 6.

[8] Employment Committee, European Commission. 2010. *The Choice of Effective Employment Policies Measures to Mitigate Jobless Recovery in Times of Fiscal Austerity*. Brussels: European Commission.

[9] OECD. 2010. *Employment Outlook, Moving Beyond The Jobs Crisis*. Paris: OECD, 11, 56 et seq.

[10] European Commission. 2010b. *Employment in Europe 2010*. Brussels: European Commission, 11.

[11] OECD. 2010. *Employment Outlook, Moving Beyond The Jobs Crisis*. Paris: OECD.

Nevertheless, commentators point out the most critical issues related to short-time work arrangements, as the fact that they may artificially maintain employment in declining industries instead of allowing an efficient reallocation of employment. There is agreement about the negative impact associated with the deadweight, substitution and displacement.[13] In order to face these distortions, some countermeasures can be taken, in particular short-time work schemes need to be provided for a shorter period and arranged on the basis of more precise criteria, notably eligibility conditions and limited duration of the scheme.

With reference to measures to create employment, job subsidies consisting in hiring incentives or reduction of non-wage labor costs are effective in terms of job creation, but they are costly measures and can lead to negative consequences in terms of deadweight effect. At the same time, public sector job creation are less likely than other policies to provide a positive impact.[14]

As regards measures to promote reintegration, training has a little impact on employment and it is more likely to be associated with times of high unemployment. In general, then, positive training effects become evident in the long run.[15]

On the contrary, job search assistance and activation measures have a positive impact on employment and are effective in the short run, but they need an economic context characterised by a growing or stable labour demand. Only if there is labour demand, is it possible to support job search and matching and help reintegration into the labour market. For this reason, such measures are mainly adopted in the recovery phase.

Generally speaking, the income support for the unemployed has a negative effect on unemployment, since they discourage job search and reintegration into the labour market. In order to reduce the negative effects in terms of efficiency, some adjustments can be made, such as: decreasing the amount of benefits and reducing the period through which such support is provided. Besides, unemployment benefit are linked to activation policies, which require active job search from jobseekers, and sanctions are applied in case of refusal to actively search for work and to

---

[12] Employment Committee, European Commission. 2010. *The Choice of Effective Employment Policies Measures to Mitigate Jobless Recovery in Times of Fiscal Austerity*. Brussels: European Commission.

[13] OECD. 2010. *Employment Outlook, Moving Beyond The Jobs Crisis*. Paris: OECD.

[14] Kluve, J. 2007. *The Effectiveness of European Active Labor Market Policy*. Bonn: IZA.

[15] Ibid.

accept suitable job offers.

6.1 Public Expenditure on Labour Market Policies

The question of effectiveness of labour market policies is fundamental not only with reference to crisis-related measures, but also for EU Member States since a rising in budgetary constraints.

In 2009 (and most likely even in 2010), European Commission has reported that EU countries increased their expenditure on labour market interventions and income support by 0.7% of annual GDP, while before the crisis, the public expenditure on labour market policies experienced a decline. In fact, in 2008, public expenditure on labour market policies in the European Union amounted to just 1.6% of total EU-27 GDP, though there was considerable variation between the Member States (Fig. 1-4).

For this reason, EU governments need to be aware of the most effective policy mix in order to direct the public expenditure.

It seems interesting to compare data on the labour market policies expenditure and the trends of the unemployment rate during the crisis. The data on public expenditure for all countries are available only 18-20 months after the reference period, thus at the moment Eurostat only provides data for the year 2008.

In any case, considering that the labour market policies impact on the labour market is not immediate, but requires a period of time to become evident, it seems reasonable to compare data on public expenditure for 2008 and unemployment rate growth over last two years.

Member States that had the lowest increase in unemployment rate in 2009 compared to 2008, were the same that in 2008 had considerable high labour market policies expenditure, notably Belgium, Germany, the Netherlands, and Austria with more than 1.8% of their GDP.

This trend is confirmed even if we compare the growth in unemployment rate between 2008 and 2010 and the labour market policies expenditure for 2008.

Fig. 1-4. Total LMP Expenditure 2008 and Unemployment Rate Growth 2009/07-2008/07

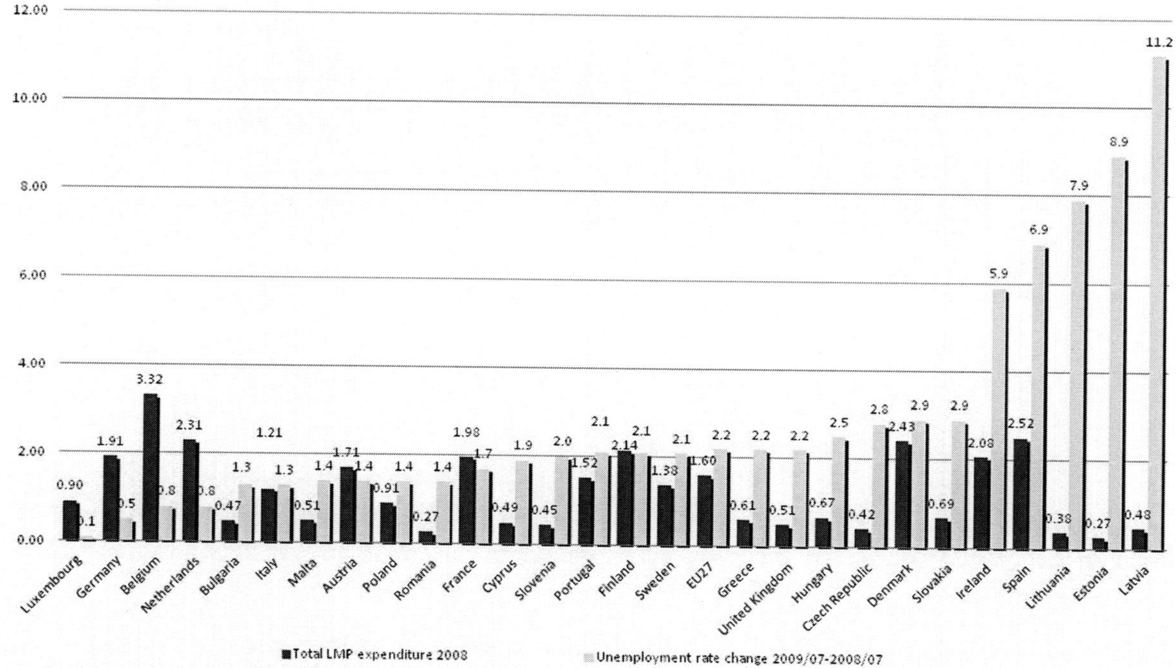

Source: Own elaboration on Eurostat data.

Fig. 1-5. Total LMP expenditure 2008 and Unemployment Rate Growth 2010/07-2008/07

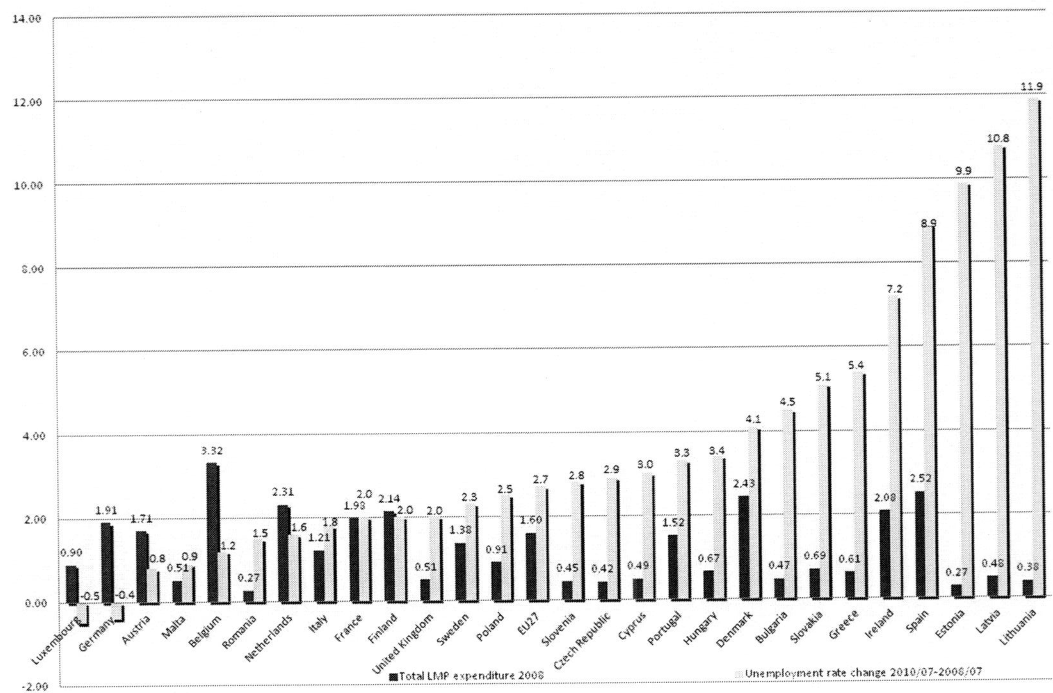

Source: Own elaboration on Eurostat data

6.2 The Effectiveness of Social Model

These figures give the opportunity for further observations and remarks. In Denmark, total public expenditure on labour market policies in 2008 was quite high (as traditionally is). It was the third highest spending country among those surveyed. Nevertheless, the rise in unemployment rate was high. This situation suggests to look at the types of policies implemented and at the social model adopted in Denmark.

Indeed, this country has been and still is an interesting case with reference to the performance of the labour market during the crisis. It is regarded as role model of flexicurity (see below), characterised by: non-restrictive dismissal protection legislation, generous unemployment benefits, consistent adoption of active labour market policies, efficient public employment services. Before the crisis, this system ensured a low unemployment rate and a quick reintegration of jobseekers into the labour market. During the crisis, however, this system proved to have some shortcomings, and Denmark had doubled the level of unemployment in September 2009: from 3.2% in July 2008 to 6.5% in September 2009 (the highest level was reached in April 2010: 7.4%).

The aim of this system is not to prevent dismissal but rather to support a quick job-to-job transition and reintegration into the labour market. Nevertheless, if the labour demand is low, the reintegration is not possible or is very difficult.

In addition, Denmark does not envisage a “real” short-time work compensation system, even though companies may use short-time work arrangements and employees involved are eligible for part-time unemployment benefits. They must fulfil the contributory requirements for eligibility to total unemployment benefits and have to be available for a new occupation despite the employment contract with the same employer is still in force. In practice, it seems that this provision is not strictly applied, if the employee has the possibility to stay in the company.

Looking at the labour market performance of the EU Member States, and by taking into consideration the two different social models adopted in Europe, some interesting remarks and comments are possible.

As regards the growth of the unemployment rate during the crisis, Austria, Belgium, Germany and, to some extent Italy, are regarded as countries with the lowest increase. The social model of all these EU Member States can be classified as new welfare system.

On the contrary, as mentioned, Denmark, which is the reference model for flexicurity, experienced a high increase in unemployment.

Table 1-3. Comparison between New Welfare System and Flexicurity Model

Systems	Employment protection legislation	Unemployment benefit	STW compensations	Effective in the crisis
New welfare	Stringent dismissal protection legislation	Non generous: • Short duration • Low replacement rate	Yes	More effective (Germany, Austria Belgium, Italy)
Flexicurity	Non–restrictive dismissal protection legislation	Generous: • Long duration • High replacement rate	No or very limited as partial unemployment benefit	Less effective (mainly Denmark, Finland, Sweden, the Netherlands)

Also Finland, Sweden, and the Netherlands (and Norway, though not a EU Member) are considered as countries adopting the flexicurity system, but they had a better labour market performance than Denmark during recession, even if they had, however, an increase of the unemployment rate amounting to more than two percent.

Actually, there is an important variation factor between Denmark and the other flexicurity countries. It is the employment protection legislation. In fact, Denmark has a liberally-oriented employment protection legislation, while the other countries have more stringent one.

Table 1-4. OECD EPL Index

Countries	OECD EPL index
Germany	2,63
Luxembourg	3,39
Malta	-
Austria	2,41
Romania	-
Belgium	2,61
Netherlands	**2,23**
Italy	2,58
Finland	**2,29**
United Kingdom	1,09
France	2,90
Sweden	**2,06**
Poland	2,41
European Union	2,41
Czech Republic	2,32
Portugal	2,84
Slovenia	2,76
Hungary	2,11
Cyprus	-
Denmark	**1,91**
Bulgaria	-
Greece	2,97
Slovakia	2,13
Ireland	1,39
Spain	3,11
Lithuania	-
Latvia	-
Estonia	2,39

Among flexicurity countries, the Netherlands is the only country being characterised by a lower rise in unemployment rate. In this case, it is worth pointing out that the Netherlands introduced short-time work compensations of a temporary nature, while Finland has a system similar to the Danish one and Sweden does not envisage any.

On the basis of these observations and considering evidence from labour market policies effectiveness, the new welfare system model appears to be more effective in facing the crisis, while the flexicurity system, as seen, had and still has difficulty in this connection and turn out to be less effective in controlling the increase in unemployment.

It is not completely clear whether this is due to short-time working arrangements or to the presence in new welfare system model of a stringent regulation against (individual or collective) dismissal. It might probably depends on both aspects, also because they are related.

Now, considering social models and labour market policy combinations applied by the EU Member States, there is not a unique "best solution" to tackle "different kinds" of economic recession. It is also important to understand the context and the legal framework in which any possible solution has to be implemented.

7. Active and Passive Labour Market Policies between Flexibility and Security

Over the last two decades, and with reference to labour market policies to be implemented by countries, the international institutions (OECD and the European Commission, among others) put emphasis on active labour market policies rather than passive ones, therefore addressing public interventions mainly towards active measures.

Looking from this standpoint at policies packages applied by the EU Member States, at the beginning of the crisis there was a critical approach towards short-time work arrangements. Observers and commentators constantly pointed out the labour market distortions and limitations associate with these schemes. A reason for that, since they are income support measures, could be the passive nature of labour market policy.

But, recently and perhaps thanks to the effectiveness in tackling the crisis, it seems that authors look at these schemes in a different way. Indeed, a recent report of the Eurofound,[16] describing the effectiveness of

---

[16] Mandl, I., J. Hurley, M. Mascherini, and D. Storriel. 2010. *Extending Flexicurity—The Potential of Short-time Working Schemes*. Dublin: European Foundation for the Improvement of Living and Working Conditions.

short-time work schemes, tries to link these measure to the flexicurity principles, by stressing how they serve the implementation of flexicurity.

In examining the functioning of short-time work schemes, it easy to see them as a tool for flexicurity, combining internal flexibility and job and income security. In fact, the possibility of a reduction of working hours (till zero hours) allows internal flexibility for employers (based exactly on flexible working time arrangements). At the same time, this provision prevents dismissals and helps employees to stay in their current position, enhancing job security. Moreover, wage compensations linked to short- time work arrangement ensure income security for the employees, thanks to the continuity of income, granted through either a wage or unemployment benefits.

Among the other types of labour market policy measures mentioned above in terms of flexicurity, those to promote reintegration and to create employment are fundamental resources for guaranteeing employment security, that is continuity of employment, not necessarily within the same employer.

On the other hand, income support for unemployed people has the obvious purpose to ensuring income security in case of dismissal and can be seen as complementary to external flexibility.

8. Concluding Remarks

While wondering if and which changes may be necessary for a national system – intended as a combination of the social security system – the employment protection legislation, the public employment services system and labour market policies applied, it can be probably useful to take into consideration the different aspects highlighted.

The crisis has created a sort of *laboratory* in which it was somehow possible to conduct experiments on the functioning of different national system.

Before the crisis, European and international institutions took in great consideration flexicurity principles dominated by external flexibility and employment security based on non- or low-restrictive employment protection legislation (and dismissal protection legislation), supported by a generous unemployment benefit system, efficient public employment services, high level of active labour market policies. From this point of view, the prevailing measures had to be those aiming at creating employment or, to be more precise, at promoting reintegration, giving momentum to job-to-job transition. By launching the EU flexicurity strategy, the European Union promoted internal and external flexicurity "accompanied by secure transition from job to job".[17]

Before the crisis, the review of the old model moving towards the flexicurity one became a matter of urgency. However, the economic downturn raised awareness of the fact that this formulation of the flexicurity strategy was suitable for a period of economic growth and to face structural unemployment, which need in particular measures to support (re-)integration by addressing job mismatch, supporting job matching by means of counselling, career guidance, search assistance, activation measures and by increasing occupability through training.

Indeed, a flexicurity strategy based on external flexibility and employment security, as described above, was not able to stand the impact of the recession. In such a situation, in order to limit the related socio-economic consequences, policy measures to maintain employment and keep employees at work turned out to be indispensable.

Therefore, by trying to plan an appropriate combination of the above mentioned elements, it is necessary to balance the different kinds of flexibility and security and to bear in mind that measures and tools should be put into place both in a period of economic growth and in recession.

References

Employment Committee, European Commission. 2010. *The Choice of Effective Employment Policies Measures to Mitigate Jobless Recovery in Times of Fiscal Austerity*. Brussels: European Commission.

European Commission. 2007. *Towards Common Principles of Flexicurity: More and Better Jobs Through Flexibility and Security*, COM(2007) 359. Brussels: European Commission.

—. 2008. *A European Economic Recovery Plan*, COM (2008) 800. Brussels: European Commission.

—. 2009. *Recovering from the Crisis—27 Ways of Tackling the Employment Challenge*. Luxembourg: European Commission.

—. 2010a. "Short Time Working Arrangements as Response to Cyclical Fluctuation," European Economy, Occasional Papers 64. Luxembourg: European Commission.

—. 2010b. *Employment in Europe 2010*. Brussels: European Commission.

---

[17] European Commission. 2007. *Towards Common Principles of Flexicurity: More and Better Jobs Through Flexibility and Security*, COM(2007) 359. Brussels: European Commission.

Hurley, J., I. Mandl, D. Storrie, and T. Ward. 2009. "Restructuring in Recession," ERM Report 2009. Dublin: European Foundation for the Improvement of Living and Working Conditions.

Kluve, J. 2007. *The Effectiveness of European Active Labor Market Policy*. Bonn: IZA.

Mandl, I., and L. Salvatore. 2009. *Tackling the Recession: Employment-related Public Initiatives in the EU Member States and Norway.* Dublin: European Foundation for the Improvement of Living and Working Conditions.

Mandl, I., J. Hurley, M. Mascherini, and D. Storriel. 2010. *Extending Flexicurity—The Potential of Short-time Working Schemes*. Dublin: European Foundation for the Improvement of Living and Working Conditions.

OECD. 2010. *Employment Outlook, Moving Beyond The Jobs Crisis.* Paris: OECD.

THE CONCEPT OF FLEXICURITY IN ESTONIAN LABOUR LAW

MERLE MUDA

1. Introduction

The development of social relations has led to a change in the nature of employment arrangements. Besides standard employment schemes, there has been widespread implementation of atypical forms of work, the result of increasing competition in the 1990s. Thus, the regulation of classical employment relations that aims to provide effective protection for employees proved insufficient to fulfil the needs of the labour market.

Over the last few years, most European countries have searched for possibilities on how to make their labour law more flexible. At the end of the 1990s, Estonia was also planning to review its labour law, with the rethinking of labour legislation that was connected with the reform of private law as a whole.[1]

Immediately after the restoration of Estonia's independence in 1991, several new labour law provisions were adopted, while the Labour Code of the Soviet Estonia was abolished. These Acts[2] were drafted and passed very quickly because the fast-developing market economy required new labour laws.[3] Once these measures were enforced, further reform was

---

[1] Muda, M. 2010. "Estonian Labour Law Reform: The Successful Implementation of the Idea of Flexicurity?" IJCLLIR 26, No. 3:347.

[2] For example, the Wages Act, the Working and Rest Time Act, the Holidays Act, and so on. The most important labour law act that determined the overall approach to labour relations regulation was the Employment Contracts Act. *Eesti Vabariigi töölepingu seadus* (TLS)/Republic of Estonia Employment Contracts Act, passed on 15 Apr. 1992—RT (*Riigi Teataja*/State Gazette) 1992, 15/16, 241; I 2009, 11, 67. The Act is available in English at www.legaltext.ee/text/en/X1056K10.htm (accessed November 1, 2011). This Act is no longer in force as of 1 July 2009.

[3] Orgo, I.-M. 1996. "Labour Law Reform in Re-independent Estonia," *Juridica International, Law Review,* Tartu: University of Tartu, 1:99-108

decided upon, in order to strengthen the regularity of rules, and align them with EU labour law.[4]

In this sense, eight draft laws regulating employment contracts were issued over the period 1996 to 2005, but none of them passed, as the scope of the reform was far from being clear. Finally, at the end of the year 2008, the Estonian Parliament—the *Riigikogu*—adopted the new Employment Contracts Act (*töölepingu seadus*—TLS).[5] The TLS entered into force on 1 July 2009.

According to the Explanatory Statement of the Draft of the TLS, the new Act builds on the concept of flexicurity.[6] The goal of the TLS was to provide a legal basis for flexible labour arrangements and carry out the extensive reform of Estonian labour relations. However, at the time of the adoption of the new Act, flexicurity was not a particularly widespread concept at a national level.

The aim of this paper is to examine the meaning of flexicurity in Estonian labour law. To this end, the author will analyse the rise of this concept in Estonia, as well as components and measures to implement it nationwide. This contribution considers Estonian labour legislation. However, the situation in the EU and other European states is also investigated when examining certain specific issues.

2. The Rise of the Concept of Flexicurity

As mentioned earlier, in the 1996-2005 time period, several draft laws regulating employment contracts were elaborated on, although there was no clear understanding of the scope of the new regulation. The authors of

(http://www.juridicainternational.eu/index/1996/vol-i/labour-law-reform-in-re-independent-estonia/, accessed November 1, 2011).

[4] See also Muda, M. 2008. "Eesti töösuhete regulatsioon vajab uuendamist / Estonian Employment Regulations Need to be Renewed," *Riigikogu Toimetised*, 17:148.

[5] *Töölepingu seadus* / Employment Contracts Act, passed on 17 Dec. 2008—RT I 2009, 35, 5; 2010, 22, 108. The Act is available in English at http://www.sm.ee/fileadmin/meedia/Dokumendid/Toovaldkond/TLS_eng.pdf, (accessed November 1, 2011). This act was elaborated during 2006-2008. See par. 2.

[6] *Seletuskiri töölepingu seaduse eelnõu juurde* / The Explanatory Statement of the Draft of the Employment Contracts Act (18 Jun. 2008), 2. Available in Estonian at www.riigikogu.ee/, (accessed November 1, 2011).

the drafts held that the new set of rules had to be harmonised with the EU labour law, while also considering ongoing social relations.[7]

Both aims were indeed rational. Since the Republic of Estonia was an associated member of the EU, the Government was obliged to ensure the conformity of national legislation to EU law. However, as the process of the labour law reform lasted long, the principles of EU law were transposed into Estonian law by amending already existing Acts.

In addition, it was necessary to ensure the conformity of the new regulation to other private law acts that had been passed after the adoption of the previous TLS. Rules on labour relations in Estonia are closely connected to the section of general principles of both civil and obligation law. The TLS is a specific body of law concerning the General Part of the Civil Code Act[8] and the Law of Obligations Act[9]. As the previous version of the TLS was not in line with these Acts, there was a lack of association between the regulation of employment relations and the principles of private law.

Thus, at the end of the 1990s and at the beginning of the 2000s, efforts were made to further widening the scope of provisions that was in force at that time, taking into account requirements of the EU law and other Estonian private law acts, as well as tendencies in national case law. In conceptual terms, there was no incongruity between Estonian and EU law.[10] Also, the harmonisation of the regulation of employment relations with other national provisions would not involve large-scale changes in labour law. Primarily, there was a need to regulate several issues concerning relationships between the parties to the employment contract in greater detail.

---

[7] Muda, M. 2004. "Impact of the European Community Labour Law on Estonian Labour Legislation," *Labour Law in United Europe. m. spalio 16-18 d. Tarptautinės mokslinės konferencijos medžiaga*, Vilnius, 92.

[8] *Tsiviilseadustiku üldosa seadus*/General Part of the Civil Code Act, passed on 27 Mar. 2002—RT I 2002, 35, 216; 06.12.2010, 1. The Act is available in English at http://www.legaltext.ee/text/en/X30082K3.htm, (accessed November 1, 2011).

[9] *Võlaõigusseadus*/Law of Obligations Act, passed on 26 Sept. 2001—RT I 2001, 81, 487; 08.07.2011, 6. The Act is available in English at http://www.legaltext.ee/text/en/X30085K2.htm, (accessed November 1, 2011).

[10] See, e.g., Muda, M. 2004. "Impact of the European Community Labour Law on Estonian Labour Legislation," *Labour Law in United Europe. m. spalio 16-18 d. Tarptautinės mokslinės konferencijos medžiaga*, Vilnius, 92-103; Muda, M. 1996. "Improving Estonian Labour Legislation on Integration with Europe," *Juridica International, Law Review,* Tartu: University of Tartu, 1:109-114 (http://www.juridicainternational.eu/index/1996/vol-i/improving-estonian-labour-legislation-on-integration-with-europe/, accessed November 1, 2011).

Hence, there was not any ideological issue associated with labour law reform. Further, members from commissions in charge of drafting new Acts did not consider transposing principles of some other European country into Estonian law,[11] due to different systems of industrial relations. In effect, because of the limited role of social partners in shaping employment relations in Estonia, the labour market is mainly regulated by legislation.[12] In the author's view, its lack of clarity from a conceptual point of view was one of the reasons behind the failure of its entry into force over the period considered (1996-2005).

In 2006, the Estonian Ministry of Social Affairs started working on the next draft law.[13] At the end of the same year, the European Commission issued the *Green Paper on Modernising Labour Law to Meet the Challenges of the 21st Century*[14] in order to emphasise the need to develop flexible labour relations and innovate labour law. The keyword of the document was flexicurity: through the implementation of this concept, it was intended that there be an increase in the adaptability of employees and enterprises and the flexibility of labour markets.[15] This was one of the aims of the Lisbon Strategy.[16]

The issuing of the Green Paper helped to renew the regulation of employment relations in Estonia, as the basis for the elaboration of the

---

[11] For example, German law was taken as a model when Estonia reviewed its legal system in the 1990s.

[12] The low incidence of collective agreements in regulating employment relationships is largely due to the fact that only 7% of employees belong to trade unions. About the role of the employees' representatives on shaping of employment relations, see Muda, M. 2009. "Estonia", in *The Laval and Viking Cases. Freedom of Services and Establishment v. Industrial Conflicts in the European Union*, eds. Blanpain, R., and A. M. Świątkowski, *Bulletin of Comparative Labour Relations*, No. 69. The Hague: Kluwer Law International, 38-42.

[13] The draft of the TLS was elaborated by the commission that consisted of the officials of the Ministry of Justice and the Ministry of Social Affairs only. The trade unions and employers' organisations were involved after the publication of the first version of the draft. Members of research institutions were not included in the compilation of the TLS.

[14] Available at.
http://eur-lex.europa.eu/LexUriServ/LexUriServ.do?uri=COM:2006:0708:FIN:EN:PDF, (accessed November 1, 2011).

[15] Muda, M. 2010. "Estonian Labour Law Reform: The Successful Implementation of the Idea of Flexicurity?" IJCLLIR 26, No. 3:348.

[16] For the present, the EU has elaborated the new growth strategy—Europe 2020. Information about this strategy is available at:
http://ec.europa.eu/europe2020/index_en.htm, (accessed November 1, 2011).

new law—the idea of flexicurity—was now clear, with the implementation process that was also justified by the need to make flexicurity work in practical terms. As mentioned above, the new TLS was therefore adopted at the end of 2008 and entered into force in 2009.

As the new Act was drafted quickly and without public discussion, there was very little research into the meaning and suitability of the idea of flexicurity in the Estonian system of labour relations.[17] Thus, it is argued in this article that the recourse to the concept of flexicurity as the main ideological framework for the TLS was hasty and occasional. When the first signs of economic crisis appeared in Estonia in the second half of 2008, employers needed more flexible working arrangements because the existing rules that provided extensive protection for employees worsened their situation. Hence, at the end of the same year, the new Act was enacted, and also supported by politically favourable conditions.

3. Content of the Concept of Flexicurity

As previously discussed,[18] the idea of flexicurity that had been described in the Green Paper issued by the European Commission inspired the drafters of the TLS to use it as the basis for the new Act. Accordingly, it can be stated that Estonia provided the same interpretation of this notion as the EU.

The idea of flexicurity consists of two elements—flexibility and security—and the main function of the concept is to strike a balance between such components in order to protect the interests of all parties to the labour market.[19] The implementation of this concept is not possible only by means of labour law reform, because relations between employees and employers are only one component of the operation of labour market.

The European Council explains that flexicurity involves the deliberate combination of flexible and reliable contractual arrangements, comprehensive lifelong learning strategies, effective active labour market

[17] Muda, M. 2010. "Estonian Labour Law Reform: The Successful Implementation of the Idea of Flexicurity?" IJCLLIR 26, No. 3:348. This does not mean that research in this area was not being done at all, but these studies were not connected with the elaboration of the TLS.
[18] See par. 2.
[19] About two elements of the idea of flexicurity, see, e.g., Madsen, P. K. 2007. "Flexicurity—Towards a Set of Common Principles?" IJCLLIR 23, No. 4:525 et seq.

policies, and modern, adequate and sustainable social protection systems,[20] with this definition that is drawn on the one provided by Denmark.[21]

The Council also emphasises that approaches in terms of flexicurity are not about one single labour market or working life model, nor about a single policy strategy: they should be tailored to specific needs of each Member State. Flexicurity implies a balance between the rights and responsibilities of all those concerned, and each Member State should devise its own flexicurity arrangements.[22]

This paper argues in favour of the Council's opinion that the exact content of the idea of flexicurity depends on social, economic, legal, and political factors in a given state, and each state has to find its own way in order to incorporate flexibility and security.

Following the notions of the EU, the Explanatory Statement of the Draft of the TLS sets forth that the purpose of the TLS is to regulate relations between employers and employees, ensuring sufficient security relying on the values of the welfare state for employees, allowing undertakings to realise their constitutional right to the freedom for business, and promoting competitiveness of national economy.[23] Also, it is important to find a reasonable way to enable employers to react to market needs quickly, as well as to ensure adequate protection for employees in the case of facing a decline in income and a rise in unemployment.[24]

In the Explanatory Statement, the drafters of the TLS enumerate the following components with regard to the concept of flexicurity: flexible labour law, contemporary social security systems, effective active labour

---

[20] Council of the European Union. 2007. *Towards Common Principles of Flexicurity. Draft Council Conclusions*. Brussels: Council of the European Union. Available at: http://ec.europa.eu/social/main.jsp?catId=117&langId=en, 5.

[21] In Denmark, the core of flexicurity consists of three elements: a flexible, highly mobile workforce, a strong income support system, and active labour market and educational policies. About Danish "Golden Triangle", see, e.g., Jørgensen, H., and P. K. Madsen. 2007. "Flexicurity and Beyond—Reflections on the Nature and Future of a Political Celebrity," in *Flexicurity and Beyond. Finding a New Agenda for the European Social Model*, eds. Jørgensen H., and P. K. Madsen. Copenhagen: DJØF Publishing, 12.

[22] Council of the European Union. 2007. *Towards Common Principles of Flexicurity. Draft Council Conclusions*. Brussels: Council of the European Union. Available at: http://ec.europa.eu/social/main.jsp?catId=117&langId=en, 5.

[23] *Seletuskiri töölepingu seaduse eelnõu juurde*/The Explanatory Statement of the Draft of the Employment Contracts Act (18 Jun. 2008), 1 and 6. Available in Estonian at www.riigikogu.ee/, (accessed November 1, 2011).

[24] Ibid.

market policy, and adequate system of lifelong learning.[25] Hence, the content making up the idea of flexicurity that represents the basis for the elaboration of the new TLS matches—almost perfectly—the definition provided by the EU. Although Estonia complies with the EU's guidelines, the overall description of elements characterising flexicurity does not help to understand the real output of this notion, casting doubts on how to implement the concept of flexicurity practically.

The Explanatory Statement of the Draft of the TLS also provides four sub-aims of the TLS:

- to harmonise labour law with the principles of private law;[26]
- to increase flexibility of labour relations;
- to enhance security of employees;
- to abolish formal provisions in labour law, to diminish the administrative burden.[27]

Thus, the new TLS is intended to provide employees with higher levels of flexibility and protection. However, the Explanatory Statement does not describe procedures for achieving these aims and how the balance between flexibility and security has been stricken, upholding the argument put forward in this paper that the implementation of flexicurity has not been realised considering the Estonian labour law reform.

Accordingly, it is not clear whether the concept of flexicurity approved by the EU and the the TLS will have an impact on the regulation of employment relations in Estonia. As mentioned above, this concept originates from the Danish system. However, unlike Estonia, Denmark is known as a welfare state with high taxes and well-established collective labour relations.[28] Whether the implementation of a similar idea of flexicurity is possible in such different countries remains to be seen.

---

[25] Ibid.

[26] This aim is not connected to the idea of flexicurity. On the background of this aim, see par. 2.

[27] *Seletuskiri töölepingu seaduse eelnõu juurde*/The Explanatory Statement of the Draft of the Employment Contracts Act (18 Jun. 2008), 2-6. Available in Estonian at www.riigikogu.ee/, (accessed November 1, 2011).

[28] See also, Jørgensen, H., and P. K. Madsen. 2007. "Flexicurity and Beyond—Reflections on the Nature and Future of a Political Celebrity," in *Flexicurity and Beyond. Finding a New Agenda for the European Social Model*, eds. Jørgensen, H., and P. K. Madsen. Copenhagen: DJØF Publishing, 12.

4. Implementing the Concept of Flexicurity

4.1 Principles of the Alteration of Labour Relations Regulation

As explained above,[29] the aim of the TLS is to make employment relations more flexible and, at the same time, provide employees with more adequate protection. The Explanatory Statement of the draft TLS sets forth that renewing the regulation of the employment contract entails the enlargement of flexibility in employment relations. Accordingly, both employers and employees attach significant importance to security.[30]

A considerable part of relevant literature[31] holds that, in the context of employment relations, both flexibility and security are regarded on an equal footing by either employees and employers. In the author's view, both parties to the employment contract need flexibility and security. However, in the framework of the implementation of the concept of flexicurity, it is not possible to guarantee similar status for the employee and employer in the employment relationship.

With reference to the relationship between the parties to the employment contract from a legal point of view, the underpinning component of the idea of flexicurity is flexible labour law, that should be characterised by high levels of flexibility. More importantly, employers should be given the opportunity to react to the needs of the labour market quickly, and they should not be seen only as individuals in charge of safeguarding employees.[32] Accordingly, in the context of the labour relation, the degree of security of employees might decrease. However, by implementing other components of the concept of flexicurity—contemporary social security systems, effective active labour market policy and effective system of lifelong learning—the role of the state as the catalyst for social protection should increase.

Pursuant to the Explanatory Statement of the draft TLS, the implementation of the concept of flexicurity means that the regulation of

---

[29] See par. 3.

[30] *Seletuskiri töölepingu seaduse eelnõu juurde*. The Explanatory Statement of the Draft of the Employment Contracts Act (18 Jun. 2008), 2. Available in Estonian at www.riigikogu.ee/, (accessed November 1, 2011).

[31] See, e.g., Madsen, P. K. 2007. "Flexicurity—Towards a Set of Common Principles?" IJCLLIR 23, No. 4:256.

[32] See, e.g., Jørgensen, H., and P. K. Madsen. 2007. "Flexicurity and Beyond—Reflections on the Nature and Future of a Political Celebrity," in *Flexicurity and Beyond. Finding a New Agenda for the European Social Model*, eds. Jørgensen H., and P. K. Madsen. Copenhagen: DJØF Publishing, 7.

labour relations should enable the parties to the employment contract to shape the relationship taking account of the needs and interests of the employer and employee to the greatest possible extent.[33] Here, it is argued that such line of reasoning is advisable, also in consideration of major shortcomings of the previous regulatory framework. Indeed, many of the rules of the previous version of the TLS were too strict[34] and the parties to the employment contract did not have enough room to manoeuvre.[35]

In comparison with the preceding regulation, the TLS extends the scope of the freedom of contract: the new Act streamlines the set of provisions to comply with for both employees and employers and allows the parties to agree freely on the content of the contract.[36] As a consequence of this amendment, the regulation of the TLS is more flexible but this flexibility is advantageous particularly for employers. As employers are the stronger party of the employment relation, they have more power to determine the content of agreements.[37]

Hence, and with the aim of implementing flexibility, the TLS reduces employees' level of security, especially when compared to the previous regulation that provided extensive protection for the employee in the framework of the traditional employment relation.

On the other hand, the implementation of the concept of flexicurity is not possible without guaranteeing enough security to employees. As set forth by one of the main principles of the TLS, it is important to ensure that undertakings realise their constitutional right to the freedom for

---

[33] *Seletuskiri töölepingu seaduse eelnõu juurde*/The Explanatory Statement of the Draft of the Employment Contracts Act (18 Jun. 2008), 2. Available in Estonian at www.riigikogu.ee/, (accessed November 1, 2011).

[34] See, e.g., Muda, M. 2006. "Termination of Employment Relationships: Legal Situation in Estonia," in *Termination of Employment Relationships: Legal Situation in the Member States of the European Union*. Brussels: European Commission. Available at
<http://ec.europa.eu/social/BlobServlet?docId=4628&langId=en>,
(accessed November 1, 2011).

[35] The old TLS was based on the Labour Code of Soviet Estonia that comprised detailed instructions for employees and employers about how to act in different situations.

[36] Muda, M. 2010. "Implementation of the Idea of Flexicurity: the Case of Estonia," *GCOE Newsletter*, No. 5, Tokyo: Tokyo University, 15.

[37] Muda, M. 2010. "Estonian Labour Law Reform: The Successful Implementation of the Idea of Flexicurity?" IJCLLIR 26, No. 3:352.

business,[38] with the onus of employees' protection that must be shared by both the employer and the state. Whereas the latter is not the party to the employment contract, it cannot interfere in the employment relation but may provide income support for persons not in employment.[39]

4.2 The Regulation of Labour Relations: A Plethora of Reform

4.2.1 More Abstract Norms

As previously discussed,[40] neither the Explanatory Statement of the draft TLS nor any other document describes how to implement flexicurity so as to make employment relations more flexible and give workers more protection. Furthermore, any hints at how to balance flexibility and security have been overlooked as well. Thus, in order to understand how the concept of flexicurity is conceived of in different provisions of the TLS, it is useful to identify the rules of the new regulation that have changed in comparison with the previous version, and to examine them alongside basic principles of flexicurity.[41]

It should be pointed out that the new set of regulation reviews the previous version of the provisions considerably.[42] In this respect, it is not clear whether the reason for such amendments is the implementation of the idea of flexicurity or the practical need to provide the norms with higher level of abstraction, the result of the interpretation of the previous TLS. From the author's viewpoint, a number of amendments have been made considering either the relation between the parties to the employment contract and the concept of flexicurity.

For instance, unlike the previous regulation, and pursuant to the TLS, the employer is not under the obligation to maintain employment record

---

[38] *Seletuskiri töölepingu seaduse eelnõu juurde*/The Explanatory Statement of the Draft of the Employment Contracts Act (18 Jun. 2008), 1. Available in Estonian at www.riigikogu.ee/, (accessed November 1, 2011).

[39] For example, persons whose employment contract has been terminated.

[40] See par. 3.

[41] However, as there are different ways of putting the idea of flexicurity into practice, the use of such method does not enable to understand the exact intention of the legislator.

[42] The aim of this article is not to make a detailed analysis of these changes but to observe the main developments in the TLS pertaining to the implementation of the concept of flexicurity. About renewals in the TLS, see also Muda, M. 2010. "Estonian Labour Law Reform: The Successful Implementation of the Idea of Flexicurity?" IJCLLIR 26, No. 3:352-366.

books[43] and personnel files because these documents are useless in practical terms. Also, employers are no longer required to notify the termination of employment in writing.[44]

In the new TLS, the set of rules on remuneration is smaller. In comparison with many other countries where wage conditions have been usually regulated by collective agreements,[45] the main principles of remuneration in Estonia must be established by law, due to less-developed collective labour relations. However, it did not seem reasonable to maintain similar norms in the new TLS, as previous regulation[46] was in some parts over detailed, as providing for several definitions (e.g. additional remuneration, additional payment, average wages, minimum wage) and declarative provisions (e.g. on the establishment of wage rates and wage systems).

The rules on employees' liability have also been amended. Prior to the entry into force of the new Act, the liability of employees was regulated under the Labour Code of the Estonian SSR,[47] that set forth a specific system of liability that was not in conformity with the principles of obligation law. At present, the corresponding regulation is more general, laying down only special provisions that safeguard employees. As it is in

---

[43] Under the old TLS, employers were required to maintain employment record books for all employees. As a rule, the employment record book only contained data on the length of employment. Until 1999, employment record books were necessary to prove the pension qualifying period. But as the pension qualifying period is now based on information about the social tax paid for the person, there is no need to keep employment record books.

[44] Pursuant to previous rules, an employer made an entry of termination in the employment contract, with a statement of the ground for termination and reference to the section, subsection and clause of the TLS, the date of termination, payment of compensation to the employee or employer and return of that which was acquired under the contract. There was no need for such formalities in practice.

[45] See, e.g., Weiss, M., and M. Schmidt. 2008. *Labour Law and Industrial Relations in Germany*. Zuidpoolsingel: Kluwer Law International, 108-109; Hasselbalch, O. 2005. *Labour Law in Denmark*. The Hague: Kluwer Law International; Copenhagen: DJØF Publishing, 127-128.

[46] Prior to the entry into force of the TLS, the Wages Act regulated issues pertaining to remuneration. *Palgaseadus*/Wages Act, passed on 26 Jan.1994—RT I 1994, 11, 154; 2008, 56, 315. The Act is available in English at http://www.legaltext.ee/text/en/X1037K6.htm, (accessed November 1, 2011). This Act is no longer in force as of 1 July 2009.

[47] *Eesti NSV töökoodeks*/Labour Code of the Estonian SSR, *Eesti NSV Justiitsministeerium*/Ministry of Justice of the Estonian SSR. Tallinn, Eesti Raamat, 1985. The Labour Code's regulation on the employee's liability is no longer in force as of 1 July 2009.

many other countries,[48] where an employee causes damages to the employer's property, norms of obligation law are applied.

According to the new TLS, the employer has no possibility to sanction the employee. Under the previous regulation,[49] the employer had the right to opt for four different sanctions[50] in the event of employee misconduct. Although the Explanatory Statement of the Draft of the TLS does not explain why rules concerning disciplinary action cannot be applied in the framework of employment relations, the new Act holds that—in considering the freedom of contract—such sanctioning mechanism is not suitable and that the room for manoeuvre to settle the grievance amicably must be extended. The new TLS specifies that the employer should issue a warning before terminating the employment contract due to a breach of duty on the part of employees, or a decrease in their work capacity. The Act does not provide for any formal procedure with regard to the warning.

As seen, norms of the new TLS are rather theoretical in discussing many issues. The parties to the employment contract can agree on action to be taken, if all circumstances are considered. Thus, in contrast with the previous regulation, labour laws are more flexible, i.e. in accordance with the concept of flexicurity. On the other hand, Estonian employees and employers are used to detailed statutory norms and general rules may bring about the misinterpretation of their rights under the law.[51]

4.2.2 Entering into Employment Contracts

In examining the notion of flexicurity, it is important to establish a simple mechanism to conclude the employment contract. This means, first

---

48 See, e.g., Weiss, M., and M. Schmidt. 2008. *Labour Law and Industrial Relations in Germany*. Zuidpoolsingel: Kluwer Law International, 117-118.

49 The Employees Disciplinary Punishments Act established corresponding rules before the new TLS entered into force. *Töötajate distsiplinaarvastutuse seadus*/Employees Disciplinary Punishments Act, passed on 5 May 1993—RT I 1993, 26, 441; 2010, 22, 108. The Act is available in English at http://www.legaltext.ee/text/en/X1042.htm, (accessed November 1, 2011). As regards employment relations, this Act is no longer in force as of 1 July 2009. It is still in effect in public service.

50 A reprimand; a fine not exceeding ten times the average daily wages of the employee; suspension from work without pay for a period not exceeding ten consecutive scheduled working days; and termination of an employment contract.

51 For the present, essential problems have not occurred in practice. However, as the TLS has been in force for two years only, it is not possible to draw wide-reaching conclusions yet.

and foremost, that there are no significant formal requirements when the employer and employee wish to enter into an employment contract.[52]

In many countries, the parties can usually sign a valid contract without complying with any formal request.[53] Pursuant to the previous TLS, the employment contract had to be concluded in writing,[54] therefore not providing high levels of flexibility.

In the author's view, the rules of the new TLS are likewise limited. Section (4)2 of the TLS sets forth that an employment contract must be entered into in writing. However, failing to comply with the formal requirement does not result in the invalidity of the employment contract and an employment contract is also deemed concluded if an employee commences work (TLS sections 4(4) and 4(2)). Thus, oral contracts are also valid. In addition to these rules, section 5 of the TLS sets forth that the employer is under the obligation to notify the employee about working conditions.[55] Thus, under the TLS, the employer has both the obligation to enter into the written employment contract and the obligation to inform the employee about the conditions of the employment contract in writing. It is not easy to understand how to implement these sections at the same time.

The drafters of the TLS explain that an employer must, first, enter into the written employment contract where provision is made for the substantial conditions (e.g., wages, working time, employee's duties, and the place of performance) of the contract and, second, inform the employee about the standard terms (that do not need agreement) in writing.[56]

Such regulation is far too complicated. It would be more understandable if the TLS did not lay down any formal requirement concerning the conclusion of employment contracts, except for some specific terms. The employer should only have the obligation to inform

[52] See, Muda, M. 2010. "Estonian Labour Law Reform: The Successful Implementation of the Idea of Flexicurity?" IJCLLIR 26, No. 3:352 et seq.

[53] Muda, M. 2009. "Increasing the Flexibility of Employment Regulation in Estonia," in *The Modernization of Labour Law and Industrial Relations in a Comparative Perspective*, ed. Blanpain, R., *Bulletin of Comparative Labour Relations*, No 70. The Hague: Kluwer Law International, 369.

[54] In addition, employers had administrative liability for failure to formalise or for the unsatisfactory formalisation of employment contracts (TLS sections 28(1) and 28(3)).

[55] This regulation is based on Directive 91/533/EEC on an employer's obligation to inform employees of the conditions applicable to the employment contract (OJ L 288, 18 October 1991, 32-35).

[56] Käärats, E., S. Suder, and T. Treier. 2011. *Selgitused töölepingu seaduse juurde/Comments on the Employment Contracts Act*. Tallinn: Sotsiaalministeerium/ Ministry of Social Affairs, 7-8.

employees about their working conditions in writing. Such a regulation would make labour relations more flexible.[57]

4.2.3 Fixed-term Employment Contracts

Following the notion of flexicurity, the regulation of employment relations should enable the implementation of atypical forms of work,[58] in order to correspond to the needs of the labour market. In Estonia, the most widespread form of non-standard work is the one provided by the use of fixed-term employment contracts.[59]

In comparison with the previous regulation, the TLS proposes two main amendments with regard to the contract of a definite term. First, it modifies the rules about entering into such agreements. In many countries, a general principle has been established according to which there must be a justified reason for concluding a fixed-term employment contract.[60] Section 27(2) of the previous TLS set forth a comprehensive list of grounds[61] enabling one to enter into a contract for a definite period.

Conversely, the new Act lays down only the general rule that entering into a fixed-term employment contract is justified by a good reason arising from the temporary fixed-term characteristics of the work (TLS section 9(1)). Thus, the new regulation is in line with the concept of flexicurity, makes it simpler and gives employers more possibilities to conclude fixed-term employment contracts.[62]

---

[57] Muda, M. 2010. "Estonian Labour Law Reform: The Successful Implementation of the Idea of Flexicurity?" *IJCLLIR* 26, No. 3:354-355. However, it seems that the parties to the employment contract would continue to enter into the written contracts in order to avoid labour disputes about the content of the employment contract.

[58] For example, part-time work, fixed-term employment contracts, telework, temporary agency work, and so on.

[59] Legal Acts do not restrict the implementation of any atypical forms of work.

[60] Muda, M. 2009. "Fixed-term Employment Contract as a Basis for Creating Flexible Labour Relation," in *Studia z zakresu prawa pracy i polityki spolecznej/Studies on Labour Law and Social Policy. Liber Amicorum* Prof. A. M. Świątkowski, Krakow: Musica Iagellonica sp. z.o.o, 363.

[61] For example, the completion of a specific task, the replacement of an employee who is temporarily absent, a temporary increase in work volume, the performance of seasonal work, and so on. If a fixed-term employment contract was entered into for reasons not recognised by the law, the contract was deemed to be open-ended.

[62] See also, Muda, M. 2010. "Estonian Labour Law Reform: The Successful Implementation of the Idea of Flexicurity?" *IJCLLIR* 26, No. 3:355-356.

On the other hand, the TLS has amended norms concerning the termination of fixed-term employment contracts on the initiative of the parties. The previous regulation did not provide for specific rules about the termination of the contract on the initiative of the employee or employer. The parties to the employment contract had the right to terminate such contracts almost in same way as they would for open-ended contracts.

In the context of this paper, the fact that an employee may not terminate a fixed-term contract without good reason (section 85(2))—as laid down in the new TLS—is regarded as positive. This is because the fixed-term employment contract is usually concluded with the intention to continue with this contract until the end of the agreed-upon term.[63]

Thus, the employer must also have a good reason for terminating the contract for a definite period. But section 100(3) of the TLS lays down a further obligation for the employer: upon termination of a fixed-term employment contract for economic reasons, employees are entitled to compensation that is tantamount to the wages he/she would receive until expiry of the term.[64] This means that if an employer terminates the employment contract for economic reasons, he/she must 'buy out' an employee.

In the author's view, the new regulation is not effective as somehow hampering the conclusion of fixed-term employment contracts. In some cases, it is more favourable for the employer to enter into an open-ended rather than a fixed-term contract.[65] The regulation on the fixed-term employment contract should not give absolute priority to the security of the parties to the employment contract: it could be a good measure to increase flexibility. The new TLS does not make use of this option.[66]

---

[63] A similar principle has also been established in many other countries. See, Muda, M. 2009. "Fixed-term Employment Contract as a Basis for Creating Flexible Labour Relation," in *Studia z zakresu prawa pracy i polityki spolecznej/Studies on Labour Law and Social Policy. Liber Amicorum* Prof. A. M. Świątkowski, Krakow: Musica Iagellonica sp. z.o.o, 369.

[64] This norm does not apply in the cases of force majeure and bankruptcy.

[65] Muda, M. 2009. "Fixed-term Employment Contract as a Basis for Creating Flexible Labour Relation," in *Studia z zakresu prawa pracy i polityki spolecznej/Studies on Labour Law and Social Policy. Liber Amicorum* Prof. A. M. Świątkowski, Krakow: Musica Iagellonica sp. z.o.o, 371.

[66] Muda, M. 2010. "Estonian Labour Law Reform: The Successful Implementation of the Idea of Flexicurity?" *IJCLLIR* 26, No. 3:357.

4.2.4 Termination of Employment Contracts

In the framework of the notion of flexicurity, it is important to lay down transparent rules on the termination of employment, particularly with regard to the one carried out at the initiative of the employer. The regulation of the termination of employment contract initiated by the employer shows the level of flexibility of labour relations.[67]

The TLS contains a series of reforms concerning the termination of employment contracts at the initiative of the employer. For example, in lieu of the exhaustive list of grounds for dismissal mentioned earlier, sections 88 and 89 of TLS set forth the general principle that—in order to terminate the contract—there must be economic reasons or reasons pertaining to the employee's capacity or conduct. The new Act also shortens the terms of advance notice to be given in the event of dismissal.[68]

In the author's opinion, and with a view to implement flexicurity, the most important alteration in the TLS is the compensation that the employer is obliged to pay in the event of lay-offs of employees. Under the previous regulation, the employer's fiscal duties were quite extensive: the amount of compensation (2, 3 or 4 months' average wages) paid to employees depended on the length of work (e.g. less than five years, 5-10 years; more than 10 years) (TLS section 90(1) 1)).

The new TLS modifies the regulation concerning the employee's income protection. In comparison with the old rules, the TLS reduces the employer's responsibility and enlarges that of the state.[69] Under section 100(1) of the TLS, in the case of lay-offs of employees, the employer is obliged to pay compensation equivalent to the average monthly wage to the employee.

In addition to the compensation paid by the employer, the TLS establishes that upon the termination of an employment contract due to a

---

[67] See also ibid., 362 et seq.

[68] For greater detail, see ibid., 362-364.

[69] Similarly, in many other countries, the statutory law usually does not provide a duty to pay compensation to the employee when the employer terminates the employment contract, or the amount of the allowance is not remarkable. Muda, M. 2009. "Increasing the Flexibility of Employment Regulation in Estonia," in *The Modernization of Labour Law and Industrial Relations in a Comparative Perspective*, ed. Blanpain, R., *Bulletin of Comparative Labour Relations*, No 70. The Hague: Kluwer Law International, 374 and Muda, M. 2010. "Estonian Labour Law Reform: The Successful Implementation of the Idea of Flexicurity?" *IJCLLIR* 26, No. 3:365.

lay-off, an employee has the right to receive an insurance benefit (section 100(2)).[70] However, unlike previous regulations, the total amount of compensation[71] has been reduced to one month's salary. In order to somehow make up for this disadvantage, the TLS has increased the amount of unemployment benefit (section 178 (10)).

The author of this article holds that the reduction of the employees' rights and employers' duties in the manner provided in the TLS is reasonable. By enlarging the state responsibility, the TLS introduces greater flexibility in the termination of employment by the employer.[72] However, the implementation of the idea of flexicurity is not successful because the enforcement of section 178 (10) of the TLS that strengthens the employee's protection in the case of unemployment has been postponed.[73]

5. Concluding Remarks

The new Estonian TLS builds on the concept of flexicurity. It has been argued that in the past, the recourse to the concept of flexicurity as the main ideological framework for the TLS was hasty and occasional. During the elaboration of the TLS, the European Commission issued the Green Paper on modernising labour law. This document was a source of inspiration for drafters of TLS as they made use of that notion of flexicurity as the basis for the Act. In order to justify the adoption of the new draft, it was stressed that the need to implement flexicurity was a matter of urgency.

In Estonia, the content of flexicurity corresponds to the concept approved in the EU. The components of flexicurity match almost perfectly with the definition provided by the EU, even though its implementation

[70] Thus, the TLS establishes a new type of benefit: insurance benefit upon lay-off which is paid under the conditions and pursuant to the procedure provided for in the Unemployment Insurance Act. *Töötuskindlustuse seadus* / Unemployment Insurance Act, passed on 13 June 2001—RT I 2001, 59, 359; 03.03.2011, 2. The Act is available in English at http://www.legaltext.ee/text/en/X50053K7.htm, (accessed November 1, 2011).

[71] That is the compensation paid by the employer plus the benefit upon lay-off.

[72] Muda, M. 2009. "Increasing the Flexibility of Employment Regulation in Estonia," in *The Modernization of Labour Law and Industrial Relations in a Comparative Perspective*, ed. Blanpain, R., *Bulletin of Comparative Labour Relations*, No 70. The Hague: Kluwer Law International, 375.

[73] The enforcement has been postponed until 1 January 2013 because of the economic crisis.

has not been thought out in the framework of Estonian labour law reform. In fact, it is not clear which measures must be used in order to strike a balance between flexibility and security in the TLS.

The new TLS contains a considerable amount of reforms. Most of amendments in the new Act have been made, first and foremost, in view of satisfying practical needs that have arisen in relations between the parties to the employment contract, as well as considering the concept of flexicurity.

In comparison with the previous regulation, rules on entering into employment contracts are not clear. Also, the termination of fixed-term employment contracts for economic reasons at the initiative of the employer is very complex. Thus, relevant provisions included in the TLS are neither flexible nor in line with the idea of flexicurity.

The implementation of the concept of flexicurity has impacted the regulation of compensation so that the employer is required to pay an employee in the event of lay-off. The TLS reduces the employer's fiscal obligations and increases the role of the state while guaranteeing protection for the unemployed. But as the enforcement of the norms concerning the responsibility of state has been postponed, the implementation of flexicurity cannot be regarded as successful.

References

Council of the European Union. 2007. *Towards Common Principles of Flexicurity. Draft Council Conclusions*. Brussels: Council of the European Union.

Hasselbalch, O. 2005. *Labour Law in Denmark*. The Hague: Kluwer Law International; Copenhagen: DJØF Publishing.

Jørgensen, H., and P. K. Madsen. 2007. "Flexicurity and Beyond—Reflections on the Nature and Future of a Political Celebrity," in *Flexicurity and Beyond. Finding a New Agenda for the European Social Model*, eds. Jørgensen, H., and P. K. Madsen. Copenhagen: DJØF Publishing.

Käärats, E., S. Suder, and T. Treier. 2011. *Selgitused töölepingu seaduse juurde/Comments on the Employment Contracts Act*. Tallinn: Sotsiaalministeerium/Ministry of Social Affairs.

Madsen, P. K. 2007. "Flexicurity—Towards a Set of Common Principles?" *IJCLLIR* 23, No. 4.

Muda, M. 1996. "Improving Estonian Labour Legislation on Integration with Europe," *Juridica International, Law Review*. Tartu: University of Tartu, No. 1.

—. 2004. "Impact of the European Community Labour Law on Estonian Labour Legislation," *Labour Law in United Europe. m. spalio 16-18 d. Tarptautinės mokslinės konferencijos medžiaga*, Vilnius.

—. 2006. "Termination of Employment Relationships: Legal Situation in Estonia," in *Termination of Employment Relationships: Legal Situation in the Member States of the European Union*. Brussels: European Commission.

—. 2008. "Eesti töösuhete regulatsioon vajab uuendamist/ Estonian Employment Regulations Need to be Renewed," *Riigikogu Toimetised*, 17.

—. 2009. "Estonia", in *The Laval and Viking Cases. Freedom of Services and Establishment v. Industrial Conflicts in the European Union*, eds. Blanpain, R., and A. M. Świątkowski, *Bulletin of Comparative Labour Relations*, No. 69. The Hague: Kluwer Law International.

—. 2009. "Fixed-term Employment Contract as a Basis for Creating Flexible Labour Relation," in *Studia z zakresu prawa pracy i polityki spolecznej/Studies on Labour Law and Social Policy. Liber Amicorum* Prof. A. M. Świątkowski, Krakow: Musica Iagellonica sp. z.o.o.

—. 2009. "Increasing the Flexibility of Employment Regulation in Estonia," in *The Modernization of Labour Law and Industrial Relations in a Comparative Perspective*, ed. Blanpain, R., *Bulletin of Comparative Labour Relations*, No 70. The Hague: Kluwer Law International.

—. 2010. "Estonian Labour Law Reform: The Successful Implementation of the Idea of Flexicurity?" *IJCLLIR* 26, No. 3.

—. 2010. "Implementation of the Idea of Flexicurity: the Case of Estonia," *GCOE Newsletter*, No. 5, Tokyo: Tokyo University.

Orgo, I.-M. 1996. "Labour Law Reform in Re-independent Estonia," *Juridica International, Law Review,* Tartu: University of Tartu, No. 1.

Weiss, M., and M. Schmidt. 2008. *Labour Law and Industrial Relations in Germany*. Zuidpoolsingel: Kluwer Law International.

FLEXICURITY—
WHERE DOES FLEXIBILITY OF LABOUR RELATIONS END AND SOCIAL SECURITY BEGIN? THE CASE OF ESTONIA

GAABRIEL TAVITS

1. Introduction

At present, discussions about flexicurity are modest. Although the European Union has published a series of documents on flexicurity and modernisation of labour law, the question about the limits of flexibilisation of labour relations and the intensity of social security remains open. There are a number of Member States where the level of flexibilisation of labour relations is quite high, but at the same time the necessary social security is inadequate or missing. A case in point is Estonia, which is characterised by a maximum level of flexibilisation in labour relations, and a modest level of social security. One can say that the long-term policy of the Government of the Republic of Estonia has been to hold the level of social benefits as low as possible in order to encourage and create incentive for the population to enter the labour market.

Here, a question can be raised as to whether there are or should be any connections between labour law and social security law. At first sight, it is difficult to find any relationships of this kind, as these are different fields of law—the former is part of private law, the latter falls within the sphere of public law. Social security law does not guarantee flexible employment conditions, but it could partly help to finance "flexible labour conditions" or cover, at least partly, the costs of the termination of the employment relations (e.g. payments of compensation in case of redundancies). On the basis of these considerations, this paper will discuss some problematic aspects of applying *flexicurity* in Estonia.

2. The Idea of Flexicurity

As already known, the concept of flexicurity consists of four parts: flexibilisation of labour relations, intensive social security protection for those who have lost their job, lifelong learning and active labour market measures for the unemployed. In order to guarantee the realisation of the idea of flexicurity, it is desirable that all four components exist. There is a considerable amount of research and literature on the topic of flexicurity,[1] but in the same vein one should say that there is no concrete idea or plan of action of how this system should function and be implemented in the European Member States. It has been stated that Denmark is an example state with regard to implementing flexicurity. Here the idea of flexicurity is one of the best developed,[2] and it is unclear if there are any other states[3] that can be identified as holding a similar exemplary model of flexicurity.

Although the principle has been clarified and described in many ways, uncertainty still exits. Nobody is able to give a solution of how to introduce and to develop the concept of flexicurity.

As it has been described in literature: "the core of the flexicurity idea is that security is a precondition for flexibility, and flexibility is a precondition for security". It has also been noted that much depends on if and how Member States take up the flexicurity ideas (if at all), the content of the policies and regulations they implement and the effects these measures have.[4] As already stated, the concept of flexicurity consists of four main parts:

- flexible and reliable contractual arrangements;
- efficient active labour market policies to strengthen transition security;

[1] e.g. Hendrickx, F., S. Bekker, and R. Blanpain, eds. 2008. *Flexicurity and the Lisbon Agenda: a Cross-disciplinary Reflection.* Antwerp: Intersentia. Also important: Rojot, J. 2007. "Security of Employment and Employability," in *Collective Labour Law and Industrial Relations in Industrialized Market Economies,* ed. Blanpain, R., (The Hague: Kluwer Law International),439 - 461.

[2] Ilsǿe, A. 2008. "The Danish flexicurity model—a lesson for the US," in *Flexicurity and the Lisbon Agenda: a Cross-disciplinary Reflection*, eds. Hendrickx, F., S. Bekker, and R. Blanpain, (Antwerp: Intersentia), 65-99.

[3] In some cases it has been stated that also the Netherlands could be an example of flexicurity e.g. Wilthagen, T., and S. Bekker. 2008. "Flexicurity: is Europe right on track?" in *Flexicurity and the Lisbon Agenda: a Cross-disciplinary Reflection*, eds. Hendrickx, F., S. Bekker, and R. Blanpain, (Antwerp: Intersentia), 33-47.

[4] Ibid.

- systematic and responsive lifelong learning;
- modern social security provisions that also contribute to good mobility in the labour market.

These four components are the usual components of flexicurity, and sometimes a fifth element is also included, that is the development of supportive and productive social dialogue.[5]

As one can see, all these measures are mainly meant to promote flexibility in the labour market in that if a person changes the place of work, he or she could soon find a new occupation. It could also mean that the "*free movement of persons inside of the state*" will be encouraged. The fifth component is not only a part of flexicurity, but it is the necessary part of employment relations as such. Therefore, this aspect of flexicurity should be developed, notwithstanding whether there is a policy of flexicurity or not.

2.1 The Case of Estonia

Estonia wanted to introduce the idea of flexicurity via the reform of individual employment law. In this sense, preparations to reform Estonian individual employment law had already began in 2007. The idea was simple: to make the individual employment contract similar to other civil law contracts, to reduce the level of formalities (e.g. employment contract in written or in oral form) and the financial burden of the employer in case of redundancy as well as to avoid any application of the system of disciplinary punishments. Although the preparation of the new Employment Contracts Act started in 2007, only in 2008 did the reasoning for reform of individual employment law contain the idea of flexicurity and ideas from the Green Paper of the European Commission on modernisation of European labour law.

The Government of Estonia attempted to be one of the first EU Member States to introduce the concept of flexicurity. In the new draft of the ECA[6] some amendments in the system of protection of the unemployed were proposed, also the system of health insurance was reformed (health insurance for the registered unemployed). From this, it seemed that Estonia would apply the method of flexicurity in a consistent manner.

---

[5] Ibid.

[6] Employment Contract Act—Riigi Teataja I (State Gazette) 2009, 5, 35. English version available at: http://www.legaltext.ee.

Prior to the enforcement of the new ECA, social security reform ceased. In 2008, in the framework of the new ECA, the following changes in the unemployment insurance system were introduced: 1) the coverage of insured persons was widened (e.g. when an employee leaves the job of his or her free will, the unemployment insurance benefit would be granted), 2) and the amount of the benefit would increase. The system of unemployment insurance remained unchanged. In addition to this, the necessary costs of the active labour market policy and lifelong learning were diminished. Although it was clear in 2008 that there would be a lack of resources to ensure better unemployment insurance protection, the Government was of the opinion that it was better to stop the social security reform instead of stopping the flexibilisation of employment relations.[7]

3. What is Meant under Flexible Employment Conditions?

One of the most important aspects of the concept of flexicurity is the part of flexible employment conditions, although it is unclear whether it means that employment conditions are flexible. One should ask—flexible to whom? If the Member States are free to choose how they are going to implement the concept of flexicurity, it should be clear what kind of flexibility in employment conditions should be applied. If we are talking about the flexibilisation of employment conditions from the perspective of an employee, it should mean the flexibility of fulfilling employment tasks, e.g. home work, telework, part-time work, in order to strike a better balance between employment tasks and family life.[8] This is a very important aspect with regard to providing employees with a more flexible position.

In similar vein, it is also obvious that nobody will examine the notion of flexibility of labour relations in the sense of flexicurity from the perspective of an employee. In most cases, what is mentioned is that an employer should have better opportunities for flexible employment conditions in order to avoid dismissal of an employee and to guarantee the continuity of employment, or to make it easier to dismiss an employee. As a consequence, the idea of flexicurity is meant to protect an employer, to

---

[7] According to trade unions it was not possible to implement ECA 2008 without any changes in unemployment insurance. The changes in unemployment insurance have been postponed to 1 January 2013.

[8] See e.g for Germany: Deich, S., A. Genenger, K. Linde, and U. Preis. 2005. *Innovative Arbeitsformen: Flexibilisierung von Arbeitszeit, Arbeitsentgelt, Arbeitsorganisation.* Cologne: Otto Scmidt.

guarantee for the employer better opportunities to change employment conditions unilaterally and to dismiss an employee without any obstacles or, better yet, without any good reason. As a result, security is a tool provided to the employee to be protected against the flexibilisation of employment conditions.

3.1 The Case of Estonia

As stated in literature, the onus is on the Member States to decide how they will develop the idea of flexible employment conditions. Estonia has developed perhaps the most radical system of flexibilisation. Here, the previous Employment Contracts Act (hereinafter ECA 1992) provided intensive protection for employees' rights (the employment contract had to be concluded in written form, there was a fixed list of reasons for the conclusion of a fixed-term contract and exact rules in case of redundancies, especially on how to choose employees for dismissal). Complaints regarding the ECA 1992 included that it was too old, and did not take into account the needs of small and medium enterprises.

The ECA 2008 changed this state of affairs. There are now no direct instructions in the law on how the employment relationship should be formed. The employer is empowered with the right to decide whether working conditions are reasonable and consider the interests of both parties. For instance, an employer is free to order an employee to conduct additional work, as long as this is done reasonably and takes into account the interests of both sides. This last point remains unclear as in day-to-day practice the employer will order additional work and the employee has to follow the employer's order.

According to the ECA 2008, it is the employers' obligation to arrange working time and—whereas necessary—they can change relevant system and rules unilaterally. There is no obligation to inform the employee about the changes in working time before the changes take effect. The mandatory information and consultation system will be applied only if the number of employees is higher than 30. One could argue that working time is an obligatory part of the employment contract and it should be agreed upon in the employment contract. In the ECA 2008 this is not the case. According to Art. No. 5 ECA 2008, an employer can make a unilateral written statement where the employment conditions are laid down and, if there is no written employment contract, the employer has to inform the employee in writing about the employment conditions. It should be done before the employee starts work. Otherwise, it could also be done at a later stage, but only upon request of the employee. This means that it is possible for an employee to be unaware of the working time system that will be used (part-time or full-time, if there are any shifts, or how many hours the shifts will last).

Although one can see that there is flexibility in organising working time, this kind of flexibility brings about more uncertainty in labour relations. An unawareness of the number of hours to be worked and the relevant remuneration will result in a source of confusion for the employee, particularly in terms of work-life balance.

This situation raises the question as to whether or not there are some limits to flexibilisation. There are no concrete answers to the question. It is argued, however, that labour law is the field of law that should protect employees against the mistreatment of the employers. If one analyses the concept of flexicurity, then it is obvious that the limits of flexibility will be established by the Member States. This means that throughout the EU Member States the level of flexibility will be different and employment conditions will vary, as well as employees' forms of protection. To the extent that the employment relationship becomes like any other relationship based on mutual consent without any additional special safeguards.

Of course, this concept needs further clarification. According to what has been laid down by the European Union, flexible employment conditions should mean flexibility in a broader sense. This involves different innovative forms of employment such as telework, part-time work, and so on. As it is the responsibility of the Member States to introduce the concept of flexicurity, it is up to them how the flexibility of labour relations will be introduced and to what extent it will be applied.

According to the OECD index, the protective measures in Estonian labour regulation were quite high. Research conducted by the Estonian Employers Association has revealed that the flexibility of labour relations is not very high. It is not common to use part-time work and telework is not widespread. It was also mentioned that administrative obligations were too high (e.g. it was necessary to agree on the internal rules of work with the labour inspectorate, to obtain consent before dismissing the employees' representative or a pregnant worker, and to formulate the termination of employment contract in written form). All those aspects were seen as disturbing in view of guaranteeing normal flexible employment relations. Starting from 2008, that is when the new Employment Contracts Act was implemented, these rules were no longer applicable. One can say that, at least at the level of law, there is a certain level of flexibilisation of employment relations, but in practice both employers and employees are not quick to resort to using the new ways and methods that the ECA 2008 introduced.

In some ways, it could be viewed that employees have obtained new rights (too much flexibility), which can be questionable. An example here could be Art. No. 38 of ECA 2008. According to this rule, an employee can leave his or her place of work temporarily for personal reasons and the employer has an obligation to pay an average wage for a reasonable period of time. What is important in that case is the fact that an employer is not allowed to ask where the employee is going, but the employer has the right to decide if he or she will pay the average salary and for what period of time.

There is a negative side to the flexibility of employment conditions. For instance, one can argue that the level of protection of pregnant workers has diminished. According to ECA 1992, it was forbidden for an employer to dismiss a pregnant worker. Even if the employer did not know about the pregnancy, still the termination of an employment contract was null and void. ECA 2008 does not forbid the redundancy of a pregnant worker, who is obliged to be mindful of her own protection against dismissal. Pursuant to Art. No. 93 of ECA 2008, a pregnant worker is protected only in case she presents a medical certificate within 14 days of receiving notification of dismissal. If this is not the case, the redundancy is regarded as legal. There are some doubts about whether such regulation is in conformity with the European and international standards of protection of maternity, but so far the Government has not been in a hurry to change the legislation.

4. How Social Security Assists the Flexibility of Employment Relations

At a certain stage, the concept of flexicurity involves the system of social security. Its main task is to help the unemployed survive during the period of unemployment or changing jobs. The social security system should diminish the risks of poverty in case of unemployment. When examining flexibility of employment conditions, there are two aspects that are significant: the existence of social protection of unemployed persons (social assistance or unemployment insurance benefits schemes) and health insurance for unemployed persons. Another important aspect is also employment services offered by the state, and it is up to the Member States to decide how to construct the unemployment protection system. In some cases, the protection of the unemployed involves active measures for unemployed persons, even though social security schemes are laid down only when passive measures are involved.

4.1 The Case of Estonia

In Estonia there are two types of schemes for the unemployed. On the one hand, there is the State guaranteed system of services and benefits regulated by the Labour Market Services and Benefits Act.[9] According to this Act, the Estonian unemployment insurance fund is responsible for guaranteeing different services and benefits for persons who are registered as unemployed, e.g. finding a new job, organising training courses in order to get additional skills and knowledge, and so on. The Estonian unemployment insurance fund is also responsible for granting state-financed benefits: unemployment assistance, financial support for unemployed persons in order to start their own economic activity, and financial support for employers to employ unemployed persons who belong to the group of persons whose opportunities to find new employment are limited, e.g. long-term unemployed persons (more than one year, young persons in the 16 to 24 age group, ex-offenders).

A person can also be registered to the unemployment insurance fund as a job-seeker, although for them there is a limited number of services available, particularly regarding information about vacancies.

The other scheme for the unemployed concerns the unemployment insurance benefits, that is usually paid if the following conditions are met:

1) there should be a certain insurance period, at least 12 months during the last 36 months. The insurance period will be calculated on the basis of unemployment insurance contributions;

2) there is no entitlement to compensation if the employment contract was terminated at the initiative of the employee (except when the reason was the breach of contract on the part of the employer), if the employment contract was terminated by mutual consent, or if the employment contract was terminated at the initiative of the employer because of the behaviour of the employee (breach of contractual obligations).

Unemployment insurance benefits amount to 100% of the employee's previous earnings. From day 101 to the 360th calendar day, the amount is reduced to 50% of the previous earnings.[10]Although both systems have

---

[9] Labour Market Services and Benefits Act—RT I 2005, 54, 430, English version available at: http://www.legaltext.ee.

[10] At the moment it is not possible to get unemployment benefits for the maximum period of 360 calendar days. The maximum amount of unemployment insurance

functioned for many years, some problems persist. The state-guaranteed unemployed protection is insufficient, particularly in educational terms, as there are not enough resources to implement educational programmes and to develop active labour market initiatives.[11] A recent survey carried out by practitioners and experts in the field has shown that three aspects of flexicurity are missing in Estonia: there is a low level of active labour market initiatives, a low level of social benefits for unemployed persons and an inefficient system of promoting and guaranteeing lifelong learning.[12]

5. Conclusions

As the situation in Estonia shows, the idea of flexicurity is misunderstood, with flexicurity that could be misused in order to introduce flexible employment conditions. Estonia has implemented only one component of flexicurity—flexible labour relations. Undoubtedly, the concept of flexicurity could be used for any reform of labour relations, but nobody resorts to the notion of flexicurity for amendments in social security law, causing the social security system to remain unchanged.

References

Deich, S., A. Genenger, K. Linde, and U. Preis. 2005. *Innovative Arbeitsformen: Flexibilisierung von Arbeitszeit, Arbeitsentgelt, Arbeitsorganisation.* Cologne: Otto Scmidt.

Hendrickx, F., S. Bekker, and R. Blanpain, eds. 2008. *Flexicurity and the Lisbon Agenda: a Cross-disciplinary Reflection.* Antwerp: Intersentia.

Rojot, J. 2007. "Security of Employment and Employability," in *Collective Labour Law and Industrial Relations in Industrialized Market Economies,* ed. Blanpain, R., (The Hague: Kluwer Law International).

---

benefit will be granted to the unemployed persons who have an insurance period of more than ten years. As the unemployment insurance scheme was introduced only in 2002, the insurance period can be maximum eight years.

[11] Turvaline paindlikkus Eestis:hetkeolukord ja arenguperspektiivid (Flexicurity in Estonia; the situation today and future developments) Tallinn, Tartu 2010, available at: http://www.eakl.ee/?&pid=470&lang=5 (accessed November 7, 2011).

[12] Turvaline paindlikkus Eestis:hetkeolukord ja arenguperspektiivid (Flexicurity in Estoni; situation today and future developments) Tallinn, Tartu 2010, available at: http://www.eakl.ee/?&pid=470&lang=5 (accessed November 7, 2011).

FLEXIBILITY AND SECURITY IN THE 21ST CENTURY LABOUR MARKET: CURRENT TRENDS IN LATVIA

KRISTĪNE DUPATE

1. Introduction

The aim of this paper is to analyse flexicurity in the Latvian context, providing general statistical figures relevant to the future of the Latvian economy, discussing the decisions taken by the Latvian legislator on account of the economic crisis and investigating the short and long-term consequences of such decisions. Finally, some proposals for moving towards flexicurity will be offered.

2. The Statistics: The Overall Situation

Generally speaking, official statistics show a demographic trend that is similar to other European countries. The demographic situation is worsening; on average, there were 2.3 million inhabitants in Latvia over the last 20 years. However, the population is shrinking year after year. The primary reason for this is the decreasing birth rate. At the end of the 1980s, there were 40,000 births per year, but by 1995 this number dropped to 20,000 births per year. Since then, there have been no considerable changes, with the situation worsening in 2010, as only 19,000 births were reported. The question that arises, is what this mean for Latvia. It has been observed that in general, the birth rate is negative, as each year there are more deaths than births. Numerically, this is around—0.35% or around—10,000 persons annually.[1]

[1] In 2009, this demographic rate was equal to -0.37%; in 2008, it was equal to -0.31%. In 2010, a negative rate of -10,750 was reported (deaths -29,970, newborns: 19,220). In total, taking into account birth and emigration rates, the figures were as follows: in 2008, -9600 persons; in 2009 -12,920 persons. http://data.csb.gov.lv/Dialog/Saveshow.asp

The second reason is emigration. No one has statistics on the real numbers of emigration. Officially, it has been estimated that 30,000 people have left the country to settle permanently in another. Unofficially, there are 200,000 persons in total who left for the West. The biggest wave of emigration to the West started when Latvia received the EU membership, also in consideration of the right to free labour movement in Europe. At the same time, and according to official data, immigration rates to Latvia is five times lower than emigration rates.[2] In addition, the economic crisis has had a negative effect on the Latvian economy. The unemployment rate was considerably affected by the crisis: from around 7% before the crisis, it increased to 20% during the crisis and it is currently around 14%. In 2009, there were 986,700 employed persons in the 15-74 age group and 473,300 recipients of old-age pension (+ 17,300 with respect to the previous year).

All these factors have led to the situation where employed persons have to bear a considerable burden in meeting the needs of the social security budget, mostly on account of old-age pensions. The table of expenses for social security purposes looks as follows:

Table 1-5. Total Expenses for Social Security Purposes[3] (in EUR)

	2008	2009
Retirement	1 246 008 845	1 398 270 357
Unemployment	117 073 893	293 140 050
Child-care/family	318 538 312	322 920 757

3. Government and Parliament Responses to the Crisis

What have the Government and the parliament done to ease this burden? On 16 June 2009, the Parliament adopted the Law on Payment of retirement pensions and allowances for the period 2009-2012,[4] that was enacted on 1 July 2009 in response to the crisis. It envisaged the following restrictions with regard to the amount of retirement pensions and benefits:

---

[2] Officially, in 2010, 10,107 persons emigrated from Latvia but only 1974 immigrated.

[3] According to ESSPOS classification, www.csb.gov.lv.

[4] OG No.100, 30 June 2009.

1) retirement[5] pensions—unemployed recipients of retirement pension are entitled to 90% of the pension, but those employed are only granted 30% of the pension;
2) A family allowance for each child—LVL 8 (EUR 11.4) monthly.[6]

Furthermore, on 1 December 2009 (enacted from 1 January 2010) the Parliament amended the said laws by imposing the following restrictions:[7]

1) child care allowance—parents of children born after 2 May 2010 are not entitled to such allowance if they remain in active employment;
2) child care, sickness, maternity, paternity allowances—paid in full up to EUR 16.3 daily, and in amount of 50% for incomes above LVL 11.51.

In addition, during 2009 and 2010 the Parliament made amendments to the State Funded Pension Law envisaging the reduction of part of social insurance contributions for old age risk transferred to the second-tier retirement insurance—to state-funded private retirement schemes.[8]

Finally, the amount of social insurance contributions was raised from 33.09% to 35.09% of gross income of an employee (24.09% paid by an employer and 11% paid by an employee).[9]

In addition to changes in social security, the Parliament adopted the decision to increase income tax[10] and statutory minimum wage.[11]

As these changes were made, there were no amendments to labour law with regard to employment conditions, which are currently very demanding for employers and do not allow for more flexible working arrangements.

---

[5] Retirement pension in the public sector is granted to certain categories of officials and public servants before statutory retirement age which, since 2008, is 62 years old.

[6] Instead of two times higher (2 x LVL 8) for the second child, and three times higher (3 x LVL 8) for the third and the following children, as provided by Art. No. 15(3) of the Law on State Social Allowances, OG No.168, 19 November 2002.

[7] OG No.200, 21 December 2009

[8] The State Funded Pension Law, OG No.78/87, 8 March 2000, as amended until 2010, OG No.206, 30 December 2010.

[9] Art. No. 18(1) of the Law on Statutory Insurance, OG No.274/276, 21 October 1997, respective amendments - OG No.205, 29 December 2010.

[10] The Law in Income Tax, OG No.32, 1 July 1993, respective amendments OG No.200, 21 December 2009.

[11] Regulation of the Cabinet of Ministers No.1096 "On statutory minimum monthly salary and minimum hourly rate", OG No.193, 7 December 2010.

4. Consequences

4.1 Social Security

After the aforementioned steps were taken by the Parliament, the Constitutional Court of Latvia was overloaded with constitutional claims. The claims were predominantly on the constitutionality of the cuts on of retirement pensions. On 21 December 2009, the Constitutional Court took its first decision declaring that norms on the cuts of retirement pensions were unconstitutional.[12]

The cut of allowances was contested only as far as it concerned the legal certainty in the cut of child care allowances for parents in active employment.[13]

This resulted in a situation where the state budget had to bear the full burden with regard to pensions, while the rights of the working population, including parents of infants decreased considerably. In particular, the amount of sick, maternity, paternity and child care allowance does not constitute the amount of real earnings, as it did before. Parents on child care leave are prevented from combining this leave with part-time employment.

The short-term effects of this state of affairs are as follows: persons on sick, maternity, paternity or child-care leave may lose a considerable part of their previous income, which would considerably affect the standard of living of their families, because an average income in Latvia only ensures daily needs, it does not allow for savings.

The long-term consequences are even more considerable. Partial protection during sickness, maternity, paternity and child care leave causes several crucial long-term negative effects. Firstly, it does not stimulate legal employment,[14] because social insurance contributions are high, while protection in case social risks occur is low. Secondly, it does not act in favour of the birth rate increase, as statistics show that the birth rate is

---

[12] Decision in case No. 2009-43-01, respective norms are incompatible with Art. No. 109 of the Constitution providing the right to social security, in particular the legislator has not chosen the least restrictive means to attain a legitimate aim—cut of budget expenses in the interests of a whole society; the decision in available in English at: http://www.satv.tiesa.gov.lv/upload/judg__2009_43_01.htm, and related cases No. 2009-76-01; 2009-88-01.

[13] Before respective legislative steps, parents were allowed to remain in active employment and receive child-care allowance.

[14] Illegal employment is unofficially estimated around 20% to 30% of employed persons.

decreasing in spite of the fact that during the current years a significant number of people have attained the age of fertility.[15] Sociological research confirms that the birth rate is affected by a decrease in family allowances. Both considerations result in lower income to the social insurance budget, currently due to illegal employment and, in the long term, to the ageing population.

Negative consequences are caused by the total ban in the social insurance system on combining working and personal life, in particular, prohibition to combine sick and child care leave with at least part-time employment. In reality, combining child-care leave or long-term (child)[16] sickness leave with part-time employment arrangements becomes increasingly possible with the development of communication technologies, as a person is not forced to leave home in order to perform work duties. Furthermore, parents on child-care leave without the possibility to remain in active employment for one year, risk losing both their job and their skills. The same applies to persons on sick leave. Alongside this, one should take into account that in 2010 labour law was amended by a provision allowing dismissal of an employee on account of long-term sick leave.[17] Such a system causes a greater burden on the social budget because of the obligation to pay child care and sickness allowances in full, at the same time it prevents income to the budget from part-time employment. In the long term, such a system may result in higher expenditure on unemployment allowances due to the exclusion of the said group of persons from the labour market.

The problem is also gender sensitive, as the majority of persons on child- care leave are women, and those using the right to sick leave on account of child's sickness are predominantly mothers.[18] In general, the latter right disadvantages women with small children in the labour market.

One more decision has been and still is sharply criticised. It is the decision concerning the reduction of a share from statutory pension contributions which are to be transferred to state funded private insurance

---

[15] Persons born at the end of the 1980s and the beginning of the 1990s when the birth rate (around 40,000 births annually) was almost twice higher than in the last 17 years (around 20,000 births annually).

[16] Right to sick leave (for maximum 3 weeks) on account of child's sickness up to the age of 14 years old.

[17] Amendments to the Labour Law, OG No.47, 24 March 2010, Art. No. 101(1)(11) provide that an employee may be dismissed on account of sick leave lasting at least 6 consecutive months or in total 1 year within the period of 3 years.

[18] Art. No. 11(5) of the Law on Maternity and Sickness Insurance, OG No.m182, 23 November 1995, as amended until 2010, OG No.m201, 21 December 2010.

schemes.[19] As pointed out by many financial experts, in the long term there is a risk of depriving the persons who are currently 30 to 50 years old of any reasonable income after the attainment of retirement age.

To summarise, the current social security law creates an enormous burden on the budget on account of retirement pensions. Rather than stimulating, it even prevents the improvement of the situation by excluding the working population from active employment and, in the long term, by hindering the increase of the birth rate.

Although such regulation is formally temporary, nothing testifies to the possibility of returning to the old system at the moment. It is more likely that the crisis model will become permanent because of the overall demographic and economic situation.

It follows that the social security system is inflexible, thus working neither in favour of individuals nor in favour of society at large.

4.2 Labour Law

Labour law[20] does not stimulate flexible forms of employment. Temporary employment is allowed only for certain types of work or a few kinds of situations strictly defined by law. There is no special regulation for on-call work, telework, or temporary agency work. This means that for these forms of work, general employment conditions apply. Flexible working arrangements are not widespread in Latvia, and the law does not encourage it, either. Instead, it creates obstacles for both employers and employees to perform work under flexible forms of employment.

A fact testifying to scarcely developed flexible work arrangements is that in 2009 only 8.8% of employed persons worked on a part-time basis.

4.3 Costs on the Labour Force

In addition to inflexible legal regulations in the field of social security and labour law, there are some decisions of the legislator that have resulted in an increase of labour costs. There has been an increase in the minimum statutory salary, income tax and social insurance contributions.

There are no exact statistics in this connection, but many employers have not been able to bear the increase in labour costs during the economic crisis. Consequently, increased labour costs may offer three choices for the

---

[19] The State Funded Pension Law, OG No.78/87, 8 March 2000, as amended until 2010, OG No.206, 30 December 2010.

[20] OG No. 105, 06 July 2001, as amended until 2010, OG No. 47, 24 March 2010.

employer: dismissals, illegal employment or insolvency of a business. Many unofficial stories testify that in a situation like this, employers opt for illegal employment rather than bankruptcy.

As a result, the direction chosen by the legislator and the Government is not the correct one, taking into account the demographic and economic situation in Latvia and global trends.

5. Propositions

By way of remedial action, there are several proposals in the field of social security and labour law that should be taken into consideration:

1) full compensation of income lost due to child care leave, which will stimulate an increase in the birth rate;
2) the possibility to combine sick leave (especially sick child care leave) and child care leave with part-time employment, which will, firstly, allow for more effective work-life balance and, secondly, will diminish the expenses of the social security budget and allow for extra income;
3) temporary and proportionate cuts of retirement pensions, which will allow the provision of child care allowance in full (full previous income from work);
4) adoption of legal regulations on flexible forms of work, which will stimulate legal employment.

THE REVIEW OF THE EU WORKING TIME DIRECTIVE: MEDIATING FLEXIBILITY AND SECURITY. THE DIALOGUE OF THE EUROPEAN LEGISLATOR, THE ECJ AND THE SOCIAL PARTNERS

CECIEL RAYER

1. Introduction

At present, within the EU and at EU level, the debate on labour law and employment policy has its focus on the economic need of enterprises for flexibility in the work organisation, on the one hand, and its consequences for the workers' security, on the other hand. For example, the EU Green Paper on labour law of 2006 states that European labour markets face the challenge of combining greater flexibility with the need to maximise security for all.[1] The flexible work organisation is expected both by EU policymakers and national governments to be successful in the perspective of competitiveness. It is hoped that this subsequently will lead to stable or higher employment rates and heightened welfare.

With regard to the flexibility and security debate about reviewing the present Directive 2003/88/EC on working time, "on-call work", the exclusions and opt out from the maximum weekly working time, and, to a lesser extent, the related aspect of work-life balance are key legislative issues that have arisen. Over the past years, this debate has unfolded as a "dialogue" between the European legislator, the ECJ and the (European) social partners, and contrasting views as regards the aim of worker protection and the employers' need for working time flexibility have come to the fore. Nevertheless, at the end of 2010, the European Commission

---

[1] European Commission. 2006. *Modernising Labour Law to Meet the Challenges of the 21st Century, COM(2006) 708 final.* Brussels: European Commission.

consulted the social partners at EU level in the second round of consultation in order to readdress negotiations on the draft Working Time Directive. The aim is to establish a new Directive, based on a social partners' agreement, which like the present one ensures minimum protection, whilst providing for flexibility "to cope with particular circumstances of countries, sectors and workers". The Commission considered several developments to justify reason for the review. In its communication about the first phase consultation of the social partners from 2010,[2] it points out that the development of the knowledge-based economy, and the autonomy that "knowledge"-workers have with regard to the organisation and location of their work might be a reason to reconsider the application of the provisions of the Directive with regard to these workers. On the other hand, the group of workers that do repetitive work experience strain and stress, especially where there is a shortage of workers. For all workers it holds that working more hours is attractive from the point of view of their income. Within undertakings working time management has become more important. For instance, the costs and adjustment to the demand lead, in the service sector to extended production time and for other sectors to another spread of the production time. Flexible schedules and shifts are utilised in this respect. Optimistically, the Commission then states the benefits of these developments. Flexible working time might also be to the advantage of the workers who wish to combine their work with their private life and for weaker groups in the labour market who would like to increase their opportunities for work and career. The primary aim of the envisaged new Working Time Directive would still contain the protection of health and safety of workers. However, according to the Commission, in light of the developments, other aims should be considered as well. Working time flexibility seems to be expressed as a possible second goal and perhaps the improvement of work-life balance could be a third one.

However, despite the Commission's intentions, so far the contrasting views of the European social partners have resulted in a deadlock on the review. A common position has not been found yet, in particular on the important legislative matters of on-call work, the individual opt out and—

---

[2] European Commission. 2010. *Communication from the Commission to the European Parliament, The Council, The European Economic and Social Committee and the Committee of the Regions, Reviewing the Working Time Directive, COM(2010), (First-phase Consultation of the Social Partners at European Level under Article 154 of the TFEU), 106 final.* Brussels: European Commission.

in the Commission communication somewhat suppositious—the matter of work-life balance.

In this paper the question that will be addressed is whether the dialogue over the past few years has only resulted in opposite points of view on different aspects of the regulation of flexible working time.[3] This paper argues for the contrary: based upon a close examination of the dialogue between the EU legislator, the ECJ and the social partners—at European and decentralised level—legal solutions for the impasse can be drawn from the interim outcomes of the dialogue between the various actors at different levels. Further, it will be argued that some issues about working time flexibility and protection as it is currently regulated are not fully explored in the dialogue between the actors yet. Certain aspects of protection in the provisions of Directive 2003/88/EC are still open to interpretation by the ECJ.

First, this paper presents an overview of the current EU working time Directive from 2003 considering aspects on security and flexibility. Secondly, the dialogue between the European legislator, the ECJ and the social partners at European and decentralised levels on such aspects of the Working Time Directive will be scrutinised. The research will show that the different actors take different positions towards the related flexibility-security nexus and each utilise distinctive legal techniques in order to achieve aims of protection and/or flexibility on the topics of on-call work, the opt out and work-life balance. Thirdly, whether certain legal outcomes of the dialogue would suit the goals of security and flexibility sustained in the new draft Directive on working time and could serve as solutions for the current legislative impasse will be tested.

2. Security and Flexibility in Directive 2003/88 on Working Time and its Review

In 1993, the first general EU Directive on Working Time was enacted. Its, contested,[4] legal base was Art. No. 118a EC on health and safety (now

---

[3] The theme of annual leave will be left out here. The focus is on the utilisation of flexible working time in a strict sense of the word.

[4] ECJ Case C-84/94 United Kingdom / Council OJ 1994 C 120/13. See Gray, M. 1998. "A Recalcitrant Partner: The UK Reaction to the Working Time Directive," in *Yearbook of European Law 1997*, eds. Barav A., and D.A. Wyatt, (Oxford: Clarendon Press), 323-362; and Barnard, C. 1997. "The Judgment of the ECJ in United Kingdom v Council: The Working Time Directive," in CELS Occasional Paper No. 2; Dashwood, A. A. 1997. "The Working Time Judgment in a Wider

Art. No. 153 TFEU). The goals of the latter were to provide minimum standards for the protection of the health and safety of the worker in relation to working time. Subsequently, in 2003, the Directive was amended in order to give a clear overview of the interim amendments of the 1993 Directive[5], which were to adjust the provisions to the need for flexible working time arrangements. Consequently, Directive 2003/88/EC was enacted. With reference to the organisation of working time in an undertaking, its expressed aim is to ensure a better level of protection of the health and safety of the worker in the work environment (Art. No. 1 par. 1 Directive 2003/88/EC). Central to this aim is the general principle of "humanisation of work": adapting the work to the worker (Art. No. 13 Directive 2003/88/EC), the limits of the daily, weekly (48 hours) and annual hours worked, for night work, and the entitlements to rest periods and annual leave. However, security aspects are crucial to enhance flexibility in the working time in undertakings. Recital 15 of the Directives' Preamble states that it is

> desirable to provide for flexibility in the application of certain provisions of this Directive, whilst ensuring compliance with the principles of protecting the safety and health of workers.

Flexibility is incorporated in the Directive via the following legal techniques:

- the use of reference periods, allowing for surpassing the maxima at the short term, provided that the extra hours will be compensated within the given reference period (Art. No. 16);
- exclusions or derogations of the key provisions of the directive for unmeasured or predetermined working time of certain type of workers (Art. No. 17 par 1 Directive 2003/88/EC, Art. No. 20 and 21[6]), for certain work, workers or sectors (Art. No. 17 par 3-5 and Art. No. 19 Directive 2003/88/EC);

Perspective," in CELS Occasional Paper No. 2; and Hepple, B. A. "Commentary," in CELS Occasional Paper No. 2.

[5] European Commission. 2002. *Directive 2000/34/EC, Proposal for a Directive of the European Parliament and of the Council Concerning Certain Aspects of the Organisation of Working Time (Codified Version), COM(2002), 336 final.* Explanatory Memorandum. Brussels: European Commission, 2.

[6] Directive 1999/63/EC on the working time of sea farers.

- options to derogate from several provisions by collective agreements of the social partners at the appropriate level in the Member State (Art. No. 18 and 19 Directive 2003/88/EC);[7]
- the individual choice of opting out from the maximum working week of 48 hours (Art. No. 22 Directive 2003/88/EC).

Thus, the Directive seems to permit for ample working time flexibility strategies, whenever the national legislation or collective agreements authorise these strategies. The hazards inflicted upon the health and safety of workers are considered to be tolerable and adequately limited and—in reference to night work and health problems—countered by specific rights to health surveillance and to a transfer to day work, respectively, as laid down in chapter three of the Directive

Hereafter, in sections 3 to 5 the paper will explore the dialogue between the legislator and the ECJ leading to the debate on the review of Directive 2003/88/EC and the current debate. The focus will be on three related important legislative topics: on-call work, the derogations and individual opt out from the maximum working time, and the issue of the work-life balance.

3. On-call Work

In 2003, the ECJ defined in the Simap and Jaeger-judgments[8] on-call work as working time as meant in Directive 2003/88/EC. The Directive only gives the definition of "normal" working time: "any period during which the worker is working, at the employers' disposal and carrying out his activity or duties, in accordance with national laws and practice (Art. No. 2 par 1 Directive 2003/88/EC). Although the definition in the Directive refers to the national laws and practice, the definition of working

---

[7] The Directive further allows the MS extensive legislative derogation for several types of workers and activities with regard to the daily and weekly rest periods, annual leave, the maximum length of night work and, to a limited extent, with regard to the maximum reference periods (Art. No. 17 and 19). Derogation is also allowed by collective agreements at national or regional level, or, in conformity with the national or regional rules, at decentralised level. MS may lay down rules for derogation by collective agreement and for the extension of these agreements (Art. No. 18).

[8] ECJ 3 October 2000, case No. C-303/98 (Simap) (hereafter: Simap) and ECJ 3 September 2003, No. C-151/02 (Jaeger) (hereafter: Jaeger). See for an overview of the judgment: Nowak, T. 2008. "The Working Time Directive and the European Court of Justice," *MJ*, 447-471.

time is not left to these Member States. As it is a Community concept, it must be autonomously interpreted.[9]

Working time, as defined in the Directive, is posed opposite to rest period, defined as any period which is not working time (Art. No. 2 par. 2 Directive 2003/88/EC). These two are mutually exclusive notions.[10] On-call work as such is not defined in the Directive. According to the ECJ the Directive must be interpreted as meaning that on-call duty (*Bereitschaftsdienst*) performed by a worker where he/she is required to be physically present at the workplace must be regarded as constituting in its totality working time for the purposes of that directive. This holds even where the persons concerned is allowed to rest at their place of work during the periods when their services are not required. The ECJ reasons that workers on call are required to be present at the place determined by the employer and to be available to the employer in order to be able to provide their services immediately in case of need.

> (...) those obligations, which make it impossible for the doctors concerned to choose the place where they stay during waiting periods, must be regarded as coming within the ambit of the performance of their duties.
>
> (an employee, CR) on-call duty is subject to appreciably greater constraints since he has to remain apart from his family and social environment and has less freedom to manage the time during which his professional services are not required. Under those conditions an employee available at the place determined by the employer cannot be regarded as being at rest during the periods of his on-call duty when he is not actually carrying on any professional activity.[11]

The ECJ adds that "interpretation cannot be called in question by the objections based on economic and organisational consequences (...)".[12] Further, the ECJ states that derogation from the definitions of working time and rest period are not allowed for.[13] The judgment is that Directive 2003/88/EC precludes legislation of a Member State which classifies employee's periods of inactivity in the context of such on-call duty as rest periods.[14] The fact that the total amount of on-call time constitutes working time does not, however, preclude national laws or collective

---

[9] Par. 48 and 50 Simap and 58 Jaeger.

[10] Par. 47 Simap.

[11] Par. 63 Jaeger.

[12] Par. 66 Jaeger.

[13] Par. 91 Jaeger.

[14] Confirmed in; ECJ 1 December 2005, nr. C- 14/04 (Dellas).

agreements to differentiate between time actually worked or on-call time during which the worker is at rest with regard to the payment for the shift.[15] Therefore, differences in payment between active and inactive hours of the on-call service are permitted.

The "black and white" approach of the ECJ in sectors where use of on-call work is made led to problems. With on-call work, the limits of the weekly working time were now trespassed.[16] When the weekly working times were adjusted to the new way of counting hours when on-call, the workers would face a reduction in payment since they would make less (fully) paid hours. In the Netherlands and ten other Member States, the solution has been to fully count the on-call work as working time and to introduce the individual opt out of the maximum weekly working time.[17] In several other Member States, despite the Courts rulings, on-call work is still not fully treated as working time. This means non-compliance with the Directive. From the European Commission's report on the implementation of the Working Time Directive, it is now clear that 14 Member States and the employers call for a more flexible approach in the Directive towards the definition of working time in case of on-call work.[18] The European trade unions, however, do not accept that the implementation of the Simap-Jaeger judgments would suffer "insuperable obstacles" and are only prepared to seek a way out when the relevant definitions remain unchanged and the use of the opt out will be restricted.[19] They refer to the protection of the Directive as based on fundamental social rights that must be respected and built upon.

The contrasting views between the European social partners, however, obscure the fact that the problem of on-call work is not new at all. Since the first occurrence of on-call work, at a decentralised level in the Member States, the social partners have concluded provisions to regulate this form of employment, the calculation of active and inactive hours as working

---

[15] ECJ 11 January 2007, nr. C-437/05 (Vorel/ Ceský Krumlov).

[16] It causes problems with the minimum rest as well: European Commission. 2010. *Report from the Commission to the European Parliament, the Council, the European Economic and Social Committee and the Committee of the Regions on the implementation by Members States of Directive 2003/88/EC ("the Working Time Directive"), COM (2010) 802 final*. Brussels: European Commission, 2.

[17] Ibid., 4.

[18] Ibid., 8-9.

[19] European Commission. 2010. *Communication from the Commission to the European Parliament, the Council, the European Economic and Social Committee and the Committee of the Regions, Reviewing the Working Time Directive (Second-phase Consultation of the Social Partners at European Level under Article 154 TFEU)*. Brussels: European Commission, 4.

time and the payment for these active and inactive hours. Usually a fixed percentage of the on-call hours calculates as working time and the active and inactive hours are pro rata being paid for. Where the un-nuanced approach of the legislator and ECJ has caused the social partners to take diametrically opposed points of view, the actors at European level could learn from their own old school results of the social dialogue at sectoral level within the Member States. A proposal for a draft new Directive on working time could just like the 2005 proposal of the Commission[20] include "adding a shade of grey": a definition of on-call work, where the actual differentiation is left to the social partners at the appropriate level within the Member States. A point of reference would be to stipulate that all of the actively worked time on-call would count as working time.

4. Maximum Weekly Working Time, Derogations and Opt-out

In order to allow for flexibility in the application of certain provisions of the Directive 2003/88/EC, the Directive permits several types of derogations. First of all, Art. No. 17 declares derogation possible from the maximum weekly working time and minimum rest, the length of night work and the reference periods for the so-called unmeasured working time and for "autonomous" workers (Art. No. 17 par 1 Directive 2003/88/EC). The latter refers to workers who can determine their working time for themselves. Barnard, Deakin and Hobbs warned earlier that whenever flexibility in the Directive is restricted, the derogation of the unmeasured working time and/or the autonomous worker will be the next escape employers would want to utilise.[21] The European Commission now proposes to avoid abuse by specifying that this derogation only applies to senior managers and other workers with "genuine and effective autonomy over both the amount and the organisation of working time".[22] A remark here would be that the demarcation between dependant and autonomous workers is always a problem. The Commission's suggestion still leaves ample leeway for interpretation of specific cases at hand. The additional

---

[20] European Commission, 31 May 2005, COM(2005)246 final.

[21] Barnard, C., S. Deakin, and R. Hobbs. 2003. "Opting Out of the 48-hour Week: Employer Necessity or Individual Choice? An Empirical Study of the Operation of Art. No. 18(1)(B) of the Working Time Directive in the UK," *Industrial Law Journal*, December.

[22] COM(2010) 801 final, 13.

specification of autonomous workers will be most helpful for the courts in deciding on such cases.

Art. No. 17 par. 3 allows for derogations of the minimum rest, length of night work and reference periods[23] (but not the maximum weekly working time!), for certain activities:

- that are at distance of the workers home (off shore work, for instance);
- that require permanent presence to protect property of persons;
- that need continuity in service or production;
- and where there is a foreseeable surge in production (agriculture or tourism, for instance).

Another type of derogation is regulated in Art. No. 17 par. 3 as well: the derogation for workers in railway transport. Further, the Directive builds in Art. No. 17 par. 3 the option to limit or exclude from application of the Directives' provisions where occurrences are due to unusual and unforeseeable circumstances, beyond the employers' control, or to exceptional events, the consequences of which could not have been avoided despite the exercise of all due care (par. 2 f) or in case there is an accident or imminent risk of accident (par. 2 g). Next, in case of shift work, certain derogations from the provisions on daily and weekly rest are allowed for (Art. No. 17 par. 4 Directive 2003/88/EC). Lastly, ample derogations are possible for doctors in training (Art. No. 17 par. 5 Directive 2003/88/EC).

For all of these derogations, it holds that in case of derogation by national law or collective agreement, the worker is entitled to equivalent periods of compensatory rest, or, in exceptional cases where that is not possible for objective reasons, workers are afforded appropriate protection. This "safety net" is one example of an unexplored element in the dialogue. In the Jaeger-case the ECJ has explained that the compensatory rest should follow immediately after the extended working time. Compensatory rest that is not immediately linked with the period of work extended does not adequately take into account the general principles of protection the safety and health of workers.[24] The Court states in Isère[25] that it only allows for alternative protection in entirely exceptional cases where granting

[23] Art. No. 19 gives further limitations on the derogation of the provisions about the reference periods of Art. No. 17 par. 3 Directive 2003/88/EC.

[24] Par. 94 and 97 Jaeger.

[25] Par. 54 and 55 ECJ 14 October 2010, Case nr. C-428/09 (Union syndicale Solidares Isère v Premier Ministre and others, hereafter: Isère).

compensatory rest is not possible for objective reasons. It is clear the ECJ interprets the provision strictly in order to provide protection, and refers to "objective reasons" or justification. It would be interesting to see in future when alternative protection is allowed and when it is not.

In Art. No. 18 yet another type of derogation is to be found. Derogations of the minimum rest, length of night work and reference periods[26] (but again not from the maximum weekly working time!), can be made by collective agreement between the two sides of industry at national or at the appropriate decentralised level. Again, in such a case, the worker is granted equivalent periods of compensatory rest, or, in exceptional cases where that is not possible for objective reasons, workers are afforded appropriate protection.

The articles on minimum rest and the length of night work do not apply to mobile workers, and off shore work (Art. No. 20), and those provisions, plus the provision on the maximum weekly working time, do not apply to workers on board of seagoing fishing vessels (Art. No. 21 Directive 2003/88/EC).

Apart from the national or collective options to derogate from the Directive, according to Art. No. 22 it is possible to opt out at individual level from the maximum weekly working time. After fierce opposition of the UK that resisted the enactment of the (1993) Working Time Directive, an individual option to "opt-out" on the maximum working week of 48 hours was incorporated in the Directive (Art. No. 22 par. 1 and 2 Directive 2003/88/EC).

At national level, the Member State can allow for this individual opt-out. If that is the case, the general principles of the protection of the health and safety of workers should be respected. This is another example of the protective nature of the Directives' provision, whose meaning is not clearly known yet. The Directive requires then that the employer obtains the worker's consent to work more than the maximum of 48 hours. In an attempt to empower the worker as much as possible with regard to the acceptance, the ECJ has interpreted this requirement of consent rather strictly.[27] The consent must be "expressly and freely" given by each worker individually in order for the 48-hour maximum period of weekly working time to be validly extended. Whenever an employee decides not

---

[26] Art. No. 19 Directive 2003/88/EC applies here as well.

[27] ECJ, 5 October 2004, cases C-397/01 to C-403/01 (Pfeiffer/ Deutsches Rotes Kreuz).

to consent, the ECJ states that in order to ensure the useful effect of the Directive, the worker in such a case is protected against victimisation.[28]

According to the ECJ, such an extension is not valid when the employment contract refers to a collective agreement which permits such an extension. Flexibility with regard to the maximum working time thus is possible, although procedurally strictly regulated. One could wonder if here the legislator and the ECJ rely too heavily on the procedural limits with regard to the opt-out and neglect the reality that an employee often will be confronted with a "*standard take it or leave it form*" at the moment of formation of the contract[29] or faces the risk that a temporary contract would not be extended. The approach of both the legislator and the ECJ and the impact the opt-out has on the worker's protection seem to call for additional collective protection. The European Commission wishes the social partners to agree upon (the limitation of) the opt-out in the review of the present Directive. Business Europe wants to keep the opt-out underlined, CEEP and UEAPME are reserved about any changes towards the opt out, although CEEP "*regrets its rapid spread in public services*".[30] The trade unions ETUC and EPSU take the opposite standpoint: the opt-out should be put to an end. [31] The problem of *de facto* "unfree" individual consent and the impasse between the social partners perhaps could be solved by at least temporarily, by finding "a middle way". That would mean upholding the opt-out, but adding security at the collective level. An idea would be to demand that, before the recourse to the opt-out at an individual level, the collective agreement between the sectoral social partners would have to permit the option to use the individual opt-out.

5. Flexible Working Time and Work-life Balance

The current working time Directive does not include any provisions on work-life balance. To support the arguments in favour of working time flexibilisation, the European Commission reasons as mentioned before that this type of flexibilisation suits the needs for flexibility in light of private care duties as well. However, that assertion seems to be rather generalising, as the concurrence of the need for and realisation of the

---

[28] ECJ, 14 October 2010, case C-243/09 (Fuss/ Stadt Halle), The ECJ relates its judgment to the fundamental right to effective judicial protection (Art. No. 47 of the Charter of Fundamental Rights of the European Union).

[29] Collins, H. 2005. "European Social Policy and Contract Law," *ERCL* 2005/1, 123.

[30] COM(2010) 801 (final), 4.

[31] Ibid.

employers' wish for working time flexibility, alongside the need for and realisation of combination security, will only take place for certain workers at a certain time. Since the interests of the workers with regard to combination and income security are diversified and will probably vary even further over time, it seems to be of utmost relevance to enhance the workers' information on and say over their working time. Communication with the employer over working time is thus essential.

Since the Directive on working time neglects the issue of combination security, there seems to be a task left for the EU to further these matches between the employers' and the employees' demands. The European Commission indeed has put the item on the legislative agenda. The Commission proposes that the social partners pay attention to this issue since the lack of protection (the lack of information rights about time schedules and lacking rights with regard to requests to individual changes of the time schedules in particular), "creates a serious challenge for reconciling work with family life and for general work/life balance".[32] The Commission suggests including in the envisaged review of the Directive:

> - encouragement for the social partners to agree at the appropriate level aimed at supporting reconciliation of work and family life;
> - a right to information well in advance about substantial change to the pattern of work;
> - an employers' obligation to examine workers' requests to change their working hours and patterns, in the light of each other's needs for flexibility, and to give reasons for refusing such requests.

The aim to improve the work-life balance suits to Art. No. 3 TEU. Within the context of a single EU market, the Community has set the social objectives to:

> (…) promote throughout the Community a harmonious, balanced and sustainable development of economic activities, *a high level of employment and of social protection*, equality between men and women, sustainable and non-inflationary growth, a high degree of competitiveness and convergence of economic performance, a high level of protection and improvement of the quality of the environment, *the raising of the standard of living and quality of life*, and economic *and social cohesion* and solidarity among Member States. (Art. No. 3 par. 3 TEU, italics added).

[32] COM(2010)801 final, 12.

The question is, however, whether the current legal base of the Directive (Art. No. 188a EC, now Art. No. 153 par. 1 sub a TFEU) could serve as the legal basis for such provisions. In the Jaeger's judgment, the ECJ states:

> In that regard it is clear from paragraph 15 of the judgment in United Kingdom v Council that the concepts of "safety" and "health" as used in Art. No. 118a of the Treaty, on which Directive 93/104 is based, should be interpreted widely as embracing all factors, physical or otherwise, capable of affecting the health and safety of the worker in his working environment, including in particular certain aspects of the organisation of working time. At the same paragraph of that judgment the Court further noted that such an interpretation derives support in particular from the Preamble to the Constitution of the World Health Organisation to which all the Member States belong. Health is there defined as a state of complete physical, mental and social well-being that does not consist only in the absence of illness or infirmity.[33]

Although the ECJ interprets the "health and safety" ground extensively, evidence that the work-life balance directly influences worker health or safety is lacking. Therefore, it is doubtful whether Art. No. 153 par 1 sub a can serve as a legal basis. In the author's view, the legal basis should be broadened, to, for instance, sub b, the working conditions. If a problem in political terms, the alternative seems to be to encourage the social partners to take on the topic and agree upon a social partner agreement (as in Art. No. 155 TFEU). The prospect of such happening seems bleak, according to the Commission's Communication about the second phase of the review, only the European Trade Union Confederation (ETUC) shows an interest in the topic. Again, legislative results at national level are discarded: for instance in the Netherlands and Germany far-reaching legislation on work-life balance and workers' requests with regard to change to working time or pattern is already in place. Perhaps the dialogue on this issue could be stimulated by Member States who have already enacted legislation on work-life balance bottom up via the national social partners.

[33] Par. 93 Jaeger.

6. Conclusion

The question addressed in this paper has been whether or not the dialogue in the past few years on different aspects of the regulation of flexible working time has resulted only in opposing views. A close examination of the dialogue between the EU legislator, the ECJ and the social partners—at European and at a decentralised level—has showed that, despite the expressed contrasting views, existing results of the dialogue between (sectoral) social partners within the Member States or national legislation might give clues for breakthroughs with regard to the contested legislative topics of on-call work, derogations, opt-out and work-life balance. With regard to on-call work, the black and white approach of the legislator and the ECJ towards the definition of working time should be more nuanced. A proposal for a draft new Directive on working time could include a definition of on-call work, where the actual differentiation is left to the social partners at the appropriate level within the Member States. The point of reference would be to stipulate that all of the actively worked time on-call would count as working time.

With regard to the derogations for the so-called autonomous worker it is noted that, in general, the demarcation between dependant and autonomous workers, in the light of protection of the former, is a well known and persisting problem in labour law. The Commission's suggestion to specify the characteristics of the autonomous worker still leaves ample leeway for interpretation of specific cases at hand. The suggested additional specification of autonomous workers will be at maximum helpful for the courts in deciding on such cases.

For most derogations in the Directive it holds that, in case of derogation by national law or collective agreement, the worker is entitled to equivalent periods of compensatory rest, or, in exceptional cases where that is not possible for objective reasons, workers are afforded appropriate protection. This "safety net" is one example of an as yet unexplored element in the dialogue. It is clear that the ECJ interprets the provision strictly in the light of the aim of protection and demands for alternative protection "objective reasons" or justification. It would be interesting to see in future when alternative protection is allowed and when it is not. With regard to the opt-out provision in the dialogue the ECJ has interpreted the provision on the opt-out strictly with regard to its procedural aspects. However, the problem of *de facto* "unfree" individual consent and the (severe) effects on worker protection remains. Currently, the social partners express contrasting views with regard to the question whether or not to keep the opt-out in place. Here, perhaps meeting "half-way" would lead to, at least a temporary solution. This would mean upholding the opt-out, but adding security at the collective level. In this paper, an idea is suggested to only allow for individual opt-out when the collective agreement between the (sectoral) social partners permits that. Finally, with regard to the issue of work-life balance, the Commission has made cautious suggestions to improve work-life balance. However, the legal base for such provisions in a health and safety Directive might be contested. The prospect of actually realising improvement in this area seems bleak, since only the ETUC shows an interest in the topic. Again, existing legislative results at the national level are disregarded at the European level. The Member States who have already enacted legislation on the work-life balance could perhaps step forward and stimulate via the national dialogue with the social partners the debate between the social partners at European level on this matter.

The dialogue on the regulation of working time will continue and will remain an interesting matter for legal debate.

References

Barnard, C. 1997. "The Judgment of the ECJ in United Kingdom v Council: The Working Time Directive," in CELS Occasional Paper No. 2.

Barnard, C., S. Deakin, and R. Hobbs. 2003. "Opting Out of the 48-hour Week: Employer Necessity or Individual Choice? An Empirical Study of the Operation of Art. No. 18(1)(B) of the Working Time Directive in the UK," *Industrial Law Journal*, December.

Collins, H. 2005. "European Social Policy and Contract Law," *ERCL* 2005/1,

Dashwood, A. A. 1997. "The Working Time Judgment in a Wider Perspective," in CELS Occasional Paper No. 2.

European Commission. 2002. *Directive 2000/34/EC, Proposal for a Directive of the European Parliament and of the Council Concerning Certain Aspects of the Organisation of Working Time (Codified Version), COM(2002), 336 final.* Explanatory Memorandum. Brussels: European Commission.

—. 2006. *Modernising Labour Law to Meet the Challenges of the 21st Century, COM(2006) 708 final.* Brussels: European Commission.

—. 2010. *Communication from the Commission to the European Parliament, The Council, The European Economic and Social Committee and the Committee of the Regions, Reviewing the Working Time Directive, COM(2010), (First-phase Consultation of the Social*

Partners at European Level under Article 154 of the TFEU), 106 final. Brussels: European Commission.

—. 2010. *Communication from the Commission to the European Parliament, the Council, the European Economic and Social Committee and the Committee of the Regions, Reviewing the Working Time Directive (Second-phase Consultation of the Social Partners at European Level under Article 154 TFEU).* Brussels: European Commission.

—. 2010. *Report from the Commission to the European Parliament, the Council, the European Economic and Social Committee and the Committee of the Regions on the Implementation by Members States of Directive 2003/88/EC ("the Working Time Directive"), COM (2010) 802 final.* Brussels: European Commission.

Gray, M. 1998. "A Recalcitrant Partner: The UK Reaction to the Working Time Directive," in *Yearbook of European Law* 1997, eds. Barav A., and D.A. Wyatt, (Oxford: Clarendon Press), 323-362.

Hepple, B. A. "Commentary," in CELS Occasional Paper No. 2.

Nowak, T. 2008. "The Working Time Directive and the European Court of Justice," *MJ*, 447-471.

Some Considerations Concerning the Flexible Shaping of Working Time and its Limitations in Light of Polish Statutory Regulations

Tatiana Wrocławska

1. General Considerations

Flexicurity consists of flexibility and security.[1] Is it possible to reconcile these two seemingly contradictory concepts? More and more frequently we hear about the politics of flexicurity,[2] based on the pursuit of the state corresponding to an almost ideal solution. For its part, on the one hand, it is about the need to respond to the ongoing changes and transformation of social relations that are determined by various factors, including those of an economic and technological nature,[3] but on the other hand, it is about the appropriate degree of safety through adequate and necessary protection of work.

The need for the introduction and use of flexible working hours arrangements especially because of the recent experience of the economic crisis, is beyond doubt. The implementation of changes appropriate to the situation in the organisation of working time[4]—flexible hours[5]—allows a

[1] E. Kryńska tries to show the balance between flexibility and security, in Kryńska, E. 2007. "The balance between flexibility and security on the Polish labour market. How to achieve the flexicurity? [in Polish]" *Monitor of Labour Law*, No. 7:340.

[2] For the concept of flexicurity see Patulski, A. 2008. "Atypical Employment. Flexibility or Stability? [in Polish]" part 1, *Monitor of Labour Law*, No. 2:66.

[3] The need for it is indicated in Bąk, E. 2009. *Atypical Employment in the Labour Market [in Polish]*. Warsaw: C.H. Bech, 1.

[4] For the definition of flexible regulation see Piecko-Mazurek, A. 2008. "Job Sharing, Work for Two, [in Polish]" *Monitor of Labour Law*, No. 12:631.

[5] Some patterns of flexible working time by A.E. Pocztowski are given in Bąk, E. 2009. *Atypical Employment in the Labour Market [in Polish]*. Warsaw: C.H. Bech, 4.

balance between the interests of both employers and employees. Reconciliation of interests in this case is down to maintaining employment in difficult periods of transition for employers. The rationale for the use of flexible working arrangements can be seen not only in situations involving transitional issues on the part of employers. The need for flexible working arrangements is also justified by economic and social transformation, especially the emergence of new forms of employment regarded as atypical.[6]

The possibility of flexible working hours arrangements can also prevent employers from opting for new forms of flexible employment, which are often less favourable to employees due to a separation from the general guarantee of employment law. Thus, it seems that the creation of an appropriate level of flexible working hours would not only prevent such situations, but, above all, would enable the adjustment of labour supply to its demand.[7] Of course, even though the change in working arrangements is conducive to retaining most of the other employee rights, it is not to be overlooked that this can also create scope for abuse by those with an economic advantage. Hence the question arises about the limits of flexible working arrangements and borders that are drawn above all the interests of both sides of the employment relationship.

2. The Constitutional and Community Guidelines for the Regulation and Flexible Shaping of Working Time

The Constitution of the Republic of Poland[8] delegates the regulation of working time standards to the Law Act, at the same time guaranteeing for employees the right to days off from work and the right to annual paid holiday leave (Art. No. 66 par. 2 of the Constitution). Moreover, the constitutional provision guarantees everyone the right to safe and healthy labour conditions. Hence, it should be assumed that the core law only generally understood the safety and health of workers as the general limitation of flexible organisation of working time.

In this basic Act there is an absence of any additional guidelines with respect to the question of the organisation of working time. Hence, the overall regulation of working time is a statutory matter, with a view to

---

[6] Atypical forms of employment are presented in Patulski, A. 2008. "Atypical Forms of Employment, [in Polish]" part 2, *Monitor of Labour Law*, No. 3:124.

[7] Skąpski, M. 2006. *Protective Function of Labour Law in a Market Economy [in Polish]*. Zakamycze: Kantor Wydawniczy, 360, 361.

[8] Constitution from 2.04.1997 (O.J. No 78, pos. 483).

achieving the constitutional guideline ensuring the health and safety of workers. As for European Union Law, since the accession of Poland to the European Union, it has become part of the binding national legislation, thus the internal legal system should be formed in accordance with the requirements and guidelines contained in these acts. Therefore, it is impossible to bypass the consideration of issues related to the regulation of working time in the sources binding for the Polish legislator.

From the viewpoint of working time, the main document is the Directive of 4 November 2003 concerning certain aspects of the regulation of working time (2003/88/EC), defining minimum standards of safety and health associated with the organisation of working time. In accordance with the Directive and Art. No. 15, there are no obstacles for the application of more stringent national solutions which guarantee better protection of the safety and health of workers, including collective agreements and other agreements concluded by the social partners. Working time, within the meaning of the Directive, is the period during which the employee is working, as well as the period of employer's disposal, in accordance with the national laws or practice, while the rest period will be any period of non-working time. The term "adequate rest" should mean regular rest periods, which are expressed in units of time and which are sufficiently long and continuous to ensure that, as a result of fatigue or other irregular working patterns, the employees do not cause injury to themselves, to fellow workers or to others and that they do not damage their health, either in the short term or in the longer term.

The minimum daily rest period shall be 11 consecutive hours per a 24-hour period. Every worker is entitled to a minimum uninterrupted weekly rest period of 24 hours plus 11 hours of daily rest, per each seven-day period. Notwithstanding, it is permissible to reduce the weekly rest period to 24 hours if this is justified by objective, technical or work organisation conditions (Art. No. 3, 5).

The average weekly working time for each seven-day period, including overtime work, shall not exceed 48 hours. A settlement period in order to give a weekly rest period shall not exceed 14 days, and with reference to the maximum weekly working time the settlement period shall not exceed four months (Art. No. 6 and 16).

The European Union legislator omitted in the matter of the Directive the definition of a "day" and the "daily norm". Only night workers whose work involves special hazards of heavy physical or mental strain do not work more than 8 hours in any period of 24 hours during which they perform night work (Art. No. 8).

Besides the mentioned minimum standards (Art. No. 4, 5, 8), exceptions from them are acceptable on account of the specific characteristics of the activities concerned, when working time is not measured or is not determined or can be calculated by workers themselves, especially in the case of managing executives or other persons with autonomous decision-making powers, and family workers or workers officiating at religious ceremonies in churches and religious communities.

It needs to be emphasised that the derogations are possible if the equivalent period of compensatory rest will be given for workers concerned or, if it is not possible, the adequate protection for the workers concerned must be ensured. How to regulate and provide derogations has been left to the Member States. Derogations could be adopted by laws, regulations or administrative provisions or by collective agreements or other agreements between the two sides of industry (Art. No. 17).

Derogations from the daily rest period, weekly rest period, the length of night work and the reference periods are also permitted on account of the specific types of activities or type of work. In accordance with Art. No. 17 of the Directive, it is possible in the case of activities when the place of work and the employee's place of residence are far from one another, in the case of security and surveillance activities (requiring a permanent presence in order to protect property and persons, particularly with regard to security guards and caretakers), in the case of activities involving the need for continuity of service or production, in cases where there are foreseeable activities (in particular in the field of agriculture, tourism, postal services), in the case of persons working in railway transport and in the cases of accident or imminent risk of accident. In addition, derogations from the compulsory daily and weekly rest periods may be made in the case of shift work activities, when the worker changes shift and cannot take daily or weekly rest periods between the end of one shift and the start of the next one, and also in the case of activities involving periods of work split up over the day (especially those of cleaning staff).

These derogations may be made by means of collective agreements or an agreement concluded between the two sides of industry at the national or regional or a lower appropriate level. The derogations shall be allowed on condition that equivalent compensating rest periods are granted to the workers concerned or, in exceptional cases where it is not possible for objective reasons to grant such periods, the workers concerned are afforded appropriate protection (Art. No. 18).

Some guidelines for the flexible extension of the reference periods are provided by Art. No. 19 of the Directive. According to it, as a general rule, the reference period should not exceed six months. However, with regard to the general principles of the protection of the safety and health of workers, it is permitted to extend the reference periods up to a maximum of 12 months in the framework of collective agreements or agreements concluded with the social partners, if this is justified by objective or technical reasons or reasons concerning the organisation of work. There are no similar restrictions in relation to other standards of working time. Therefore, it should be noted that the other limitation in the field of flexible organisation of working time could be provided by social partners by collective agreements (other agreements), in concluding that the social partners have the freedom to organise working time, restricted by general guidelines concerning the appropriate protection of workers and the objective reasonableness of flexible organisation of working time.

Attention should also be given to Art. No. 22 of the Directive, setting out the opportunity to make derogation from the maximum weekly working time on the basis of the consent of a worker, taking into account the general principles of the protection of the safety and health of workers. The way for exceeding the maximum weekly rest period is the consent of the worker to such an organisation of working time. In addition, however, it must be stressed that the consent of the employee could not be a result of coercion from the employers, therefore it is necessary to provide documentation of work in such conditions and ensure control by a competent authority with the possibility of prohibiting or restricting the exceeding of the maximum weekly working time.

3. The Restrictions of Flexible Shaping of Working Time in Light of the Polish Statutory Regulations

3.1 Day Definition

The definition of a working day, referred to in Art. No. 128, paragraph 3 of the Labour Code,[9] provides the significant limitation of flexible working time. This also concerns the flexible forms of working time presented below. The term of the day should be further understood as 24 consecutive hours, starting from the hours in which the employee begins work in accordance with the working time schedule. The work week is understood as seven consecutive calendar days, starting from the first day of the reference period. Both, the working day and the week must not overlap with the astronomic day or calendar week. The work performed on

[9] Labour Code from 24.04.1974 (O.J. from 1998, No 21, pos. 94 with amendments).

the same day after the normal working hours of the employee, in accordance with Art. No. 151 of the Labour Code, should be understood as overtime work. Therefore, the employer planning the distribution of working time of the employee should have regard to the expiry of the 24 hours, counted from the commencement of the work, otherwise he could be obliged to pay the worker (for working time that falls in the same day) the allowance for overtime hours. In addition, it should be noted that the planning overtime work conflicts with the basic premise of applying it. The overtime work is permitted for the specific needs of an employer and may not be scheduled in advance. Hindrance in appropriate organisation of work because of the aforementioned definition of a working day is visible, especially in the case of shift work. There is no possibility of flexible planning of working time until 24 hours day work has expired. That is why it is necessary to indicate the difficulty of the work performed in the removable working time, flexitime, in which an employee performs work for the next 8 hours, with a choice of starting and ending work time in established schedule.

Also it should be stressed that the daily working time standard shall be 8 hours per day. The exceeding of the daily working time may take place only because of an adequate system of working time. For example, in equivalent working time system, it is allowed to extend the working time up to 12 or to 16 (supervision of devices) or up to 24 hours a day (security guards). Extension of work in each kind of activity mentioned is balanced by a shorter daily working time on other days or by giving free days of work. The equivalent working time system provides the general requirements, i.e. requirements concerning the general weekly standards in the appropriate reference period. In addition, the possibility of exceeding the daily working time takes place also in a short-week working time system and in the system of weekend-work, when it is allowed to exceed the daily working time up to 12 hours.

3.2 Weekly Working Time

Weekly working time of employees shall be 40 hours in an average of five days a week. Both, the average 40-hour standard and the average five-day working week allow the employer for free management of working time. This means that an employee may work 6 days in certain weeks and 4 days in others, however, on average he/she needs to perform work for 5 days a week. Limitation of free choice of days of work is provided by the Holidays Act. Sunday, according to the Labour Code, is a public holiday and work on that date is allowed only in the cases expressly provided for.

Also, the maximum average weekly working time, including overtime, does not exceed 48 hours in a seven-day period. It does not prejudice the flexible planning of work and reflects the provisions of Art. No. 6 of the Directive. It is important that the main restrictions of using the average weekly norms are provided by the reference periods.

3.3 Reference Periods

The legislator determines that, in principle, working time should be settled in a period not exceeding four months. This period is called the basic maximum settlement period. The derogations from the basic reference period (by using the shorter and longer periods of settlement), have been clearly identified in the Labour Code and are possible only in the specified situations. Longer periods are allowed only in agriculture and breeding, as well as in guarding of property or persons. It is acceptable to use the period of 6 months, or even 12 months, if it is further justified by the atypical organisation of work or technical constraints affecting the work process (Art. No. 129 of L.C.). The foregoing solution is not permitted in the case of systems of equivalent working time. For the equivalent working time system, in principle, the settlement periods do not exceed one month. An exception is possible only in particularly justified cases and in activities dependent on the season or weather conditions. Then the settlement period may be extended to 3 months, or up to 4 months, when it comes to the second of the given conditions.

3.4 Daily and Weekly Rest Period

A daily rest period shall be 11 hours and a weekly rest period shall be 35 hours and must not be interrupted (Art. No. 132 and 133 of L.C.). Adaptation of such rigidly defined standards of rest periods means that, in principle, an employee can perform work for a maximum of 13 hours. The provided restriction does not concern the work periods, in which an ability of performing work for a greater number of hours exists (equivalent working time systems).

The legislator predicted derogations of obligatory and interrupted daily and weekly rest periods. The daily rest period may be interrupted in the events defined specifically by the legislator. This applies to the situation in relation to the need to carry out rescue operations in order to protect human life or health, protection of property or the environment, or removal of breakdown, as well as in the case of managers undertaking work on behalf of the employer. In presented cases the employees are entitled to equivalent rest period in the adopted settlement period. It should be emphasised that the derogations from the weekly rest period are also acceptable for the reasons previously specified and, in addition, also in case of shift work, in situations when the worker changes shift and cannot take a weekly rest period between the end of one shift and the start of the next one. Then the weekly rest period may be reduced to 24 hours. Due to the nature of work under an equivalent system of working time, with the possibility of extending the daily working time to 16 (operating equipment supervision) and 24 (work at guarding of property or persons) hours per day, a daily rest period is granted immediately after the work during the extended daily working time, adequately to the period corresponding to at least the number of performed hours, regardless of the 11-hours daily rest period.

3.5 Working Time Systems

The Polish legislator provided several systems of flexible organisation of working time. We shall remember about the definition of a daily work time and the necessity of providing a period of compulsory rest time to all employees within the borders of flexible organisation of work time.

Excessive use of casuistic provisions governing the systems of working time restricts the flexible shaping of working time.[10] The choice of a particular system of work was fortified with a duty of meeting a number of conditions. A clear example of the adaptive evolution of working time is the system of task working time. It allows for flexible formation of working time, bearing in mind the needs of the employer and the employee. However, it needs to be stressed that the scheme of working time must provide such a task assignment that allows their execution within the framework of the basic standards presented earlier. The employer, after a consultation with an employee, shall determine the time necessary to carry out the tasks assigned, bearing in mind the basic standards of working time. The freedom of work in the framework of the system of task time manifests itself in the absence of an obligation of recording (evidence) the work time by the employer. An employee decides about the beginning of work, breaks and completion of work. This is beneficial to the interests of both the employee and the employer. The

---

[10] Rycak, M. 2008. "Legal Considerations of the Flexible Working Time Developments in Poland—Proposals for Amendments, [in Polish]" *Monitor of Labour Law,* No. 1:14.

employer shall, in principle, not meet the costs related to the work being done in overtime (unless the tasks were assigned incorrectly—in such a way that they were implemented out of the framework of the basic standards of working time), while the employees have the possibility of convenient shaping of working time that allows them to reconcile additional employment with family responsibilities. Significant constraints on the possibility of the introduction of a task system of working time are constituted by the circumstances determining the admissibility of its application. According to Art. No. 149 of the Labour Code, the system of task working time may be used in cases justified by a type of activity, a work organisation or a place where the work is performed. It is not hard to notice that the phrases which are used by the Polish legislator are not fully specified, hence, whether it is justified can be settled by the collective agreements or other agreements concluded by employers and employees. Certainly, the usage of the task system of working time will be unacceptable in cases when an employee is under the constant supervision of an employer and also in a permanent place of work—because it is in contradiction with the essence of a system of task working time as a system which allows for the employee to work away from an employer. However, it raised a question about the relevance of excluding the ability of a system of task working time, in cases where the parties of employment are so agreed, of giving more freedom to those concerned.

It should be noted that a similar premise, like the above mentioned, as the type of activity or work organisation occurs in the interrupted system of working time. Application of an interrupted work time is additionally hedged by the obligation of its implementation by a collective agreement, which excludes its application with reference to employers who are not covered by the agreement. In addition, however, the possibility of applying the interrupted system of working time is anticipated for employers who are individuals engaged in the field of agriculture and breeding, where the trade unions do not function. Then the interrupted work time shall be introduced on the basis of an employment contract.

Equivalent systems of work time can be introduced in cases determined in Art. No. 135-137 of the Labour Code. In situations which are justified by work organisations or type of work, there exists an ability of extension of working hours up to 12 hours. However, in cases of execution of work with equipment supervision, it is acceptable to extend the working hours up to 16 hours, but in the event of work involving guarding the property or people—up to 24 hours.

The system of weekend working time and the system of a reduced working week are introduced in the contract of employment on the basis of a previous agreement (request) submitted by an employee. The legislator does not specify in what form the application (request) should be submitted with the only restrictions for the use of such system of working time by request of employee. This means that without the consent of the employee (application), the employer cannot introduce and apply these working time systems.

In the field of flexible organisation of working time, the Labour Code conceived of introducing an individual scheme of working time in a frame of applied working time system and this should be highlighted. With regard to starting and finishing work in other hours than those that are in force at the workplace. Individual time work schemes are implemented upon the request of the employee. In this case, an employee's consent in a written form constitutes the restriction of flexible working time.

At the end of the presentation of Polish regulatory laws, the adopted possibility of extending weekly working hours under the opt-out clause cannot be omitted. Thus, only medical staff who are on call may exclusively have the use of such an organisation of working time. It raised a question about purposefulness of extending the possibility on other employees. Such a solution meets with a reasonable criticism in literature. In the opt out clause it is noticed as an attempt to return to the 19th century perception of working time as a free contract and exploitation of the employees. Thus, the protection of an employee's interest in a form of obtaining his consent to extend the maximum weekly working time may be puzzling.[11]

It seems that in cases of flexible regulation of working time, the leading role should be performed by the representatives of the parties of an employment relationship (from the employee's side—trade unions or workers' representatives). Taking into account an established possibility of exceeding the weekly working hours, one cannot see the danger of the weakening of employee's protection. It was accurately noticed that the requirement of the employee's consent (agreement to perform work for more than 48 hours) as a measure to make derogations from the maximum weekly working standards, although the principle *volenti non fit iniuria* or, *anyone knows better what is good for him*, calls into question the rationality of the usage of the above mentioned regulation. This question becomes important in the context of ongoing discussion of implementation

[11] Rycak, M. 2009. "The Institution of the Opt-out, Attempting to Return to 19th Century Perception of Working Time, [in Polish]" *Monitor of Labour Law*, No. 10:11.

of a similar concept in the Labour Code.[12] Therefore, I believe that an objective justification for the implementation of such a solution, i.e. the optional derogations and exceptions from the maximum working time standards, would be guaranteed only through the participation of the social partners (trade unions or worker's representatives).

With regard to the Polish statutory regulations in the field of working time, it needs to be noted that the legislator had largely regulated the organisation of working time. In the Polish Labour Code the wide statutory regulations in matters of working time are quite visible. Participation of social partners is small and is limited, in principle, to some written cases, when the flexible shaping of working time is possible. The possibility of flexible shaping of working time given by the Directive is not fully exploited.

4. Flexible Shaping of Working Time in Light of the Provisions of the Act on Mitigating the Effects of the Economic Crisis

Law of 1 July 2009 on mitigating the effects of the economic crisis for employees and entrepreneurs,[13] as the title indicates, bearing in mind the consequences of the economic crisis, has provided many new solutions in the field of flexible shaping of working time. The provisions provided by this Act (commonly named as anti-crisis Act) shall apply exclusively to entrepreneurs in its meaning and only for a transitional period to 2012. The "anti-crisis" Act distinguishes the entrepreneurs with transitional financial difficulties and all other entrepreneurs (employers who are entrepreneurs within the meaning of Art. No. 4 the Act of 2 July 2004 on the freedom of economic activity).[14] The provisions of the Act concerning the flexible shaping of working time are applicable to both mentioned categories of entrepreneurs. Quite a complicated definition of entrepreneur with transitional financial difficulties is provided by Art. No. 3 of this Act. Outside the scope of application of the Act there are other entities which employ workers, so its provisions could not be applicable to other employers within the meaning of Art. No. 3 of the Labour Code.

---

[12] Rycak, M. 2009. "The Institution of the Opt-out, Attempting to Return to 19th Century Perception of Working Time, [in Polish]" *Monitor of Labour Law*, No. 10:11.

[13] Official Journal from 17.08 2009, No 125, pos. 1035.

[14] O.J. from 2007, No 155, pos. 1095 with amendments.

The Act has established the rules for the prolongation of the reference period and for the application of an individual schedule of working time that state a clear example of flexible shaping of working time and that are beyond the restrictions determined in the Labour Code.[15]

The reference period, pursuant to Art. No. 9 of the commented Act, may be extended up to a maximum of 12 months, if it is justified by objective or technical reasons or reasons concerning the organisation of work. The extension of the reference period has not been limited to a particular system of working time, it is therefore admissible regardless of the system of working time. The extension of the reference period is possible in compliance with the general principles relating to the protection of the safety and health of workers. Moreover, using an extended reference period could not affect the right of an employee to daily and weekly rest periods. Therefore, an important restriction on the usage of the flexible organisation of working time provides the rigid standard of daily rest. The extension of the reference period could involve determining the individual work schedule. The right to determine the individual work schedule should be closed under the current system of working time.[16]

During the extended reference period, the individual working time schedule may provide the differentiated number of hours for work in referred months. Longer periods of work are compensated for by the shorter working time or by non-working time in the adopted reference period. During each month of the extended reference period the remuneration of employees shall not be less than the minimum remuneration and also the individual work schedule shall not be prepared for less than the reference period of 2 months.

An extension of the reference period may be made by collective agreements or by consultation with trade union organisations. However, if it is not possible to achieve the agreement with all trade union organisations, the entrepreneur shall make an agreement with representative trade unions

---

[15] The comments concerning the new regulations adopted by anti-crisis Act are presented in the following publications: Baran, K.W. 2009. "The General Characteristic of the Anti-crisis Legislation in the Light of the Functions of Labour Law [in Polish]," *The Labour and the Social Security (LSS)*, No. 9:18; Stelina, J., and M. Zieleniecki. 2009. "The Anti-crisis Act [in Polish]," *The Labour and the Social Security (LSS)*, No. 10: 2; Sobczyk, A. 2010. "The Extended Reference Periods [in Polish]," *The Labour and the Social Security (LSS)*, No. 10:13.

[16] Frączek, M., and R. Lisicki. 2009. "Consultations and Clarifications [in Polish]," *The Labour and the Social Security (LSS)*, No. 11: 42.

within the meaning of the Labour Code. If the trade unions do not function, the reference period may be extended by an agreement with other representatives of the workers who were selected within procedures accepted by the entrepreneur. The entrepreneur shall send a copy of the agreement to the competent labour inspector during the 3 working days period counted from the conclusion of the agreement. It should be noted that the application of new reference periods by collective labour agreements can be quite difficult for an employer with a view to amending the work conditions. It seems that the most appropriate form would be the agreement, which in accordance with Art. No. 9 of this Act, provides an alternative form of the application of the flexible organisation of working time.

An individual schedule of working time, determined by the entrepreneur, may provide for different hours of starting and finishing of work. In these cases, the work on the same day may not be understood as overtime work. The individual work schedule must ensure the right of an employee to the minimum daily and weekly rest periods (Art. No. 10).

An employee, caring for the child under the age of 14 or caring for a family member requiring personal care, may submit a written request to their employer for an individual working time schedule. The employer shall take into account the request of the employee, unless this is impossible due to the organisation of work or type of work. The employer shall inform the employee in writing about the reason for refusal (Art. No. 11).

Additionally, it is possible to reduce working time to not more than half of the full working time. In such cases the remuneration shall be proportionally reduced. The presented solution could be provided in the same way as before: in collective agreements or other agreements. Collective agreements or other concluded agreements should include the definitions of the time period of the reduced working time application, occupations covered by the reduced working time and reduced working hours. A reduction of working time does not require the submission of the notice that allows an employer to implement the solutions without an unnecessary waiting period (Art. No. 12).

5. The Interests of the Employee and the Employer as a Guideline for Flexible Shaping of Working Time

With respect to the considerations above, some final conclusions were made. It seems that the policy of safe and flexible shaping of working time should be striving to reconcile the interests of both parties, which, in principle, could be possible by involvement of the social partners. A Community Directive recognises the importance of the role of the social partners that is especially visible in the option to make derogations and exceptions from the general standards. It was previously noted that the participation of social partners in flexible shaping of working time, in particular through the collective agreements or other agreements, would ensure that the general account would be taken to reconcile the interests of workers and employers.[17] As was written before, the role of the social partners has been recognised by regulations established in the "anti-crisis" Act. There are no doubts that the length of reference period and the possibility of making derogations from the daily and weekly rest periods must be granted by adequate law provisions, guaranteeing the possibility to make it by the way of collective agreements or agreements concluded between the two sides of employment.[18]

Although in the marginal, I would like to make one more consideration relating to the issue of flexible shaping of working time by way of collective agreements. Taking into account the possible delegation of the flexible shaping of working time also for workers' representatives and the lack of representation of the trade unions in many workplaces, it is important that the adopted solution allows for derogations from the provisions in force not only in the sphere of collective agreements (without notice of termination of working conditions). Choosing adequate measures and solutions constitutes the basic condition of an appropriate way for flexible shaping of working time.

6. Final Remarks

The reasonableness of the deregulation of statutory regulations of working time is visible not only in cases of protection of the interests of employers as persons delivering work, but also from the point of view of employees.

The concept of flexibility is multidimensional. It is possible to extract several planes of flexible working time arrangements: the concept of the flexible working time, flexible dimension and flexible working time[19] have been distinguished. Flexible regulation of working time should lead to the possibility for organisation of work according to current needs, in

[17] Latos-Mikowska, M. 2009. "The Flexibility of Working Time [in Polish]," *Monitor of Labour Law*, No. 3:121.
[18] Ibid., 122.
[19] Latos-Mikowska, M. 2009. "The Flexibility of Working Time [in Polish]," *Monitor of Labour Law*, No. 3:118.

accordance with the interest of the employment parties. At first glance, it may seem that a flexible shaping of working time primarily serves the interests of employers. However, it should be noted that the widely understood interest of the employer may not be considered in isolation from the interest of workers.[20] Striving to achieve maximum profit often results in employment reductions (especially in situations related to the deterioration of economic activity), that could be prevented through the flexible forms of working time, which should interest both parties concerned. A flexible shaping of working time should therefore reconcile the interests of both parties of employment.

Of course, the application of flexible working time should not be used only as the result of the financial crisis, although such remedial measure are especially needed in these situations. The flexible shaping of working time could be used as an alternative form to other forms of non-standard employment (atypical employment), particularly in the cases related to the changes in employment base (into self-employment) that are prone to abuse. Flexicurity should be understood as a measure to reconcile quite different interests of both parties of employment. An ability to change the organisation of working time by flexible regulations of working time should lead to the maintenance of more existing entitlements of workers, which is very important for them as the "weaker" part of the employment relationship.

Flexicurity in the example of the regulations of working time means the appropriate measure for ensuring the balance between the interests of the employer and the employees. In the view of the different possibilities of flexible shaping of working time the limitations will not be rigid. The adopted guidelines should take into account the "legitimate interest" of both parts of employment relationship that is also difficult to interpret. However, I believe that a decisive role in the verification of the borders of flexible organisation of working time should be given to the social partners (representatives of employees), who through negotiations and dialogue could reach the respective compromises.[21]

---

[20] Compare Florek, L. 2003. "The Limits of Liberalization of Labour Law [in Polish]," in *The Boundaries of the Liberalization of the Labour Law. Problems of Social Security*, eds. Bielak E., and H. Lewandowski, (Lodz: University of Łódź), 10 and 11.

[21] The need of the wider limits in case of participation of the social partners is maintained in L. Florek. 2003. "The Limits of Liberalization of Labour Law [in Polish]," in *The Boundaries of the Liberalization of the Labour Law. Problems of Social Security*, eds. Bielak, E., and H. Lewandowski (Lodz:University of Łódź), 23.

References

Bąk, E. 2009. *Atypical Employment in the Labour Market [in Polish]*. Warsaw: C. H. Bech.

Baran, K.W. 2009. "The General Characteristic of the Anti-crisis Legislation in the Light of the Functions of Labour Law [in Polish]," *The Labour and the Social Security (LSS)*, No. 9:18.

Florek, L. 2003. "The Limits of Liberalization of Labour Law [in Polish]," in *The Boundaries of the Liberalization of the Labour Law. Problems of Social Security*, eds. Bielak, E., and H. Lewandowski, (Lodz: University of Łódź), 10 and 11.

Frączek, M., and R. Lisicki. 2009. "Consultations and Clarifications [in Polish]," *The Labour and the Social Security (LSS)*, No. 11: 42.

Kryńska, E. 2007. "The balance between flexibility and security on the Polish labour market. How to achieve the flexicurity? [in Polish]" *Monitor of Labour Law*, No. 7:340.

Latos-Mikowska, M. 2009. "The Flexibility of Working Time [in Polish]," *Monitor of Labour Law*, No. 3:121.

Patulski, A. 2008. "Atypical Employment. Flexibility or Stability? [in Polish]" part 1, *Monitor of Labour Law*, No. 2:66.

—. 2008. "Atypical Forms of Employment, [in Polish]" part 2, *Monitor of Labour Law*, No. 3:124.

Piecko-Mazurek, A. 2008. "Job Sharing, Work for Two, [in Polish]" *Monitor of Labour Law*, No. 12:631.

Rycak, M. 2008. "Legal Considerations of the Flexible Working Time Developments in Poland—Proposals for Amendments, [in Polish]" *Monitor of Labour Law,* No. 1:14.

—. 2009. "The Institution of the Opt-out, Attempting to Return to 19th Century Perception of Working Time, [in Polish]" *Monitor of Labour Law*, No. 10:11.

Skąpski, M. 2006. *Protective Function of Labour Law in a Market Economy [in Polish]*. Zakamycze: Kantor Wydawniczy.

Sobczyk, A. 2010. "The Extended Reference Periods [in Polish]," *The Labour and the Social Security (LSS)*, No. 10:13.

Stelina, J., and M. Zieleniecki. 2009. "The Anti-crisis Act [in Polish]," *The Labour and the Social Security (LSS)*, No. 10: 2.

FIXED-TERM EMPLOYMENT CONTRACTS IN POLAND: IN SEARCH OF EQUILIBRIUM BETWEEN FLEXIBILITY AND PROTECTION

ŁUKASZ PISARCZYK

1. Introductory Remarks

In a number of countries, one of the most relevant consequences of the global crises has been the growing instability of labour markets. Employers now search for forms of employment which respond to the real demand for work,[1] and this leads to some dangerous phenomena such as growth in the informal economy or illegal employment.[2] The crisis has also stimulated changes within employment relationships encouraging the emergence of atypical forms of employment. One example of this within the employment relationship is the decreasing number of open-ended contracts and the rise in the use of fixed-term employment.

2. Fixed-term Contracts and Flexicurity Policy

In an attempt to adjust labour law to the changing circumstances, the legislator has to search for a compromise between the market's and the employees' expectations as regards the stability of employment and its conditions. As a result, national labour laws become more and more flexible. The notion of flexibility covers numerous aspects of the legal relationship existing between the parties to the employment contract, such

---

[1] Mialon, M.-F. 2003. "Flexible Rules or Rigid Labour Relations?" in *Changing Industrial Relations and Modernisation of Labour Law*, eds. Blanpain, R., and M. Weiss, (The Hague: Kluwer Law International), 282.

[2] See Owens, R. "Regulatory Frameworks and Law Enforcement in New Forms of Employment," XIX World Congress of Labour and Social Security Law, Sydney, Australia, 2009.

as flexible working hours, wage flexibility, arrangements concerning the workplace (internal flexibility), and part-time, temporary work or fixed-term employment relationships (external flexibility).[3] The importance of special flexible forms of employment in various countries depends on their tradition and current situation. In some of them, part-time work plays the most important role, while in others, efforts are directed towards making their working time regulations more flexible.[4] On the other hand, working conditions remain the key point of social policy of the European Union and its Member States. Art. No. 31 of the Charter of Fundamental Rights of the European Union clearly states that every worker has the right to work in adequate conditions for his/her health, with safety and dignity. This resulted in a *flexicurity* policy and the European Employment Strategy which combines both, more freedom for entrepreneurs and protection of employees.

The search for equilibrium between the above various expectations also took place in Poland. As a result, over the last decade the Polish legislator has introduced (in some instances only temporarily) a number of legal instruments aimed at encouraging the growth of employment which *inter alia* includes:

- more flexible working hours (daily working time may be extended to 12 hours with further exceptions in case of jobs of special nature);
- longer reference periods (up to 12 months) which could be applied till the end of the year 2011;
- the promotion of part-time work;
- the possibility to temporarily worsen working conditions (to protect working places);

---

[3] See e.g. Rojot, J. 2004. "Security of Employment and Employability," in *Comparative Labour Law and Industrial Relations in Industrialized Market Economies*, ed. Blanpain, R., (The Hague: Kluwer Law International), 380 and Reichold, H., and S. Krauch. 2008. "The Impact of New Forms of Labour on Industrial Relations and the Evolution of Labour Law in Germany," *Europäische Zeitschrift für Arbeitsrecht,* 4:486-494.

[4] The finest example of the application of part-time work is the Netherlands, where the level of part-time workers exceeds 40%. For more details see Jacobs, A. 2004. *Labour Law in the Netherlands.* The Hague: Kluwer Law International, 78-79. In the year 2009 it amounted to 48.3%. As regards the flexibility of working hours, major developments have been observed over the recent years: International Labour Organization. 2005. *Hours of Work: From Fixed to Flexible? [International Labour Conference, 93rd Session 2005].* Geneva: ILO, 8-12.

- the possibility to suspend the employment relationship and to shorten working time (employees' interests are protected by payments from public funds)—those instruments were provided temporarily (till the end of the year 2011);
- the promotion of lifelong learning (particularly during the economic crisis).

Consequently, labour law has become more flexible and more friendlier towards employers. However, the main purpose of labour legislation remained the protection of the employee as a weaker party to the employment relationship. Employees are now protected in a slightly different way than in the past. The law intends to develop employee's adaptability and employability focusing on education and vocational training. For instance, the anti-crisis regulations provide for the funding of different forms of training, mainly as regards workers employed by employers in financial difficulties. The law also promotes social dialogue which should replace a part of protective laws created by the state[5] in the years to come. In general, the above mentioned social action may be considered to be a Polish version of flexicurity policy leading to the creation of a flexible, but also secure, labour market.

First of all, growing flexibility of employment is connected with the application of fixed-term contracts. According to statistics the rate of fixed-term workers amounted to 27.9% in the fourth quarter of 2006 and 28.4% in the fourth quarter of 2007. The rate of fixed-term employment contracts decreased slightly in the fourth quarter of 2008 (26.9%), the result of a significant improvement of the economic situation in Poland.[6] In the year 2009, however, Poland overtook Spain and became the leading country within the EU as regards the rate of fixed-term contracts.[7] This

---

[5] See e.g. Seweryński, M. 1999. *Polish Labour Law from Communism to Democracy*. Warsaw: Dom Wydawniczy ABC, 210-214.

[6] The number of fixed-term employees amounted in 2006: 3 171 000 out of 11 380 000 employees, in 2007: 3 403 000 out of 12 001 000 employees and in 2008: 3 351 000 out of 12 447 000 employees. Data based on the statistics prepared by the Central Statistical Office: *Quarterly Information on the Labour Market, 4th quarter 2008*: www.stat.gov.pl/cps/rde/xbcr/gus/PUBL_lip_quarterly_inf_on_the_labour_market_4q_2008.pdf.

[7] According to the Eurostat in the year 2009 the rate of fixed-term contracts in Poland remained at the level higher than 26% while the rate of employment contracts for a definite duration in Spain decreased to about 25%. Another country with a relatively high rate of fixed-term contract is Portugal (more than 20%). On the other hand, in some European countries the rate of employment contracts for a

data clearly indicates the considerable importance of employment contracts for a definite duration, which have replaced partly traditional open-ended employment. Consequently, it is necessary to raise the question concerning reasons for such a situation. The main source of the discussed problem is, beyond doubt, the economic and social situation, among which the most important is the growing unemployment rate.

In the past, the promotion of fixed-term contracts was treated as one of the most important factors encouraging the creation of new jobs. The finest example of such a policy was the suspension of the law limiting the possibility of the use of successive fixed-term contracts. The law was suspended from November 2002 to May 2004 as an element of the Government's policy which aimed to combat unemployment. The situation had changed slightly after the accession to the European Union because Poland is obliged to limit fixed-term employment according to European regulations.[8] Despite the existence of the European standards, the rate of contracts remains exceptionally high (twice as high as it is in the entire European Union). Therefore, one should raise the question about the social consequences of the ongoing transition from open-ended to fixed-term employment. The most important issue is whether the employees engaged on a fixed-term basis are granted the protection, which would be sufficient from the point of view of the social market economy principle.

3. Various Types of Fixed-term Contracts

The Polish law recognises three different types of fixed-term employment contracts. According to Art. No. 25 of the Labour Code (L.C.) an employment contract may be concluded for a probationary

---

definite duration was lower than 3%: Estonia (2.5%), Lithuania (2.2%) and Romania (1%). In the United Kingdom it amounted to 5.5%. In the entire European Union it was about 13%.

[8] See Framework Agreement on fixed-term work of 18 March 1999 implemented by the Council Directive 99/70 of 28 June 1999 concerning the framework agreement on fixed-term work concluded by ETUC, UNICE and CEEP, OJ L 175, 10 July 1999, hereinafter referred to as "Agreement". The Agreement sets out a general framework for fixed-term work protecting employees against discrimination. It recognises, however, that contracts of an indefinite duration remain the general form of employment and a very important element in the protection system. Because of this the fixed-term contract must be considered to be the exception. See more in Blanpain, R. 2008. *European Labour Law*. The Hague: Wolters Kluwer, 430-432.

period which may last for a maximum of three months, for a specific duration (the expiration of the contract is usually connected with a calendar date) and for a completion of a particular task.[9] Each of these contracts is regulated in a slightly different manner. The main body of the regulation on fixed-term contracts is placed in the Law of June 26, 1974—the L.C.,[10] that has been amended a number of times i.e. under the influence of the changing economic conditions and the need for the adjustment of the Polish law to European labour law. The general laws concerning fixed-term contracts apply in both, private and public sectors, unless otherwise provided. The list of exceptions is comprised of a number of *leges speciales*. First, special anti-crisis regulations concerning entrepreneurs were in force until the end of the year 2011. The law temporarily modified the way of employees' protection (maximum period of employment instead of number of renewals). Secondly, there are also special laws on fixed-term contracts in public administration. Thirdly, since 2003 there has been a separate legal act relating to temporary employment (employment through temporary employment agencies).[11] Temporary workers are not treated as fixed-term employees in the strict sense because there is no direct contractual link between the actual employer and the employee. Moreover, some important regulations concerning fixed-term employment appeared in the case of collective redundancies.[12]

4. Termination of Fixed-term Employment Contracts

The relatively high popularity of fixed-term contracts among employers reflects, first of all, flexibility connected with the methods of

---

[9] For further details, see Florek, L. 2005. "Labour Law," in *Introduction to Polish Law*, eds. Frankowski, S., and A. Bodnar (The Hague: Kluwer Law International), 279, who indicates the main difference between the contract for a definite period and the contract for a period necessary to perform a particular task. The point is the way in which the period of operation of the contract is fixed (the calendar date versus the accomplishment of a task).

[10] Journal of Laws 1998, No. 21, item 94, as amended. An English language version of the Labour Code may be found in Michałowska, K. 2003. *Polish Labour Code, Bilingual edition Polish-English.* Warsaw: C.H. Beck (with English translation).

[11] Employment of Temporary Workers Act 2003, Journal of Laws 2003, No. 166, item 1608, as amended.

[12] Collective Redundancies Act 2003, Journal of Laws 2003, No. 90, item 844, as amended, hereinafter referred to as "CRA".

termination of such contracts. The non-permanent character of employment eliminates some disadvantages appearing for employers in the case of the worsening of their economic situation. As a rule, fixed-term contracts expire, by virtue of law, at the end of the term for which they were made, and on the date when the work for which it was concluded is completed. As a consequence, no period of notice is required. The flexibility of fixed-term employment increases due to the relatively easy possibility to terminate the contract before its expiration date. This solution distinguishes the Polish law from numerous legal systems which allow such a termination, apart from mutual agreement of parties, only in extraordinary cases such as *force majeure* or serious misconduct of one of the parties to the contract. In Poland the manner of the termination depends on the circumstances in which the termination occurs and the type of employment contract.

The earlier termination with a period of notice of each fixed-term contract is provided for in specific situations such as: liquidation or insolvency of the employer (Art. No. 41^1 par. 2 L.C.) and, if the employer employs not less than 20 employees, for the reasons not related to individual employees (i.e. on economic or organisational grounds). The possibility to terminate the employment contract in such a way is provided in Art. No. 5.7. and Art. No. 10.1. CRA. The only disadvantage is that the employer is obliged to pay a severance allowance which depends on the period of employment with a given employer and amounts to: 1-month wages, if the employee has been employed less than 2 years; 2-months wages, if the employee has been employed not longer than 8 years; 3-months wages, if the employee has been employed longer than 8 years (Art. No. 8.1. CRA). The relatively low level of severance payment does not create an important obstacle in the termination of an employment relationship. In addition, the entitlement to severance payment is not provided if a fixed-term contract expires by virtue of law, even if the reasons for which it is not renewed are based on the employer's decision. Thanks to this solution the employer may match the total amount of work to the actual needs, realising a flexible policy of employment.

Further regulations concerning the termination of fixed-term employment relationships with a period of notice depends on the type of the contract which was chosen by the parties. The employment contract for a probationary period may be terminated by each party with a given period of notice. No justification is required. The high flexibility reflects the assumption that the main objective of the probationary period is to facilitate for the employer the recognition of the employee's skills and abilities before he/she enters the employment relationship of permanent character. In the case of the earlier achievement of the above mentioned target the employer is not obliged to continue the employment relationship. The law of the greatest importance is Art. No. 33 L.C., which concerns the employment contracts for a definite duration. This regulation stipulates that if the employment contract is concluded for a period longer than six months the parties may terminate it with two weeks notice.[13] The termination requires neither justification nor consultation with the trade union representing the employee. The above mentioned conditions have to be met in case of the termination of the employment relationship for an indefinite duration (according to Art. No. 38 and Art. No. 45 L.C.).[14] If the requirements determined in Art. No. 33 L.C. are fulfilled, the employer may terminate the employment contract at any moment (even if the employment relationship lasts less than 6 months)[15] and just by issuing the declaration of will concerning the termination of the employment relationship with a period of notice. The clause allowing the earlier termination may be introduced not only at the time of the conclusion of the contract but also at a later date.[16] On the other hand, the parties can limit the right to terminate the contract with a period of notice by determining the situation in which the termination will be allowed (e.g. if important reasons occur). Also an appropriate compensation may be provided.

Moreover, many fixed-term contracts are concluded for relatively long periods (even for 10 or 15 years). It guarantees the stability of the workforce (employees exercise the right to dissolve their contracts rather rarely) while the employer is still entitled to terminate the contract at any

---

[13] The introduction of the clause provided for in Art. No. 33 L.C. depends theoretically on the will of both parties to the employment contract. Practically, it appears in nearly all fixed-term contracts concluded in Poland. Because of the difficult situation on the labour market the employer is able to dictate the employment conditions, and the nature of employment contract becomes rather adhesive.

[14] The requirements for justified reason and the consultation with a trade union organisation constitute the general protection against the termination of employment contract conferred upon all employees employed for an indefinite period. The fixed-term employees are, however, covered by the special protection existing in case of the employee's particular situation (e.g. pregnancy, maternity leave, military service etc.). For more details see Florek, L. 2005. "Labour Law," in *Introduction to Polish Law*, eds. Frankowski, S., and A. Bodnar (The Hague: Kluwer Law International), 283.

[15] The ruling of the Supreme Court of September 7, 1994, I PZP 35/94, Official Journal 1994, No. 11, item 173.

[16] The ruling of the Supreme Court of June 14, 1994, I PZP 26/94, Official Journal 1994, No. 8, item 126.

time, without justification and with a period of notice which amounts to 2 weeks only. In numerous cases it leads, in fact, to the evasion of the laws relating to permanent employment which provides for a much higher level of protection. The employees are forced, by the economic situation, to consent to such conditions without any guarantee of future cooperation. They are protected only to a limited extent by the judiciary when fixed-term contracts are concluded for a relatively long time (7, 9 or 10 years) without objective justification and with the possibility of the earlier termination with period of notice. In such situations the Supreme Court has declared fixed-term contracts null and void as they intended to evade the regulations on general protection against dismissal which is provided for as regards employment contracts for indefinite duration.[17] As a consequence the contractual clause which determines the termination date does not exist and the contract is considered to be concluded for an indefinite duration.[18] Long lasting fixed-term contracts are allowed when they are objectively justified or concluded without the termination clause. This type of protection is not, however, efficient enough. In the cases when the employment contract concluded for the replacement of the absent worker no contractual clause is required and the period of notice is extremely short amounting just to three working days. Also in this situation the termination requires neither justification nor consultation with the trade union which represents the employee.

A completely different situation exists as far as the employment contract for the completion of a specific task is concerned. As a rule this type of employment contract cannot be terminated before the target is reached (the task is completed). For that reason the conclusion of the discussed type of contract gives the employer a relatively low level of flexibility. As a consequence, the employment contract concluded for the completion of a particular task has not become a popular form of employment in Poland.

Each employment contract for a definite duration can be terminated without a period of notice if situations of extraordinary character take place. The employer is entitled to terminate the employment relationship in that way in cases of serious misconduct or a crime committed by the employee, the loss of the qualifications necessary to perform work through the fault of the employee (Art. No. 52 L.C.) and in case of the long absence of the employee (Art. No. 53 L.C.). It is also to be stressed that

[17] The ruling of the Supreme Court of September 7, 2005, II PK 294/04, Official Journal 2006, No. 13-14, item 207.

[18] The ruling of the Supreme Court of October 25, 2007, II PK 49/07, Official Journal 2008 No. 21-22, item 317.

even if a legal act terminating the fixed-term contract is contrary to the law, the goal, i.e. the termination of the contract, is achieved.

To summarise, fixed-term contracts constitute in Poland a very flexible form of employment. The Polish legislator accepts the precarious nature of this type of employment because of the relatively high rate of unemployment and high employment costs, hoping that the discussed advantages of contracts for a definite duration encourage the employers to engage new workers. From this perspective fixed-term employment reflects the weakness of the labour market,[19] only to some extent being an instrument of real flexibility improving the position of employees.

Consequently, the phenomenon of the enormous use of fixed-term employment has changed the Polish labour market creating two different standards of protection: relatively high in the case of permanent workers and much lower in the case of fixed-term employees. This part of the Polish labour market has dangerously approached the *hire and fire* model. The lack of stabilisation seems to be highly disputable in light of the principles of the social market economy (Art. No. 20 of the Polish Constitution) and the protection of work (Art. No. 24 of the Polish Constitution) which should imply a certain level of protection, including stability of employment. On the other hand, the Constitutional Court stated that the special rules concerning the termination of fixed-term contracts reflect the unique nature of these contracts and, as a consequence, do not contradict the constitutional principle of equal treatment.[20] The way to the maintenance of particularly high level of fixed-term employment is therefore open.

5. The Need for Special Protection of Fixed-term Employees

On the one hand, the legislator does not lean towards the elimination of fixed-term contracts, recognising that they are a feature of employment in certain sectors, occupations and activities which can suit both employers and workers. The application of employment contracts of a definite duration are also treated as contributing to a flexible labour market. On the other hand, instability of the situation of the employees engaged on a

[19] This aspect of fixed-term employment is stressed by de Grip, A., J. Hoevenberg, and E. Willems. 1997. "Atypical Employment in the European Union," *International Labour Review,* No. 1:70.

[20] The ruling of the Constitutional Court of December 2, 2008, P 48/07, Journal of Laws 2008, No. 219, item 1409.

fixed-term basis was the main reason of the action aimed at improving their working conditions. The employees should not be excluded from the benefits of stable employment. The employment contracts of an indefinite duration remain the key element in the protection of workers and the fixed-term contracts should be treated as the exception accepted in justified cases. As a consequence, the legislator adopted measures ensuring the application of the principle of non-discrimination and established a framework to prevent abuse arising from the use of successive fixed-term employment contracts or relationships.

6. Protection against Abuses

The key element of the legal regulation of fixed-term employment is the elimination of potential abuse accompanying the application of employment contracts for a definite duration. In this area the phenomenon of "chain fixed-term contracts" has been particularly common. It leads to the long-lasting fixed-term employment replacing in fact open-ended contracts. To prevent abuses various protective measures are adopted.[21] The impression arises that the method of the regulation depends, to a great extent, on the objectives assumed by the legislator. If fixed-term contracts are to be an instrument to increase the rate of employment, the laws try to avoid the requirement for the justification indicating the maximum length of employment or the maximum number of renewals. Due to such regulations the employer gains an advantageous, flexible form of employment which makes their position towards the employee much stronger. From this perspective, a fixed-term contract becomes one of the elements of the active labour market policy aimed at combating unemployment. On the other hand, figures show that the actual role of the fixed-term employment in this area is rather limited. As a rule, it contributes to the creation of the jobs of a lower quality which cease to exist when the period of prosperity or public support ends. Very often deregulation did not lead directly to the increase in the number of jobs available changing rather the dynamics and structure of employment.[22]

---

[21] Clause 5(1) of the Agreement requires the Member States to introduce one or more of the following measures: objective reasons justifying the renewal of such contracts or relationships; the maximum total duration of successive fixed-term employment contracts or relationships; the number of renewals of such contracts or relationships.

[22] International Labour Organisation, 2000. *Termination of Employment Digest*. Geneva: ILO, 11-12.

The Polish legislator decided to introduce the mixed method of the regulation depending on the character of employment contracts and the nature of work to be performed. In a number of cases, when it is justified by objective reasons, fixed-term contracts may be concluded without further restrictions. The justification for the conclusion and renewal exists in relation to contracts concluded to substitute an absent employee, seasonal works or works performed on a periodical basis (Art. No. 25^1 par. 3 L.C.) as well as employment contracts for the completion of a specific task. In the above mentioned situation there are no limits concerning the total duration of fixed-term employment or the number of renewals. If there are no objective grounds for the conclusion or renewal of the contracts Art. No. 25^1 par. 1 L.C. only allows two successive part-time contracts. The employment contracts are considered to be successive if the period of time between the termination of the previous employment relationship and the conclusion of the subsequent employment contract is no longer than one month. The conclusion of the third successive employment contract for definite duration shall have the same legal consequences as the conclusion of an employment contract for an indefinite period. According to Art. No. 25^1 par. 2 L.C., the alternation of the date of the expiration of the contract shall be treated as a conclusion of the successive employment contract. The objective of the discussed regulation is the elimination of the possible evasion of law by determining the new expiration date instead of concluding a new contract which happened in the past.[23] The contract expires at the originally determined date. From the next day the following employment contact (for a definite or indefinite period) comes into force.[24] The problem is that in practice this rule may be quite easily avoided. The chain can be disrupted by the conclusion of a civil law contract or even by a fixed-term employment contract based on objective grounds irrespective of the duration of such a contract. In some circumstances the conclusion of such a contract may be, however, considered as an evasion of law.

---

[23] Instead of concluding a new contract employers offered to employees the alternation of the ending date of a contract. If they attended to evade the law on fixed-term contracts, the provisions were considered by the courts as null and void unless the alternation was justified by objective reasons. See e.g. the ruling of the Supreme Court of November 21, 2000, Official Journal 2002, No. 11, item 270.

[24] The ruling of the Supreme Court, October 10 2002 , I PKN 546/01, PiZS 2003, No. 5, p. 37.

The time limit of fixed-term employment is provided, but only temporarily, by anti-crisis laws[25] which apply to entrepreneurs. Until the end of the year 2011 the successive contracts for specified durations could not exceed in total 24 months. Contracts are considered to be successive if the period of time between the termination of the previous employment relationship and the conclusion of the subsequent employment contract is no longer than three months. Employment contracts which are in force on 1 January 2012 are covered by basic protective mechanism provided for in Art. No. 25^1 par. 1 L.C.

Apart from the measures directly protecting against abuse, the employers shall inform fixed-term workers about vacancies which become available in the undertaking or establishment (Art. No. 94^2 L.C.) to ensure that they have the same opportunity to secure permanent positions as other workers. The duty should be carried out in accordance with the procedures applicable to the employer. Information may be provided by way of a general announcement at a suitable place in the undertaking or establishment.

7. Protection against Discrimination

It seems to be of great importance that the law in Poland does not differentiate employees' positions because of the character of employment contract. The Polish law forbids any form of direct or indirect discrimination based on the character of employment. From the general provisions of the L.C., it may be inferred that in respect to employment conditions fixed-term workers shall not be treated in a less favourable manner than comparable permanent workers solely because they have a fixed-term contract or relationship, unless different treatment is justified on objective grounds.

The general regulations establishing the principle of equal treatment and non-discrimination are accompanied by more particular regulations determining the consequences of potential infringements. First of all, the Polish legislator tends to eliminate the discriminating provisions of collective agreements and internal regulations applied in a given undertaking[26] if they introduce provisions differentiating the position of

---

[25] Mitigation of the Impact of the Economic Crisis on Employees and Entrepreneurs Employment Act 2009, Journal of Laws 2009, No. 125, item 1035, as amended.

[26] The Labour Code provides for two main types of internal regulations concerning remuneration (Art. No. 77^2) and work order (Art. No. 104-104^3). The character of internal regulations is similar to collective agreements. They are issued by the

workers due to the character of employment, e.g. limiting access to vocational training only to permanent employees. To avoid such situations, Art. No. 9 par. 4 L.C. provides that the provisions of collective agreements or internal regulations which breach the principle of equal treatment are not binding. In the case of collective agreements the registrar (minister competent in labour affairs or competent district labour inspector) may intervene to eliminate the provisions breaching the law (Art. No. 241^{11} L.C.). As far as the individual employment contract is concerned Art. No. 18 par. 3 L.C. provides that provisions upon which an employment contract interferes with the principle of equal treatment and shall be invalid. The appropriate provisions of labour law[27] shall be applied instead. If there are no appropriate regulations of law, less favourable clauses of the contract shall be replaced by the parties with appropriate provisions of anti-discriminatory character. The appropriate provisions may be introduced by the court as well. In the case of the violation of the principle of equal treatment the employee, being a victim of the employer's misconduct, is entitled to compensation not lower than the one-month minimum wage. The protection against discrimination is strengthened by the regulation concerning the burden of proof (Art. No. 18^{3b} par. 1 L.C.). When an employee considers him- or herself wronged because of the breach of the principle of equal treatment, it is for the employer to prove that the difference in treatment can be justified on objectives grounds (the employee must, however, indicate the manifestations of unequal treatment and his/her reason).

8. Conclusions

To summarise, fixed-term employment plays a particularly important role in the Polish labour market—more than one quarter of all Polish workers are employed on a fixed-term basis. The scale of the phenomenon is closely connected with the flexibility which fixed-term employment gives to the employers. There is no entitlement to severance payment in case of the expiration of the contract, the employee enjoys no protection

---

employer upon the trade union's agreement or unilaterally if in a given establishment trade unions do not exist. See further Florek, L. 2005. "Labour Law," in *Introduction to Polish Law*, eds. Frankowski, S., and A. Bodnar (The Hague: Kluwer Law International), 277-278.

[27] The concept of labour law is used in a broad sense covering, according to Art. No. 9 par. 1 L.C., provisions of laws, as well as the provisions of collective agreements, internal regulations and statutes which set out the rights and obligations of parties to an employment relationship.

against earlier dismissal either. As a consequence, the worsening of the employer's market position may entail flexible changes in the workforce. This emphasises the particularly precarious nature of fixed-term employment in Poland. Because of that, it is the employee who bears the risk of alternation in the market situation of the undertaking.

The side effect of the current policy is the segmentation of the labour market with different standards of protection—higher, in case of open-ended employment, and much lower as far as fixed-term workers are concerned. The long-lasting acceptance for relatively easy use of employment for definite duration may make the elimination of "fixed-term employment culture" extremely difficult. The further growth in fixed-term employment will lead to the domination of flexibility over security. Such a situation would be contrary to the basic rules of the labour law system in the social market economy.

As a result, it is necessary to undertake legal action which would eliminate the appearing threats. To conclude, the process of the creation of legal frameworks for fixed-term contracts has not been finished yet. The main task for the years to come is to eliminate the existing gap by the limitation of the number of fixed-term workers or improvement in their working conditions. It becomes clear, however, that any further progress in this area depends only to some extent on legislative measures, being rather closely connected with the economic situation.[28] Economic growth constitutes the key condition for the decrease in the number of fixed-term contracts.

References

Blanpain, R. 2008. *European Labour Law*. The Hague: Wolters Kluwer.

Compa, L. "Trade Liberalization and Labour Law," World Congress of Labour and Social Security Law, Paris, France, 2006.

de Grip, A., J. Hoevenberg, and E. Willems. 1997. "Atypical Employment in the European Union," *International Labour Review,* No. 1:70.

Florek, L. 2005. "Labour Law," in *Introduction to Polish Law*, eds. Frankowski, S., and A. Bodnar (The Hague: Kluwer Law International).

---

[28] The situation on labour markets depends not only on labour law but also on fiscal or economic instruments. See e.g. Compa, L. "Trade Liberalization and Labour Law," World Congress of Labour and Social Security Law, Paris, France, 2006, 3.

International Labour Organisation, 2000. *Termination of Employment Digest*. Geneva: ILO.

—. 2005. *Hours of Work: From Fixed to Flexible? [International Labour Conference, 93rd Session 2005]*. Geneva: ILO, 8-12.

Jacobs, A. 2004. *Labour Law in the Netherlands*. The Hague: Kluwer Law International.

Mialon, M.-F. 2003. "Flexible Rules or Rigid Labour Relations?" in *Changing Industrial Relations and Modernisation of Labour Law*, eds. Blanpain, R., and M. Weiss, (The Hague: Kluwer Law International).

Michałowska, K. 2003. *Polish Labour Code, Bilingual edition Polish-English.* Warsaw: C.H. Beck.

Owens, R. "Regulatory Frameworks and Law Enforcement in New Forms of Employment," XIX World Congress of Labour and Social Security Law, Sydney, Australia, 2009.

Reichold, H., and S. Krauch. 2008. "The Impact of New Forms of Labour on Industrial Relations and the Evolution of Labour Law in Germany," *Europäische Zeitschrift für Arbeitsrecht,* 4:486-494.

Royot, J. 2004. "Security of Employment and Employability," in *Comparative Labour Law and Industrial Relations in Industrialized Market Economies*, ed. Blanpain, R., (The Hague: Kluwer Law International).

Seweryński, M. 1999. *Polish Labour Law from Communism to Democracy*. Warsaw: Dom Wydawniczy ABC.

CHAPTER TWO:

PARTICULARLY PROBLEMATIC LABOUR LAW ISSUES

TERMINATION OF EMPLOYMENT CONTRACTS IN POLAND

LUDWIK FLOREK

The employment contract in Poland may be terminated by expiration or dissolution. Expiration takes place for reasons other than legal actions. The situation in which an employment relationship expires is defined in labour law in great detail. Specifically, expiration may result from the employee's death or the employer's death, if the employing establishment is not taken over by a successor. The contract of employment expires after an employee's three months' absence at work due to a temporary arrest, unless the employer had terminated the contract of employment without notice due to the employee's fault. The employer, regardless of the expiry of the contract of employment due to a temporary arrest, is obliged to reinstate the employee if the criminal proceedings have been terminated or if he/she has been acquitted, and the employee reports their return to work within seven days from the date when the decision becomes valid. Expiration may also result from other occurrences mentioned by the legal regulations applicable to specific public professions (e.g., loss of Polish citizenship or public rights or dismissal from public service).

Dissolution is a result of legal actions undertaken by one or both of the parties to the employment contract. First of all, an employment contract may be terminated by agreement of the parties. Such an agreement may be initiated by either party. The dissolution takes place on the date set by the parties. The agreement is not subject to any restrictions. In particular, it is not necessary to provide reasons for the dissolution or to consult a trade union. Understandably, in such instances the employee is not entitled to any form of protection against dismissal.

An employment contract may also be terminated when either party expresses an intention to terminate the employment relationship. In particular, the Polish Labour Code[1] makes provision for the termination of an employment contract without notice. Such notice is a unilateral

[1] Act of 26 June 1974 (Journal of Laws 1998, No. 21, Item 94 with subsequent amendments).

statement made by either party to the employment relationship, resulting in dissolution of the contract upon the lapse of the time period indicated in the statement (the so-called period of notice). This is the basic method of dissolution for contracts concluded for an unspecified period. Giving notice is also a standard method by which trial-period contracts and contracts for specified periods exceeding six months are terminated, assuming that the parties have provided for this form of termination. According to the Art. No. 33 of the Labour Code, where a contract of employment is concluded for a definite period, longer than six months, the parties may provide for an earlier termination of the contract with a two-week period of notice.[2] Regardless of the period for which contracts have been concluded, notice to terminate contracts for a specified period or contracts for completion of a particular task may be given for reasons attributable to the employer (e.g., bankruptcy or liquidation of the employment establishment).

The party's statement to terminate the employment contract must be in writing. The employer's notification of termination must give the reasons for termination and also advise the employees of their right to appeal the termination decision to the labour court.

The period of notice is a period after which the employment relationship ceases to exist by virtue of the statement of the party terminating the employment contract. The period must not be shorter than the period provided for in the Code and its specific length depends on the type of contract and, in the case of a contract for an unspecified period, on the length of service with a given employer. The length of service with a previous employer, when the new one is the legal successor, must also be taken into account. In a case of dismissal with notice due to the business necessity of an enterprise, an employer may shorten the legally required period of notification from three to one month. In such a case, the worker is entitled to a compensation (severance pay) for the remaining two months (Art. No. 36^1 par. 1 of the Labour Code).

During the period of notice the employees shall be entitled to paid time off to look for a job. The amount of time off shall be: 1) two working days—for a period of notice not longer than one month, 2) three working days—for a three-month period of notice (Art. No. 37).

Protection against the termination of an employment contract may be either of a general or special nature. General protection covers all employees. Special protection covers only those employees whose

[2] Małyszek, S. 2009. *Polnisches Arbeits- und Sozialversicherungsrecht.* Munich: C. H. Beck, 85.

situation justifies temporary restriction on the employer's right to terminate their employment contract during protective periods. It can also apply due to a special personal, life or family situation of the employee, or the employee's social or State obligations. The protection may consist either in a complete prohibition on terminating the employment relationship by notice or making notice conditional on obtaining approval from certain bodies. These restrictions on the right to give notice to terminate employment contracts apply only to employers. In contrast, employees enjoy full freedom to exercise their right to terminate employment, which derives from the principle of freedom of work (Art. No. 11).[3]

General protection against termination applies to employees hired under employment contracts for an unspecified period. These employees are protected against arbitrary termination of such contracts because the employer's notice to that effect is subject to two limitations. First, notice to terminate the contract may be given only after a proper consultation procedure with a trade union has been completed (Art. No. 38). The employer, shall inform in writing the trade union of the establishment of the intention of giving an employee a notice of termination of the contract of employment concluded for an indefinite time, including reasons for the termination of the contract. If the trade union body of the establishment decides that such termination would be unjustified, it may present the employer with substantiated objections in writing within five days of receiving the notice.

An employer is only entitled to give termination notice for justified reasons (Art. No. 45). Since the Labour Code provides only a general clause of a just cause, the decision as to what does and what does not justify a dismissal has been left entirely, in case of a dispute, to the discretion of a labour court upon consideration of factual circumstances. As a result, jurisprudence has determined quite precisely what kind of issues can be valid reasons for dismissal. Generally speaking, this can be connected with the capacity or conduct of the worker or based on the operational requirements of the undertaking resulting in employment rate. As it is in a number of national legislations in Europe, any of these reasons should be true and serious.

Special protection against termination consists of the prohibition on terminating the contract or the obligation to obtain prior approval from the proper representative body of employees or the appropriate State body.

---

[3] ILO, Profile of Polish legislation on termination of employment: http://tinyurl.com/66rfm6.

The prohibition on giving termination notice is in force during some protective periods or with regard to some categories of employees. In some situations both giving notice of termination and terminating the contract are prohibited. This means that during protective periods the contract may not be terminated. Moreover, the employment relationship must not cease even if notice was given before the beginning of the protective period. The prohibition on giving notice of termination applies, for example, when an employee is on leave or is absent from work for good cause. Other situations include the pre-trial detention of the employee for a period of up to three months upon the lapse of which the employment contract expires (Art. No. 66, par. 1), pregnancy or maternity leave. The employer may not terminate the contract of employment with employees who will reach the retirement pension age in less than four years, should they then acquire the right to pension.

The obligation to obtain approval from the appropriate body (usually the one in which the employee performs a given function) to terminate the contract applies especially to persons who are members of the trade union's executive board or members of the employees' council. The prohibition also applies with respect to deputies to the Sejm (one of the two chambers of Parliament), senators (during their term and within two years of its expiration) or members of a local self-government.

An employer may also terminate an employment contract without notice for reasons attributable to the employee, some of which may be related to the employee's fault. It is thus possible to terminate an employment contract without notice for fault-related reasons in the event of the employee's gross violation of professional duties, the employee's culpable loss of authorisation necessary for performance of work at a given position and the commission of an offence during the period of the employment contract (the offence must be of a nature that precludes further employment at a given position assuming that the commission of the offence is evident or has been established by a final court judgment).

Notice to terminate an employment contract for fault-related reasons may not be given if one month has passed since the employment establishment obtained information regarding the circumstances that justified dissolution of the contract. The trade union organisation should be notified of the reasons justifying dissolution of the contract and must issue an advance opinion for the dissolution to become valid.

An employer may also terminate an employment contract without notice and without any fault of the employee when the employee's absence, although justified, is of long duration. In particular, it is possible to terminate an employment relationship after a three, six, nine or twelve month absence caused by illness (depending on the employee's length of service and the kind and course of the illness). An employment contract may also be terminate after an employee's sixty-day absence caused by caring for a child or isolation ordered in connection with an infectious disease or in the event of justified absence from work due to other reasons if the absence has lasted for over one month. An employment contract must not be terminated without notice once the employee resumes work as soon as the reasons for the absence cease to exist.

A separate set of rules governs the modification of the terms of employment. Giving notice to modify terms of work or remuneration is considered a unilateral legal action of the employer (Art. No. 42, par. 1). This action aims at either replacing, upon lapse of the period of notice, the original terms of employment (including remuneration) or at terminating the employment relationship upon lapse of that period if the employee rejects the new terms of employment. The notice to modify the original terms of work is valid if the new terms have been communicated to the employee in writing (Art. No. 42, par. 2). The termination of recent conditions of work or remuneration shall not be required if the employee is assigned, when it is justifiable by the interest of the employer, work other than that specified in the contract of employment for a period not longer than three months in a calendar year, if that does not result in lower remuneration and corresponds with the qualifications of the employee.

Apart from the general regulation of the termination of an employment contract, the law provides for special terms for lay-offs for reasons not attributable to the employee.[4] This type of lay-off is regulated by the 2003 Law on the Special Rules on Terminating Employment Relationships for Reasons not Attributable to the Employee.[5] The law addresses both group lay-offs and individual redundancies. Its provisions are designed to help adjust employment to the employer's needs and capacity which sometimes involves restricting the scope of protection against employment termination. Furthermore, the regulations provide for information and consultation procedure with respect to group lay-offs and also grant certain rights to the individuals being laid off, including the right to a severance payment and, in the case of group lay-offs, the opportunity to return to work.

The law applies to establishments employing at least 20 employees. Smaller employers are exempt and may lay off employees on general principles. The law applies when the lay-offs are "not attributable to

---

[4] Raczkowski, B. 2009. "Poland", in *Collective Redundancies Guide*, (Brussels: Ius Laboris), 163.

[5] J.L. 2003, No. 90, Item 844 with subsequent amendments.

employees", which usually implies reasons attributable to the employer. Special reasons necessitating lay-offs include the liquidation or bankruptcy of the employer, which, as a rule, involves laying off the entire workforce, unless some part or the entire establishment is taken over by another entity.

Mass lay-offs are defined as the termination of employment agreements within 30 days of at least 10 employees out of a total under 100 employees, 10 per cent of employees out of a total of between 100 and 300 employees, and 30 employees out of a total of at least 300 employees. The aforementioned rules also apply to terminations by the parties' mutual consent if at least five employees are involved.

In the case of group lay-offs, the employer is obliged to inform the trade unions functioning in the establishment of the reasons for the lay-offs, the number and profile of the employees to be laid off, the lay-off period, the criteria for selecting the employees to be laid off, the order in which the lay-offs will be implemented and of any additional employee rights connected with the lay-off (i.e., the right to retrain in another profession or receive compensation). The same information has to be furnished to the local labour bureau. Trade unions may submit proposals on the avoidance of the contemplated lay-offs or reduction in their scope (e.g., by a temporary voluntary reduction in remuneration).

No later than 20 days after the information referred to above has been provided, the employer and the trade unions should initiate talks in order to reach an agreement, which is to specify the procedure to be followed in the case of the lay-offs and also as the rights to be observed by the employer (e.g., the payment of higher severance pay to the employees). If no agreement has been reached, the employer announces termination rules, which should be substantially similar to the terms of the failed agreement. If there are no trade unions in a given employment establishment, the intention to conduct lay-offs and the announcement of the lay-off rules must be communicated to employee representatives selected according to a procedure applicable to a given employer. After the agreement has been reached or the lay-off rules have been announced, the employer is obliged to notify the local labour bureau. Lay-offs may follow after the lapse of 30 days from such a notification, which is designed to give the labour bureau enough time to find new jobs for the laid off employees.

The aforementioned procedure does not apply in case of individual lay-offs for reasons not attributable to the employees when the number of laid off individuals is smaller than what is defined as a group lay-off. Finally, the new law grants certain rights to the employees laid off in accordance with the procedure specified therein. First of all, this includes the right of all employees laid off individually or as a group to receive a severance payment. The severance payment is equal to one, two or three month's remuneration to employees who have worked for a given employer for up to two, between two and eight and over eight years, respectively.

The 2003 law provides for benefits to which a dismissed employee is entitled. In particular, every employee dismissed for the above mentioned reasons has the right to discharge money (severance pay). Discharge money is calculated as vacation leave and would be paid in the following amount:

- one-month pay, if an employee's total period of employment is under 10 years,
- two-months' pay, if any employee's total period of employment is 10 or more years but less than 20,
- three-months' pay, if an employee's total period of employment is 20 or more years.[6]

It should be stressed that this benefit is granted to all the employees dismissed for reasons not attributable to the employee and not only those dismissed as a result of mass lay-offs. An employee dismissed as a result of mass lay-offs should be re-employed in the case of new employment of employees from the same professional group, if the employee informs the employer of his intention to be re-employed within a year after the termination of employment contract.

The Code provides for the equal treatment of employees, which means they may not be discriminated against with respect to the termination of the employment contract, on the grounds specified in Arts. 11^3 and 18^{3a} namely: gender, age, disability, race, religion, nationality, views (in particular political or religious), trade union membership, ethnic background, denomination and sexual orientation. Employees should be treated equally with respect to the initiation and termination of the employment relationship, employment terms, promotion opportunities and access to training.

An undertaking or its part can be transferred to the new employer (change of the employer). Under Art. No. 23^1 of the Labour Code, when part of the employing establishment is transferred to another employer, the latter becomes, by operation of law, the party to the existing labour relationships. This corresponds to Art. No. 3 of the Council Directive

---

[6] ILO's Industrial and Employment Relations Department (DIALOGUE). Available at http://www.ilo.org/public/english/dialogue/ifpdial/info/termination/countries/poland.htm (accessed November 7, 2011).

2001/23/EC of 12 March 2001 on the approximation of the laws of the Member States relating to the safeguarding of employees' rights in the event of transfers of undertakings, businesses or parts of undertakings or businesses.[7]

The transfer of the undertaking, shall not in itself constitute grounds for dismissal of the employee. This provision shall not stand in the way of dismissals that may take place for economic, technical or organisational reasons entailing changes in the workforce. Within two months of the above notification, each employee may terminate his/her labour relationship without notice, seven days in advance.[8]

An employee who considers that his employment has been unjustifiably terminated may appeal to the labour court, that is empowered to examine the reasons given for the termination and other circumstances relating to the case and to render a decision whether the termination was justified. If a contract of employment has been terminated by notice in violation of the mentioned law, a worker is entitled to claim either his reinstatement on the previous conditions or the payment of compensation. The court may disregard the demand of the employee to order the notice of termination ineffective or to order the reinstatement in the job if it determines that it is impossible or aimless to consider such a demand due to a liquidation or bankruptcy of the establishment or due to organisational or production changes connected with reductions in employment in the employing establishment; in such cases the court shall order a due compensation. The employee who has taken up employment in result of a reinstatement shall have the right to remuneration for the period when he was unemployed, however, for not longer than two months, and if the period of notice is three months, for not longer than one month. Where the contract of employment has been terminated with the employee four years before his/her pension or with an employee who is pregnant or on maternity leave, the remuneration shall be paid for the entire period of unemployment; the above shall apply also in cases when the termination of the contract of employment is subject to restrictions by virtue of special provisions. Where a contract of employment concluded for a definite period or for time of performance of a specified task has been terminated in violation of the provisions on termination of such contracts, the employee shall be entitled to due compensation only. Employees who have had their contracts of employment terminated without notice in violation of the provisions of terminating contracts of employment

[7] Official Journal L 08 , 22/03/2001 P. 0016 – 0020.

[8] Jaroslawska, K. 2011. "Polish Labour Law for the UK and US readers, Transfer of Undertakings: the Concept of Transfer," Polish Labour Law Blog.

according to this procedure shall be entitled to reinstatement on former conditions or to a due compensation.[9] In the case of the employee who has taken up employment due to a reinstatement, the time of unemployment for which remuneration has been awarded shall be included in the period of employment. The period of employment for which remuneration has not been awarded shall be deemed an interruption in employment resulting in the loss of rights depending on uninterrupted employment. The employee who has received due indemnity shall have the time of unemployment, for which indemnity was awarded, included in the period of employment.

References

Jaroslawska, K. 2011. "Polish Labour Law for the UK and US readers, Transfer of Undertakings: the Concept of Transfer," Polish Labour Law Blog.

Małyszek, S. 2009. *Polnisches Arbeits- und Sozialversicherungsrecht.* Munich: C. H. Beck.

Raczkowski, B. 2009. "Poland," in *Collective Redundancies Guide*, (Brussels: Ius Laboris), 163.

Swiatkowski, A. M. 2006. *Termination of Employment Relationship: The Legal Situation in Poland.* Employment Protection Legislation Database: European Union.

[9] Swiatkowski, A. M. 2006. *Termination of Employment Relationship: The Legal Situation in Poland.* Employment Protection Legislation Database: European Union. Available at ec.europa.eu/social/BlobServlet?docId=4633.

UKRAINIAN LEGISLATION AND THE REGULATION OF UNFAIR COMPETITION PREVENTION IN LABOUR RELATIONS

OLENA RYM

The reform of the Ukrainian labour legislation—as in other developed market economies—requires taking preliminary steps to ensure that numerous legal institutions are laid down to regulate labour relations—particularly those safeguarding certain rights for both employees and employers. In this sense, improvements are needed when it comes to preventing unfair competition in labour relations.

Unfortunately, national labour legislation does not envisage special norms serving as preventive measures, as well as instruments to assess responsibility for the disclosure and misuse of trade secrets on the part of employees regarding their employers, including any previous employers.

Insufficient research has been carried out which would allow for the possibility to include provisions on the prohibition of competition in employment contracts.[1] In the same vein, and in the light of the recent reform of domestic labour legislation, the importance attached to this issue is increasingly significant, particularly in the sphere of work organisation in the public sector.

Despite major shortcomings in the regulatory framework, it is however possible to limit the competition activity of employees that might be detrimental to their employers, for example, by prohibiting them to hold two jobs. It is worth recalling that in the majority of the developed countries, simultaneous employment of workers hired by competitors of their employer is considered as one of the forms of unfair competitive activity and therefore, it is subject to limitations.

---

[1] Pylypenko, P. D. 2003. *Grounds for Creation of Individual Employment Relationships* [in Ukrainian]. Kiev: "Znannya" Publishing, 80-85.

As said, labour legislation currently in force does not envisage restrictions on the holding of multiple jobs. There are some special provisions for civil servants, deputies and managers performing in state-owned enterprises, establishments, organisations, public prosecution bodies, as well as for notaries and some other categories of workers who, pursuant to national legislation, are not allowed to maintain two positions, or to carry out certain types of jobs simultaneously.

In all other cases, including managers of non-state-owned enterprises, workers have the right to work simultaneously under a few employment contracts. Nevertheless, part 2 Art. No. 21 of Labour Code of Ukraine, which actually abolished limitations, states that employees can perform their working activity by concluding an employment contract with one or, at the same time, with several enterprises, establishments, or organisations—when not prohibited by legislation, collective agreement or the employment contract itself concluded between the parties. This means that the Legislator allows for an employment arrangement which might include the prohibition for an employee to work for other employers simultaneously.[2] Such prohibition can only be set for the duration of the employment contract, with this aspect being emphasised in the letter of the State Committee of Ukraine on matters regarding regulatory policy and enterprise No. 010-541 from 27.05.2002 "Concerning prohibition for the employee to conclude employment contracts with the competitors of his employer". Accordingly, lengthening the duration of such prohibitions might be seen as a limitation of the right to work.[3]

It is important to note that an additional condition is set, that is the absolute prohibition to perform an occupation "after hours", with the possibility of laying down only certain restrictions on work when some employment contracts with other employers are concluded.

As a rule, an employer who proposes such conditions at the conclusion of an employment relationship is entitled to receive maximum output and the highest levels of productivity from the employee. Therefore, as a mandatory condition for the conclusion of the employment contract—somehow counterbalancing the one regarding the prohibition of holding two jobs—it can be expected that the worker demand a higher salary as a

[2] Labour Code of Ukraine. 10 December, 1971 No. 322-VIII. http://zakon.rada.gov.ua/cgi-bin/laws/main.cgi?nreg=322-08 (accessed November 7, 2011)

[3] Letter of the State Committee of Ukraine on matters regarding regulatory policy and enterprise "Concerning the prohibition for employees to conclude labour contracts with competitors of their employer" No. 010-541 from 27.05.2002 http://zakon.nau.ua/doc/?uid=1152.673.0 (accessed November 7, 2011).

compensation for the limitation of their labour rights. Apart from the prohibition of holding a second job, therefore working for a competitor employer, there is also another aspect that can be explicitly provided in the contract, that is the duty of workers not to disclose trade secrets. The inclusion of this clause is made possible by Art. No. 162 of the Commercial Code of Ukraine and 505-506 of the Civil Code of Ukraine. Here, in particular, the definition of trade secrets is given, and it is envisaged that the content and amount of the information making up such a secret, as well as the procedural order of its defence can only be determined by its proprietor—and on behalf of a legal entity—by the manager of the enterprise. Therefore, such matter can be dealt with considering contract law at a local level. On the contrary, provisions for assessing the responsibility for disclosing information—which makes up the trade secret—as well as instruments to guard such information are both laid down in national legislation.[4]

Apart from contractual limitations concerning after hours work and the disclosure of the employer's trade secrets, there are statutory provisions which forbid certain categories of workers from disclosing or using employer's confidential information, because of the type of work performed. For instance, Art. No. 61 of the Law of Ukraine "On banks and banking activity", sets forth duties for bank managers and clerks in terms of not disclosing or making use of confidential information for their own benefit. As the law does not make any reference to criteria for assessing when a piece of information is confidential, it can be only assumed that under certain circumstances the disclosure or use of information of commercial, professional, manufacturing or other nature takes place when the employer as a participant of the competitive market might be negatively affected as a result of such disclosure.

Art. No. 23 of the Law of Ukraine "On Business Associations" lays down the obligation for public servants of business associations, especially for the chairman and the members of the executive body, the head of the supervising committee, the chairman and members of the executive board, not to disclose trade secrets and confidential information. From 17 September 2008, such duty also applied to employees of joint-stock companies, according to part 2 Art. No. 62 of the Law of Ukraine "On joint-stock companies".

The reflections on current domestic laws cause one to infer that legal restrictions on the realisation of competition activity—disclosure and use

---

[4] Pylypenko, P. D. 2003. *Grounds for Creation of Individual Employment Relationships* [in Ukrainian]. Kiev: "Znannya" Publishing, 80.

of trade secrets and confidential information for certain categories of workers—do exist. Nevertheless, it is worth mentioning that the terms of validity of such limitations are determined by the duration of the employment contract. At the end of the employment relationship, the obligation is no longer applicable.

In surveying the several approaches dealing with competition between a worker and an employer that have been implemented in the majority of developed countries, the need to provide governmental control of competition within the employment relation is the most established one. The obligation on ensuring fair competition, and for setting the necessary limitations to the freedom on certain parties realising competitive actions is considered the responsibility of the Government. Taking this into account, it is important to point out the necessity to resort to governmental control to regulate competition between the parties to the employment contract, particularly in Ukraine. Thus, the main task of domestic law should be to strike a balance between the interests of the employer—as the proprietor of the trade secrets—and the employee.

In practice, the need to strike such a balance results in certain difficulties. In legal terms, it is possible to acknowledge the existence of the employee's duty not to disclose and not to use trade secrets without any warning (as occurs, for instance, in Bulgaria and Italy), an aspect that however limits the occupational development of workers. On the other hand, an attempt to differentiate the expertise gained by workers from the awareness of a trade secret (so that they understand a particular method) and those that are not aware is likely to lead to the disclosure of such a secret. Unfortunately, this attempt proves unrealistic, due to the difficulty in finding objective criteria to conceive this difference. In the author's view, the establishment of a number of contractual mutual obligations on the prohibition to disclose the trade secret either during the duration of the employment contract and after its termination can be a useful instrument to balance the interests of the parties. Such contractual duties must be set forth at the time of hiring, and ensure that the content of unfair competitive labour relations by the parties of the employment contract fully corresponds to their interests. Moreover, the establishment of obligations about restrictions in terms of competition represents a compromise to resolve the issue that workers consciously limit their occupational growth, and the proprietor of trade secrets faces additional charges which are, however, of much smaller value if compared to those they would bear, should the secret be used by another person.

The establishment of mutual obligations can occur either by concluding special agreements or by including specific conditions in the employment contracts. Nowadays, such a possibility can result in the most effective way to provide fair competition both during the duration of the employment contract and after its termination, also in Ukraine.[5] Thus, it is advisable to conclude non-competition agreements between the parties, or to include proper conditions in the employment contract.

However, the limitations for the employee to disclose trade secrets must be provided by law. In most countries which have provided the legal regulation of competition relations between the parties of the employment contract, the duty of the worker not to disclose the employer's trade secrets arises from the law.[6] In fact, the disclosure of such information against the will of its legal proprietor needs to be regarded as illegal, as this kind of conduct infringes upon the right of ownership of the employer, which usually consists of three elements: the right for the domain of information, the right for the use and the right to dispose of information. The distribution of a trade secret, that thus becomes available to third parties, can be interpreted as a worker taking on the disposition of it, determining its legal and actual fate. This right, however, can only belong to the proprietor, who is considered the unique holder of these absolute rights. In fact, third persons cannot hinder this realisation, as an absolute subjective duty is laid upon them, which ensures that this right will not be violated.[7]

The right to disclose the trade secret can be realised by the employer in two forms: sharing the trade secret with a limited amount of people who are subjected to the conditions of confidentiality (a trade secret is kept safe and guarded in the future); and spreading this information, which will make it available to everyone.[8] Therefore, despite the fact that workers have legally obtained information which makes up a trade secret, they are not allowed to acquaint third parties with such information without the consent of the employer. Their contribution to its creation is not a reason for granting them any property rights on it. Access to information which makes up a trade secret is provided exclusively for executing their duties—according to the employment contract—or for carrying out other

---

[5] Kuzmin, A. Y. 1992. "Legal Protection of Trade Secret [in Ukrainian]," *Pravovedeniye* No. 5, http://pravoved.jurfak.spb.ru/old/default.asp?cnt=382 (accessed November 7, 2011).

[6] Such countries, in particular, include Estonia, Latvia, Lithuania, Bulgaria and others.

[7] Dzera, O. V., and N.S.Kuznetsova, eds. 2002. *Civil Law of Ukraine: Textbook. In 2 volumes* [in Ukrainian]. Kiev: Yurinkom Inter Publishing, Volume 1, 85.

[8] Kotlyar, D. 2004. "The Legal Nature of Trade Secret and Approaches to Regulating such Relations [in Ukrainian]," *Parliament,* No. 3:35.

tasks on behalf of the employer. The degree of access every worker has to such information is determined by the employer on an independent basis, while the terms of use are set by local legislation or the employment contract itself.

Equally useful would be to devise a clause in the Labour Code of Ukraine, creating an obligation on the worker with knowledge of a trade secret to not to disclose the information which makes up its content, both during the duration of the employment contract and after its termination, during the term of the employer's right of intellectual property on the trade secret. According to Art. No. 508 of the Civil Code of Ukraine, such a term is determined by the period of existence of specific features of the trade secret.

The above has been successfully realised in Estonia, Latvia, Poland and some other countries, also taking into account their unique national features. A comparison with relevant legislation in foreign countries can contribute to further improve the bill of the Labour Code of Ukraine, which is being discussed in the Supreme Council of Ukraine, and it should translate into the possibility of the national government to draw on the experience of other European states. Undoubtedly, it is impossible to compare certain procedures which are unique to some national legal systems, though a trend towards the regulation of competition has been witnessed.

In particular, considerable interest has been evoked by the numerous forms of unfair competition reported by workers concerning their employers, which has been regulated by foreign legislation. In Hungary, for example, employees are not allowed to hold two jobs, to conclude any civil legal agreement with the contractors of the employer, to be the founder of economic companies or to be a member of the observant board of state enterprises, or to disclose confidential information of the employer. In Poland, the legislator foresees another type of activity as a form of unfair competition, that is the involvement of an activity on the part of the employee which is analogous to the one in which the employer is engaged, in practice the prohibition to carry out entrepreneurial activity that has been discussed above.

Regardless of the way these activities are labelled in foreign legislation, they can all be grouped into two categories: the activity directed towards disclosing the trade secrets of employers against their will, and the practices concerning the use of such information.

It is important to note that the use, as well as disclosure will be considered as unfair forms of display of competitive activity only when carried out against the will of the legal proprietor of the trade secret. The proposed division of the forms of unfair competitive activity does not only hold theoretical meaning, but—taking into account their content—will also lead to the opportunity to choose the right method of legal regulation. As for unauthorised use of information which makes up the content of the trade secret, it is advisable to grant the participant to employment relations the possibility to act at their own discretion, by way of special permission. Therefore, on the basis of mutual consent, the worker and the employer can limit the competitive activity between them.

In relation to unauthorised disclosure of a trade secret, a method of prohibitions needs to be applied with the purpose of placing on the participants of the relationship a duty to refrain from certain actions. In fact, as already mentioned, the access of workers to trade secrets cannot be considered as a reason for any property rights on this information.

It is worth noting that the norms governing competition in an employment relationship can be regulated by provisions pertaining to different fields of law—labour, competition, civil, and economic law, to mention a few. The reason for this is, mainly, the absence of a labour code (e.g. Italy) or the fact that the legal regulation of competition is considered exclusively the sphere of the so-called competition or economic legislation which takes into account the features of labour relations (e.g. Germany).

Current labour legislation in Ukraine is undergoing a massive process of reform, thus it is important to examine the experience of other countries with developed market economies, where relevant legislation already exists. Taking as a starting point their accomplishments in the sphere of determining the forms of unfair competition between the employee and the employer—e.g. the establishment of compensational payments for a certain period after the discontinuation of legal labour relations, which is limited to a certain period of time—will further develop the regulation of competition in Ukraine, the subject of research in the field of labour law.

References

Dzera, O. V., and N.S.Kuznetsova, eds. 2002. *Civil Law of Ukraine: Textbook. In 2 volumes* [in Ukrainian]. Kiev:Yurinkom Inter Publishing, Volume 1, 85.

Kotlyar, D. 2004. "The Legal Nature of Trade Secret and Approaches to Regulating such Relations [in Ukrainian]," *Parliament,* No. 3:35.

Kuzmin, A. Y. 1992. "Legal Protection of Trade Secret [in Ukrainian]," *Pravovedeniye* No. 5.

Pylypenko, P. D. 2003. *Grounds for Creation of Individual Employment Relationships* [in Ukrainian]. Kiev: "Znannya" Publishing.

TRANSFER OF UNDERTAKINGS IN LATVIA

IRENA KALNINA

1. Introduction[1]

The "transfer of undertakings" is one of the most complex legal institutions in European labour law and its primary aim is to grant the necessary protection to employees in the event of a change of employer, in particular, to ensure that their rights are safeguarded.[2] The transfer of undertakings acts as a legal tool for achieving one of the aims of the "Europe 2020" Strategy as well as raising employment levels at the European Union level in a secure and decent manner.[3] As Professor Roger Blanpain precisely pointed out:

> EU has no choice, we have to support the Lisbon strategy knowing that it will be extremely difficult to obtain "smart, sustainable and inclusive growth". The road is narrow and steep. But we must try. It is not forbidden to dream and sometimes dreams come true.[4]

---

[1] Published in Official Journal L 82, 22.03.2001, 16. The author would like to express her gratitude to professor Dr. iur. Tomas Davulis (Vilnius University) for valuable intellectual support in drafting this article.

[2] Par. 3 of Council Directive 2001/23/EC on the approximation of laws of the Member States relating to the safeguarding of employees' rights in the event of transfers of undertakings, businesses or parts of businesses. Complexity of transfer of undertakings is proven by a number of judgements concerning directive 2001/23 in the European Union Court—47 judgements as on 31 January 2011.

[3] One of the strategic aims of the European Union, embodied in the Lisbon Strategy Europe 2020, is increasing the percentage of the population aged 20-64 employed to 75%. Currently this figure is 60%. See European Commission. 2010. *Europe 2020: A Strategy for Smart, Sustainable and Inclusive Growth.* Brussels: European Commission, http://ec.europa.eu/eu2020/index_en.htm, (Accessed October 1, 2011).

[4] See in this volume Blanpain, R. "In Need of Flexicurity and Security in a Global Economy".

The Transfer Directive's goals are mainly implemented through Latvian labour law[5] (LL).[6] At present, there are three judgements concerning transfers of undertakings that have interpreted these norms in Latvia: one from the Supreme Court of Latvia and the other two from the court of first instance.[7] Thus, these norms are open to further interpretation and practical application.

2. Relevant Concepts in the Transfer of Undertakings

2.1 Undertaking

Art. No. 5 of the LL defines an "undertaking" as any organisational unit in which an employer employs his or her employees. Latvian commercial law goes on to define an "undertaking" as an organizational economic unit. However, commercial and labour law approaches should be distinguished for the following reasons.

First, both legal acts differ with regard to their purpose. Commercial law governs the commercial activities of merchants, while LL is designed to regulate legal employment relations between employees and employers.[8]

---

[5] Art. No. 117-121 of the Labour Law of Latvia.

[6] Labour Law of Latvia [Darba likums], adopted on 6 July, 2001, in force since 1 June 2002, published in the Official Gazette "Latvijas Vēstnesis", Number 105 (2492) 06.07.2001.

[7] Judgement of the Supreme Court of Latvia in case No. 798/2007, 19 December 2007 *[2007. gada 19. decembra LR AT spriedums lietā SKC-798/2007];* Judgement of Riga Regional Court of Civil Matters in case No. C32084105 (CA – 2317/07) 23 may 2007 *[2007. gada 23. maija Rīgas apgabaltiesas Civillietu kolēģijas spriedums lietā Nr. C32084105 (CA – 2317/07)]*; Judgement of the Supreme Court of Latvia in case No. SKC-134, 14 March 2007 *[2007. gada 14. marta LR AT spriedums lietā SKC-134]*; Judgement of Riga Regional Court of Civil Matters in case No. C32084105 (CA 2078/20) *[2006. gada 5. oktobra Rīgas apgabaltiesas Civillietu kolēģijas spriedums lietā C32084105 (CA 2078/20)];* Judgement of Riga Ziemelu district Court in case No. C-32084105 (C-84105/9) 25 April 2005 *[2005. gada 25. aprīļa Rīgas pilsētas Ziemeļu rajona tiesas spriedums lietā Nr. C-32084105 (C-84105/9)]*; Judgement of Riga Regional Court of Civil Matters in case No. C33294309, 20 August 2010 *[2010. gada 20. augusta Rīgas apgabaltiesas spriedums lietā Nr. C33294309]*; Judgement of Bauska citu court in case No. C100421/10, 3 June 2010 (appealed) *[2010. gada 3. jūnija Bauskas rajona tiesas spriedums lietā Nr. C100421/10 (iesniegta apelācijas sūdzība)].*

[8] Kalnina, I. 2007. "Transfer of Undertakings in Latvia," in *Employment Law,* eds. Alibekova, A., Center for International Legal Studies, and D. Campbell, (The Netherlands: Kluwer Law International).

Secondly, LL views an undertaking as "a place of work" engaged in the pursuit of particular working objectives. Commercial law has a completely different view of the nature of an undertaking, stating that an undertaking includes both tangible and intangible assets belonging to a merchant, as well as other economic benefits (value), which are utilised by the merchant to perform commercial activities.[9] Under commercial law, a more precise term would be "company", meaning an organisational unit with the object of making a profit.[10] More than one undertaking may form a company.[11]

Thirdly, the linguistic approach distinguishes differences between the two. For example, commercial law uses the term "reorganisation" to describe the activities of merging and restructuring, whereas the LL uses the term "transfer".

On the basis of the above three points, it is clear that there are distinct differences between the commercial and labour aspects of the process of business succession and the concept of transfers of undertakings. This article will only deal with the transfer of undertaking in the light of LL norms.

As there is no European Union standard with regard to the notion an "undertaking",[12] a review of the text of the Transfer Directive in English, French and German could help reveal the true scope of the notion in question.

The English version includes two notions: an "undertaking" and a "business" which differ from the wording in French ("d'entreprise and "d'établissement") and in German ("Unternehmen" and "Betrieb"). It seems that a more appropriate term in English could also be "enterprise". The Latvian translation of the Transfer Directive[13] contains "uzņēmums" and "uzņēmējsabiedrība" following the line of the English version of the Transfer Directive.

The problem with the Latvian version of the Transfer Directive being translated from English as well as the terminology of Art. No. 117 of the

---

[9] Commercial Law of Latvia, Art. No. 18.

[10] Halbach, G., N. Paland, R. Schwedes, and O. Wlotzke. 1992. *Labour Law: An Overview*. 4th revised and extended edition, Bonn: Federal Ministry for Labour and Social Affairs, 42.

[11] Ibid.

[12] Nor Treaty, neither the Directive includes this notion. Barnard, C. 2006. *EC Employment Law*. New York: Oxford University Press, par. 7.8.

[13] Available at Gateway to the European Union, http://eur-lex.europa.eu /Result.do?T1=V3&T2=2001&T3=23&RechType=RECH_naturel&Submit=Mekl %C4%93t, (accessed September 26, 2006).

LL which directly implements the relevant norms of the Transfer Directive is finding a precise term for a "business", which could be either an entity or a process. It seems that French, German and Latvian versions refer to the term "business" as an entity and not a process. Following this line of thought, LL only refers to "undertaking"[14] which in the light of Art. No. 5 of the LL should also include businesses.

By way of contrast, the case law of the European Union Court[15] and legal doctrine[16] implies that the term business is a wider notion which includes transfers of undertakings and/or its branches.

In the end, it should be added that the wording of the document is the first and not the last matter to analyse, since the most important factor is the aim[17] of the transfer rules in conjunction with all relevant circumstances of a particular case.

In addition to this, the International Labour Organization standards do not contain special regulations for employees in the case of transfers of undertakings, which means that it is much more difficult to find consensus on this matter at the international rather than at the European level.

2.2 Branch of an Undertaking

The issue of the nature of the branch of an undertaking arises when the transfer of an undertaking is partial. This question is of major relevance in cases of outsourcing.[18] Transfer rules are attributable to the outsourcing process only in cases when this activity has its own resources used for a specific objective.[19]

---

[14] In Latvian – "uzņēmums".

[15] Case 24/85 *Jozef Maria Antonius Spijkers v Gebroeders Benedik Abattoir CV et Alfred Benedik en Zonen.*

[16] Halbach, G., N. Paland, R. Schwedes, and O. Wlotzke. 1992. *Labour Law: An Overview.* 4th revised and extended edition, Bonn: Federal Ministry for Labour and Social Affairs,137-138.

[17] See pre-last paragraph of the Introduction of this article.

[18] Outsourcing is a new management method used by companies wishing to "refocus" on their core activity. Outsourcing consists of delegating subsidiary or ancillary, but necessary activities that were previously performed internally, such as cleaning, catering, premises security. Desprès, P; and G. L. Nouel. 2005. "French and European Law on Transfers of Undertakings and Protection of Employment," in The Comparative Law Yearbook of International Business, 27:90-91.

[19] Ibid.

LL states[20] that the transferable branch of undertaking should be autonomous, that is capable of functioning in an independent manner and/or relatively easily transferable from transferor to transferee.[21] The Federation of European Employers suggests that such an economic entity should be stable, tangible and identifiable.[22]

The European Union Court in the *Spijkers* case concluded[23] that the decisive criterion for an entity to be independent is retention of its economic identity whose operation will be continued or resumed.[24] French authors suggest that the entity's degree of autonomy is mainly characterised by the presence of separate staff and a separate organisation.[25]

In general, the *Spijkers* case criteria are applicable to "business succession". It is possible to identify the nature of the transferable branch of an undertaking by applying these criteria since the notion of "business succession" is the widest term, especially taking into account that wording of the LL. Therefore, the *Spijkers* case criteria could be used also in assessing the nature of a branch of an undertaking.[26]

Neither the Transfer Directive, nor LL or legal authorities explain this notion, except by providing some examples such as, transfers of undertakings rules would not cover the sale of equipment alone or when a

---

[20] Labour Law of Latvia, Art. No. 117(1).

[21] Art. No. 1(1)b of the Transfer Directive only refers to an economic entity which retains its identity, meaning an organized grouping of resources which has the objective of pursuing an economic activity, whether or not that activity is central or ancillary

[22] Official Website of the Federation of European Employers http://www.fedee.com/transferrules.html, (accessed on September 25, 2006).

[23] Case 24/85 *Jozef Maria Antonius Spijkers v Gebroeders Benedik Abattoir CV et Alfred Benedik en Zonen.*

[24] *Spijkers*-case criteria (the type of undertaking, whether tangible assets are to be transferred (buildings, movable property and stocks); the value of the intangible assets (know-how, goodwill) at the time of transfer; whether the majority of the undertaking's employees are taken; new employer; whether or not customers are transferred; the degree of similarity between the activities carried on before and so on.

[25] Desprès, P; and G. L. Nouel. 2005. "French and European Law on Transfers of Undertakings and Protection of Employment," in The Comparative Law Yearbook of International Business, 27:82-83.

[26] The European Union Court refers to the widest norm "transfer of business," which includes also transfer of autonomous branches of undertaking.

person acquires the stock of a company but the employer remains the same, so, the Transfer Directive does not become applicable.[27]

2.3 Transfer

According to Art. No. 117 (1) of the LL, a transfer refers to an undertaking or its autonomous branch shifting to another person on the basis of a contract or non-contractual legal ground (*law, judgment, administrative act or other legal ground (inheritance, personal servitude)* as well as the reorganisation of the enterprise.

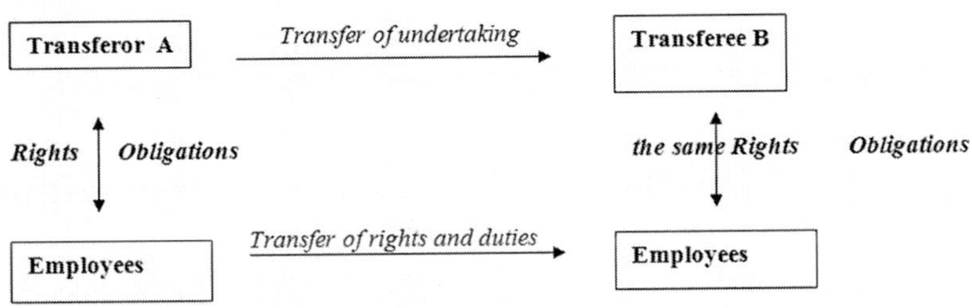

Source: Barnard, C. 2006. *EC Employment Law*. New York: Oxford University Press, par. 7.6., figure 7.1.

A major difference should be emphasised between rules that have been in place for four years and those enforced for 24 years within the national legal system as LL rules on transfer have hardly been interpreted by national courts. In contrast, transfers of undertakings in the United Kingdom within legislation have been in force since 1981. Furthermore, the new Regulation on Transfer of Undertakings (Protection of Employees) adopted in 2006 includes an extended notion of transfers of undertakings.[28]

The European Union Court has ruled that there is no need for the Transfer Directive to be applicable to any direct contractual relationship

[27] McMullen, J. 2006. "Transfer of Undertakings (Protection of Employment) Regulations 2006," *Industrial Law Journal* 35, No. 2:118 and 125.

[28] The extended definition also encompasses service provision changeovers stating that a transfer includes service activities ceased by the transferor and taken by the transferee if prior to the changeover there was an organised grouping of employees carrying out those activities on behalf of the client: McMullen, J. 2006. "Transfer of Undertakings (Protection of Employment) Regulations 2006," *Industrial Law Journal*, Volume 35, No. 2:118 and 125.

between the transferor and the transferee.[29] Until 25 March 2010 Art. No. 117(1) of the LL only contained a contract as a legal basis for a transfer since it is the main possible legal ground for transfers in the national legal system. This inconsistency with the European Union standards was corrected and now legal transfers include all possible contractual and non-contractual legal grounds for the transfer.

Art. No. 117 (2) of the LL excludes from the scope of transfers the reorganisation of state administrative institutions or of local government administration, as well as transfer of administrative functions of one institution to another institution. Transfer rules of LL are not applicable to sea-going vessels.[30]

2.4 Transferor and Transferee

According to Art. No. 118 (2) of the LL, the transferor of an undertaking may be any natural or legal person who as a result of the transfer of an undertaking loses the status of employer. The same norm also defines the transferee or the acquirer of an undertaking as any natural or legal person who as a result of the transfer of an undertaking acquires the status of employer.

In conformity with Art. No. 4 and 28(1) of LL[31] the status of the employer is obtained after the conclusion of an employment contract.[32]

2.5 Representatives of Employees

The most effective method of representation of employees is via qualified representatives, e.g. trade unions.[33] Another possibility could be

---

[29] Case C-172/99 Oy Liikene AB v Pekka Liskojarvi and Pentti Juntunden [2001] ECR I-745, para 29.

[30] Labour Law of Latvia, Art. No. 117(3).

[31] Art. No. 4 of the LL provides that: “an employer is a natural or legal person or a partnership with legal capacity that, on the basis of an employment contract, employs at least one employee”;
Art. No. 28(1) of the LL—“an employer and an employee shall establish mutual legal employment relationships by an employment contract”.

[32] As well as employee—Art. No. 3 of the LL provides that “an employee is a natural person who, on the basis of an employment contract for an agreed work remuneration, performs specific work under the guidance of an employer”.

[33] Law on Trade Unions [Likums "Par arodbiedrībām"] adopted on 13 December, in force since 2 January 1991, published in Official Gazette “Ziņotājs” Number 3 in 31.01.1991.

elected representatives (usually works councils), but this institution is not recognised nor widespread in Latvia. Art. No. 121 of the LL grants employees' representatives an unchangeable status during the business succession process, stating that if an undertaking or a branch of it retains its independence after transfer of the undertaking, the status and functions of employee representatives affected by such transfers shall be retained with the same provisions that were applicable up to the moment of transfer of the undertaking.

An exception made is in the case of the completion of preconditions for the re-election of employee representatives or for the re-establishment of employment representation.

3. Information and Consultation

It is recognised that the involvement of employees, if effective, constructive and timely,[34] should strengthen the competitiveness of the enterprise. Art. No. 11 of the LL[35] states that consultation shall mean the exchange of views and dialogue between employee representatives and the employer for the purpose of achieving agreement.

The transfer of undertakings and collective redundancy information and consultation procedures are frequently compared at the European Union level, thus it is easy to notice similarities also in the national legal system.

As is in cases of collective redundancy, provided in Art. No. 106 of the LL,[36] Art. No. 120 of the LL obliges the parties engaged to provide full information and take part in consultations prior to transfer activities.

---

[34] Art. No. 27 of the EU Charter of Fundamental Rights whose source of inspiration are Directives 77/187/EC (transfers of undertakings), 98/59/EC (collective redundancies) and 94/45/EC (European Works Council) should be mentioned here.

[35] Implementing Directive 2002/14/EC of the European Parliament and of the Council of 11 March 2002 establishing a general framework for informing and consulting employees in the European Community.

[36] Art. No. 106 (1) of the LL states that an employer who intends to carry out collective redundancy shall in good time commence consultations with employee representatives in order to agree on the number of employees subject to the collective redundancy, the process of the collective redundancy and the social guarantees for the employees to be made redundant. During consultations the employer and the employee representatives shall examine all the possibilities of avoiding the collective redundancy of the employees employed in the undertaking or of reducing the number of employees to be made redundant and how to alleviate the effects of such redundancy by taking social measures that create the possibility

Both the transferor and transferee of an undertaking have a duty to inform their employee representatives at least one month before the date of transfer of the undertaking or the expected date of transfer, providing the reasons for the transfer of the undertaking, the legal, economic and social consequences of the transfer, as well as of the measures which will be taken with respect to employees.[37]

Not later than three weeks in advance, the transferor or transferee intending to take organisational, technological or social measures in the undertaking with respect to employees has a duty to commence consultations with his or her employee representatives in order to reach agreement on such measures and their procedures.[38]

4. Transfer of Rights and Duties Arising from Employment Relations

4.1 Employment Contracts

In conformity with Art. No. 118(1) of the LL, rights and duties of the transferor of an undertaking that arise from legal relationships of employment, including employment contracts applicable at the moment of transfer of the undertaking, shall devolve to the acquirer of the undertaking. This means that a transfer of an undertaking or its branch may not result in dismissal of employees unless other economic reasons exist.[39]

Here clarification as to whether or not the transfer of employment contracts is "automatic" is required, since existing employment relationships are part of the economic entity[40] transferred, but at the same time in conformity with the principle of freedom of a contract, an employee is entitled to refuse further employment with a transferee.[41] A partial answer was given in the *Temco* case, stipulating that a worker is entitled to object

---

to further employ or retrain the employees made redundant. This norm implements Council Directive 98/59/EC of 20 July 1998 on the approximation of the laws of the Member States relating to collective redundancies.

[37] Labour Law of Latvia, Art. No. 121 (1) and (2).

[38] Labour Law of Latvia, Art. No. 121 (3).

[39] See Chapter (5)b.

[40] Joined Cases 144/87 and 154/87 Harry Berg and others, par. 13.

[41] Also in Cases 144/87 and 154/87 Harry Berg and others, par. 12 it was stated that it is not the purpose of the Transfer Directive to ensure that the contract of employment or the employment relationship with the transferor is continued where the undertaking's employees do not wish to remain in the transferee's employment.

to continued employment with a transferee.[42] At present in Latvia, there are a number of atypical employees (formally qualified contractors, self-employed—*de facto* employees) who also deserve the protection of labour law in the event of transfer of undertakings. For this reason it is necessary to re-define the notion of an employee and find common standards at the European Union level or broaden the application of transfer of undertakings rules to include atypical employees.

If the employee has decided of his own accord not to continue with the contract of employment, Latvia[43] has no statutory provisions stating that the contract of employment must be regarded as terminated either by the employee or by the employer or that the contract or employment relationship should be maintained with the transferor. Thus, this is covered by general rules on termination of employment.

Therefore, in conformity with the LL, it is the employer's duty to ensure opportunities for further employment, but not the work itself for the employees subject to transfer of undertakings.

4.2 Collective Agreements

The LL provides continuity of the collective agreement (binding at the moment of transfer of undertaking). Art. No. 118(4) of the LL stipulates that after transfer of an undertaking the acquirer of the undertaking shall continue to comply with the provisions of the collective agreement entered into previously and applicable at the moment of the transfer of the undertaking up to the moment of termination of such a collective agreement, or until the moment a new collective agreement enters into effect, or until the moment of application of the provisions of another collective agreement.

The article also states that amendments of the provisions of the collective agreement should not be to the detriment of employees within one-year period from the transfer of the undertaking. Nevertheless, the Transfer Directive as well as the LL does not oblige the transferee to continue to observe the terms and conditions agreed in any collective

---

[42] *Temco Case*, C-51/00, par. 37.

[43] According to the European Commission it is at a discretion of the Member State to determine further activities. European Commission. 2004. "Memorandum on Rights of Workers in Cases of Transfers of Undertakings," Commission Services' Working Document. Brussels: European Commission.

agreement in respect of workers who are not employed by the undertaking at the time of the transfer.[44]

4.3 Exceptions: Insolvency of the Transferor

With regard to insolvency proceedings two aspects should be mentioned: exception from devolution of rights and duties arising from the employment relations and prohibition of abuse. Art. No. 119 of the LL provides for the devolution of rights and duties from transferor to transferee, information duty and duty to comply with collective agreements in force at the moment of transfer shall not be applicable to the transfer of an undertaking within the scope of bankruptcy proceedings.

Abuse of insolvency proceedings by a transferor of an undertaking for the purpose of restricting or depriving the rights of employees provided for by the LL is not permitted.

5. Termination of the Employment Contract

The LL restricts sending notice of termination of an employment contract solely on the basis of a transfer of undertaking. It is also clear from the text of Art. No. 101 and 118 (5) of the LL, and the Transfer Directive and Art. No. 4 of the ILO Convention Number 158[45] interpreted by the ILO Recommendation No. 166 that transfers of undertakings themselves cannot be the only legal basis for an employer's unilateral termination of the employment relations.

Still, this restriction does not apply in the situation where the employer's initiative to end employment is based on economic, organisational, or technological performance or similar measures in the undertaking.[46] Thus exceptions from this prohibition (dismissals owing to economic, organisational or technical necessities) are too broadly formulated.

It seems that only Latvia, out of 27 European Union Member States, has safeguarded the norm which prohibits an employer to give notice of termination of an employment contract to an employee—member of a trade union—without prior consent of the relevant trade union in cases

---

[44] Blanpain, R. 2001. *Comparative Labour Law and Industrial Relations in Industrialized Market Economies*. The Hague: Kluwer Law International, 172.

[45] Art. No. 4 of the ILO Convention Number 158 allows dismissals only on three grounds: inadequate capacity or conduct of the worker or operational requirements of the undertaking, establishment or service.

[46] Labour Law of Latvia, Art. No. 118 (5).

determined by law.[47] If the trade union does not agree with the notice of termination of an employment contract, the employer may, within a one-month period from the date of receipt of the reply, bring an action to the court for termination of the employment contract.[48]

6. Findings

1. Transfers of Undertakings are one of the legal tools for achieving one of the aims of the "Europe 2020" Strategy and raising employment levels at the European Union level in a secure and decent manner.

2. For the purposes of protecting atypical employees it is necessary to find a common legal standard of the notion of an "employee".

3. The Latvian concept of "undertaking" includes the missing term "business" in the text of Art. No. 117 of LL, which is an unusual approach compared to European Union Court practice where a business is a wider notion including transfers of undertakings and/or its branch.

4. A clear notion of transfers of undertakings is not completely settled either by legislative or judicial processes at the European level, thus these uncertainties appear also in the national systems of Latvia.

5. The wording in Latvian labour law and/or the *Transfer Directive* is the first, but not the last matter to look at since the most important factor is the aim of the legislative act concerned and circumstances of a particular case.

6. The *Spijkers case* criteria could be used not only in determining whether or not a situation can be classified as business succession, but also in assessing the nature of branch of the undertaking: whether it is autonomous or non-autonomous.

7. The ILO standards, *the Transfer Directive* and the LL prohibit utilising transfers of undertakings as legitimate grounds for dismissal; the exceptions from this prohibition (dismissals upon economic, organisational or technical necessities) are currently too broadly formulated thus causing

[47] Labour Law of Latvia, Art. No. 110.

[48] Labour Law of Latvia, Art. No. 110(4); in 21 September, 2006 the Parliament of Latvia *(Saeima)* has adopted amendments to this norm providing that if a trade union will not submit its answer to employer's request within seven days, this silence could be interpreted as confirmation of the dismissal. This derives from Art. No. 1430 of Civil Law of Latvia stating that "silence shall not be considered to be either consent or dissent, except in those cases when law specifically requires the breaking of silence in order that it not be considered to be consent". These changes could take effect from October 2006.

one of the biggest controversies in employee protection in the event of transfers of undertakings.

References

Blanpain, R. 2001. *Comparative Labour Law and Industrial Relations in Industrialized Market Economies.* The Hague: Kluwer Law International.

Desprès, P; and G. L. Nouel. 2005. "French and European Law on Transfers of Undertakings and Protection of Employment," in The Comparative Law Yearbook of International Business, 27

European Commission. 2004. "Memorandum on Rights of Workers in Cases of Transfers of Undertakings," Commission Services' Working Document. Brussels: European Commission.

—. 2010. *Europe 2020: A Strategy for Smart, Sustainable and Inclusive Growth.* Brussels: European Commission, http://ec.europa.eu/eu2020/index_en.htm, (Accessed October 1, 2011).

Halbach, G., N. Paland, R. Schwedes, and O. Wlotzke. 1992. *Labour Law: An Overview.* 4th revised and extended edition, Bonn: Federal Ministry for Labour and Social Affairs.

Kalnina, I. 2007. "Transfer of Undertakings in Latvia," in *Employment Law,* eds. Alibekova, A., Center for International Legal Studies, and D. Campbell, (The Netherlands: Kluwer Law International).

McMullen, J. 2006. "Transfer of Undertakings (Protection of Employment) Regulations 2006," *Industrial Law Journal* 35, No. 2:118 and 125.

CHAPTER THREE:

SOCIAL SECURITY LAW

THE COORDINATION OF NATIONAL SOCIAL SECURITY SYSTEMS OF EU MEMBER STATES: EC REGULATION NO. 883/2004

ANDRZEJ MARIAN ŚWIĄTKOWSKI

1. The Function of European Social Security Regulations[1]

European legislation governs social security rules and procedures for the implementation of national systems of social security laws for insured persons (employees, the self-employed and their families) moving within the European Union. The European Union legislature provides the rules of European social security law, which coordinates different national social security schemes, so as not to deprive anyone entitled to social security benefits under national legal systems of social security entitlements. Furthermore, it protects the rights acquired and ensures that insured persons applying for benefits from another Member State receive equal treatment with the nationals of that Member State, and in this way prevents the accumulation of social security benefits. The specificity of the coordinating standards used by the EU institutions is based on the selection of appropriate national legislation of social security law from competent bodies administering social security benefits in the Member States. These are the bodies authorised to determine the length of service needed to receive insurance, and from which national social security provisions ensure the entitlement to social security benefits by virtue of social insurance in another Member State. Council Regulation (EC) No. 1408/71 of 14 June 1971 on the application of social security schemes to

---

[1] This paper is a part of study entitled "European Union Private International Labour Law" submitted for publication on April the 18th, 2011 to the Jagiellonian University Press.

employed persons and their families moving within the Community[2] was replaced on 1 May 2010 by the European Parliament and Council Regulation (EC) No. 883/2004 of 29 April 2004 on the coordination of social security systems[3] which was enforced through the implementation of Regulation (EC) No. 987/2009.[4]

Council Regulation (EEC) No. 1408/71 of 14.06.1971 has undergone numerous amendments and updates. The reason for these changes stems from the European Court of Justice rulings and developments in national social security legislation of EU Member States. These factors contributed to the complexity and the excessive build-up of the EU rules on coordination of national social security legislation. In par. 3 of the Preamble to Regulation No. 883/2004 of 29 April 2004, it was concluded that in order to guarantee the free movement of persons within the European Union, it was necessary to change, modernise and simplify the rules on the coordination of national social security systems. The general principle applied by the provisions of coordinating national social security systems is to subject the social security relationship with a foreign element to the national social security law of the Member State, in which the person carries out the work in an employment relationship or as a self-employed individual, or as one conducting commercial activities or services.[5] This basic determinant identifying the relevant national social security legislation is applied to all. The application of *Lex loci laboris* in solving conflicts of substantive labour law has been used when determining the relevant national legislation in social security. However, there are exceptions from the above rule, governed by the provisions of Title II of Regulation No. 883/2004. The guiding principle to this was expressed in par. 17 to the Preamble of the Regulation, stating that the insured person who moves within the EU should submit to the social security system, which applies in the country where his or her work is being carried out. The application of this principle results from the ideas formulated in the Preamble to par. 15 of the Regulation that an insured person moving within the European Union should be covered by the social security system of only one Member State. This principle was reaffirmed in Art. No. 10 of Regulation No. 883/2004, a provision that does not

---

[2] Official Journal of the European Union L 149 of 5.07.1971, 2, as last amended by European Parliament and Council Regulation (EC) No. 1386/2001, Official Journal of the European Union L 187, 10.07.2001, 1.

[3] Official Journal of the European Union L 166 / 1, 30.04.2004, 72.

[4] Official Journal of the European Union L 284/1, 30.10.2009.

[5] In par. 17 of the Preamble to Regulation No. 883/2004 the term "employee" is used.

confer or does not allow the insured to retain a number of social benefits of the same type and for the same period of compulsory insurance.

As a result of the movement of workers, persons who are self-employed and are moving between Member States are subjected to at least two national systems of social security, therefore the principle formulated in par. 15 in the Preamble to Regulation No. 883/2004 must be interpreted in such a way that ensures it is impossible for the same social security relationship to be subjected to the social security laws in force in two or more Member States. This does not mean that the social security relationship, where there are foreign elements, will not be subject to social security laws in force in many Member States. Theoretically speaking, the social security relationship of one insured person who during the period of their working life is covered and moves within all Member States of the European Union is regulated by the national social security legislation in force in each Member State of the Union. The principle formulated in par. 15 in the Preamble to Regulation No. 883/2004 prevents the simultaneous use of social security legislation of two or more Member States in the period in which the insured is professionally active in the territory of two or more Member States. In this case, the provisions of Regulation No. 883/2004 coordinating the implementation of national social security systems takes the form of the conflict rules *sensu stricto*. An example of such a standard is the provision of Art. No. 13 of the analysed regulation, which includes the determinants indicating the appropriate national system of social security in the event of simultaneous performance of work by the insured person operating in two or more Member States of the European Union. The peculiarity of social security laws is evident in the close liaison of a social security relationship with the individual labour relationship and other legal relations under which insured persons pursue occupational activities. Accordingly, in the case when one remains in the employment of one employer and is covered by the national social security system of the country in which the workplace employing the worker is located, the only foreign element is the place of work. An employee changing his/her place of work to another EU Member State means that the employee will be covered by the social security law of another Member State. For this reason, it should be mentioned that the principle laid down in par. 15 of the Preamble to Regulation No. 883/2004 shall not preclude the application of one social security relationship to two or more national social security systems of different Member States of the Union. This rule prevents the simultaneous use of the same social security system, where there are foreign elements (to perform the work within the territory of two Member States), and where national social security legislation is in force in thosc countries in which the insured worker carries out his/her work. Subjecting persons moving within the European Union to only one national system of social security has been introduced in Regulation No. 883/2004 in order to avoid overlapping of national social security legislation in force between two or more Member States, which would be applicable because of the simultaneous work in two or more Member States. Due to the fact that the situation whereby an employee performs the same work in the two or more Member States cannot be avoided, it was necessary to identify in Art. No. 13 of Regulation No. 883/2004 the appropriate national system of social security legislation. The overall determinant of *lex loci laboris* does not allow in this particular case, for the emergence of a national social security system.

The provisions coordinating the national social security systems require equal treatment of insured persons, subject by virtue of employment under the employment or professional activities in a particular Member State. The general principle of equal treatment of policyholders is particularly applicable to employees who are not resident in a Member State in which they carry out work (Preamble par. 8). The national social security legislation ensures that the granting of benefits is dependent on the conditions of insurance, which is usually identified with the period of employment or professional activity. However, the above conditions may take the form of requirements relating to the period of residence in a Member State.[6] In this case, persons employed in that country, living in another country, whose social security laws entitle them to social security benefits from the period of residence would not be subject to social security in any of the countries. The provisions coordinating national social security systems to employees and the professionally active, ensure equal treatment with nationals who are subject to social security law in a Member State, even if they do not meet the requirements for the submission of social security relations in which there are elements of the foreign social security laws in force in place of work or occupational activities. Paragraph 16 of the Preamble of the Regulation states that, in principle, there is no justification for the European Union to make entitlements to social benefits dependent on the residence of the persons concerned. However, in specific cases, in particular with regard to social

---

[6] For example, the full Danish pension benefits are paid after a ten-year period of residence in Denmark. For this reason, in Annex X of Regulation No. 883/2004 it has been decided that the rules prevent the same kind of benefits applying to the amount which does not depend on the length of periods of insurance or residence, as defined in Art. No. 54 par. 2 point "A" of the Regulation lists the old age benefits acquired after 10 years of residence in Denmark prior to 1/10/1989.

benefits associated with the economic and social situation of the person concerned, the place of residence of the applicant to social security benefits may be taken into account when making decisions by the competent social security body.

Equal treatment of insured persons includes:

1) equality in matters relating to benefits, income and circumstances of acquiring entitlements to the benefits (Preamble, par. 9);

2) the obligation of insurers to use "legal fiction" that one's circumstances or events occurring in the territory of another Member State in which the insured has been employed, resided or met other conditions for this to be a social security scheme in country A, from which the national provisions of social security legislation are in force in country B, in which the employee is employed, making the acquisition, maintenance, or multiplying the entitlement to social security which shall be considered fulfilled, as if they were in place in the territory of country A. In particular, the equal treatment of the insured, commits the appropriate social security bodies for the aggregation of insurance periods, employment in an employment relationship, or in professional self-employment, completed under the national social security legislation in one Member State to the same periods completed under the social security legislation in force in another Member State in which the insured has worked, lived or ran a occupational activity. In paragraph 10 of the Preamble to Regulation No. 883/2004 it has been decided that, "the periods completed under the legislation of another Member State should be taken into account only by applying the principle of aggregation";

3) the conduct by persons moving within the European Union and the expectations of the acquired rights to social security benefits (par. 13 of the Preamble).

A necessary condition for the implementation of the principle of equal treatment of the insured persons is the summation by the competent institutions administering social security benefits in the Member States of the European Union of all the periods taken into account by the various national social security systems, which during the occupational activity or residence in different Member States the insured was subjected to during the decision making process in matters relating to the acquisition, retention and expectation of rights to benefits, as well as due to the calculation of social security benefits (par. 14 of the Preamble).

Specific rules of conduct were set out in Regulation No. 883/2004 on matters relating to maternity benefits, family benefits, retirement benefits, health care, unemployment benefits, and alimony benefits. Regulation No. 883/2004 adopted a uniform rule and regulation of maternity benefits and their equivalents to be benefited by those who are entitled, namely parents or legal guardians in the first months of the infant's life (Preamble, par. 19). It was considered that in terms of insurance benefits for illness, maternity and equivalent benefits for the father of a newborn, the insured persons, as well as members of their families, living or staying in another Member State should have the assured care (par. 20 of the Preamble). For the differences between various national social security schemes in the Preamble of Regulation No. 883/2004, it recommended that the authorities of the Member States require, wherever possible, that members of the families of workers living across borders will benefit from medical care in the Member State in which the employee carries out the work (par. 23). Subjecting the insured to the social security system of one Member State, the regulation declares that it is necessary to lay down specific rules governing the accumulation of non-cash and in-kind benefits granted in the case of illness covering the same risk (Preamble, par. 24).

Regulation No. 883/2004, containing the coordinating rules of national social security systems, considers it necessary to develop a system of coordination of disability benefits, which are specific features of national legislation. In particular, it concerns the national social security systems in matters relating to the determination of the degree of bodily injury, the degree of the disability and its further development (Preamble, par. 26). It is necessary to develop a system of granting social security benefits for pensioners as well as benefits for their dependents in cases where the persons concerned are subject to social security law of more than one Member State (par. 27 in the Preamble). The subject of coordination at the European Union level should also include provisions specifying the amount of social security benefits, the rules for collecting such benefits in conjunction with other pecuniary benefits (remuneration for work). In order to protect workers, especially migrant workers and their dependants against an overly strict application of national social security legislation on matters concerning the reduction, suspension or withholding of payment of social security benefits. Regulation No. 883/2004 requires Member States' authorities to apply a uniform method for calculating retirement benefits and pensions by summing up insurance periods and calculating the proportionate amount of benefits depending on the length of periods of insurance regulated by the national social security legislation of the Member States in which the insured was actively working or living in (Preamble, par. 28). One of the purposes of the coordination of national social security legislation is to protect the insured against overly strict application of national rules concerning reduction, suspension or interruption of benefits. In paragraph 29 of the Preamble to the Regulation it was considered necessary to introduce strict regulations governing the application of such rules. These rules may not be established at the EU level. The Council of the European Union is not empowered to set rules that impose a restriction on the accumulation of two or more retirement schemes or pensions acquired in different Member States. In particular, the European social security law, coordinating national social security systems, cannot set the rules that cause a reduction in the amounts of pensions acquired solely on the basis of the national legislation of the Member States of the European Union (par. 30 of the Preamble). Establishing such rules should be within the exclusive competence of the national legislature. However, the legislative authority of the European Union has set the limits in which national social security provisions concerning matters relating to the reduction, suspension, or withholding of payments of social security benefits should apply (par. 31 of the Preamble).

More effective coordination is required for the cover of insurance schemes in the event of loss of employment. With a view of supporting workers' mobility, it is particularly important to help the unemployed seek employment in the various Member States of the European Union. Therefore, it is necessary to ensure coordination between the systems of unemployment insurance and employment services of all Member States (par. 32 in the Preamble).

The autonomy of certain matters relating to the regulation of particular social security benefits in the national social security schemes of the Member States means that the coordination of benefits such as pre-retirement and family benefits should be regulated in a separate manner. Regulation No. 883/2004 states that the principle of aggregation of insurance periods should not be applied in respect of employment, self-employment or residence in a particular Member State, the length of which is conditional to the entitlement of pre-retirement benefits. Statutory pre-retirement systems exist, indeed, in a very limited number of Member States of the European Union. However, the subject of coordination provisions under Regulation No. 883/2004 should be an issue of equal treatment of policyholders entitled to retirement benefits, the granting of family and health benefits and enabling them to export pre-retirement benefits (par. 33 of the Preamble). In the case of family benefits, paragraph 35 of the Preamble of the Regulation emphasises the need to define the rules of priority in cases of overlapping entitlements to these, which are granted under the provisions of the applicable legislation of the appropriate Member State and of the State in which the family members reside.

The coordination of social security benefit principles is not applicable to alimony benefits. Paragraph 36 of Regulation No. 883/2004 states that these benefits are repayable since they are designed to compensate for the failure of one of the parents of the child to pay alimony as part of their legal obligation to provide financial support for the child according to family law. Therefore, these alimony payments should not be considered as direct benefits "under the joint support for families". For this reason, the coordination governed by the provisions of the Regulation should not apply to such benefits.

The rules for the coordination of social security benefits can either prevent or impede the export of social benefits. Therefore, the interpretation of the national social security provisions which derogate from that principle must be interpreted strictly. This means that the prohibitions or limitations on the export of social security benefits can be applied to certain social benefits. As it is clear from the provisions of Chapter 9 of Title III of the Regulation, prohibitions or limitations on the export of social security benefits may apply only to benefits that are "both specific and non-contributory" (Preamble, par. 37). These benefits were determined by the Parliament and the Council before the enforcement of Regulation No. 883/2004.

To address any administrative matters arising from the application of the Regulation and interpretation of its provisions, in paragraph 38 of the Preamble provision was made for the appointment of the Administrative Commission. The Commission is composed of representatives of the Governments of the Member States of the European Union (Preamble, par. 38). The development and use of services for data processing to exchange information on matters governed by the standards required the establishment of the coordination of the Technical Commission of the Administrative Commission (Art. No. 39 of the Preamble). A necessary condition for the effective functioning of this Commission, is that Member State's authorities ensure that the documents exchanged between the competent administrative institutions managing the social security benefits in each Member States or electronically issued by the institutions be accepted as the equivalent of original, hard copy documents (par. 40 of the Preamble). Issues related to the implementation of Regulation No. 883/2004 have been dealt with in the draft regulation issued by the Commission and presented to the Council on 31 January 2006. It had been adopted on 16 September 2009 in the legal form of regulation No. 987/2007.

The European Commission's proposal to enact Regulation (EC) No. 883/2004 on the coordination of social security schemes, and accept as a basic assumption that Regulation No. 883/2004 modernises the coordination of national social security systems of EU Member States, measures and simplifies procedures of the coordination of national social security systems. The task of the regulation is to establish detailed and effective policy implementation measures and procedures laid down in Regulation No. 883/2004. Basic principles of the proposed Implementing Regulation are set out in the Preamble. First, the need for the use of electronic means was mentioned to permit rapid and reliable exchange of data between the social security institutions in the Member States. It was also noted that in the process of electronic personal data exchange, social security institutions should benefit from all of the guarantees laid down in the EU regulations concerning the protection of individuals in matters relating to the processing of personal data and the free movement of such data (par. 3). The Commission is of the opinion that the accessibility of contact data, including electronic, of the particular institutions of the Member States of the European Union that are able to participate in the implementation of Regulation No. 883/2004 will facilitate the exchange between social security institutions of Member States (par. 4). Strengthening certain procedures will bring the users of the Regulation No. 883/2004 more advantages and assurances of a higher level of legal security. In particular, setting common deadlines for fulfilling certain obligations specified in the provisions of Regulation No. 883/2004 or completing certain administrative proceedings for social security benefits will help to clarify the legal situation of persons applying for social security benefits, and "give the appropriate structure of relations between insured persons and the institutions" (par. 5). The explanation of this general formulation was included in the sixth par. of the Preamble. It follows from this that the authorities of the Member States and relevant authorities and social security institutions of those countries should be allowed to establish simplified procedures and administrative arrangements in matters relating to the exchange of information and decision-making on social security benefits issues. Implementing Regulation No. 987/2009 does not specify those procedures. Using the "open method of coordination" permits the authorities of the Member States and institutions administering social security benefits the right to choose the simplified procedures, those most adapted to national social security system of the Member States concerned. With a view to simplifying procedures and speeding up proceedings, the implementation of Regulation No. 987/2009 for Regulation No. 883/2004 requires Member State's authorities, in the event of a conflict of social security legislation for its resolution by the concerned competent social security institutions of Member States in which the insured person applying for social security benefits has been either employed, conducted business activity, trade or services, or lived and—for one of these reasons—was insured, to temporarily assign the applying person for social security to one of two or more national social security systems of the EU Member States, in which the insured seeking benefits from social security is or had social insurance and made use of it (par. 8).

The objective of Implementing Regulation No. 987/2009 for Regulation No. 883/2004 is to increase the transparency of the criteria with which social security institutions of Member States use in their decisions to grant a right to social security benefits in the legal relations governed by the national social security legislation of two or more countries. Detailing the criteria for making decisions on these matters is clear from the European Court of Justice decisions and from the Administrative Commission rulings with over 35 years of experience in applying the standards of coordinating the national social security provisions. Extending the scope to all insured persons, including persons economically inactive, but involved in community service activities (care for children) requires the introduction and use of certain specific rules and procedures to identify the relevant national legislation according to which social security will be addressed. This would be for periods devoted to bringing up children by persons who have never worked or are not in a self-employed business, or in a trade and services in the Member States of the European Union in which they have lived. Implementing Regulation No. 987/2009 for the Regulation No. 883/2004 lays down procedures which are designed to balance the weight of health care protection between the Member States. The established procedures should take into account the situation of Member States who bear the costs of adopting the insured persons as a result of giving them the benefit of the national health system, organised in the Member State in which these persons reside and settle the costs of benefits in-kind received by persons insured with the social security system of another Member State. The institutions administering social security benefits in the Member States calculate the costs and expenses incurred in the social benefits of social security paid to legally insured persons.

In order to maintain confidence in matters relating to the exchange of data required for the above mentioned calculations and to allow the competent national social security institutions to effectively manage the delivery of social services, Regulation No. 987/2009 introduces more restrictive calculations than those being used to calculate payments so far, between the relevant social security institutions of the Member States of the European Union. In particular, Implementing Regulation No. 987/2009 for Regulation No. 883/2004 decided that the procedures for payment claims should be strengthened relating to benefits in respect of incapacity for work due to illness and loss of employment. The legal mechanisms should be regulated for effective recovery of claims relating to undue benefits. Procedures for mutual assistance between social security institutions should be regulated in accordance with the provisions of Council Directive 2008/55/EEC of 26 May 2008 on mutual assistance for the recovery of claims relating to certain levies, duties, taxes and other charges.[7]

2. The Determinants of Coordinating Laws

Art. No. 11, par. 1 of Regulation No. 883/2004 as a basic principle uses legislation of only one Member State when applying laws to an insured person. The national social security legislation applicable to the insured is indicated by using determinants listed in Title II, "Determination of the applicable legislation" of the regulation (Art. No. 11—Art. No. 16). Under the provisions of Art. No. 12 to Art. No. 16 of the Regulation:

1) Persons in a Member State carrying out employment or self-employment are subject to national social security law in force in the country in which the work is carried out. The law applicable to the social security of the persons (*lex securitatis*) consists of the provisions of creating the insurance status in the workplace (*lex loci laboris*) (Art. No. 11 par. 3 point "a");

2) Civil servants subject to the legislation of a Member State to which the administration employing them is subjected to (Art. No. 11 par. 3 point "b"). If a civil servant carries on business in another Member State, the competent social security institution informs the pre-designated institution in that Member State. Two phrases used in Art. No. 15 of Implementing Regulation No. 987/2009 are the terms "competent institution" and "designated institution", which are defined in the glossary of legal terms set out in Art. No. 1 of Regulation No. 883/2004. The term "institution" means any body or authority responsible for implementing all or part of the legislation relating to social security branches and schemes specified in Art. No. 3 par. 1 of the Regulation. The term "competent institution" is used in the Regulation to specify the institution where the person concerned is insured at the time of application, or from which the person concerned has the right to obtain social benefits or would if such a law of

[7] Official Journal L 150, 10.06.2008, 28.

the insured or members of their family were resident in a Member State in which such an institution was located. The competent institution is also the institution designated by the authority of another Member State. Art. No. 15 of Implementing Regulation No. 987/2009 describing the procedure of exercising Art. No. 11 par. 3 point "b" of the Regulation No. 883/2004 requires Member State authorities, in which a civil servant—subject to social security legislation of the country whose rules apply to the administration employing him—is subjected to, in connection with the activities of territorial change, social security law in force in another country;

3) The person receiving unemployment benefit, living in a different Member States other than the "competent State", i.e. the State in whose territory the competent institution of social security, the social security is subject to the provisions in force in the country of residence (*lex domicilii*) (Art. No. 11 par. 3 point "c");

4) A person called up or recalled for service in the armed forces or for civilian service in a Member State shall be subject to the legislation of that Member State (Art. No. 11 par. 3 point "d").

Other insured persons not mentioned in the article referred to above, Art. No. 11 par. 3 points "a" to "d" of the Regulation are subject to national social security law in force in the Member State in which such persons are domiciled (*lex loci habitationis*). Subjecting these persons to the provisions in force in the Member State in which their place of residence does not deprive these people of the entitlement to social benefits and the collection of such benefits under the national social security legislation in force of one or more Member States (Art. No. 11 par. 3 point "e").

Insured persons in employment or self-employment on board a ship at sea flying the flag of a Member State shall be considered as working or employed in a Member State under whose flag the ship is sailed. However, a person employed on board a vessel flying the flag of a Member State and remunerated for such activity by an undertaking or a person whose registered office or place of business is in another Member State shall be subject to the legislation of the latter Member State if he/she resides in that State (Art. No. 11 par. 4). This regulation requires that the insured person is subjected to the applicable law of the employer's registered office or his/her place of business activity from the place of residence in the same Member State of the employee or the self-employed, employed on a sea vessel.

According to *lex loci delegationis* employees and the self-employed posted by the employer to work in another Member State are eligible for social security. Art. No. 12 par. 1 and 2 of Regulation No. 883/2004 states that the said persons shall remain subject to the legislation of the Member State in which they are employed or pursuing a business activity in spite of their assignment to work abroad, provided that the anticipated duration of employment in another Member State shall not exceed 24 months. A further condition for the maintenance of social security legislation in force, is a fixed place of employment of the delegated person. This may include persons posted to work as a substitute for another employee, previously seconded to the provision of such work. A necessary condition for the application to the insured person's social security legislation in force in the country to which they are posted to is that they are a temporary employee for not longer than a 24 months in a business, or conducting a commercial or service activity by an employer employing foreign workers. The same rules apply to persons employed on their own account, going to another Member State in order to perform the same or similar activity to that which they would normally carry out in another Member State. The submission of social security provisions in force in the home state of these persons is dependent on not exceeding 24 months of postings abroad. In order to prevent the misuse of the extension of the posting, Implementing Regulation No. 987/2009 to Regulation No. 883/2004 requires that the self-employment not be "similar" to activities normally conducted in another Member State based on the criterion of the actual nature of this business and not a legal basis for the exercise and the fact that these activities qualify for the sub-category of work, provided under an employment relationship (employment) or self-employment.

The procedure for implementing the obligations referred to in Art. No. 12 of Regulation No. 883/2004 has been determined in the provision of Art. No. 14 and the article of Implementing Regulation No. 987/2009. The employer posting the employee to another Member State is obliged to pre-notify to the competent social security institution of that Member State whose social security provisions are applicable to the posted worker. The competent social security institution informs the other institution in the Member State where the worker is being posted to about the posting. Identical obligations are imposed by Art. No. 16 par. 2s of Implementing Regulation No. 987/2009 on the self-employed persons, working abroad for a period of 24 months in another EU Member State.

Workers employed simultaneously in two or more Member States are under social security law of that Member State in which they reside, provided that they carry out a considerable part of their work in this country. If they are employed by various undertakings or various employers whose registered office or place of business is in different

Member States, the worker is subject to the legislation of the Member State of residence (Art. No. 13 par. 1 point "a"). A necessary condition to change the determinant in applying the regulations in force at the place of the registered office of the employer or place of business, rather than the place of residence, is to carry out a smaller part of the work in the country in which the insured has his/her habitual residence (Art. No. 13 par. 1 point "b"). A person who normally performs their activities as self-employed in two or more Member States is subject to social security legislation in force in the Member State in which the person resides, provided that they pursue a significant part of their activity in that country (Art. No. 13 par. 2 point "a"). This determinant is used when an insured person does not live in one of the Member States, where they pursue a significant part of their work (Art. No. 13 par. 2 point "b"). The article uses subjective terms such as "a substantial part". Art. No. 14 par. 2 of Implementing Regulation No. 987/2009 defines the above terms by paying attention to the relationship between the material in a quantitative form of the activity of the employee or self-employed in relation to all of the activity. According to Art. No. 14 par. 2-3 of Implementing Regulation No. 987/2009, a "substantial part" is not necessarily the largest part of the activity. According to Implementing Regulation No. 987/2009, part of the activity is not in any event considered to be material if it covers less than 25% of the total activity performed by the worker or a professional person who is self-employed. The measure used to calculate the relationship between work or activity carried out in a Member State and the total amount of activities of an employee or self-employed person is the turnover of the self-employed person, the working time of an employee, the amount of remuneration for the work performed in the different Member States or—in the case of the self-employed—profits from the activity. As an alternative determinant in Art. No. 13 par. 2 point "b", the national social security legislation in force in the country in which the focus of the activities performed is indicated.

According to Art. No. 14 par. 9 of Implementing Regulation No. 987/2009 in Art. No. 13 par. 2 point "b" of Regulation No. 883/2004 when selecting the appropriate national social security legislation of one of two or more Member States what is considered is the professional "centre of interest" of the insured. This centre, referred to as the seat or place of business shall be determined by taking into account all elements involved in the activity of the insured person, such as a place where there is a permanent place of business of the insured, the type, nature or duration of the activity, the Member State in which the person is employed or self-employed, and subjected to tax regardless of the source of income.

Implementing Regulation No. 987/2009 requires that the will of the interested persons covered by social insurance is also taken into account. If a person operates in two or more Member States for the employer, who is located outside the European Union, and when the insured is resident in a Member State of the Union and does not perform in their major activities in that country, they are subject to social security legislation of that Member State where they reside (Art. No. 14 par. 11). In case of overlapping periods of insurance in respect of employment under the co-employment relationship and professional self-employed in different Member States of the European Union, the insured is subject to social security of the State in which the subordinate carries out his work as an employee (he/she is employed under a contract of work). Then, when the insured performs work under an employment relationship in between two or more Member States, the collision of national standards of social security provisions is solved in accordance with Art. No. 13 par. 1 of Regulation No. 883/2004, by using determinants of a place of residence or the seat of the employer or the place of work.

Coordinating laws of national social security provisions set out in the provisions of Art. No. 11—Art. No. 13 of Regulation No. 883/2004 shall not apply to voluntary insurance, unless with respect to one of the branches of social security listed in Art. No. 3 par. 1 of the Regulation in question there is only a voluntary system of social security in place in a particular Member State (Art. No. 14 par. 1). In accordance with the previously outlined principle, an insured person subjected to compulsory insurance in one Member State cannot also be subject to a voluntary social insurance scheme in another Member State of the European Union. In all other cases in which, for a given branch, there is a choice between several voluntary insurance schemes, the person concerned shall only join the scheme of his/her own choice, choosing between several systems of voluntary social insurance (Art. No. 14 par. 2). Art. No. 14 par. 3 of the Regulation however, provides an exception to this, in respect of invalidity, old age and survivors' benefits. In relation to these benefits, the person concerned has the right to join the voluntary system of social insurance in one Member State, even if he/she is covered by mandatory social insurance in another Member State. The implementation of this right is dependent upon the employment under an employment relationship or professional self-employment and the social security provisions of the Member State firstly mentioned. A necessary condition for derogating from the principle of participation in the social security system of one Member State is an express or implied acceptance of the accumulation of invalidity benefits, retirement and family benefits and the social security legislation in force in the first of the two mentioned Member States (Art. No. 14 par. 3 *in fine*). National social security legislation of a Member State may make joining the voluntary insurance system dependent upon residency. In this case, formulated in the provision of Art. No. 5 point “b” the principle of equal treatment of the insured person residing in another Member State which requires the competent institution of social security to the treatment of certain circumstances or events upon which the national social security laws make certain legal consequences in cases of the social benefits of the voluntary social security scheme should be included, only if the insured person has previously been subjected to social security law in that Member State, in which he/she is now entering into a voluntary system of social insurance (Art. No. 14 par. 4).

The principles outlined above have limited application to the insured persons who are employed as support personnel in the institutions of the European Communities. Members of the support personnel of the EU institutions are also subject to the provisions of one national social security scheme of a European Union Member State. Their separate treatment according to the coordinating laws of national social security systems governed by the provisions of the Regulation, is based on granting a limited choice of national systems of social security legislation of a Member State, to which, before joining the staff in the institutions have been or are bound by virtue of current or former employment or citizenship. They finally have the right to choose the social security laws of a European Union Member State, in which they are citizens. The limited nature of the right to choose the national system of social security law is also expressed in the choice between all the listed in Art. No. 3 par. 1 of Regulation No. 883/2004 branches of social security, except for family benefits (Art. No. 3 par. 1 point “j”). Conditions for acquiring benefits and payments are governed by separate provisions of social security, which apply only to the support staff of European Communities. Members of the support staff of the EU institutions select the competent national social security system at the time of entering into the employment contract. The right to choose may be made only once and become effective from the date of employment (Art. No. 15 *in fine* of Regulation No. 883/2004). The authorities of the EU institutions notify the designated institution of the Member State whose social security laws are deemed as appropriate, with the exception of the rules governing entitlements to family allowances, by the support personnel member of the European Communities (Art. No. 17 *in fine* of Implementing Regulation No. 987/2009).

3. Conclusion

1. Coordinating standards of social security benefits included in the Regulation No. 883/2004 shall be guided by similar principles, which were formulated in Regulation No. 1408-1471. They are:

1) exclusivity and unity used as the appropriate national social security scheme;

2) the binding nature of the social security legislation of that Member State, which has been identified on the basis of determinants listed in Regulation No. 883/2004;

3) the obligation to equal treatment of persons entitled to cash benefits and use of social security benefits in kind;

4) respect by the national social security institutions of Member States of the acquired rights and expectations to benefits from social security;

5) aggregation of periods, from which national social security regulations make the acquisition, maintenance, growth and size of social security benefits;

6) export of social security benefits within the European Union.

2. Regulation No. 883/2004 contains two types of rules of private international labour law: coordinating standards and substantive standards, setting out how the relevant social security institutions should assess the situation of applicants to determine the powers and to provide cash benefits and social security in-kind and make decisions to grant or refuse the payment of these benefits. Both types of standards qualify for the recognition of *sui generis* of conflicts of substantive labour law, which are part of private international labour law, because in the Polish system of law, social security is part of labour law and the norms of the law governing the legal relations between the persons covered by social protection, guaranteed by the state and the institutions managing the provision of social security.

3. Coordinating standards contained in Regulation No. 883/2004 ensure the continuation of conduct developed by the European Court of Justice on the basis of Regulation No. 1408/71.

References

Bińczycka-Majewska, T. 1999. *Koordynacja systemów zabezpieczenia społecznego (Coordination of Social Security Systems).* Kraków: Zakamycze.

Bińczycka-Majewska, T. 2011. "Koordynacja systemów zabezpieczenia społecznego w UE na progu XX w (Coordination of Social Security

Systems in the EU at the Beginning of the 21st Century)," in *Prawo pracy w świetle przepisów integracji europejskiej* (*Labour Law in the Light of Legal Regulation of the European Integration*), eds. Wratny, J., and M. B. Rycak, (Warsaw: Wolters Kluwer Polska).

Dzienisiuk, D. 2004. *Zabezpieczenie społeczne w Unii Europejskiej—koordynacja świadczeń (Social Security in European Union—Coordination of Benefits).* Warsaw: Centrum Doradztwa i Inforamcji Difin Sp. z o.o.

Mitrus, L. 2011. "Zakres przedmiotowy koordynacji systemów zabezpieczenia społecznego w Unii Europejskiej (Material Scope of Coordination of Social Security within the European Union)," in *Z zagadnień prawa pracy i prawa socjalnego (Miscellanea of Labour Law and Social Law),* eds. Kubot, Z., and T. Kuczyński, (Warsaw: Difin).

Pennings, F. 2003. *European Union.* The Hague: Kluwer Law International.

—. 2003. *Introduction to European Social Security Law.* Antwerp-Oxford-New York: Intersentia.

—. 2005. "Co-ordination of Social Security on the Basis of the State-of-Employment Principle: Time for an Alternative?" *Common Market Law Review,* 42.

—., ed. 1994. *Introduction to European Social Security Law.* Deventer-Boston: Intersentia.

Szurgacz, H. 2011. "Zakres przedmiotowy przepisów o koordynacji świadczeń z zabezpieczenia społecznego w UE (Material Scope of Coordination of Social Security Benefits within the EU)," in *Prawo pracy w świetle przepisów integracji europejskiej* (*Labour Law in the Light of Legal Regulation of the European Integration*), eds. Wratny, J., and M. B. Rycak, (Warsaw: Wolters Kluwer Polska).

Świątkowski, A.M. 2000. *Europejskie prawo socjalne (European Social Law), Vol. III Europejskie prawo ubezpieczeń społecznych (European Social Security Law).* Warsaw: Dom Wydawniczy ABC.

Uścińska, G. 2011. "Instrumenty prawne swobody przemieszczania się obywateli UE. Koordynacja systemów zabezpieczenia społecznego. Aktualne problemy i wyzwania (Legal Instruments of Freedom of Movement of UE Citizens. Coordination of Social Security Systems. The Most Current Problems and Challenges)", in *Prawo pracy w świetle przepisów integracji europejskiej* (*Labour Law in the Light of Legal Regulation of the European Integration*), eds. Wratny, J., and M. B. Rycak, (Warsaw: Wolters Kluwer Polska).

CONTRIBUTORS

Roger Blanpain, Full Professor at the University of Tilburg, The Netherlands and Honorary President of the International Society for Labour and Social Security Law.

Tomas Davulis, Associate Professor Vilnius University, Lithuania.

Marc De Vos, Professor at Ghent University, Itinera Institute, Belgium.

Kristīne Dupate, Lecturer at the University of Latvia, Latvia.

Ludwik Florek, Professor at the University of Warsaw, Poland.

Irena Kalnina, PhD Candidate, University of Latvia, Latvia.

Yaraslau Kryvoi, London School of Economics and Political Science, UK.

Merle Muda, Associate Professor at the University of Tartu, Estonia.

Daiva Petrylaitė, Associate Professor Vilnius University, Lithuania.

Łukasz Pisarczyk, University of Warsaw, Poland.

Ceciel Rayer, LLM Radboud University Nijmegen, the Netherlands.

Robert Rebhahn, Professor of Labour Law at the University of Vienna, Austria.

Olena Rym, Associate Professor at the Ivan Franko National University of Lviv, Ukraine.

Walerian Sanetra, Professor at the University of Bialystok, Poland.

Arkadiusz Sobczyk, Legal Advisor and Lecturer at the The Jagiellonian University, Poland.

Silvia Spattini, Adapt Director and Senior Research Fellow, Italy.

Andrzej Marian Świątkowski, Professor at the Jagiellonian University, Poland.

Gaabriel Tavits, Associate Professor at the University of Tartu, Estonia.

Michele Tiraboschi, Full Professor of Labour Law, University of Modena and Reggio Emilia, Italy.

Bernd Waas, Professor at the J.W. Goethe University of Frankfurt/Main, Germany.

Manfred Weiss, Professor at the J.W. Goethe University of Frankfurt/Main, Germany.

Tatiana Wrocławska, University of Lodz, Poland.

Marcin Wujczyk, PhD Candidate, Jagiellonian University, Poland.

INDEX